lonely planet

SOUTH AMERICA

TOP SIGHTS, AUTHENTIC EXPERIENCES

Regis St Louis
Isabel Albiston, Robert Balkovich, Alex Egerton, Ant
Ham, Mark Johanson, Brian Kluepfel, Tom Masters, C
McCart
bur

Contents

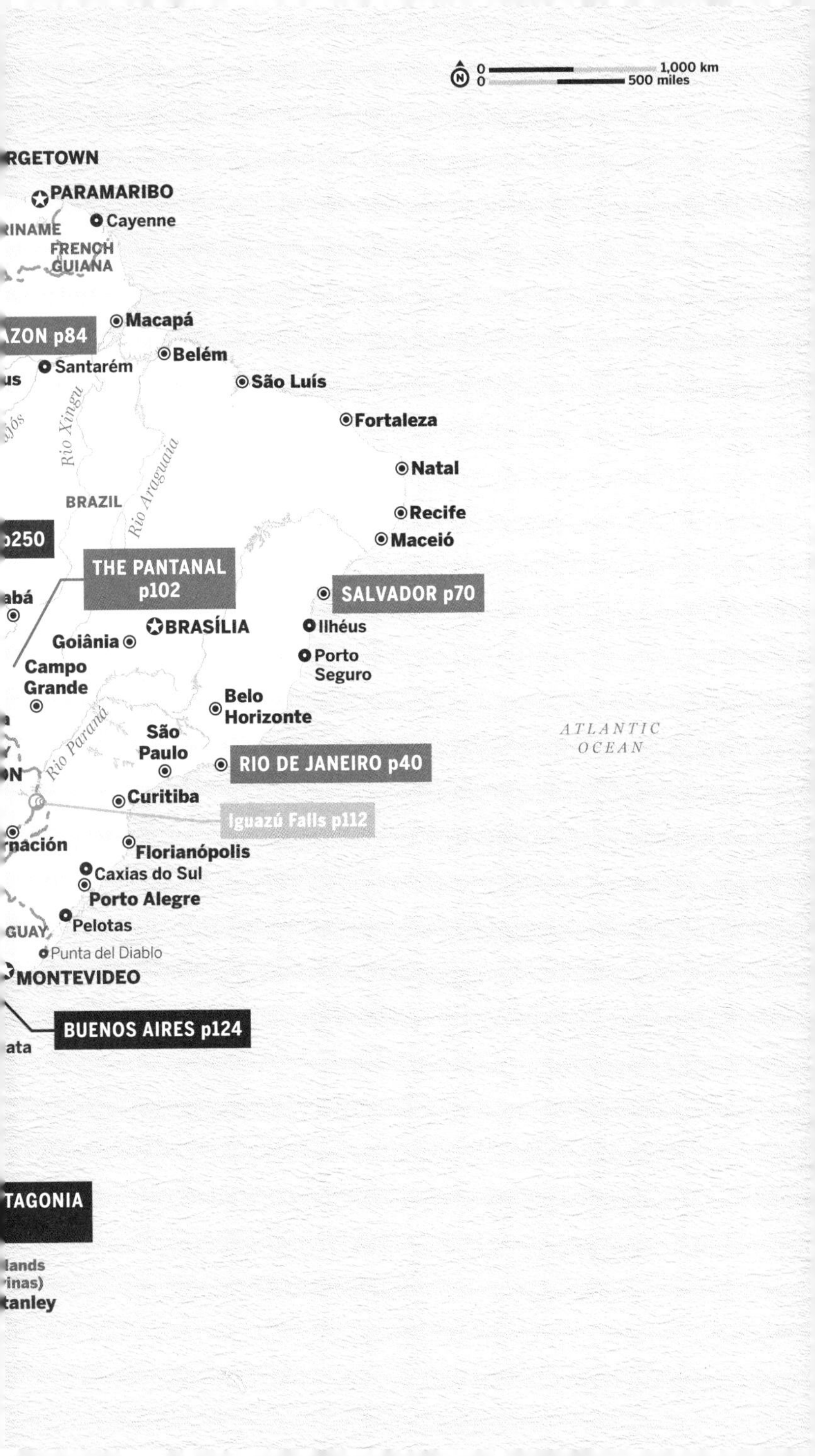

0 1,000 km
0 500 miles
RGETOWN
PARAMARIBO
Cayenne
RINAME
FRENCH GUIANA
ZON p84
Macapá
Santarém
Belém
us
São Luís
Rio Xingu
Fortaleza
Natal
Rio Araguaia
BRAZIL
Recife
p250
Maceió
THE PANTANAL p102
SALVADOR p70
abá
BRASÍLIA
Ilhéus
Goiânia
Porto Seguro
Campo Grande
Belo Horizonte
São Paulo
Rio Paraná
ATLANTIC OCEAN
RIO DE JANEIRO p40
Curitiba
Iguazú Falls p112
rnación
Florianópolis
Caxias do Sul
Porto Alegre
Pelotas
GUAY
Punta del Diablo
MONTEVIDEO
BUENOS AIRES p124
ata
TAGONIA
lands
inas)
tanley

Welcome to South America

Andean peaks, Amazonian rainforest, Patagonian glaciers, Inca ruins, colonial towns, white-sand beaches and vertiginous nightlife: the wonders of South America set the stage for incredible adventures.

From the snow-capped peaks of the Andes to the undulating waterways of the Amazon, South America spreads a dazzling array of natural wonders. This is a continent of lush rainforests, towering volcanoes, misty cloud forests, bone-dry deserts, red-rock canyons and ice-blue glaciers. Take in some of the incredible natural wonders found in every country in South America, then head to the coast for an idyllic retreat among palm-fringed, white-sand beaches and photogenic tropical islands.

Such settings offer tantalizing adventures. You can hike past ancient temples first laid down by the Incas, contemplate the awe-inspiring power of Iguazú Falls, or spend the day watching wildlife from a dugout canoe on one of the Amazon's countless *igarapés* (narrow waterways).

South America's diversity doesn't end with landscapes. You'll find colonial towns whose cobblestone streets lead past gilded churches and stately plazas little changed since the 18th century. You can haggle over colorful textiles at indigenous markets, share meals with traditional dwellers of the rainforest and follow the pounding rhythms of Afro-Brazilian drum corps. South America is home to an astounding variety of modern and ancient cultures, and experiencing it first hand is as easy as showing up.

The wonders of South America set the stage for incredible adventures.

Tourists at Iguazú Falls (p112), Brazil
R.M. NUNES / GETTY IMAGES ©

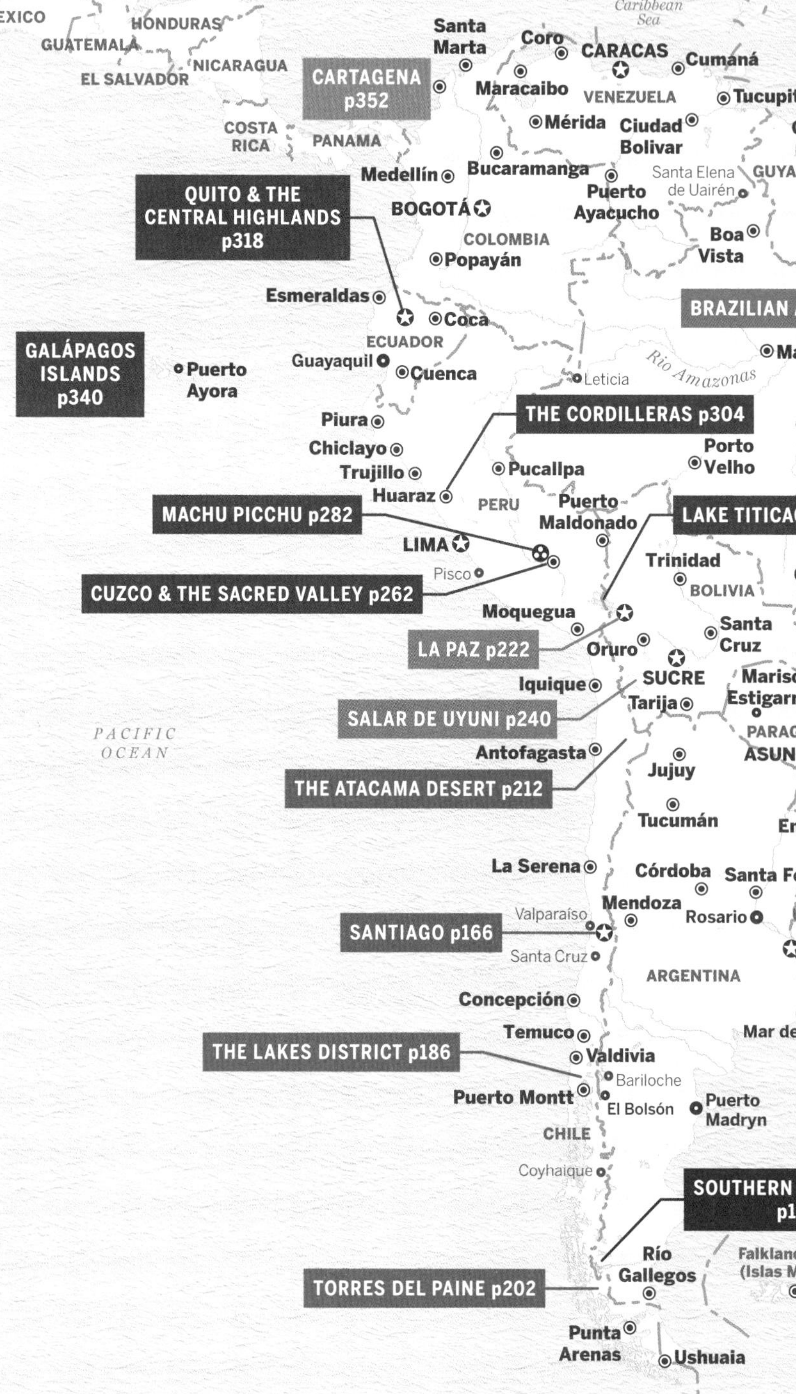

MEXICO
HONDURAS
GUATEMALA
NICARAGUA
EL SALVADOR
COSTA RICA
PANAMA
Caribbean Sea
Santa Marta
Coro
CARACAS
Cumaná
CARTAGENA p352
Maracaibo
VENEZUELA
Tucupita
Mérida
Ciudad Bolívar
Bucaramanga
Medellín
Santa Elena de Uairén
GUYAN
QUITO & THE CENTRAL HIGHLANDS p318
BOGOTÁ
Puerto Ayacucho
COLOMBIA
Boa Vista
Popayán
Esmeraldas
BRAZILIAN A
Coca
ECUADOR
GALÁPAGOS ISLANDS p340
Puerto Ayora
Guayaquil
Cuenca
Leticia
Río Amazonas
Piura
THE CORDILLERAS p304
Chiclayo
Trujillo
Pucallpa
Porto Velho
Huaraz
PERU
MACHU PICCHU p282
Puerto Maldonado
LAKE TITICAC
LIMA
Pisco
Trinidad
CUZCO & THE SACRED VALLEY p262
BOLIVIA
Moquegua
Santa Cruz
LA PAZ p222
Oruro
SUCRE
Iquique
Tarija
Estigarri
SALAR DE UYUNI p240
PACIFIC OCEAN
PARAGU
Antofagasta
ASUNC
Jujuy
THE ATACAMA DESERT p212
Tucumán
La Serena
Córdoba
Santa Fe
Mendoza
Valparaíso
Rosario
SANTIAGO p166
Santa Cruz
ARGENTINA
Concepción
Temuco
Mar del
THE LAKES DISTRICT p186
Valdivia
Bariloche
Puerto Montt
El Bolsón
Puerto Madryn
CHILE
Coyhaique
SOUTHERN P
p15
Río Gallegos
Falkland (Islas Ma
TORRES DEL PAINE p202
Punta Arenas
Ushuaia

Alpaca on the Inca Trail (p296), Peru
MAX MAXIMOV MM / SHUTTERSTOCK ©

South America's Top 20

Machu Picchu, Peru

South America's fabled Inca ruins

This fantastic Inca citadel (pictured; p282), lost to the world until its discovery in the early 20th century, stands as a ruin among ruins. With its emerald terraces backed by steep peaks and Andean ridges echoing on the horizon, the sight simply surpasses the imagination. This marvel of engineering has withstood six centuries of earthquakes, foreign invasion and howling weather. Discover it for yourself: wander through its stone temples and scale its dizzying heights.

JOEL SHAWN / SHUTTERSTOCK ©

1

Right: Girls dressed in traditional Peruvian clothing, Machu Picchu

AGUSTAVOP / GETTY IMAGES ©

STREETFLASH / GETTY IMAGES ©

Brazilian Amazon

2

The world's greatest rainforest

Home to the greatest collection of plant and animal life on earth, the awe-inspiring Amazon (pictured; p84) has outdoor excursions of all sorts: from easy nature hikes to scaling 50m trees, from luxury lodges to makeshift camps in the forest. Spend your day plying the winding waterways in a canoe, slow-boating between towns or scanning the canopy for monkeys. Whatever your interest, there's a jungle trip in the Amazon waiting to blow your mind. Top: Toucan

MAKINGSAUCE / GETTY IMAGES ©

Galápagos Islands, Ecuador

Enchanting islands packed with wildlife

The famous Galápagos Islands (p340), with their volcanic, otherworldly landscapes, are a magnet for wildlife lovers. Here, you can get up close and personal with massive lumbering tortoises, scurrying marine iguanas (the world's only seagoing lizard), prancing blue-footed boobies and a host of other unusual species. On snorkeling trips, you'll see playful doe-eyed sea lions, lightning-fast penguins and graceful sea turtles winging through the equatorial waters. Sea lions

3

Iguazú Falls, Brazil & Argentina

A jaw-dropping array of 275 waterfalls

The thunderous roar, the dramatic cascades, the refreshing sprays, the absolute miraculous work of Mother Nature – nothing prepares you for that first moment you set eyes upon Iguazú Falls (pictured; p112). On the Brazilian side, enjoy the wide-eyed view of the whole astounding scene stretching out before you in all its panoramic wonder. In Argentina, get up close and personal with the deafening Devil's Throat for a mind-blowing experience.

Rio de Janeiro, Brazil

Samba-charged city of beaches and mountains

On privileged real estate flanked by striking Atlantic-blue waters, sugary-white sands and a mountainous backdrop of Crayola-green rainforest, Rio's (p40) cinematic cityscape has few rivals. And once its soundtrack kicks in – a high-on-life siren song of bossa nova and samba – Rio's raw energy seizes you with the come-hither allure of a tropical fantasy. You'll have no choice but to follow. Right: View of Cristo Redentor (Christ the Redeemer; p48) and Pão de Açúcar (Sugarloaf Mountain; p46)

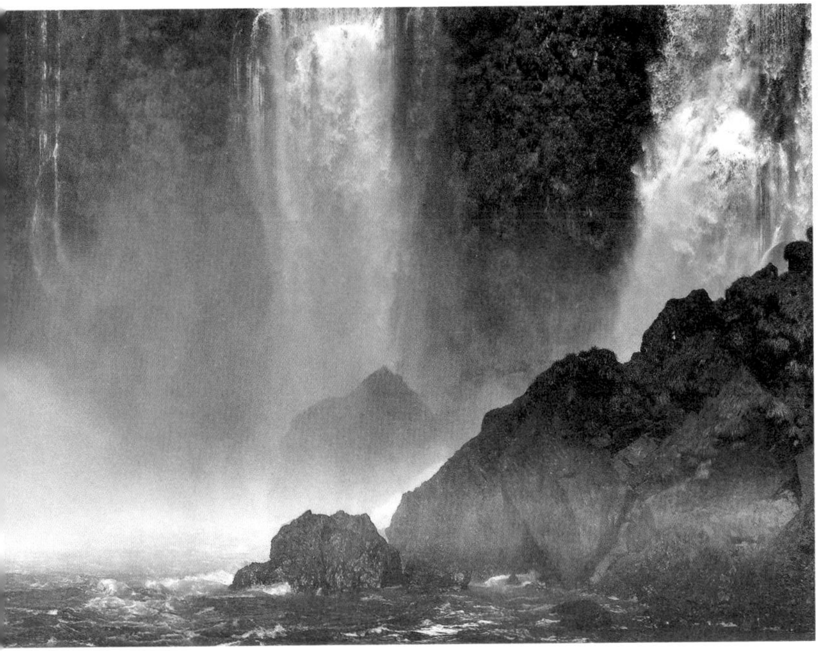

JPSANCHEZ / GETTY IMAGES ©

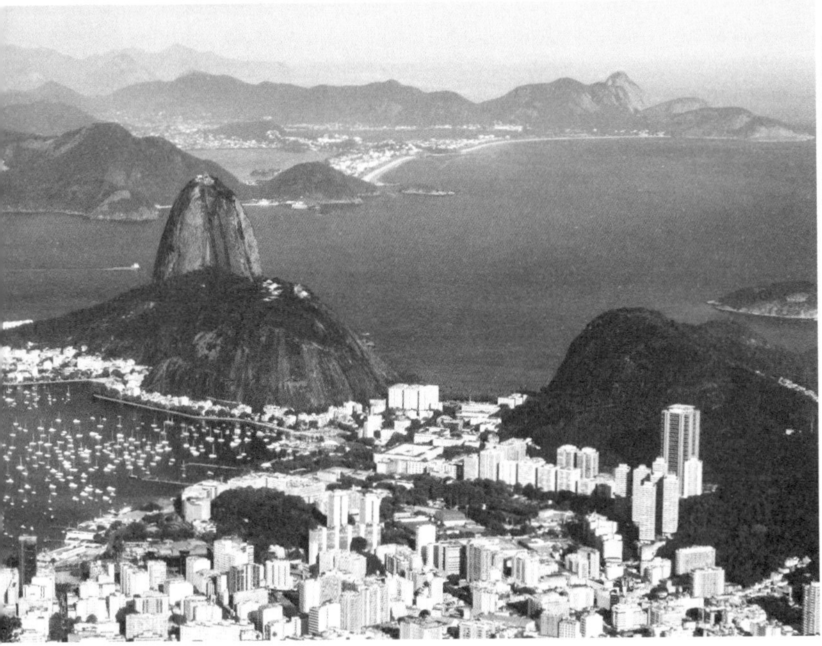

R.M. NUNES / SHUTTERSTOCK ©

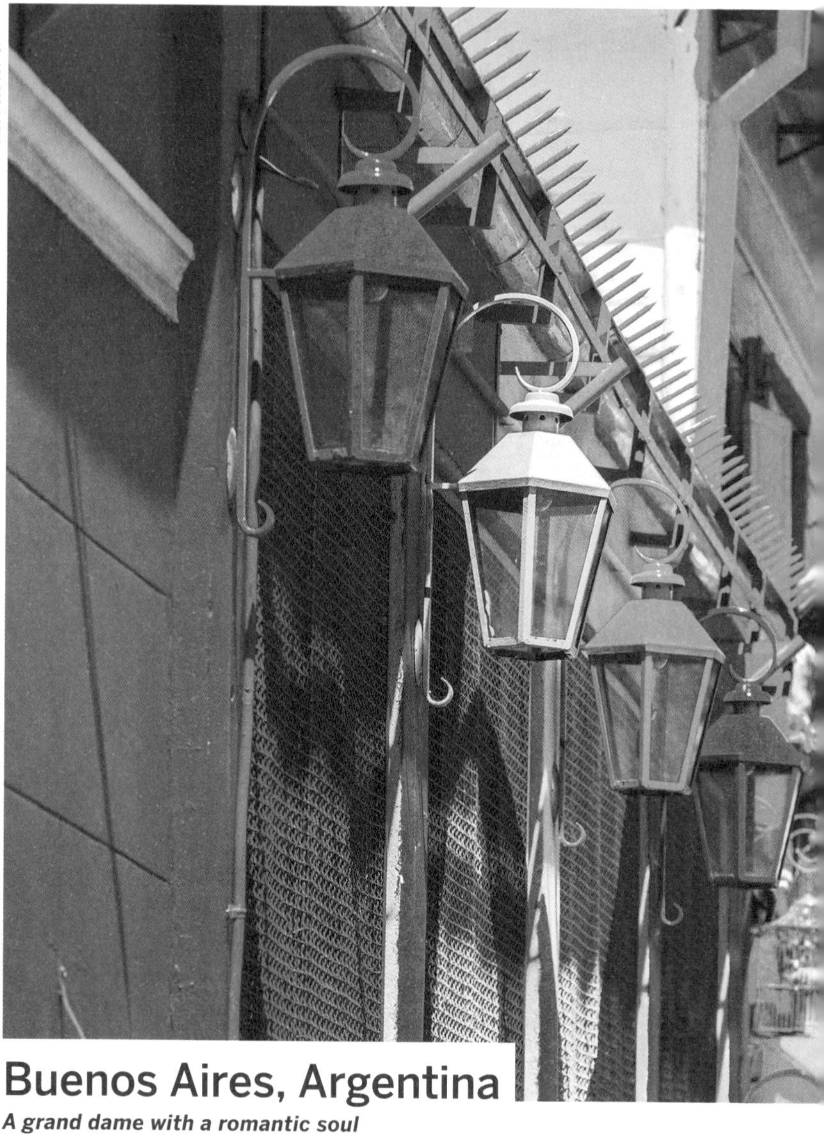

STUART DEE / GETTY IMAGES ©

Buenos Aires, Argentina

6

A grand dame with a romantic soul

Whip together a beautiful Argentine metropolis with gourmet cuisine, awesome shopping, frenzied nightlife and gorgeous locals, and you'll get Buenos Aires. It's a European-like, cosmopolitan city encompassing both slick and unsafe neighborhoods, but that's the appeal. You can experience classic cafes, amazing steaks, surprising architecture, energizing *fútbol* games and, of course, that sultry tango. Buenos Aires (p124) is elegant, seductive, emotional, confounding, frustrating and chock-full of attitude. A colorful facade in La Boca

MICHELE FALZONE / GETTY IMAGES ©

Torres del Paine, Chile

7

Hike amid dramatic Patagonian landscapes

The wind whips dark clouds overhead as the trail suddenly opens to reveal a stunning vista of granite spires soaring high above the Patagonian steppe. These are the Torres del Paine (p202), the proud centerpiece of Chile's famous national park. Trekking through this Unesco Biosphere Reserve isn't for the faint of heart – guides say the park sees all four seasons in a single day – but hiking the 'W' remains a rite of passage for adventurous travelers.

Hiker enjoying the view of Cuernos del Paine and Lake Pehoé

Cuzco & the Sacred Valley, Peru

Former capital of the Inca empire

With ancient cobblestone streets, grandiose baroque churches and the remnants of Inca temples with centuries-old carvings, no place looms larger in Andean history than Cuzco, a city that has been inhabited continuously since pre-Hispanic times. Mystic, commercial and chaotic, this unique city is still a stunner. It's also the gateway to the picturesque Sacred Valley, with its famed temples and colorful markets, as well as Machu Picchu just beyond. Right: Quechua woman in Cuzco (p262)

PAOLO MARCHETTI / GETTY IMAGES ©

Southern Patagonia, Argentina

Walk beside glaciers and shark-tooth summits

The rugged, mountainous wilderness of Southern Patagonia (p152) is a world-class trekking destination. In the Fitz Roy Range, you can plan challenging multiday treks, or plan shorter outings to take in stunning views just a day's hike from town. South of Fitz Roy, Perito Moreno (pictured far left; p156) is one of the most accessible glaciers on the planet. Watch from steel catwalks as building-sized icebergs calve from the face and crash into Lago Argentino.

Left: Magellanic penguin

JESS KRAFT / SHUTTERSTOCK ©

PXHIDALGO / GETTY IMAGES ©

ALESSANDRO_PINTO / GETTY IMAGES ©

Quito & the Central Highlands, Ecuador

10

Architectural jewel and gateway to Andean adventure

History lurks around every corner of Quito's (p318) vibrant Centro Histórico. Delve into the past by stepping off the cobblestones into beautifully maintained museums, historic mansions and jaw-dropping sanctuaries. Afterwards, join the festivities on lively La Ronda. Head further afield to outdoor adventures (and thermal springs) in Baños or the snowcapped scenery of Cotopaxi (pictured bottom left; p330). Top: Plaza Grande (p324); Bottom right: Quito's colonial-style facades

PAULO COSTA / 500PX ©

Lakes District, Chile

11

Adventure playground of lakes and mountains

While turquoise glacial lakes dominate the landscape, they're hardly the only attraction in this photogenic southern Chile region (p186). Play on towering, perfectly conal, snowcapped volcanoes. Visit charming lakeside hamlets such as Frutillar. Admire the green umbrella of national parks like Parque Nacional Huerquehue. A long list of outdoor adventures and a unique, German-influenced Latin culture make for a cinematic region that appeals to all. Top: Pier at Frutillar (p200)

LAZYLLAMA / SHUTTERSTOCK ©

Salvador, Brazil

12

World capital of Afro-Brazilian culture

Salvador (p70) is famous for *capoeira* (martial-art dance; pictured above), Candomblé, Olodum, colonial Portuguese architecture, African street food and one of the oldest lighthouses in the Americas. The city's past, marked by gritty stories of Portuguese seafaring and the heartbreaking history of the African slave trade, is one of hardship, but today's lively Bahian capital offers a unique fusion of two vibrant cultures. The music and nightlife scene culminates when Salvador hosts one of Brazil's best Carnavals.

HELDER GERALDO RIBEIRO / SHUTTERSTOCK ©

JOHN WARBURTON-LEE / GETTY IMAGES ©

PAKAWAT THUNGCHAROEN / GETTY IMAGES ©

The Atacama Desert, Chile

13

Otherworldly landscapes in northern Chile

See the desert don its surrealist cloak as you stand atop a giant sand dune, with the sun slipping below the horizon and multicolored hues bathing the sands, all with a backdrop of distant volcanoes and the rippling Cordillera de la Sal. This is just one small part of the Atacama Desert (p212), a mesmerizing landscape that encompasses red rock formations, jagged mountains, glittering salt lakes and sputtering geysers, plus dazzling star-filled skies. Top: Salar de Atacama (p218); Bottom left: Mountain biking in the desert (p219); Bottom right: Tourists at El Tatio Geysers (p217)

GALYNA ANDRUSHKO / SHUTTERSTOCK ©

The Cordilleras, Peru

14

Ground zero for outdoor adventure in Peru

The Cordilleras (pictured; p304) are one of the preeminent hiking, trekking and backpacking spots in South America. Every which way you throw your gaze, perennially glaciated white peaks razor their way through expansive mantles of lime-green valleys. The Cordillera Blanca is one of the highest mountain ranges in the world and boasts the enigmatic 3000-year-old ruins of Chavín de Huántar.

WALTER MARIO STEIN / SHUTTERSTOCK ©

The Pantanal, Brazil

15

Wildlife-watching in the wetlands

Few places on earth can match the wildlife-watching of the Pantanal (p102), a wondrously remote wetland in the heart of Brazil. From cute capybaras to stately storks, the animal life simply abounds and is remarkably easy to see in the open marshy surroundings, whether you are traveling on foot, on horseback or by boat. Among the big draws is the elusive jaguar (pictured above) – this is one of the best places in South America to spot one.

F11PHOTO / SHUTTERSTOCK ©

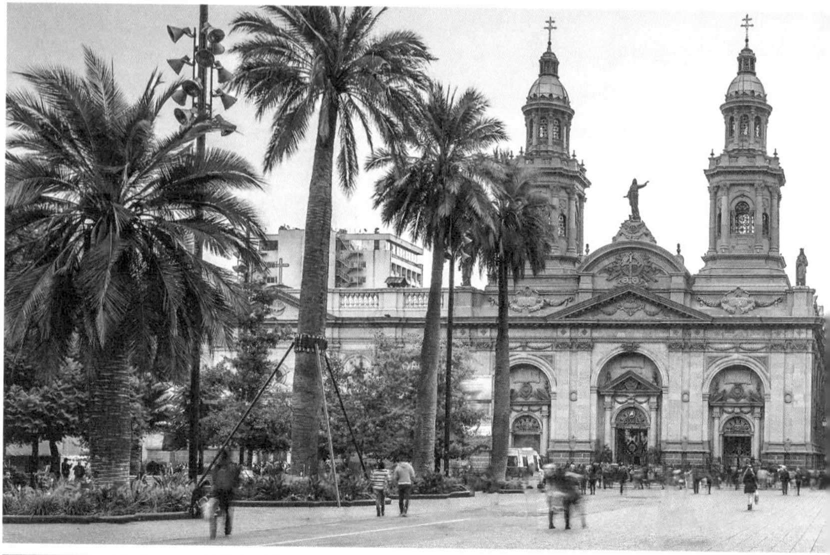

HEDONIMAGES / GETTY IMAGES ©

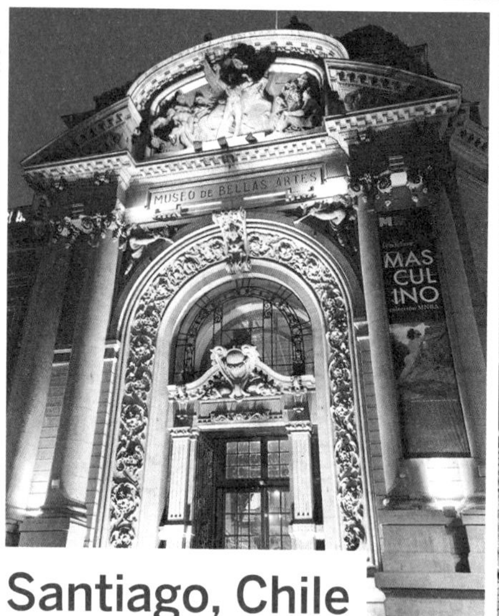

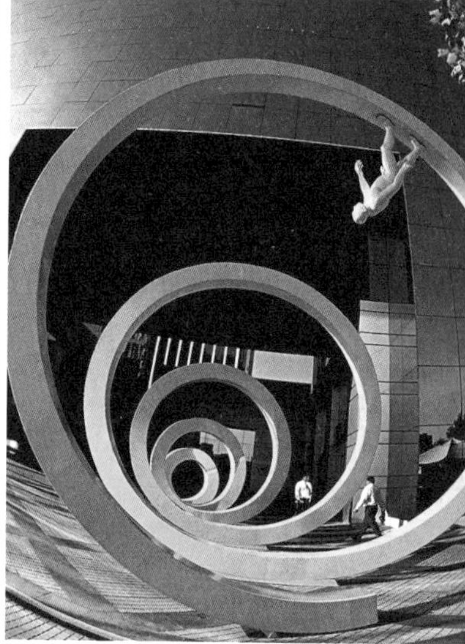

KRZYSZTOF DYDYNSKI / GETTY IMAGES ©

16

Santiago, Chile

Chile's art- and food-loving capital

Santiago (p166) is the center of the nation's cultural and intellectual universe. See the places that inspired the great poet Pablo Neruda, followed by visits to the grand collections in the Museo Nacional de Bellas Artes (pictured bottom left). By evening delve into Santiago's avant-garde restaurant scene, followed by a late night exploring raucous beer halls, candlelit poetry houses and just about anything else your inner Bacchus desires. Top: Plaza de Armas and the Catedral Metropolitana de Santiago; Bottom right: 'Yellow Spiral' sculpture by Osvaldo Pena

ANTONIO SALINAS L / GETTY IMAGES ©

Salar de Uyuni, Bolivia

17

The surreal salt flats of Bolivia

While a three-day jeep tour through the world's largest salt flat (pictured; p240) will leave your bones chattering, it could quite possibly be the defining experience of your Bolivian adventure. The vastness, austerity and crystalline perfection of the salt flat will inspire you. An early-morning exploration of rock gardens, geyser fields and piping-hot springs along with the camaraderie of three days on the road with your fellow 'Salterians' will create a lasting memory.

OLGA GAVRILOVA / SHUTTERSTOCK ©

Lake Titicaca, Peru

18

Floating reed islands and traditional living

Less a lake than a highland ocean, Titicaca (p250) is home to fantastical sights – none more surreal than the floating islands crafted entirely of tightly woven totora reeds. Requiring near constant renovation, the reeds are also used to build thatched homes and elegant boats. There are plenty of other islands to choose from, such as Isla Taquile, where rural Andean life from centuries long gone lives on, and where the quinoa soup recipe has been perfected. Puno (p260)

19

Cartagena, Colombia

Colonial grandeur on the Caribbean

The hands of the clock on the Puerta del Reloj wind back 400 years in an instant as visitors enter the walled old town of Cartagena (p352). Strolling the cobblestone streets is like stepping into the pages of a Gabriel García Márquez novel. The pastel-toned balconies overflow with bougainvillea and the streets are abuzz with food stalls around magnificent Spanish-built churches, squares and historic mansions. Right: Colonial building facade

20

La Paz, Bolivia

High-energy city famed for its markets

The world's highest capital city, La Paz (p222) is a dynamic whirl of tootling taxis, bustling indigenous markets and fast-moving pedestrians all mixing it up beneath the blinding *altiplano* sun. Welcome to one of South America's most fascinating cities: a strangely intoxicating metropolis of rich ethnographic museums and stunning hilltop lookouts with a packed festival calendar. La Paz is also the gateway to intriguing pre-Columbian ruins outside of town. Right: Women in traditional Bolivian clothing

RAFAL CICHAWA / SHUTTERSTOCK ©

PEEK CREATIVE COLLECTIVE / SHUTTERSTOCK ©

Need to Know

When to Go

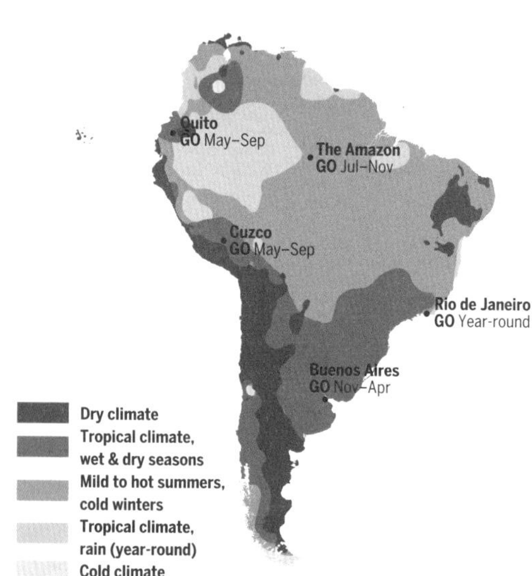

High Season (Dec–Mar)

- It's high season in Brazil and the Atlantic coast; beaches and festivals (such as Carnaval) are big draws.
- The best time to visit Patagonia, though expect higher prices.

Shoulder (Oct–Nov)

- It's dry season in the Amazon, making for fine wildlife-watching.
- Fewer crowds and lower prices make this a good time to visit Buenos Aires, Rio and other coastal destinations.

Low Season (Jul–Aug)

- In Chile and Argentina, many services close at beach resorts, and mountain passes can be blocked by snow.

Currency

Argentine peso (AR$)
Bolivian boliviano (B$)
Brazilian real (R$)
Chilean peso (CH$),
Colombian peso (COP$)
Ecuador: US dollar (US$)
Peru: nuevo sol (S)

Languages

Portuguese, Spanish, and over 500 indigenous languages

Visas

Visas are sometimes required, or in some cases other charges must be paid, for example for reciprocity fees or tourist cards.

Money

ATMs are available in major towns and cities; stock up on funds before visiting remote areas. Credit cards are widely accepted.

Cell Phones

Local SIM cards can be used in unlocked European and Australian (GSM) phones. Or you can purchase a phone when you arrive.

Time

Ranges from GMT minus three hours (Brazil's east coast) to GMT minus six hours (the Galapagos Islands).

Daily Costs

Budget: Less than US$50

- Dorm beds: from US$12
- Double rooms: from US$30
- Shopping at markets, eating inexpensive set meals: from US$5

Midrange: US$50–120

- Budget jungle lodge in the Amazon per day: US$50–80
- Hiking and cycling tours per day: from US$50
- 3½-day Manaus–Belem boat trip (hammock fare): from US$100

Top End: More than US$120

- Hiking the Inca Trail (four-day trek) per person: US$600
- Multiday Galápagos cruise per day: around US$200

Useful Websites

Lonely Planet (www.lonelyplanet.com/south-america) Destination information, hotel bookings, traveler forum and more.

Latin American Network Information Center (www.lanic.utexas.edu) Links to all things Latin American.

UK Foreign Travel Advice (www.gov.uk/foreign-travel-advice) Travel advisories.

US State Department (www.state.gov) Travel advice and warnings.

Thorn Tree (lonelyplanet.com/thorntree) Get trip recommendations and destination tips from other travelers.

Opening Hours

On Sunday, nearly everything is closed. In the Andean countries, businesses tend to close earlier.

Banks Monday to Friday (for money changing).

Businesses 8am or 9am–noon and 2pm–8pm or 9pm Monday to Friday. Shorter hours on Saturday.

Arriving in South America

Aeropuerto Internacional Ministro Pistarini, Buenos Aires (p401)

Frequent shuttle buses head downtown (AR$240); taxis cost around AR$1200.

Aeropuerto Internacional Arturo Merino Benítez, Santiago (p402)

Frequent shuttle connections go to downtown Santiago hotels (40 minutes, CH$7000), plus local buses (one hour to downtown, then transfer to the metro or Transantiago bus; CH$1700) and taxis (CH$18,000).

Galeão International Airport, Rio de Janeiro (p401)

Bus 2018 (R$16, one to two hours, every 30 minutes) goes to Copacabana and Ipanema. Radio taxis cost R$130 (45 to 90 minutes). Metered yellow-and-blue *comum* (common) taxis cost between R$82 and R$100. Shuttle service costs R$25.

Getting Around

Bus Extensive services throughout the continent, except for the Amazon. You'll find reclinable seats (and super-powered air-conditioning on long hauls).

Plane Useful for crossing immense distances; can save days of travel; prices are generally high, but airfare promotions are frequent.

Car Useful for traveling at your own pace, though cities can be difficult to navigate and secure parking is a must.

Boat Slow, uncomfortable, but brag-worthy transport between towns in the Amazon, with trips measured in days rather than hours. You'll need a hammock, snacks, drinking water and a high tolerance for boredom.

Train Limited networks, generally geared toward tourists.

For more on **getting around**, see p403 

Hot Spots for...

MATT MUNRO / LONELY PLANET ©

Dramatic Scenery

Thundering waterfalls, volcanoes and otherworldly desert landscapes. When gazing upon these natural wonders, you might feel like you've stepped back a few million years.

Iguazú Falls (pictured; p112)
Spread between Argentina and Brazil, these are some of the most spectacular waterfalls on earth.

Garganta del Diablo (p116)
A close-up view of the powerful torrent.

Torres del Paine (p202)
In southern Patagonia, sparkling glaciers, topaz lakes and sheer granite cliff-faces dominate the landscape.

The 'W' (p206)
Photographing the dramatic scenery on this multiday trek.

Salar de Uyuni (p240)
The world's largest salt flats are a dazzling remnant of a vast prehistoric lake.

Isla Incahuasi (p244)
Gazing over the cacti and endless salt horizon.

TETIANA TUCHYK / SHUTTERSTOCK ©

Urban Allure

Life spills into the streets with pop-up graffiti murals, sprawling food markets, and buzzing music-filled cafes in South America's colorful city neighborhoods.

Rio de Janeiro (pictured; p40)
The Cidade Maravilhosa is full of lovely beaches, samba-fueled nightlife and jaw-dropping scenery.

Pão de Açúcar (p46)
Admire the view over one of the world's most captivating cities.

Buenos Aires (p124)
A place that's hard to leave, with old-world cafes, sultry tango clubs, and French and Italianate architecture.

Esquina Carlos Gardel (p130)
Nothing captures the city's essence like the tango.

Santiago (p166)
Grand architecture, vast green spaces and a thriving arts scene: Chile's capital has it all.

Centro Gabriela Mistral (p177)
Grab the cultural pulse at this performing-arts center.

Wildlife

South America is home to more plant and animal species than any other place on earth; it has countless settings to watch wildlife.

GUENTERGUNI / GETTY IMAGES ©

The Amazon (p84)
An unforgettable experience whether you slow-boat along the river or base at an upscale jungle lodge.

Mamirauá Reserve (p90)
Marveling at the abundant wildlife in this remote reserve.

The Pantanal (p102)
At these wildlife-rich wetlands, you can spot countless birds and mammals.

Pantanal Jaguar Camp (p108)
Spotting felines at this aptly named wilderness lodge.

The Galápagos (pictured; p340)
These volcanic islands are home to creatures so tame, you'll practically be tripping over all the sea lions.

Rancho Primicias (p345)
Admiring tortoises as they lumber through the highlands.

Outdoor Adventures

Get your adrenaline fix clambering past snow-capped peaks, paddling along rushing rivers or mountain biking down slopes. There are many ways to get your heart racing.

CHRISTIAN KOBER / ROBERTHARDING / GETTY IMAGES ©

Volcan Cotopaxi (pictured; p330)
If you're fit you can try for the ascent. Or go horseback riding from a hacienda.

Condor Trekk (p333)
Take a guided trek to the summit for a magnificent sunrise.

Lakes District (p186)
Against a mountainous backdrop, you can take an adventure-filled trip on class IV rapids.

Al Sur (p191)
Splashing through the white water on a guided rafting trip.

The Atacama Desert (p212)
The desert oasis town of San Pedro de Atacama offers daytime adventures followed by nights of stargazing.

Valle de la Muerte (p216)
Sandboarding down dunes against a red-rock backdrop.

Essential South America

SL PHOTOGRAPHY / SHUTTERSTOCK ©

Activities

There's a whole range of adventures awaiting in South America. You can go hiking amid the soaring peaks of the Andes, go rafting along rushing jungle-lined rivers and overnight in a rainforest lodge with the sounds of the Amazon all around you. And you'll find many more astounding options in every country on the continent. There's memorable diving off of the Galápagos, trekking and mountaineering in the Andes, wildlife-watching in the Pantanal and legendary mountain biking outside of La Paz.

Shopping

South America has a treasure trove of arts and crafts. All across the continent, you'll find lively markets packed with crafts and clothing. In the Andes, you'll find alpaca wool sweaters and scarves, woven textiles, ceramics, masks and gold and silver jewelry. Brazil has its own enormous crafts scene, with some of the finest works emerging from the Northeast. Neighboring Argentina has myriad temptations for shoppers, from street fairs and antique shops to indie clothing boutiques. Wherever you roam, when you need essentials, large North American–style malls and sizable supermarkets can be found in the big cities.

Eating

South America has staggering variety when it comes to cuisine. You'll find sizzling steaks in Buenos Aires, creative twists on age-old dishes in the Andes, and tender freshwater fish in the Amazon. Every country has its own specialties, and within countries you'll find a great range (with coastal recipes quite different from cooking traditions in the interior). The capitals and big cities of South America are all fertile grounds for foodies, though increasingly, you can also find fantastic meals in smaller towns. Memorable meals can sometimes be had at markets, as well.

LARISA BLINOVA / SHUTTERSTOCK ©

Drinking & Nightlife

You'll find dynamic nightlife in all of South America's big cities, particularly in Rio, Buenos Aires and Santiago. You'll find easy-going beach bars, DJ-fueled clubs, stylishly decked speakeasies and cocktail bars, as well as craft-beer bars tapping into the recent craze for local microbrews. Wine bars are all the rage in Argentina and Chile, and nearly every region has its specialty drinks – from *canelazo* (a hot rum, cinnamon and orange juice concoction) in the Andean highlands to *mate* (hot *yerba mate* drunk from a special gourd) in Argentina, Chile and southern Brazil.

Entertainment

Live music is the lifeblood of South America. Brazil's music scene is unrivaled, with buzzing samba clubs in Rio and heart-pounding drum corps filling the streets of Salvador. Buenos Aires has its magnificent tango scene, which can mean watching or dancing depending on the place (plenty of places offer lessons), while Peru and Bolivia have their *peñas*, venues for traditional folkloric music. Aside from live rhythms, there are countless other draws in South America, including theater, dance and indie cinema, as well as live football matches, which bring die-hard fans to local (sometimes massive!) sporting arenas in every corner of the continent.

★ Live Music Venues

Rio Scenarium (p67)
Tango Porteño (p129)
Espaço D'Venetta (p74)
Jallalla (p237)
Café Havana (p366)

From left: Traditional Peruvian handmade textiles; Peruvian ceviche

Month by Month

January

It's peak season in Brazil and Argentina. Expect higher prices, bigger crowds and sweltering temperatures as city dwellers head to the coast. This is also the most popular time to travel to Patagonia.

☆ Santiago a Mil

This 17-day theater and dance fest (www.fundacionteatroamil.cl/en/santiagoamil) features dozens of shows and events around the Chilean capital, staged by international and local companies.

February

The sizzling summer is still in full swing in the southern half of the continent, with exorbitant prices and sparse accommodations during Brazilian Carnaval. Elsewhere, it's fairly wet in the northern Andes and the Amazon region.

Carnaval

The famous bacchanalian event happens across South America, though the pre-Lenten revelry is most famous in Brazil. Rio (p40) and Salvador (p70) throw the liveliest bashes, with street parades, costume parties and round-the-clock merriment.

Fiesta de la Virgen de Candelaria

Celebrated across the highlands in Bolivia and Peru, this festival features music, drinking, eating, dancing, processions and fireworks. Some of the liveliest celebrations take place in Puno (Peru). The big day is February 2.

March

While the weather is still warm in the south, the crowds thin and prices fall a bit at beach destinations. It's still rainy in the northern Andes.

Above: Carnaval in Rio de Janeiro (p40)

EFE NEWS AGENCY / ALAMY STOCK PHOTO ©

☆ Lollapalooza Chile

Chile's rock fest (www.lollapaloozacl.com) kicks off in Santiago in late March or early April, and features an impressive line-up of homegrown and international groups on par with the North American version of Lollapalooza.

Concurso Nacional de Belleza

Also known as the Carnaval de Cartagena, this beauty pageant and festival (www.srtacolombia.org), Cartagena's most important annual bash, celebrates the city's independence day and the crowning of Miss Colombia. Festivities include street dancing, music and fancy-dress parades.

April

In the Andes, crowds and high-season prices mark Holy Week, a boon of national tourism in March or April. Elsewhere on the continent, you'll find generally fewer crowds and good post-summer prices.

★ Best Festivals

Carnaval, February

Fiesta de la Virgen de Candelaria, February

Inti Raymi, June

Tango BA Festival y Mundial, August

Reveillon, December

Semana Santa

Throughout Latin America, Holy Week is celebrated with fervor. One of the most colorful processions happens in Quito (Ecuador) when purple-robed penitents parade through the streets on Good Friday.

May

Buenos Aires and Rio head into low season, with cooler weather and lower prices; the rain begins to taper off in the Andes, making it a fine time to go trekking.

Above: Lenny Kravitz performing at Lollapalooza Chile

La Festividad de Nuestro Señor Jesús del Gran Poder

Held in late May or early June, La Festividad de Nuestro Señor Jesús del Gran Poder in La Paz involves candle processions, elaborate costumes and dancing.

June

High season in the Andean nations corresponds with the North American summer (June to August), when the weather is also sunniest and driest. Book major tours (such as hiking the Inca Trail) well in advance.

Inti Raymi

This millennia-old indigenous celebration of the solstice and harvest is celebrated in many Andean towns. In Cuzco it's the event of the year, attracting thousands of visitors for street fairs, open-air concerts and historical reenactments.

August

It's dry in many parts of the continent, making August a fine time to visit the Amazon, the Pantanal or the Andes. It's chilly to freezing south of the Tropic of Capricorn.

☆ Tango BA Festival y Mundial

World-class tango dancers perform throughout Buenos Aires during this two-week festival (http://festivales.buenosaires.gob.ar). Competition is fierce for the title of 'world's best tango dancer.' You can also hone your own moves at classes and workshops.

September

The weather remains dry and sunny (but chilly) in the Andes, though you'll find fewer crowds. September is also a good (less rainy) time to visit the Amazon.

Fiestas Patrias

Chilean Independence is feted during Fiestas Patrias (week of September 18), with a week of big barbecues, *terremotos* (potent wine punch) and merrymaking all over Chile.

October

Heavy rains make for tough traveling in Colombia, while the Andes generally have milder weather. In Bolivia, Brazil, Chile and Argentina, temperatures are mild, making it a pleasant time to visit.

Oktoberfest

Join the swillers and oompah bands in Puerto Varas, Chile, for live music in lederhosen and beer festivals.

November

Rainier days are on the horizon in the Amazon. Generally November nets better prices, good weather and fewer crowds than December in most parts of South America.

Puno Week

Starting November 5, this week-long festival involves several days of spectacular costumes and street dancing to celebrate the legendary emergence of the first Inca, Manco Cápac.

☆ Buenos Aires Jazz Festival Internacional

BA's big jazz festival (www.buenosairesjazz.gob.ar) showcases the talents of more than 200 musicians who play in 70 different concerts around town.

December

December marks the beginning of summer, with beach days (and higher prices) on both the Atlantic and Pacific coasts. It's fairly rainy in the Andes.

Founding of Quito Festival

Quito's biggest bash is a much anticipated event, with parades, street dances and open-air concerts throughout town.

Reveillon

There are many great spots in South America to celebrate New Year's Eve, but Rio is a perennial favorite. Some two million revelers, dressed in white to bring good luck, pack the sands of Copacabana Beach to watch fireworks light up the night sky.

Get Inspired

CIRCUMNAVIGATION / SHUTTERSTOCK ©

Read

Gabriel García Márquez & Mario Vargas Llosa García Márquez *(Love in the Time of Cholera)* and Vargas Llosa *(War of the End of the World)*, both Nobel Prize winners, are among the continent's greatest writers.

Jorge Luis Borges This legend of modern literature is best known for his labyrinthine tales and playful melding of myth and truth, such as in *Ficciones*.

Jorge Amado Colorful, ribald stories set in Bahia, such as the classic *Dona Flor and Her Two Husbands*.

Bruce Chatwin Poignant and beautifully written travel narrative, *In Patagonia*, blends fact and fable.

Watch

The Motorcycle Diaries (2004) The road trip that made a revolutionary.

Central do Brasil (1998) Moving tale of a homeless boy and an older woman on a journey across Brazil.

Neruda (2016) The communist Chilean poet goes on the run.

Aguirre, the Wrath of God (1972) Werner Herzog's historical masterpiece about a fruitless search for El Dorado.

Amargo Mar (1984) Highly regarded look at the loss of Bolivia's coastline to Chile.

Qué Tan Lejos (2006) Road movie about two women in the Ecuadorian highlands.

Listen

África Brasil (Jorge Ben Jor) Celebratory album from the 1970s that blends funk, samba and blues.

Amanecer (Bomba Estéreo) A blend of African, indigenous and vibrant dance beats by an inventive Colombian band.

Lunático (Gotan Project) Brilliant fusing of tango with electronic grooves.

Roots of Chicha (various artists) Wild Peruvian cumbias that channel psychedelic, rock and melodic sounds.

Tropicália ou Panis et Circencis A famed Brazilian collaboration between Gilberto Gil, Caetano Veloso, Gal Costa and Tom Zé.

Above: Glaciar Grey (p208), Torres del Paine, Chile

Seven-Day Itineraries

Forests, Falls & Urban Allure

Careful planning will allow you to take in some of the continent's most majestic sights on a one-week itinerary. You'll get a taste of the Amazon, see awe-inspiring waterfalls and explore two of South America's most dynamic cities.

1 **The Amazon** (p84) Delve into the mother of all rainforests on a two-day wildlife-watching excursion in Brazil. ✈ 4¼ hrs to Rio

2 **Rio de Janeiro** (p40) Spend two days enjoying beaches, live samba, and lofty views atop Cristo Redentor. ✈ 2 hrs to Iguazú Falls

3 **Iguazú Falls** (p112) On a full day, take in one of South America's great wonders, the thundering waterfalls of Iguazú. ✈ 2 hrs to Buenos Aires

4 **Buenos Aires** (p124) The last two days enjoy colorful neighborhoods, tango-fueled nightlife, and the continent's best restaurants in Argentina's steamy capital.

Colonial Towns & Lava Landscapes

On a seven-day trip in the northwest, you can visit two colonial cities followed by a memorable cruise around the Galápagos Islands. The varied terrain encompasses the Caribbean Sea, jagged Andean peaks and volcanoes in the Pacific.

1 **Cartagena** (p352) Wander through the cobblestone streets of this romantic, Unesco-listed town on the Caribbean. ✈ 4¼ hrs to Quito

2 **Quito** (p318) Over two days, explore the magnificent colonial center of this Ecuadorian jewel fringed by the Andes. ✈ 2 hrs to Baltra

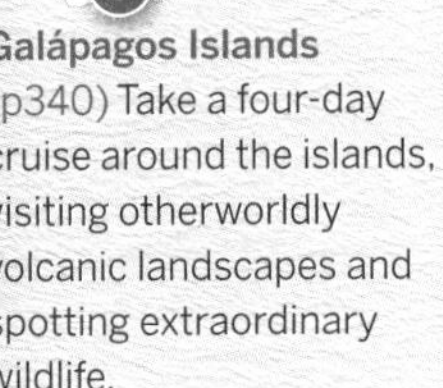

3 **Galápagos Islands** (p340) Take a four-day cruise around the islands, visiting otherworldly volcanic landscapes and spotting extraordinary wildlife.

FROM LEFT: ROCHAR BEIRO / SHUTTERSTOCK ©; WESTEND61 / GETTY IMAGES ©

10-Day Itinerary

Grand Adventures in the South

A paradise for lovers of the great outdoors, the south beckons with glacial lakes and dramatic peaks. You'll get a dose of city life before heading down to Chile's photogenic Lakes District, then on to the big open skies of Patagonia.

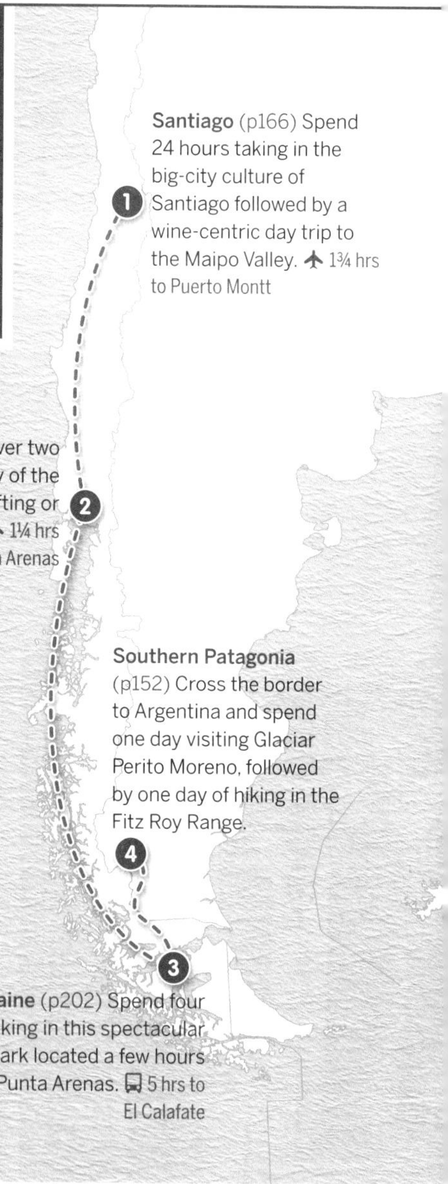

1 **Santiago** (p166) Spend 24 hours taking in the big-city culture of Santiago followed by a wine-centric day trip to the Maipo Valley. ✈ 1¾ hrs to Puerto Montt

2 **The Lakes District** (p186) Over two days, take in the pretty scenery of the Lakes District, followed by a rafting or mountain-biking adventure. ✈ 1¼ hrs to Punta Arenas

3 **Torres del Paine** (p202) Spend four days trekking in this spectacular national park located a few hours north of Punta Arenas. 🚌 5 hrs to El Calafate

4 **Southern Patagonia** (p152) Cross the border to Argentina and spend one day visiting Glaciar Perito Moreno, followed by one day of hiking in the Fitz Roy Range.

FROM LEFT: JOSE LUIS STEPHENS / EYEEM / GETTY IMAGES © ICYS / GETTY IMAGES © MICHELE FALZONE / GETTY IMAGES ©

Two-Week Itinerary

From the Andes to the Atacama

Over two weeks, you'll join an unforgettable hike along the Inca Trail and experience Andean wonders: ancient indigenous temples, floating islands, and one (literally) breathtaking metropolis. The trip ends amid the otherworldly landscapes of the Atacama Desert.

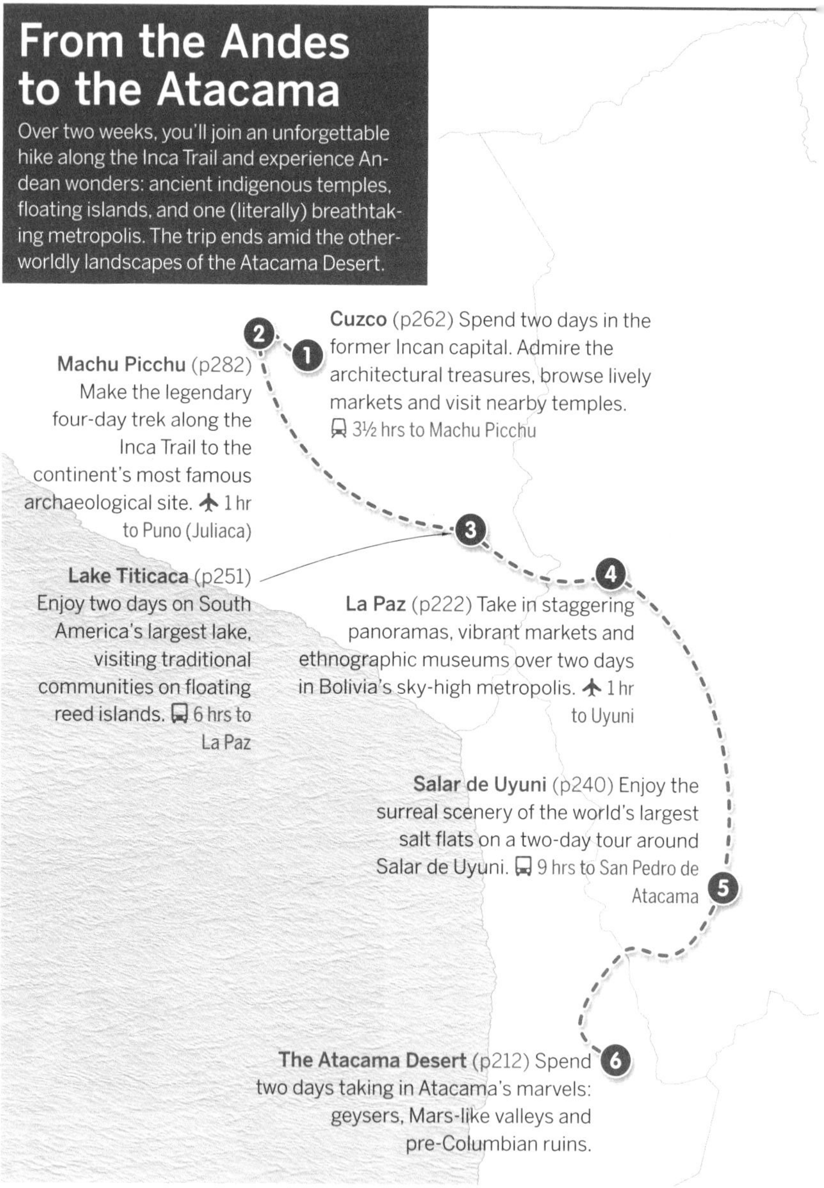

1 **Cuzco** (p262) Spend two days in the former Incan capital. Admire the architectural treasures, browse lively markets and visit nearby temples. 3½ hrs to Machu Picchu

2 **Machu Picchu** (p282) Make the legendary four-day trek along the Inca Trail to the continent's most famous archaeological site. 1 hr to Puno (Juliaca)

3 **Lake Titicaca** (p251) Enjoy two days on South America's largest lake, visiting traditional communities on floating reed islands. 6 hrs to La Paz

4 **La Paz** (p222) Take in staggering panoramas, vibrant markets and ethnographic museums over two days in Bolivia's sky-high metropolis. 1 hr to Uyuni

5 **Salar de Uyuni** (p240) Enjoy the surreal scenery of the world's largest salt flats on a two-day tour around Salar de Uyuni. 9 hrs to San Pedro de Atacama

6 **The Atacama Desert** (p212) Spend two days taking in Atacama's marvels: geysers, Mars-like valleys and pre-Columbian ruins.

2

5

6

FROM LEFT: SUNSINGER / SHUTTERSTOCK © KAZUKI KIMURA / EYEEM / GETTY IMAGES © DANTE BUSQUETS / SHUTTERSTOCK ©

Family Travel

In general, wherever you roam in South America, you'll find a warm welcome when traveling with children. Family culture is strong in Latin America and locals generally do their best to accommodate young travelers. That said, infrastructure can be lacking. Baby-change facilities are rare outside of big cities and pushing strollers (prams) around can be a challenge amid broken pavements and missing sidewalks (a wearable baby carrier is a better idea). Public transport can often be quite crowded. For insider tips check out Lonely Planet's *Travel with Children*.

Lodging

The great majority of hotels accept children without any problems; the most upscale may even offer babysitting services. The only places with possible minimum age restrictions are small boutique hotels or guesthouses. During summer, reserving a hotel with a pool can be a good idea. Also look for places with kitchenettes.

Apartments are available in nearly every city; in less-urban holiday destinations you can look for *cabañas* (cabins) with full kitchens. Larger campgrounds often have *cabañas,* common cooking facilities and sometimes play structures.

Hostels are usually not the best environment for kids, but a few welcome them.

Dining

While restaurants don't offer special kids' meals, most offer a variety of dishes suitable for children; none are spicy. It is perfectly acceptable to order a meal to split between two children or an adult and a child; most portions are abundant.

The only challenge to dining families is the late hours in Argentina and Chile, where restaurants open for dinner no earlier than 7pm, sometimes 8pm, and service can be quite slow. Bring a journal or scribble book and crayons for the kids to pass the time.

Local snacks are handy for hungry little ones. Empanadas make good, healthy

DFLC PRINTS / SHUTTERSTOCK ©

snacks that are fun to eat. You'll find tropical juices, coconut water and snacks such as *pão de queijo* (cheese bread), served at ubiquitous juice bars in Brazil. And ice cream is found everywhere on the continent – an essential treat on hot days!

★ Best Destinations for Kids

Galápagos Islands (p340)

Iguazú Falls (p112)

Buenos Aires (p124)

Santiago (p166)

Rio de Janeiro (p40)

Before You Go

Keep the kids in mind as you plan your itinerary or include them in the trip planning from the get-go. If renting a car, ask ahead if you can book a child's seat, as they are not always available. It's not necessary to be tied down to a schedule while traveling in the continent; plenty of activities can be booked just a few days in advance.

Need to Know

- Disposable diapers (nappies) are found in big-city supermarkets, but variety may be limited, so come prepared.
- Cribs (cots) aren't widely available in hotel rooms.
- Children get in free or half-price to most major sights around South America.
- Baby formula isn't always available outside major cities; bring your own supply.
- In Argentina and southern Chile, outdoor activities are best experienced outside the winter months of June through August (with the exception of skiing, of course).

From left: Tourist photographing marine iguanas on Isla Fernandina (p349), Galápagos Islands; Parque Bicentenario (p177), Santiago, Chile

RIO DE JANEIRO, BRAZIL

In this Chapter

Rio de Janeiro, Brazil

Flanked by gorgeous mountains, golden beaches and verdant rainforests fronting deep-blue sea, Rio de Janeiro occupies one of the most spectacular settings of any metropolis in the world. Tack on one of the sexiest populations on the planet and you have an intoxicating tropical cocktail.

Rio's residents, known as cariocas, have perfected the art of living well. Prepare to be seduced as you stroll world-famous beaches like Copacabana and Ipanema, enjoy the views from atop Corcovado or Pão de Açúcar, and join the party at dance halls, bars and open-air cafes, which proliferate around the city.

Two Days in Rio de Janeiro

Spend the first day enjoying the sand and sun off Ipanema Beach. Have dinner at **Zazá Bistrô Tropical** (p60) and drinks at **Nosso** (p66). On day two, get active along Copacabana Beach, followed by a trip to **Pão de Açúcar** (p47) for fabled views over the city. Cap the day with live samba at **Rio Scenarium** (p67) in Lapa.

Four Days in Rio de Janeiro

On your third day, visit the lush **Jardim Botânico** (p53), then head skyward for fabulous views beneath open-armed Cristo Redentor. End the day with drinks at lakeside **Palaphita Kitch** (p66). On the last day, check out the museums and baroque churches of Centro, art-gaze along the **Boulevard Olímpico** (p53) and have a sunset dinner and drinks at atmospheric **Xian** (p64).

Previous page: Aerial view of Rio de Janeiro

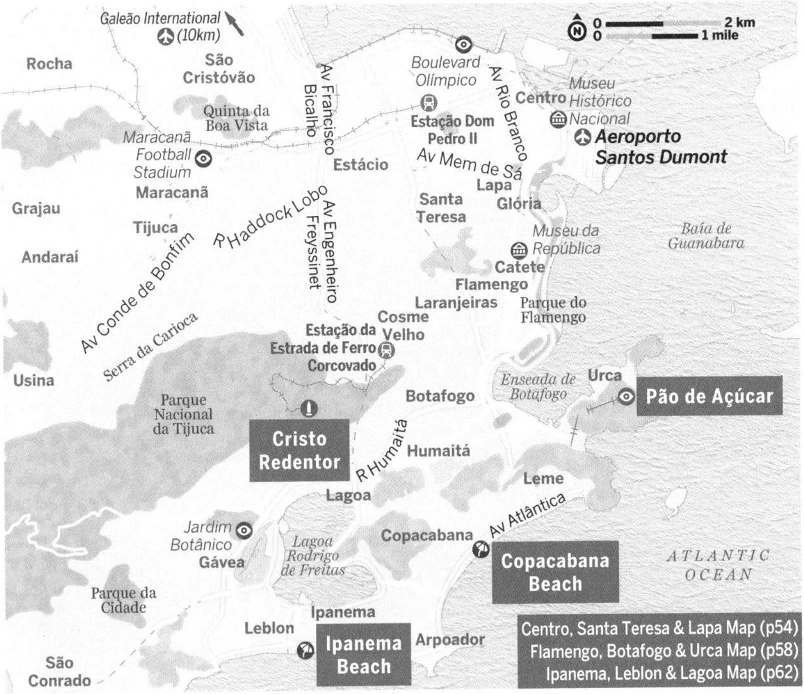

Galeão International (10km)
Rocha
São Cristóvão
Quinta da Boa Vista
Maracanã Football Stadium
Maracanã
Grajau
Tijuca
Andaraí
Usina
Av Francisco Bicalho
Estácio
R Haddock Lobo
Av Engenheiro Freyssinet
Av Conde de Bonfim
Serra da Carioca
Parque Nacional da Tijuca
Boulevard Olímpico
Estação Dom Pedro II
Av Rio Branco
Centro
Museu Histórico Nacional
Aeroporto Santos Dumont
Av Mem de Sá
Lapa
Glória
Santa Teresa
Museu da República
Baía de Guanabara
Catete
Flamengo
Laranjeiras
Parque do Flamengo
Cosme Velho
Estação da Estrada de Ferro Corcovado
Cristo Redentor
Botafogo
Enseada de Botafogo
Urca
Pão de Açúcar
R Humaitá
Humaitá
Leme
Lagoa
Av Atlântica
Jardim Botânico
Gávea
Lagoa Rodrigo de Freitas
Copacabana
Copacabana Beach
ATLANTIC OCEAN
Parque da Cidade
Ipanema
Leblon
Ipanema Beach
Arpoador
São Conrado

Centro, Santa Teresa & Lapa Map (p54)
Flamengo, Botafogo & Urca Map (p58)
Ipanema, Leblon & Lagoa Map (p62)

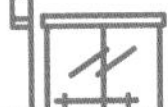

Arriving in Rio de Janeiro

Rio's main airport, **Galeão international airport (GIG; p401)**, is 15km north of the city center. Bus 2018 links the airport with Copacabana, Ipanema, Leblon and other neighborhoods (75 minutes to two hours, R$16). Radio taxis charge a set fare of R$130 to Copacabana and Ipanema (45 to 90 minutes). Less-expensive metered yellow-and-blue taxis cost around R$100. Ride-sharing services cost around R$60. There's also shuttle service (R$25).

Where to Stay

Rio has a wide range of lodgings, including B&Bs, hostels and guesthouses; there are dozens of high-end high-rises with ocean views, particularly in Copacabana. An abundance of options keeps rates from going sky high, except during Carnaval and other major events.

For information on what each Rio neighborhood has to offer, see the table on (p69).

Surfing at Ipanema Beach

GIOVANI CORDIOLI / GETTY IMAGES ©

Copacabana & Ipanema Beaches

Rio's loveliest beaches are a magnificent confluence of land and sea, with golden sands anchored by green peaks. The city's sun-kissed backyard has amusements of all kinds, from surfing and jogging to sitting back, agua de côco (coconut water) in hand, and watching Rio at play.

Great For...

☑ Don't Miss

Enjoying the sunset from Ponta do Arpoador, a rocky outcropping at Ipanema's eastern end.

Beachside Activities

Aside from frolicking in the waves and people-watching, the main attraction for visitors to the beach is running or cycling the beach path; the beachside lane closes to traffic on Sundays. Early risers can greet the sunrise while exercising. Another way to get physical is to have a go on a stand-up paddle board, which you can hire from the south end of Copacabana Beach. Hire outfits also offer lessons if you need a bit of a primer.

The Scene

The beaches are demarcated by *postos* (posts), which mark off subcultures as diverse as the city itself. Ipanema's Posto 9, near Rua Vinícius de Moraes, is Garota de Ipanema, where Rio's most lithe and tanned bodies tend to migrate. In front of Rua

Aerial view of Copacabana Beach

STUART DEE / GETTY IMAGES ©

Need to Know

Reach Copacabana Beach via the metro stations of Cardeal Arcoverde, Siqueira Campos and Cantagalo. For Ipanema Beach, use NS da Paz and General Osório metro stations.

Take a Break

Pick up sandwiches with fresh grilled chicken plus cold drinks from **Barraca do Uruguai** (Map p62; Posto 9; sandwiches R$14-20; noon-5pm) on Ipanema Beach.

★ Top Tip

Go early to stake out a spot, and bring just enough cash for the day.

Farme de Amoedo the beach is known as Praia Farme, and is the stomping ground for gay society. Arpoador, at Ipanema's eastern end, is Rio's most popular surf spot.

In Copacabana, young football and *futevôlei* (soccer volleyball) players hold court near Rua Santa Clara. Postos 5 and 6 are a mix of favela kids and *carioca* retirees, while the spot next to Forte de Copacabana is the *colônia dos pescadores* (fisherfolk's colony). As Copacabana Beach curves north you get into the quieter sands of Leme (Av Princesa Isabel forms the boundary between Copacabana and Leme).

Beach Kiosks

By afternoon and nightfall, the beach kiosks – particularly in Copacabana – are great places to relax, rehydrate over *agua de côco*, and refuel before the night begins. On weekends there's also live music. Things get decidedly livelier when football games are screened, with kiosks setting up TVs, and passers-by and beach-goers joining the celebratory crowds over ever-flowing drinks.

Relaxing & Refreshment

Once on the beach, head to your favorite *barraca* (beach stall), where you can hire chairs and a sun umbrella. There are also food and drink stalls, though roving vendors will come to you, proffering cold drinks (try the sweet tea-like *maté*) and snacks (such as crunchy *globos* – a crispy biscuit made from manioc flour).

If you're in the mood for something more substantial, head up to one of the kiosks lining the beachfront. Some Copacabana kiosks have full menus (the kitchens are cleverly concealed underground).

Cable car to Pão de Açúcar

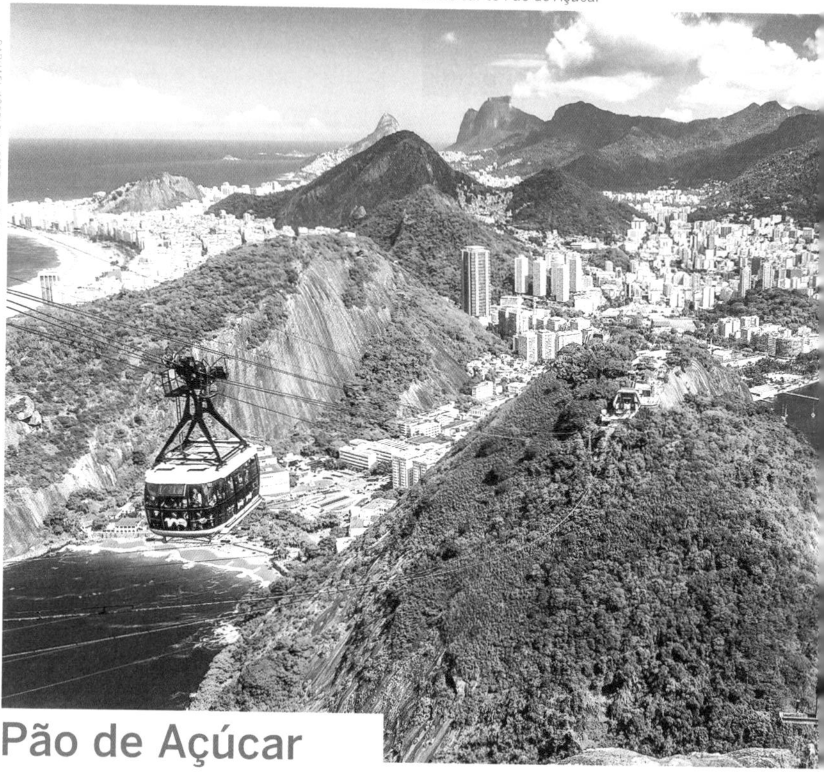

RAPHAEL KOERICH / GETTY IMAGES ©

Pão de Açúcar

From the summit of Pão de Açúcar (Sugarloaf Mountain), it's clear why Rio is called the Cidade Maravilhosa (Marvelous City). Following the ascent by aerial cable car up the mountain, you'll be rewarded with magnificent views over Rio.

Great For...

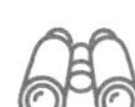

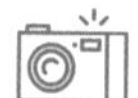

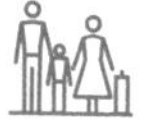

☑ Don't Miss

The view of planes landing beneath you at Santos Dumont Airport in Guanabara Bay.

The Ascent by Cable Car

The most traditional way to reach the top is to board the two-stage cable car that departs from Urca every 20 minutes or so. The glass-and-steel cars ascend 215m to Morro da Urca and are good fun in themselves. From here, you can see Baía de Guanabara and along the winding coastline; on the ocean side of the mountain is Praia Vermelha, in a small, calm bay. Aside from the traditional visit, you can also arrange for a guided tour that delves into the history of the sight; there's also a backstage tour that allows a behind-the-scenes look at the cable-car engine rooms.

Morro da Urca has a restaurant, souvenir shops, outdoor theater and a helipad. In the summer, concerts are sometimes staged in the amphitheater. The second cable car continues up to Pão de Açúcar.

The View

At the top, the city unfolds beneath you, with Corcovado mountain and Cristo Redentor off to the west, the twinkling lights of Niteroi across the bay to the east, and the long curve of Copacabana Beach to the south. If the breathtaking heights unsteady you, there's a stylish restaurant and bar on hand serving caipirinhas and snacks.

For prime views of the Cidade Maravilhosa, go around sunset on a clear day.

Climbing to the Top

Those who'd rather take the long way to the top should sign up with one of the granite-hugging climbing tours offered by various outfits in Rio, including **Crux Eco** (21 3322-8765, 21 99392-9203; www.cruxeco.com.br;). Morro da Urca is much easier to climb and you can do it on your own.

Need to Know

Sugarloaf Mountain; Map p58; 21 2546-8400; www.bondinho.com.br; Av Pasteur 520, Urca; adult/child R$85/42; 8am-8pm

Take a Break

Linger over cocktails and excellent snacks from the mountaintop **Clássico Beach Club** (Map p58; 21 2542-8966; www.classicobeachclub.com/urca; Av Pasteur 520; 9am-9pm).

★ Top Tip

To avoid queues, come first thing in the morning or late in the day. Save 10% by purchasing a ticket online.

The short but steep path takes about 30 minutes to climb. You'll find the unmarked trail along the Pista Cláudio Coutinho.

What's Nearby

Praia Vermelha

Beneath Morro da Urca, narrow Praia Vermelha has superb views of the rocky coastline from the shore. Its coarse sand gives the beach the name *vermelha* (red). Because the beach is protected by the headland, the water is usually calm.

Pista Cláudio Coutinho

This paved 1.2km trail winds along the southern contour of Morro da Urca. It's a lush area, with the craggy mountain rising on one side, and waves crashing on rocks below. To get here, walk 100m north along the edge of Praia Vermelha (with your back to the cable-car station) and you'll see the entrance to the path straight ahead, just past the beach.

SAN HOYANO / SHUTTERSTOCK ©

Cristo Redentor

One of Rio's most identifiable landmarks, the magnificent 38m-high Cristo Redentor (Christ the Redeemer) looms large atop the forest-covered mountain of Corcovado. From the statue's base, you'll have mesmerizing views over all of Rio.

Great For...

☑ Don't Miss

The splendid views from the Cog Train (sit on the right side of the train for the best scenery).

The Views

Corcovado, which means 'hunchback,' rises straight up from the city to a height of 710m, and at night the brightly lit statue is visible from nearly every part of the city. When you reach the top, you'll notice the Redeemer's gaze directed at Pão de Açúcar (Sugarloaf Mountain), with his left arm pointing toward the Zona Norte; Maracanã football stadium crowds the foreground. You can also see the international airport on Ilha do Governador just beyond and the Serra dos Órgãos mountain range in the far distance. Beneath Christ's right arm you can see Lagoa Rodrigo de Freitas, Hipódromo de Gávea, Jardim Botânico, and over to Ipanema and Leblon.

S J FRANCIS / SHUTTERSTOCK ©

Parque Nacional da Tijuca
Estação da Estrada de Ferro Corcovado
Mirante Dona Marta
Corcovado
Paineiras
Cristo Redentor

Need to Know

Christ the Redeemer; Map p58; 21 2558-1329; www.tremdocorcovado.rio; cog train station, Cosme Velho 513; adult/child R$75/49; 8am-7pm

Take a Break

Although touristy, the restaurant just below the statue serves decent Brazilian food and the terrace views are fabulous.

★ Top Tip

Avoid going on weekends when the crowds are biggest, and don't go on overcast days.

Cog Train

The most popular way up to the statue is to take the red narrow-gauge train that departs every 30 minutes from the cog station. Note that you must buy your cog train tickets in advance (either online or at various sale points in town). It takes approximately 20 minutes to get to the top. To reach the cog station, take any 'Cosme Velho' bus; from Copacabana, Ipanema or Leblon bus 583 will get you here.

Historical Background

The Redeemer, which opened in 1931, is considered to be the world's largest art deco statue. It's not a gift from the French, as is popularly believed. However, chief sculptor Paul Landowski was of French-Polish origin and carried out much of the construction in France. He collaborated with the Rio architect-engineer Heitor Silva Costa (1873–1947) on the project. Many organizations helped make the statue a reality, including several individuals who went door-to-door asking for contributions.

The idea of the statue originated in 1921 when a group called Círculo Carioca held a competition for a religious monument to commemorate Brazil's upcoming 100 years of independence. Heitor's winning project, which took 10 years to build, was considered particularly ambitious at the time – naysayers doubted whether it could be accomplished at all. Heitor's original idea depicted Christ as a vertical form with a long cross held against his side but the committee wanted something recognizable from a great distance, so the crosslike outstretched arms were chosen instead. Today it's one of Brazil's most frequented attractions, welcoming more than one million visitors a year.

Walking Tour: Historic Centro

A mélange of cobblestone streets and colonial architecture, Centro is a fine place to delve into Rio's past. Weekdays are the best time to visit, as the area is deserted (and unsafe) on weekends.

Start Praça Floriano
Length 3km
Distance 4 hours

4 Stop in **Confeitaria Colombo** (Map p54; www.confeitariacolombo.com.br) for caffeine, pastries and art nouveau surroundings.

Classic Photo: Interior of the Real Gabinete Português de Leitura

5 Real Gabinete Português de Leitura (Map p54; www.realgabinete.com.br) is a historic reading room that seems straight out of 19th-century Portugal.

3 On the hill above Largo da Carioca, **Igreja São Francisco da Penitência** (Map p54; www.conventosantoantonio.org.br) is an 18th-century church with a jaw-dropping gilded interior.

Take a Break...

Cais do Oriente (p64) is set in a charming mansion from the 1870s and features gastronomic delights.

7 One of Centro's oldest lanes, the **Travessa do Comércio** (Map p54), springs to life at workday's end with open-air bars on the cobble-stone streets.

6 Once the seat of the Portuguese rulers in Brazil, the **Paço Imperial** (Map p54; www.amigosdopacoimperial.org.br) today houses cafes and intriguing art exhibitions.

2 One of Rio's finest buildings, the neoclassical **Theatro Municipal** (Map p54; www.theatromunicipal.rj.gov.br) has a lavish interior and stages opera, dance and classical concerts.

1 The heart of downtown is the **Praça Floriano** (Map p54), a scenic plaza dotted with outdoor cafes and framed by grand architecture.

SIGHTS

Gávea, Jardim Botânico & Lagoa

Lagoa Rodrigo de Freitas Lake

(Map p62) One of the city's most picturesque spots, Lagoa Rodrigo de Freitas is encircled by a 7.2km walking and cycling path. Bikes are available for hire from stands along the east side of the lake, as are paddleboats. For those who prefer *caipirinhas* (cocktails made from limes, sugar, ice and high-proof sugarcane alcohol) to plastic swan boats, the lakeside kiosks on either side of the lake offer alfresco food and drinks, sometimes accompanied by live music on warm nights.

Flamengo

Museu da República Museum

(Map p43; 21 2127-0324; http://museudarepublica.museus.gov.br; Rua do Catete 153; R$6, Wed & Sun free; 10am-5pm Tue-Fri, 11am-6pm Sat & Sun) The Museu da República, located in the Palácio do Catete, has been wonderfully restored. Built between 1858 and 1866, and easily distinguished by the bronze condors on its eaves, the palace was home to the president of Brazil from 1896 until 1954, when President Getúlio Vargas committed suicide here. The museum has a good collection of art and artifacts from the Republican period. It also houses a small cafe, an art-house cinema and a bookstore.

Parque do Flamengo Park

(Map p58; Av Infante Dom Henrique) Officially called Parque Brigadeiro Eduardo Gomes, Parque do Flamengo was the result of a landfill project that leveled the São Antônio hill in 1965. It now spreads all the way from downtown Rio through Glória, Catete and Flamengo, and on around to Botafogo. The 1.2 sq km of land reclaimed from the sea now sees every manner of outdoor activity by *cariocas*.

Centro & Praça Mauá

Museu Histórico Nacional Museum

(Map p54; 21 3299-0324; http://mhn.museus.gov.br; off General Justo, near Praça Marechal Âncora; adult/child R$10/5, Sun free; 10am-5:30pm Tue-Fri, 1-5pm Sat & Sun) Housed in the colonial arsenal, which dates from 1764, the impressive Museu Histórico Nacional contains relics relating to the history of Brazil from its founding to its early days as a republic. Highlights include gilded imperial coaches, the throne of Dom Pedro II, massive oil paintings depicting the horrific war with Paraguay and a full-sized model of a colonial pharmacy.

Museu de Arte do Rio Museum

(MAR; Map p54; 21 3031-2741; www.museudeartedorio.org.br; Praça Mauá 5; adult/child R$20/10, Tue free; 10am-5pm Tue-Sun) Looming large over Praça Mauá, the MAR is an icon for the rebirth of Rio's once derelict port. The huge museum hosts wide-ranging exhibitions that focus on Rio in all its complexity – its people, landscapes, beauty, challenges and conflicts. Start by taking the elevator to the top (6th) floor and absorbing the view over the bay. There's also an excellent restaurant here. Then work your way down through the galleries, taking in a mix of international and only-in-Rio exhibitions.

Museu do Amanhã Museum

(Map p54; www.museudoamanha.org.br; Rodrigues Alves 1; adult/child R$20/free, Tue free; 10am-6pm Tue-Sun) Designed by famed

---

Rio's Iconic Streetcar

The **bonde** (Map p54; return ticket R$20; 9am-5pm Mon-Fri, 10am-5:30pm Sat, 11am-4:30pm Sun; M Carioca) is the last of the historic streetcars that once crisscrossed the city. Its romantic clatter through the cobbled streets is the archetypal sound of bohemian Santa Teresa. Currently the bonde travels every 15 to 20 minutes from the cable-car station in Centro over the scenic Arcos da Lapa and as far as Largo do Guimarães in the heart of Santa Teresa.

Spanish architect Santiago Calatrava, this thoughtfully conceived science museum has interactive exhibitions on outer space, the earth and its biodiversity, humans (and our impact on the world), and the major global trends and challenges that lie in the future. In all, the museum takes a somewhat pessimistic view of the human species and its long-ranging impact on the world.

Boulevard Olímpico Area

(Map p54) Rio's formerly derelict port district has been reborn as a wide promenade lined with massive street art. A handful of renowned artists have painted spectacular murals on the old warehouses, though Brazilian artist Eduardo Kobra (www.eduardokobra.com) deserves special mention for his jaw-dropping work entitled *Etnias* (Ethnicities). The massive mural stretches for 190m and features photogenic portraits of indigenous people from around the globe.

Centro Cultural Banco do Brasil Cultural Center

(CCBB; Map p54; ☎21 3808-2020; www.culturabancodobrasil.com.br; Primeiro de Março 66, Centro; ⏰9am-9pm Wed-Mon) FREE Housed in a beautifully restored 1906 building, the Centro Cultural Banco do Brasil hosts some of Rio's top exhibitions. Facilities include a cinema, two theaters and a permanent display of the evolution of currency in Brazil. There is always something going on, from exhibitions and lunchtime and evening concerts to film screenings, so look up details in *O Globo's* entertainment listings or the 'Veja Rio' insert in *Veja* magazine before you go.

Santa Teresa & Lapa

Escadaria Selarón Landmark

(Map p54; btwn Joaquim Silva & Pinto Martins, Lapa) One of Rio's best-loved attractions, the steps leading up from Joaquim Silva became a work of art when Chilean-born artist Jorge Selarón decided to cover them with colorful mosaics. A dedication to the Brazilian people, the 215 steps are a vivid riot of color.

Jardim Botânico

The exotic 137-hectare **botanical gardens** (Map p62; ☎21 3874-1808; www.jbrj.gov.br; Jardim Botânico 920; R$15; ⏰noon-6pm Mon, 8am-6pm Tue-Sun), with more than 8000 plant species, was designed by order of the Prince Regent Dom João (later to become Dom João VI) in 1808. The garden is quiet and serene on weekdays and blossoms with families on weekends. Highlights of a visit here include the row of palms (planted when the garden first opened), the Amazonas section, the lake containing the huge Vitória Régia water lilies and the enclosed *orquidário*, home to 600 species of orchids.

Before or after a visit to the gardens, you can grab a bite or a drink at **Jarbô** (Map p62; ☎21 2259-2924; www.jarbocafe.com; mains R$38-67; ⏰noon-6:30pm Mon, 8am-6:30pm Tue-Sun; 📶 ✍). It's set in a lovely colonial building and has outdoor seating on a peaceful veranda.

Avenue of Royal Palms

Arcos da Lapa Landmark

(Map p54; Lapa) A much-photographed symbol of Lapa, the arches date back to the mid-18th century, when the structure served as an aqueduct to carry water from the Carioca River to downtown Rio. In a style reminiscent of ancient Rome, the 42 arches stand 64m high. Today the arches carry the bonde (p52) cable car on its way between Centro and Santa Teresa. Located near Av Mem de Sá.

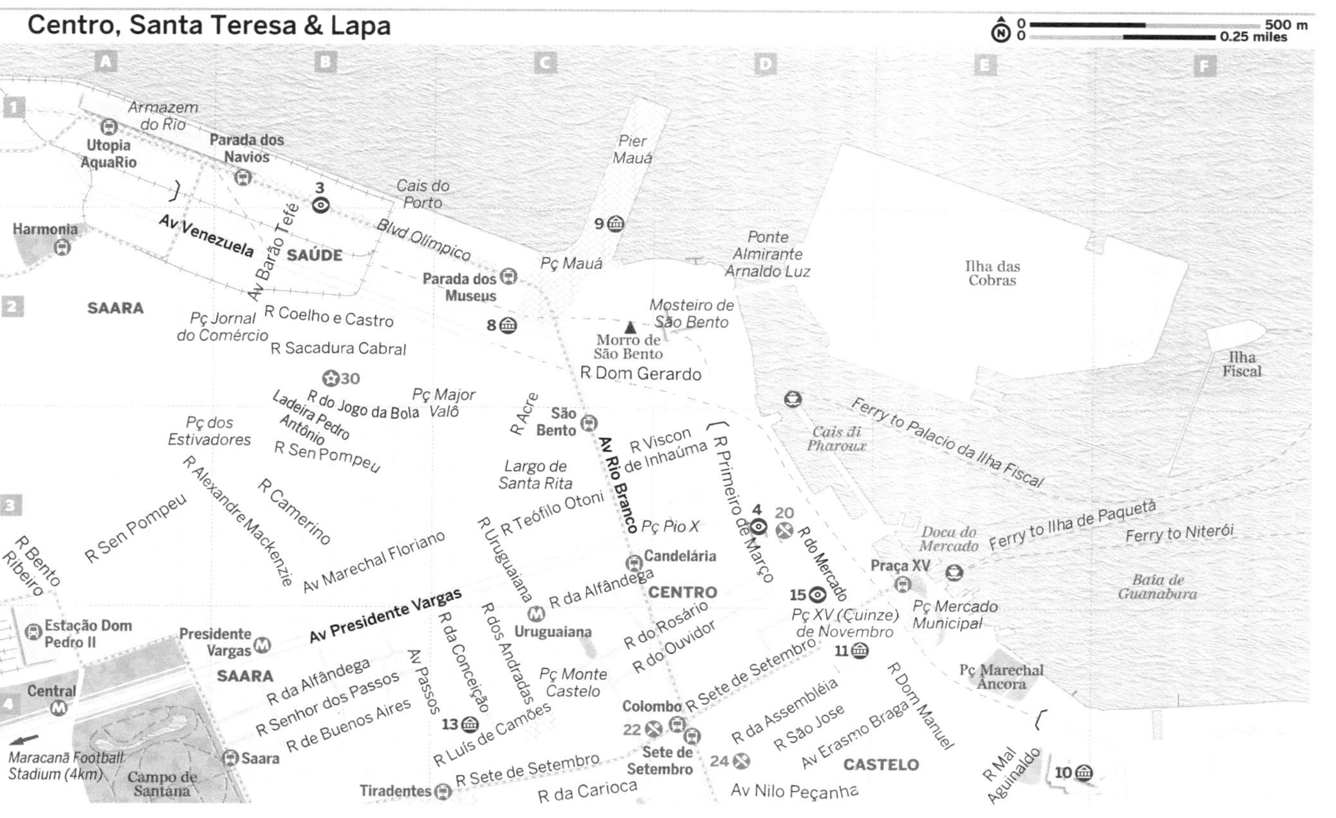
Centro, Santa Teresa & Lapa
500 m
0.25 miles
Ilha Fiscal
Ilha das Cobras
Ferry to Niterói
Baía de Guanabara
Ferry to Ilha de Paquetá
Ferry to Palacio da Ilha Fiscal
Doca do Mercado
Cais di Pharoux
Ponte Almirante Arnaldo Luz
Pier Mauá
Pç Mauá
Mosteiro de São Bento
Morro de São Bento
Cais do Porto
Blvd Olímpico
Armazem do Rio
Utopia AquaRio
Harmonia
Parada dos Navios
Parada dos Museus
SAÚDE
Av Venezuela
Av Barão Tefé
SAARA
Pç Jornal do Comércio
R Coelho e Castro
R Sacadura Cabral
Pç dos Estivadores
Pç Major Valô
R do Jogo da Bola
Ladeira Pedro Antônio
R Sen Pompeu
R Camerino
R Alexandre Mackenzie
Av Marechal Floriano
R Dom Gerardo
São Bento
R Acre
Largo de Santa Rita
R Visconde de Inhaúma
R Primeiro de Março
Av Rio Branco
Pç Pio X
Candelária
CENTRO
R Teófilo Otoni
R Uruguaiana
Uruguaiana
R da Alfândega
R do Rosário
R do Ouvidor
Pç Monte Castelo
R dos Andradas
R da Conceição
Av Presidente Vargas
Av Passos
R Luís de Camões
R Sete de Setembro
Tiradentes
Colombo
Sete de Setembro
R da Carioca
R Sete de Setembro
R da Assembléia
R São José
R Erasmo Braga
Av Nilo Peçanha
CASTELO
R Dom Manuel
Praça XV
Pç XV (Quinze) de Novembro
Pç Mercado Municipal
R do Mercado
Pç Marechal Âncora
R Mal Aguinaldo
Presidente Vargas
SAARA
R da Alfândega
R Senhor dos Passos
R de Buenos Aires
Saara
Campo de Santana
Estação Dom Pedro II
Central
R Bento Ribeiro
Maracanã Football Stadium (4km)
A
B
C
D
E
F
1
2
3
4
3
8
9
10
11
13
15
20
22
24
30

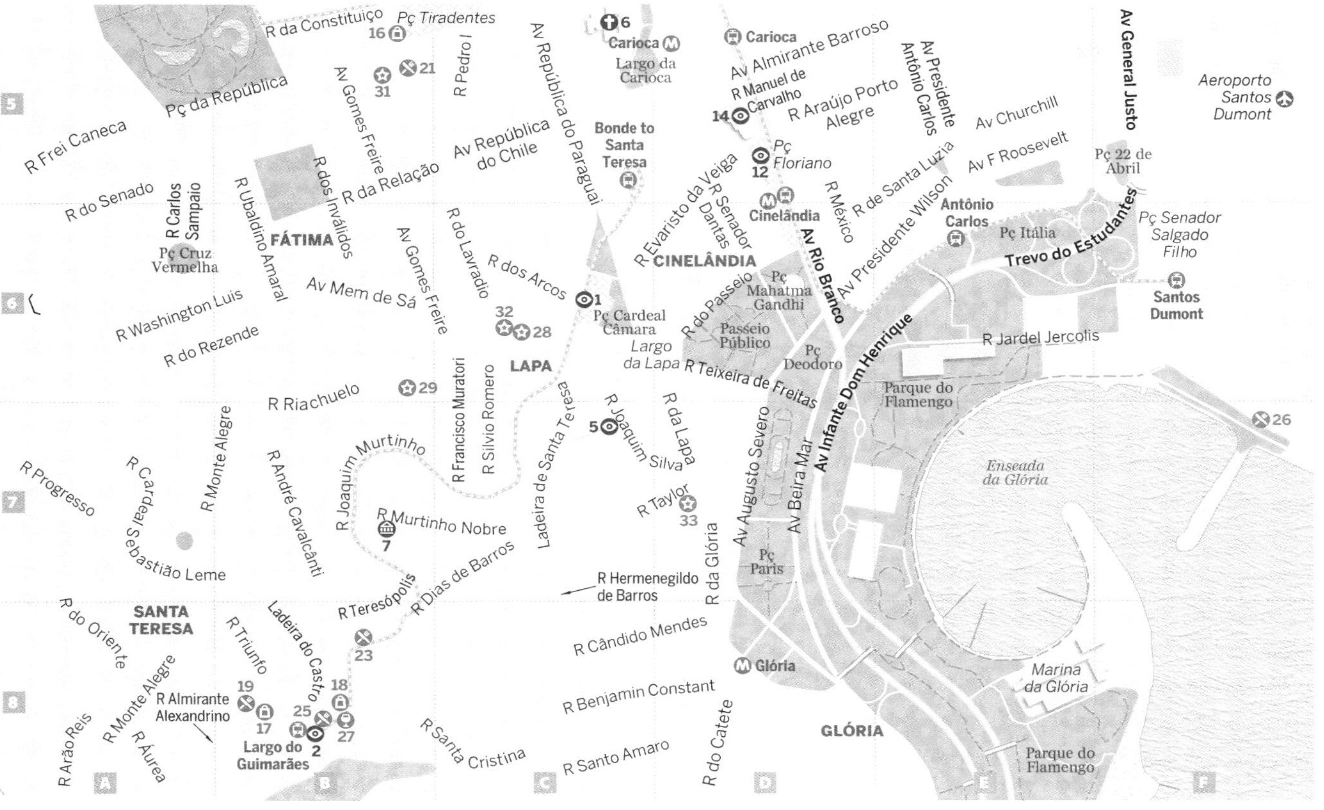
R da Constituição
Pç Tiradentes
Pç da República
R Frei Caneca
Av Gomes Freire
R Pedro I
Av República do Paraguai
Carioca
Largo da Carioca
Bonde to Santa Teresa
Carioca
Av Almirante Barroso
R Manuel de Carvalho
R Araújo Porto Alegre
Av Presidente Antônio Carlos
Av Churchill
Av General Justo
Aeroporto Santos Dumont
Av F Roosevelt
Pç 22 de Abril
R do Senado
R Carlos Sampaio
R Ubaldino Amaral
R dos Inválidos
R da Relação
Av República do Chile
Pç Floriano
R de Santa Luzia
Pç Cruz Vermelha
FÁTIMA
R do Lavradio
R Evaristo da Veiga
R Senador Dantas
Cinelândia
R México
Av Presidente Wilson
Antônio Carlos
Pç Itália
Pç Senador Salgado Filho
Trevo do Estudantes
Av Mem de Sá
R dos Arcos
CINELÂNDIA
Av Rio Branco
Pç Mahatma Gandhi
Santos Dumont
R Washington Luis
Pç Cardeal Câmara
R do Passeio
Passeio Público
Av Infante Dom Henrique
R Jardel Jercolis
R do Rezende
Largo da Lapa
LAPA
Pç Deodoro
R Teixeira de Freitas
Parque do Flamengo
R Riachuelo
R Francisco Muratori
R Silvio Romero
Ladeira de Santa Teresa
R Joaquim Silva
R da Lapa
Av Augusto Severo
Av Beira Mar
R Joaquim Murtinho
Enseada da Glória
R Progresso
R Cardeal Sebastião Leme
R Monte Alegre
R André Cavalcânti
R Murtinho Nobre
R Taylor
R da Glória
Pç Paris
R Dias de Barros
R Hermenegildo de Barros
R do Oriente
SANTA TERESA
R Triunfo
Ladeira do Castro
R Teresópolis
R Cândido Mendes
Glória
Marina da Glória
R Monte Alegre
R Almirante Alexandrino
R Benjamin Constant
R Arão Reis
R Áurea
Largo do Guimarães
R Santa Cristina
R Santo Amaro
R do Catete
GLÓRIA
Parque do Flamengo
A
B
C
D
E
F
5
6
7
8

Centro, Santa Teresa & Lapa

Sights

1 Arcos da Lapa ... C6
2 Bonde ... B8
3 Boulevard Olímpico ... B1
4 Centro Cultural Banco do Brasil ... D3
5 Escadaria Selarón ... C7
6 Igreja São Francisco da Penitência & Convento de Santo Antônio ... C5
7 Museu Chácara do Céu ... B7
8 Museu de Arte do Rio ... C2
9 Museu do Amanhã ... C2
10 Museu Histórico Nacional ... E4
11 Paço Imperial ... D4
12 Praça Floriano ... D5
13 Real Gabinete Português de Leitura ... C4
14 Theatro Municipal ... D5
15 Travessa do Comércio ... D3

Shopping

16 CRAB ... B5
17 Favela Hype ... B8
18 La Vereda ... B8

Eating

19 Bar do Mineiro ... B8
20 Cais do Oriente ... D3
21 Casa Momus ... B5
22 Confeitaria Colombo ... D4
23 Espírito Santa ... B8
24 Govardhana Harí ... D4
25 Sobrenatural ... B8
26 Xian ... F7

Drinking & Nightlife

27 Explorer Bar ... B8

Entertainment

28 Carioca da Gema ... C6
Favela Hype ... (see 17)
29 Lapa 40 Graus ... B6
30 Pedra do Sal ... B2
31 Rio Scenarium ... B5
32 Sacrilégio ... C6
33 TribOz ... D7

Museu Chácara do Céu Museum

(Map p54; 21 3970-1093; www.museuscastromaya.com.br; Murtinho Nobre 93; adult/child R$6/free, Wed free; noon-5pm Wed-Mon) The former mansion of art patron and industrialist Raymundo Ottoni de Castro Maya contains a small but diverse array of modern art, formerly Ottoni's private collection, which he bequeathed to the nation. In addition to works by Portinari, Di Cavalcanti and Lygia Clark, the museum displays furniture and Brazilian maps dating from the 17th and 18th centuries, and hosts temporary exhibitions.

ACTIVITIES

If you weigh less than 100kg (about 220lb) and have a spare R$500, you can do the fantastic hang glide off 510m Pedra Bonita – one of the giant granite slabs that tower above Rio – onto Pepino Beach in São Conrado. Flights last about seven to 10 minutes, and no experience is necessary. Guest riders are secured in a kind of pouch that is attached to the hang glider.

A reliable operator is **Just Fly** (21 3593-4362; www.justflyinrio.blogspot.com; R$520).

TOURS

Jungle Me Hiking

(21 4105-7533; www.jungleme.com.br; tours from R$195;) This top-notch outfit offers excellent hiking tours through Parque Nacional da Tijuca led by knowledgeable guides. The eight-hour Tijuca Circuit (Peaks & Waterfalls tour) offers challenging walks up several escarpments with stunning views of Rio, followed by a refreshing dip in a waterfall. The Prainha & Grumari tour consists of a hike between scenic beaches in Rio's little-visited western reaches.

Rio by Bike Cycling

(Map p62; 21 96871-8933; www.riobybike.com; Av NS de Copacabana 1085, Copacabana; tours R$100-135) Two Dutch journalists operate this biking outfit, and their excellent pedaling tours combine scenery with cultural insight. It's a great way to get an overview of the city, with guides pointing out landmarks and describing key events that have shaped Rio. Tours generally last three to four hours and travel mostly along bike lanes separated from traffic.

Eat Rio Food Tours Walking

(www.eatrio.net; tours from US$75) On these highly recommended small-group tours, you'll visit markets, snack bars and other foodie hot spots to taste a wide range of fruits, juices and street food little known outside Brazil. The English-speaking guides are excellent and provide culinary as well as cultural insights. The cost of the tour covers all food, including snacks and a big meal at the end.

Sail in Rio Boating

(Map p58; ☎21 99998-3709; www.sailinrio.com; Av Pasteur 333, Iate Clube do Rio de Janeiro; sailing tours from R$250) This recommended outfit offers memorable sailing tours around Rio. When the weather cooperates, there are daily departures (at 11am) from the yacht club in Urca. You can also arrange your own private sailings with up to 10 people; you choose the date and help design the itinerary (private sailings cost R$1500 for three hours, R$1800 for five hours).

SHOPPING

CRAB Arts & Crafts

(Map p54; ☎21 3380-1850; www.facebook.com/crabsebrae; Praça Tiradentes 69; ⏰10am-5pm Tue-Sat) One of Rio's best new handicraft stores stocks an exquisite collection of pieces from every corner of Brazil. You'll find ceramics with pre-Columbian imagery found in the Serra da Capivara, lovely eco-jewelry made of seeds and nuts from indigenous groups and brightly painted folk art from the Northeast, as well as sustainably made animal-free bags, vegetable-fiber woven textiles and all-rubber footwear.

There's much to discover here, and all of the products are fair trade.

Pé de Boi Arts & Crafts

(☎21 2285-4395; www.pedeboi.com.br; Ipiranga 55, Laranjeiras; ⏰10am-7pm Mon-Fri, to 1pm Sat) Although everything is for sale here, Pé de Boi feels more like an art gallery than a handicrafts shop, owing to the high quality of the wood and ceramic works, and the tapestries, sculptures and weavings. This is perhaps Rio's best place to see one-of-a-kind pieces by artists from Bahia, Amazonia, Minas Gerais and other parts of Brazil.

Don't miss the upstairs area, which has photos of some of the artists whose work is on sale.

Maracanã Football Stadium

Rio's **Maracanã stadium** (Map p43; ☎21 2334-1705; www.suderj.rj.gov.br/maracana.asp; Av Maracanã, São Cristóvão) is hallowed ground among football lovers. The massive arena has been the site of legendary victories and crushing defeats. Maracanã played a starring role both in the 2014 World Cup and the 2016 Summer Olympics. No matter who takes the field, the 78,800-seat arena comes to life in spectacular fashion on game days. Seeing a game is the best way to experience the excitement; you can also get a behind-the-scenes look during a stadium tour with **Maracanã Tour** (☎21 98341-1949; www.tourmaracana.com.br; tour guided/unguided R$60/50; ⏰9am-4:30pm), available daily.

Gilson Martins Fashion & Accessories

(Map p62; ☎21 2227-6178; shop.gilsonmartins.com.br; Visconde de Pirajá 462; ⏰9am-8pm Mon-Fri, to 7pm Sat) Designer Gilson Martins transforms the Brazilian flag and silhouettes of Pão de Açúcar (Sugarloaf Mountain) and Corcovado into eye-catching accessories in his flagship store in Ipanema. This is the place for unique glossy handbags, wallets, passport covers, key chains

Flamengo, Botafogo & Urca

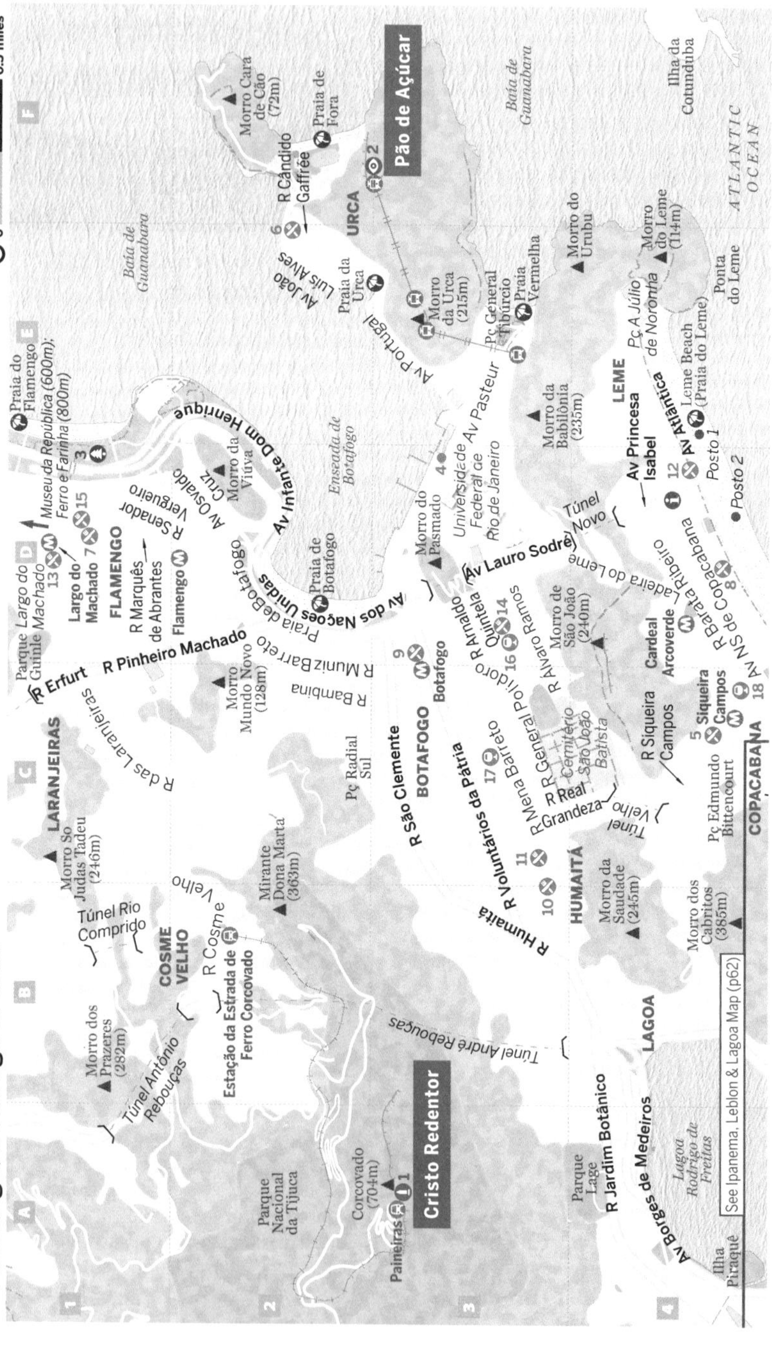

See Ipanema, Leblon & Lagoa Map (p62)

Flamengo, Botafogo & Urca

Sights

1 Cristo Redentor....A3
2 Pão de Açúcar....F2
3 Parque do Flamengo....D1

Activities, Courses & Tours

4 Sail in Rio....D3

Eating

5 Adega Pérola....C4
6 Bar Urca....E2
7 Brou....D1
8 Churrascaria Palace....D4
9 Marchezinho....D3
10 Meza Bar....B3
11 Oteque....C3
12 Salomé....D4
13 Sírio Libaneza....D1
14 South Ferro....D3
15 Tacacá do Norte....D1

Drinking & Nightlife

Bar Urca....(see 6)
Clássico Beach Club....(see 2)
16 CoLAB....D3
17 Comuna....C3
18 Pavão Azul....C4

and iPad covers. Products are durable and use recycled and sustainable materials – and are not available outside Rio.

Osklen Clothing

(Map p62; 21 2227-2930; www.osklen.com; Maria Quitéria 85; 9am-8pm Mon-Fri, 10am-7pm Sat, 11am-5pm Sun) One of Brazil's best-known fashion labels outside the country, Osklen is notable for its stylish and well-made beachwear (particularly men's swim shorts and graphic T-shirts), sneakers and outerwear. The company was started in 1988 by outdoor enthusiast Oskar Metsavaht, the first Brazilian to scale Mont Blanc.

Lenny Niemeyer Fashion & Accessories

(Map p62; 21 2227-5537; www.lennyniemeyer.com; Garcia d'Ávila 149; 10am-8pm Mon-Fri, to 6pm Sat) When it comes to swimwear, few designers have earned a following like Lenny Niemeyer. She creates beautiful, form-fitting bikinis and one-pieces in both classic and avant-garde styles. You'll also find plenty of other essentials for street and beach, including dresses, tops, caftans and sarongs.

Maria Oiticica Jewelry

(Map p62; 21 3875-8025; www.mariaoiticica.com; Av Afrânio de Melo Franco 290, Shopping Leblon; 10am-10pm Mon-Sat, 1-9pm Sun) Using native materials found in the Amazon, Maria Oiticica has created some lovely handcrafted jewelry inspired by indigenous art. Seeds, plant fibers and tree bark are just some of the ingredients of her bracelets, necklaces, earrings and sandals. There are even sandals and handbags made from fish 'leather.'

Chocolate Q Chocolate

(Map p62; 21 2274-1001; www.chocolateq.com; Shop B, Garcia d'Ávila 149; 10am-8pm Mon-Sat) This is serious chocolate. Cacao beans, harvested from a single, environmentally conscious grower in Bahia, are processed into a range of exquisite dark-chocolate products (milk chocolate fans be advised, there is nothing for you here). All the bars and pastilles are beautifully packaged, with colorful illustrations of Brazilian wildlife, making them eminently gift-worthy.

La Vereda Arts & Crafts

(Map p54; 21 2507-0317; www.lavereda.art.br; Almirante Alexandrino 428, Santa Teresa; 10am-8pm) La Vereda stocks a colorful selection of handicrafts from local artists and artisans in a spot near Largo do Guimarães. Handpainted clay figurines by Pernambuco artists, heavy Minas ceramics, delicate sterling-silver jewelry and loosely woven tapestries cover the interior of the old store.

Favela Hype Fashion & Accessories

(Map p54; www.facebook.com/favelahype; Paschoal Carlos Magno 103, Santa Teresa; 10am-11pm Tue-Sun) This ultrahip but very friendly gathering spot is part fashion boutique, part restaurant and (at certain times) all

Hippie Fair

The Zona Sul's most famous market, the **Hippie Fair** (Map p62; Praça General Osório; 9am-6pm Sun) has artwork, jewelry, handicrafts, clothing and souvenirs for sale. Stalls in the four corners of the plaza sell tasty plates of *acarajé* (croquettes made from mashed black-eyed peas, with a sauce of *vatapá* – manioc paste, coconut and *dendê* oil – and shrimp), plus excellent desserts. Don't miss it.

Performer at Hippie Fair
JOHN MAIER JR / LONELY PLANET ©

party space. The art-filled shop sells swimwear, dresses, jewelry, sunglasses, ecofriendly flip-flops, floral-print button-downs (for the guys) and original artworks. Most products are made by local designers.

EATING

Ipanema & Leblon

Vero Ice Cream $

(Map p62; 21 3497-8754; Visconde de Pirajá 229; ice creams R$11-16, pizza slices R$13-16; 10am-12:30am;) This artisanal Italian-run gelateria whips up Rio's best ice cream. You'll find more than two dozen rich and creamy temptations, including *gianduia* (chocolate with hazelnut), *caramelo com flor de sal* (caramel with sea salt), *figo com amêndoas* (fig with almond) and classic flavors such as *morango* (strawberry).

Quitéria Brazilian $$

(Map p62; 21 2267-4603; www.ipanemainn.com.br/en/quiteria; Maria Quitéria 27; mains around R$53, lunch buffet weekday/weekends R$39/53; 7am-11pm) Inside the Ipanema Inn, this humble-looking place serves delectable contemporary Brazilian cooking. Seasonal, high-quality ingredients feature in the extensive lunch buffet, which draws mostly locals. By night the à la carte menu offers hits such as nicely turned out pork ribs with mashed baroa potatoes and cashew sauce, or grilled catch of the day with creamy rice and black-eyed beans.

Zazá Bistrô Tropical Fusion $$$

(Map p62; 21 2247-9101; www.zazabistro.com.br; Joana Angélica 40; mains R$65-87; 7pm-midnight Mon-Thu, from noon Fri-Sun) Inside an art-filled and whimsically decorated converted house, Zazá serves beautifully prepared dishes with Asian accents, and uses organic ingredients when possible. Favorites include chicken curry with jasmine rice, flambéed prawns with risotto, and grilled fish served with caramelized plantain. Don't miss brilliantly creative cocktails like the Caramba Carambola, with Amazonian gin (or vodka), *carambola* (star fruit), ginger, mint and lemon.

Zuka International $$$

(Map p62; 21 3205-7154; www.zuka.com.br; Dias Ferreira 233; mains R$76-120; 7pm-1am Mon, noon-4pm & 7pm-1am Tue-Fri, 1pm-midnight Sat & Sun) One of Rio's best restaurants, Zuka prepares mouthwatering cuisine. Try zingy ceviche with Brazilian *piquinho* pepper or the confection-like delicacy of Zuka's original foie gras to start, followed by tender octopus over a roast potato crisp, honey-glazed duck breast with Moroccan couscous, grilled fish of the day with truffle sauce, or one of many other outstanding dishes.

Giuseppe Grill Brazilian $$$

(Map p62; 21 2249-3055; www.bestfork.com.br; Bartolomeu Mitre 370; mains R$88-150; noon-4pm & 7pm-midnight Mon-Thu, noon-1am Fri & Sat, noon-11pm Sun) One of Rio's best restaurants, Giuseppe Grill aims for perfection and it rarely disappoints. Chargrilled meat and fish plates are outstanding, as are Brazilian classics like *bobó de camarão* (manioc paste with dried shrimp and coconut milk). The setting is all class, with black-garbed waitstaff, dark-wood tables and artful touches (an open kitchen, a soaring bar that reaches to the ceiling and a Zen-like wall of water near the entrance).

Copacabana & Leme

Salomé Bistro $$

(Map p58; 21 2541-2416; www.facebook.com/salomebistro; Av Atlântica 994; mains R$48-65; 6:30pm-midnight Tue-Thu, noon-midnight Fri-Sun;) Run by the same people behind Ipanema's enormously popular Canastra (p64), Salomé brings a dash of style to the Leme beachfront. The easygoing open-sided bistro has vintage mirrors and curious wall hangings, potted palms and atmospheric lighting – though on fine days, the outdoor tables are the best place to enjoy high-quality small plates, grilled meats and seafood, and wines by the glass.

Adega Pérola Tapas $$

(Map p58; 21 2255-9425; www.facebook.com/adegaperolariodejaneiro; Siqueira Campos 138; sharing plates R$24-46; 11am-1am Mon-Thu, to 2am Fri & Sat) Going strong since 1957, this atmospheric bottle-lined eating and drinking den serves outstanding Spanish and Portuguese small plates, including marinated octopus, whole sardines, stuffed olives, codfish balls, fried squid and marinated shrimp. Just step inside and check out the culinary bounty on the long front counter.

Churrascaria Palace Churrascaria $$$

(Map p58; 21 2541-5898; www.churrascariapalace.com.br; Rodolfo Dantas 16; all you can eat R$140; noon-midnight;) This elegantly set dining room is one of the best *churrascarias* (traditional barbecue restaurants) in town. Aside from juicy, high-quality cuts of meat, the included buffet nearly steals the show with fresh oysters, grilled heart of palm, sushi and sashimi, rice with wild mushrooms and goji berries, codfish casseroles, smoked fish, grilled prawns and octopus and amazing salads.

Snacking on the Seawall

Bar Urca (Map p58; 21 2295-8744; Cândido Gaffrée 205, Urca; 6:30am-11pm Mon-Sat, 8am-8pm Sun) is a much-loved neighborhood snack spot with a marvelous setting near Urca's bayside waterfront. At night, young and old crowd along the seaside wall to enjoy cold drinks, appetizers and fine views. For something more upscale, Bar Urca's elegant upstairs **dining room** (mains R$57-170; noon-3pm & 7-11pm Mon-Sat, noon-8pm Sun) serves outstanding seafood.

JOHN MAIER JR / LONELY PLANET ©

Botafogo & Urca

Marchezinho Cafe $$

(Map p58; www.facebook.com/marchezinho; Voluntários da Pátria 46, Botafogo; sandwiches R$28-38; 9am-1am Mon-Wed, to 2am Thu & Fri, 10am-2am Sat) This multipurpose space operates as a cafe, bar and minimarket. The owner's French roots show through on the menu and store shelves, with the excellent cheese, bread and coffee. The carefully selected ingredients and produce are exclusively Brazilian, however, with most coming from small local producers. Come for creative tapas, delectable sandwiches, craft beers and first-rate cocktails.

Meza Bar Tapas $$

(Map p58; 21 3239-1951; www.mezabar.com.br; Capitão Salomão 69, Humaitá; tapas R$16-42; 6pm-1am) Humaitá's see-and-be-seen hot spot serves delectable, Brazilian-slanted

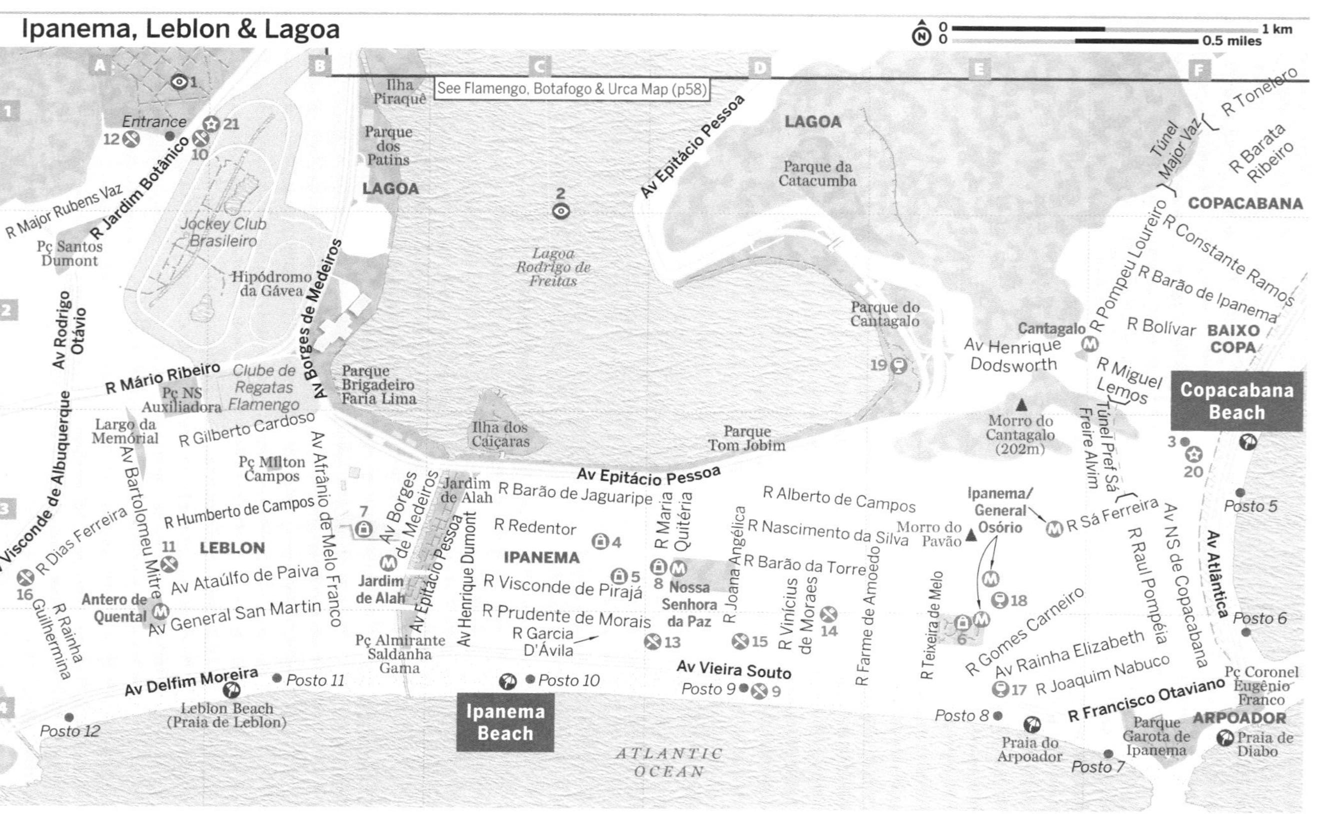
Ipanema, Leblon & Lagoa
0.5 miles
1 km
See Flamengo, Botafogo & Urca Map (p58)
LAGOA
Parque da Catacumba
Parque do Cantagalo
Cantagalo
Av Henrique Dodsworth
Morro do Cantagalo (202m)
Túnel Pref Sá Freire Alvim
R Miguel Lemos
R Pompeu Loureiro
R Barão de Ipanema
R Bolívar
BAIXO COPA
R Constante Ramos
Túnel Major Vaz
R Barata Ribeiro
R Toneleiro
COPACABANA
Copacabana Beach
Posto 5
Posto 6
Av Atlântica
Av NS de Copacabana
R Raul Pompéia
R Sá Ferreira
Ipanema/ General Osório
Morro do Pavão
R Gomes Carneiro
Av Rainha Elizabeth
R Joaquim Nabuco
R Francisco Otaviano
Pç Coronel Eugênio Franco
ARPOADOR
Praia de Diabo
Parque Garota de Ipanema
Posto 7
Praia do Arpoador
Posto 8
R Teixeira de Melo
R Farme de Amoedo
R Alberto de Campos
R Nascimento da Silva
R Barão da Torre
R Vinícius de Moraes
R Joana Angélica
R Maria Quitéria
Nossa Senhora da Paz
Av Vieira Souto
Posto 9
ATLANTIC OCEAN
Parque Tom Jobim
Av Epitácio Pessoa
Lagoa Rodrigo de Freitas
Ilha dos Caiçaras
R Barão de Jaguaripe
R Redentor
IPANEMA
R Visconde de Pirajá
R Prudente de Morais
R Garcia D'Ávila
Posto 10
Ipanema Beach
Jardim de Alah
Av Henrique Dumont
Av Borges de Medeiros
Pç Almirante Saldanha Gama
Ilha Piraquê
Parque dos Patins
Parque Brigadeiro Faria Lima
Clube de Regatas Flamengo
Hipódromo da Gávea
Jockey Club Brasileiro
Entrance
R Jardim Botânico
Pç Santos Dumont
R Major Rubens Vaz
Av Rodrigo Otávio
Av Visconde de Albuquerque
R Mário Ribeiro
Pç NS Auxiliadora
R Gilberto Cardoso
Av Afrânio de Melo Franco
Pç Milton Campos
R Humberto de Campos
LEBLON
Av Ataúlfo de Paiva
Av General San Martin
Largo da Memória
Av Bartolomeu Mitre
Antero de Quental
R Dias Ferreira
R Rainha Guilhermina
Av Delfim Moreira
Leblon Beach (Praia de Leblon)
Posto 11
Posto 12
1 2 3 4 5 6 7 8 9 10 11 12 13 14 15 16 17 18 19 20 21
A B C D E F
1 2 3 4

Ipanema, Leblon & Lagoa

Sights

1 Jardim Botânico A1
2 Lagoa Rodrigo de Freitas C1

Activities, Courses & Tours

3 Rio by Bike F3

Shopping

4 Chocolate Q C3
5 Gilson Martins C3
6 Hippie Fair E4
Lenny Niemeyer .... (see 4)
7 Maria Oiticica B3
8 Osklen D3

Eating

9 Barraca do Uruguai D4
10 Casa Camolese A1
11 Giuseppe Grill A3
12 Jarbô A1
13 Quitéria D4
14 Vero D4
15 Zazá Bistrô Tropical D4
16 Zuka A3

Drinking & Nightlife

17 Baretto-Londra E4
18 Canastra E3
Nosso .... (see 8)
19 Palaphita Kitch E2

Entertainment

20 Bip Bip F3
21 Clube Manouche B1

tapas to a sophisticated and trendy crowd. Creative cocktails and delightful staff round out the fun.

South Ferro — Asian, Pizza $$

(Map p58; ☎21 3986-4323; www.facebook.com/pg/SouthFerro; Arnaldo Quintela 23, Botafogo; mains R$41-62; ⏲11:30am-3pm Mon, 11:30am-3pm & 6:30-11pm Tue-Sat;) Chef Sei Shiroma made his name with Ferro e Farinha (p63), widely regarded as Rio's best pizza place. South Ferro, Shiroma's second restaurant, adds a healthy pinch of Asian spice in vegetable dumplings, tempura, fish curry and outstanding bowls of ramen. You'll also find a few pizza selections and well-made cocktails (R$32).

Oteque — Gastronomy $$$

(Map p58; ☎21 3486-5758; www.oteque.com; Conde de Irajá 581; 8-course tasting menu R$250; ⏲7:30-11:30pm Tue-Sat) Much to the delight of *cariocas*, celebrated São Paulo chef Alberto Landgraf recently moved to Rio and opened this small, beautifully designed restaurant, complete with a theatrically lit open kitchen. The menu changes daily but features exquisite seafood (grilled octopus, scallops, monkfish, oysters) artfully prepared with Brazilian accents like hearts of palm and *tucupi* (a sauce made from wild manioc).

Flamengo

Sírio Libaneza — Middle Eastern $

(Map p58; ☎21 2146-4915; Largo do Machado 29, Loja 16-19; snacks R$6-28; ⏲8am-11pm Mon-Sat;) Always packed, this bustling place serves tasty and cheap Syrian-Lebanese cuisine and great juices. Try the hearty *kibe de forno* (an oven-baked ground-beef dish with spices), a hummus platter or *kafta* (spiced meat patty), followed by baklava and other sweets. It's inside the Galleria Condor on Largo do Machado.

Tacacá do Norte — Amazonian $

(Map p58; ☎21 2205-7545; Barão do Flamengo 35, Flamengo; tacacá R$27; ⏲9am-11pm Mon-Sat) In the Amazonian state of Pará, people order their *tacacá* late in the afternoon from their favorite street vendor. In Rio, you don't have to wait until the sun is setting. The fragrant soup of manioc paste, lip-numbing leaves of *jambú* (a Brazilian vegetable), and fresh and dried shrimp isn't for everyone. But then again, neither is the Amazon.

Ferro e Farinha — Pizza $$

(Andrade Pertence 42; pizzas R$40-50; ⏲7-11:30pm Tue-Sat, from 6:30pm Sun) Sei Shiroma, an expat from NYC, and a dexterous team of dough handlers serve Rio's best pizza at this atmospheric and delightfully

Ipanema's Best Street Party

Run by a trio of Frenchmen, **Canastra** (Map p62; Jangadeiros 42; 6:30pm-1am Tue-Sat) has become one of the top nightlife destinations in Ipanema. Most nights, the crowd spills out onto the streets, and plenty of socializing *cariocas* never even make it inside. This, however, would be a mistake, as the food (cheese and charcuterie plates, grilled squid and octopus) and drinks (Brazilian wines, sangria, caipirinhas) is outstanding. There's also a hidden bar downstairs – an artfully decorated speakeasy where you can escape the chattering crowds. The big night is Tuesday, when fresh oysters from Santa Catarina arrive (a fine deal at R$40 a dozen).

Caipirinha

MARKO POPLASEN / SHUTTERSTOCK ©

ramshackle spot in Catete. Seats are few, with just a handful of bar stools crowding around the pizza makers and oven at center stage, plus a few outdoor tables, so go early to try to beat the crowds.

Brou Brazilian $$

(Map p58; 21 2556-0618; www.facebook.com/casa.brou; Senador Vergueiro 2, Flamengo; mains lunch R$18-30, dinner R$32-56; 11:30am-3pm & 6pm-midnight) A brilliant new addition to Flamengo, this bright and attractive eating and drinking spot features a daytime menu of creative salads topped with grilled veggies, salmon or roast meat, as well as quiches and soups. By night, crowds come for nicely prepared prime rib, grilled octopus and thin-crust pizzas fired up in a wood-burning oven.

Centro & Praça Mauá

Xian Asian $$

(Map p54; 21 2303-7080; www.xianrio.com.br; top fl, Almirante Silvio de Noronha 365, Bossa Nova Mall; mains R$65-90; noon-11pm Mon-Thu, to midnight Fri & Sat, noon-10pm Sun;) One of Rio's loveliest new additions is this spacious, theatrically decorated dining room, open-air cocktail bar and nightclub, set rather dramatically on the edge of the bay. Come for mouthwatering seafood and tender meats with Asian accents, such as fresh oysters with ponzu sauce, salmon truffle tartar or marinated pork ribs with miso.

Cais do Oriente Brazilian $$

(Map p54; 21 2203-0178; www.caisdooriente-rj.com.br; Visconde de Itaboraí 8, Centro; mains R$55-75; 11am-10pm Mon-Sat, to 5pm Sun) Brick walls lined with tapestries stretch high to the ceiling in this almost-cinematic 1870s mansion. Set on a brick-lined street, hidden from the masses, it blends elements of Brazilian and Mediterranean cooking in dishes such as duck breast with Brazil-nut *farofa* (garnish of manioc flour sautéed with butter) and *açaí* sauce.

Govardhana Harí Vegetarian $$

(Map p54; 21 2544-2636; 2nd fl, Rodrigo Silva 6; lunch R$35; 11:30am-3:30pm Mon-Fri;) Amid artwork and decorations from India, the always-welcoming Hare Krishnas whip up delicious vegetarian dishes made with care. The restaurant is tucked down a narrow lane just off Rua São José and is always packed, so arrive early to get a seat.

Santa Teresa & Lapa

Casa Momus Mediterranean $$

(Map p54; 21 3852-8250; www.casamomus.com.br; Rua do Lavradio 11, Lapa; mains R$42-58; 11:30am-5pm Mon, to midnight Tue & Wed, to 2am Thu-Sat) One of the best and loveliest restaurants in Lapa, Casa Momus has a small but well-executed menu of Mediterranean-influenced dishes. Start with prawn croquettes, fried polenta with spicy Gorgonzola or a Moroccan lamb *kafta* (spiced meat patty) with tabbouleh and yogurt sauce, then feast on oxtail risotto with watercress, seared tuna with couscous, grilled beef tenderloin, and other rich main courses.

Bar do Mineiro Brazilian $$

(Map p54; ☎21 2221-9227; Paschoal Carlos Magno 99, Santa Teresa; mains R$65-125, weekday lunch special R$22-35; ⏰noon-2am Tue-Sat, to midnight Sun) Black-and-white photographs of legendary singers cover the walls of this old-school *boteco* (small open-air bar) in the heart of Santa Teresa. Lively crowds have been filling this spot for years to enjoy traditional Minas Gerais dishes. The *feijoada* (bean-and-meat stew served with rice) is tops and served every day, along with appetizers, including *pasteis* (savory pastries).

Espírito Santa Amazonian $$$

(Map p54; ☎21 2507-4840; www.espiritosanta.com.br; Almirante Alexandrino 264, Santa Teresa; mains R$55-98; ⏰noon-11pm) At this beautifully restored mansion, you can sit on the back terrace with its sweeping views or in the charming, airy dining room, and feast on rich, expertly prepared meat and seafood dishes from the Amazon and Northeast. Top picks include the *moqueca* (fish stew), made with pintado (a delicious river fish), and the slow-roasted pork ribs served with sweet potato.

Sobrenatural Seafood $$$

(Map p54; ☎21 2224-1003; Almirante Alexandrino 432, Santa Teresa; mains for 2 R$80-155; ⏰noon-11pm Thu-Tue) The old hardwood ceiling and exposed brick set the stage for feasting on *frutas do mar* (seafood). Lines gather at weekends for crabmeat appetizers, fresh grilled fish and flavorful platters of *moqueca* (fish stew). During the week, stop by for tasty lunchtime specials. There's live music most nights.

Lively crowds have been filling this spot for years...

Bar do Mineiro

DRINKING & NIGHTLIFE

Palaphita Kitch Lounge

(Map p62; 21 2227-0837; www.palaphitakitch.com.br; Av Epitácio Pessoa s/n; 6pm-midnight Mon-Fri, from 10am Sat & Sun) A great spot for a sundowner, Palaphita Kitch is an open-air, thatched-roof wonderland with rustic bamboo furniture, flickering tiki torches and a peaceful setting on the edge of Lagoa Rodrigo de Freitas. It's a popular spot with couples, who come for the view and the creative (but pricey) cocktails: the caipirinhas, made from unusual fruits from the Northeast and Amazonia, are a hit.

Nosso Cocktail Bar

(Map p62; 21 99619-0099; www.facebook.com/nossoipanema; Maria Quitéria 91, Ipanema; 7pm-1am Tue-Thu, to 2am Fri & Sat, 6-11pm Sun) Located in the heart of Ipanema, this supremely stylish cocktail bar and restaurant, complete with swanky rooftop terrace, feels like it has been plucked directly from downtown Manhattan. The meticulously crafted cocktails are made with high-quality spirits and often arrive adorned with foams and dehydrated fruit slices. The menu offers equally intricate yet delicious dishes.

Pavão Azul Bar

(Map p58; 21 2236-2381; Hilário de Gouveia 71, Copacabana; noon-midnight Mon-Sat, to 8pm Sun) A Copacabana classic, Pavão Azul is a simple open-sided bar where huge crowds gather on the sidewalk out front to drink ice-cold *chope* (draft beer) and chat late into the night. It's been so successful in fact that the owners have opened a similar *boteco,* Pavãzinho, across the street. Don't miss the fantastically good, inexpensive *pataniscas* (codfish fritters).

CoLAB Bar

(Map p58; 21 3592-0470; www.colab-rio.com; Fernandes Guimarães 66; 10am-1am Tue-Sat) CoLAB is one of Botafogo's increasing number of lively bar/restaurants attracting a predominantly young crowd with a combination of international cuisine, cocktails

The intimate space has an enchantingly illuminated bar...

Baretto-Londra

JOHN MAIER JR/LONELY PLANET / GETTY IMAGES ©

and craft beers. The menu features curries (both Indian and Thai) as well as samosas, falafel sandwiches, burgers and other temptations. Calm by day, CoLAB picks up in the evenings – with DJs and the occasional band keeping things lively.

Comuna Bar

(Map p58; ☎21 3579-6175; www.facebook.com/comunacc; Sorocaba 585, Botafogo; ⊙noon-1am Tue-Fri, 6:30pm-1:30am Sat, 6:30pm-midnight Sun) This creative space is equal parts bar, art gallery and independent bookseller (and indie publishing house). There's always something afoot in the delightfully off-the-beaten-path locale, with workshops, music sessions, readings, exhibitions and fashion shows. It's also just a great spot for a local microbrew and a bite (try one of the award-winning burgers).

Explorer Bar Cocktail Bar

(Map p54; ☎21 3264-9665; www.explorerbar.com; Almirante Alexandrino 399, Santa Teresa; ⊙5pm-midnight Tue-Fri, from 2pm Sat & Sun) A gorgeous multilevel garden with fairy lights is the centerpiece of this charming cocktail bar. Beautifully conceived cocktails (around R$30) showcase exotic flavors in elixirs like TLV, with orange, tamarind, ginger foam and grated nutmeg. The first-rate food menu features an eclectic mix of Sicilian seafood pasta, *sabich* (a roasted eggplant and hummus sandwich) and other globally inspired dishes (mains R$32 to R$56).

Baretto-Londra Lounge

(Map p62; ☎21 3202-4000; www.fasano.com.br/gastronomia/baretto-londra; Av Vieira Souto 80, Hotel Fasano; ⊙8pm-2am Thu-Sat) You'll find one of Rio's most glam bars here inside the **Hotel Fasano**, offering a vision of decadence matched by few of the city's night spots. The intimate space, designed by Philippe Starck, has an enchantingly illuminated bar, leather armchairs and divans, and a DJ spinning world electronica.

Samba Clubs in Lapa

Samba is the great soundtrack of Rio. It plays all across town, but if you're looking for its heart, you'll probably find it in the bohemian neighborhood of Lapa. In this neighborhood, addictive rhythms spill out of old-fashioned dance halls, drawing music lovers from far and wide.

Rio Scenarium (Map p54; ☎21 3147-9000; www.rioscenarium.art.br; Rua do Lavradio 20, Lapa; R$35-60; ⊙7pm-4am Tue-Sat) One of the city's most photogenic nightspots, Rio Scenarium has three floors, each lavishly decorated with antiques. Balconies overlook the stage on the 1st floor, where dancers keep time to the jazz-infused samba filling the air.

Carioca da Gema (Map p54; ☎21 2221-0043; www.barcariocadagema.com.br; Av Mem de Sá 79, Lapa; R$20-40; ⊙7:30pm-1:30am Sun-Tue & Thu, to 3am Fri, from 9pm Sat) One of Lapa's pioneers, this small, warmly lit club still attracts some of the city's best samba bands, and you'll find a festive mixed crowd filling the dance floor most nights.

Sacrilégio (Map p54; ☎21 3970-1461; www.sacrilegio.com.br; Av Mem de Sá 81, Lapa; R$20-40; ⊙7pm-2am Tue-Thu, to 6am Fri, 8pm-6am Sat) A short stroll past the Arcos da Lapa you'll find a key spot for live samba in an intimate setting. The garden makes a fine setting for a few cold chopes while the music filters through the windows.

Rio Scenarium

ENTERTAINMENT

Bip Bip — Live Music

(Map p62; 21 2267-9696; www.facebook.com/barbipbip; Almirante Gonçalves 50, Copacabana; 7pm-midnight Sun-Fri) For years Bip Bip has been one of the city's favorite spots to catch a live *roda de samba* (informal samba played around a table), despite it being just a storefront with a few battered tables. As the evening progresses the tree-lined neighborhood becomes the backdrop to serious jam sessions, with music and revelers spilling into the street.

Pedra do Sal — Samba

(Map p54; Largo João da Baiana, Gamboa; 8pm-midnight Mon & Fri) The Monday- and Friday-night street parties here are major draws for lovers of samba, whether they're Brazilian or foreign, rich or poor. The lively *samba da mesa* features a handful of changing players who belt out well-known songs to swaying, joyful crowds surrounding the tiny plaza.

TribOz — Jazz

(Map p54; 21 2210-0366; www.triboz-rio.com; Conde de Lages 19, Lapa; R$15-30; 6-8pm & 9pm-1am Thu-Sat) Not for lazy ears, this avant-garde jazz house known to the sonic cognoscenti is unique in Rio for its serious approach to performances. Run by an Australian ethnomusicologist, it sits in a shadier part of old Lapa in a signless mansion, which transforms into a beautiful showcase space.

Clube Manouche — Live Music

(Map p62; www.casacamolese.com.br; Jardim Botânico 983; R$60-90) Downstairs from the main restaurant in **Casa Camolese** (Map p62; 21 3514-8200; mains R$42-70; noon-midnight Mon-Sat, to 11pm Sun;), Clube Manouche is an intimate music bar designed in the tradition of West Village clubs in New York City. Sight lines are excellent no matter where you sit, and you can order drinks throughout the show. The club lines up some top-notch jazz artists, as well as eclectic sounds from Brazil and beyond.

Lapa 40 Graus — Live Music

(Map p54; 21 3970-1338; www.lapa40graus.com.br; Rua do Riachuelo 97, Lapa; R$20-50; 8pm-4am Thu-Sat) This impressive multistory music venue and pool hall has tables for lounging on the 1st floor, more than a dozen pool tables on the 2nd floor, and a small stage and dancing couples on the top floor. There are usually two shows nightly. Pop, rock, samba and *choro* (romantic, improvised, samba-related music) typically kick off around 9pm.

INFORMATION

Riotur's multilingual website (www.visit.rio) is a good source of information. Its offices distribute maps and guides about major events; the main branch is in **Copacabana** (Map p58; 21 2541-7522; Av Princesa Isabel 183; 9am-6pm Mon-Fri).

GETTING THERE & AWAY

Rio's main airport is Galeão international airport (p401), located 15km north of the city center on Ilha do Governador.

Aeroporto Santos Dumont (Map p54; 21 3814-7222; www4.infraero.gov.br; Praça Senador Salgado Filho), used by some domestic flights, is by the bay, in the city center, 1km east of Cinelândia metro station.

GETTING AROUND

Metro The most convenient way to get around. Trains run from 5am to midnight Monday through Saturday, and from 7am to 11pm on Sunday and holidays. Single rides cost R$4.30.

Bus Buses are frequent and cheap; destinations are listed above the windscreen. Fares are around R$3.50.

Taxi Useful at night. Fares start at R$5.50, plus R$2.50 per kilometer. Rates rise to R$3 per kilometer at night and on Sunday.

Bike Rio's bike-share scheme has numerous stations around town. You'll need a local cell phone (mobile) number to release the bikes at each station.

Ride-sharing apps Uber, but not Lyft, is widely available in Rio de Janeiro.

Where to Stay

Rio has a wide range of lodging, including B&Bs, hostels and guesthouses, plus scores of luxury hotels, particularly in Copacabana. Abundant options keeps rates from soaring, except during Carnaval and other major events. Book well ahead during high season.

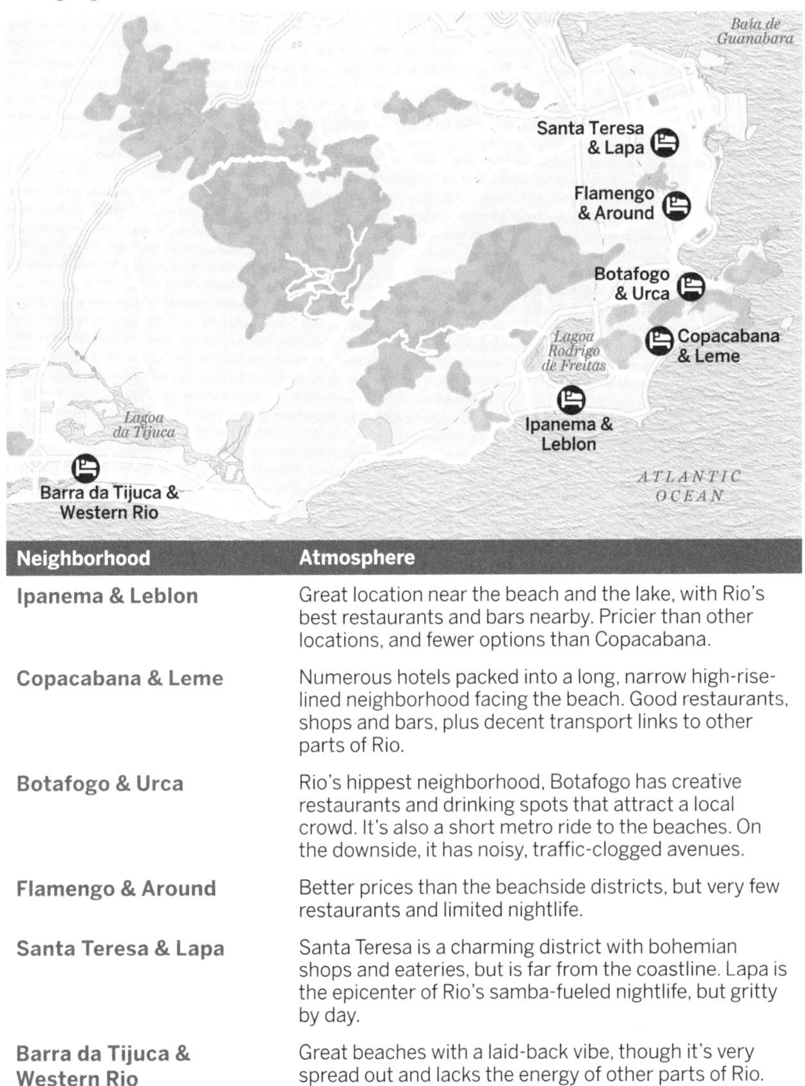

Neighborhood	Atmosphere
Ipanema & Leblon	Great location near the beach and the lake, with Rio's best restaurants and bars nearby. Pricier than other locations, and fewer options than Copacabana.
Copacabana & Leme	Numerous hotels packed into a long, narrow high-rise-lined neighborhood facing the beach. Good restaurants, shops and bars, plus decent transport links to other parts of Rio.
Botafogo & Urca	Rio's hippest neighborhood, Botafogo has creative restaurants and drinking spots that attract a local crowd. It's also a short metro ride to the beaches. On the downside, it has noisy, traffic-clogged avenues.
Flamengo & Around	Better prices than the beachside districts, but very few restaurants and limited nightlife.
Santa Teresa & Lapa	Santa Teresa is a charming district with bohemian shops and eateries, but is far from the coastline. Lapa is the epicenter of Rio's samba-fueled nightlife, but gritty by day.
Barra da Tijuca & Western Rio	Great beaches with a laid-back vibe, though it's very spread out and lacks the energy of other parts of Rio.

VISA
VISA

SALVADOR, BRAZIL

In this Chapter

Salvador, Brazil

Salvador da Bahia has an energy and unadorned beauty that few cities can match. Once the magnificent capital of Portugal's New World colony, today Salvador is the pulsating heart of the country's Afro-Brazilian community. Its brilliantly hued center is a living museum of 17th- and 18th-century architecture and gold-laden churches. Wild festivals happen frequently, with drum corps pounding out rhythms against the backdrop of colonial buildings almost daily. Aside from the many attractions within Salvador, a gorgeous coastline lies right outside the city – a suitable introduction to the tropical splendor of Bahia.

Two Days in Salvador

Spend two full days exploring the Pelourinho. Visit baroque churches like **Igreja e Convento São Francisco** (p76) and learn about Salvador's Carnaval traditions at the **Casa do Carnaval da Bahia** (p78). Take a cooking class and indulge in Bahian delicacies at **Restaurante do Senac** (p81) and catch a performance at the famed **Balé Folclórico da Bahia** (p74).

Four Days in Salvador

On your third day, go souvenir shopping and snacking at the **Mercado Modelo** (p78), browse modern art and catch a concert at the **Solar do Unhão** (p79).

On the fourth day visit the **Igreja NS do Bonfim** (p82), then head down to Barra for fun on the **beach** (p79), a **lighthouse visit** (p79) and seafood at **Du Chef Arte e Gastronomia** (p81).

Previous page: Colorful buildings, Pelourinho (p76)

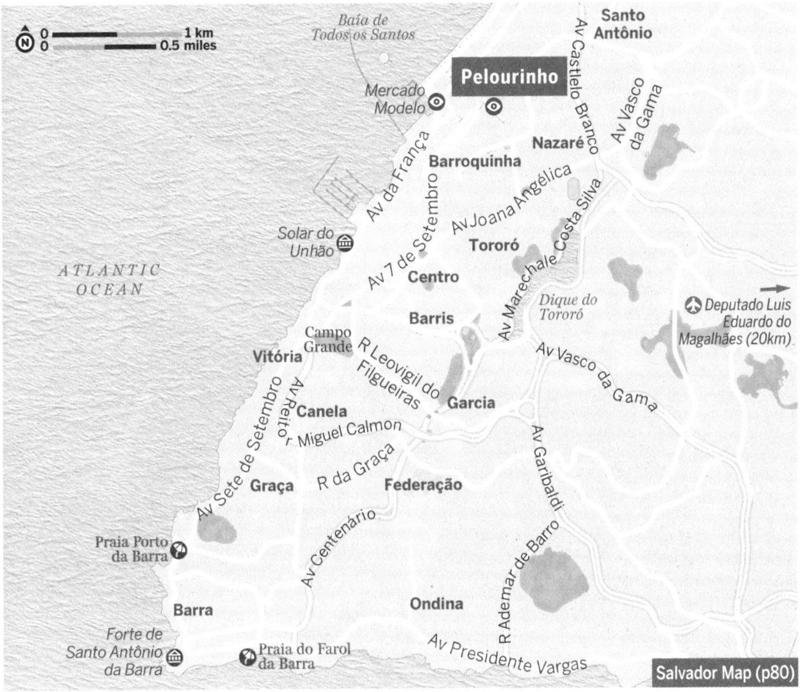

Salvador Map (p80)

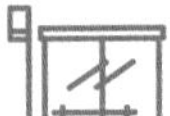

Arriving in Salvador

The airport is located about 30km east of the center. For a taxi going to Barra or the Pelourinho (40 to 60 minutes), you'll pay around R$140 in advance at the airport via the official Taxi COMTAS and Taxi COOMETAS stands.

An executive bus called First Class (www.firstclassbus.com.br) travels between the airport and key tourist points (R$25 per person).

Where to Stay

Staying in the Pelourinho means being close to the action, but the beach suburbs are mellower (and just a short bus or taxi ride away). Santo Antônio is a peaceful neighborhood with classy *pousadas* (guesthouses) in renovated old buildings just a short walk from the Pelourinho. Reservations during Carnaval are essential.

Balé Folclórico da Bahia

Afro-Brazilian Rhythms

Salvador is the pulsing center of an incredible music and dance scene, which blends African and Brazilian traditions in a wide range of musical styles including live percussion and samba.

Great For...

☑ Don't Miss

Live outdoor concerts at Largo de Tereza Batista, Largo do Pedro Arcanjo and Praça Quincas Berro d'Água.

Balé Folclórico da Bahia

The most astounding professional show is put on by this world-renowned **folkloric ballet company** (☎71 3322-1962; www.balefolcloricodabahia.com.br; Gregório de Mattos 49, Teatro Miguel Santana; R$60; ⏲shows 8pm). Incredibly talented performers showcase dances of the *orixás* (the gods in the Afro-Brazilian religion of Candomblé), *capoeira* (a dance-like martial art) and *maculêlê* (stick dance) among many other highlights.

Espaço D'Venetta

This buzzed-about cultural center, bar and **art space** (www.dvenetta.com.br; Rua dos Abodes 12, Santo Antônio; cover varies; ⏲6pm-midnight Wed-Fri, noon-midnight Sat, noon-6pm Sun) in Santo Antônio features live samba, samba de roda and jazz. Some events are free.

ℹ Need to Know

During the high season, there are almost nightly concerts in the inner courtyards of the Pelourinho.

✕ Take a Break

A good place for creative Bahian and international fare is at **Bar Zulu** (Rua das Laranjeiras 15; mains R$22-56; ⌚11am-10pm; ☰✎) in the Pelourinho.

★ Top Tip

You can frequently hear drum corps, which rehearse by walking through the Pelourinho and gathering a following as they go.

Teatro Castro Alves

For the biggest acts, keep your eye on Salvador's finest venue, the **Teatro Castro Alves** (www.tca.ba.gov.br; Praça 2 de Julho, Campo Grande). Its Concha Acústica (amphitheater) has weekly concerts throughout summer.

Jam no MAM

Saturday-evening jazz and bossa nova at **MAM** (www.jamnomam.com.br; Av Contorno s/n, Museu de Arte Moderna; adult/child R$8/4; ⌚6-9pm Sat) is a must for music lovers. Go early to see the museum first and catch the views at sunset. Though the venue is located within walking distance of the Pelourinho, muggings are common along this quiet stretch; taking a taxi is recommended.

Topázio

The popular show that used to be staged at the Solar do Unhão, featuring 18 dancers, musicians and *capoeiristas*, now happens here after dinner at **O Coliseu** (☎71 3321-5585; www.ocoliseu.com.br; 2nd fl, Cruzeiro de São Francisco 9; lunch buffet per person R$65, dinner & cultural show R$200; ⌚11:30am-4pm & 7-10pm Mon-Sat; ✎). Dinner starts at 7pm and the show begins around 8:30pm. Reserve ahead.

Olodum

Founded in 1979, Olodum is famous for its *afro bloco*, which takes inspiration from the musical styles of reggae, salsa and Brazilian samba. Catch them playing around town, or take a peek into the group's headquarters, the **Escola Olodum** (☎71 3321-4154; www.olodum.com.br; Gregório de Mattos 22; tours by donation, workshops free; ⌚9am-6pm Mon-Fri, to 1pm Sat).

Pelourinho

Packed with colorful buildings and magnificent churches, the cobblestone-lined Pelourinho is not just for tourists. Cultural centers and schools of music, dance and capoeira pack these colonial buildings.

Great For...

☑ Don't Miss

The lavish interior of the Igreja e Convento São Francisco, one of Brazil's most magnificent churches.

Largo do Pelourinho

Picture-perfect Largo do Pelourinho is a sloping, triangle-shaped square, once the site of the *pelourinho* (whipping post) – one of several nearby locations where slaves were exposed and punished. After slavery was outlawed in 1835, the neighborhood fell into disrepair; in the 1990s major restoration efforts were initiated to preserve the cobblestone square's colonial houses and churches. Today, the square is the heart of Salvador's historic center.

Igreja e Convento São Francisco

The baroque **Igreja e Convento São Francisco** (Cruzeiro de São Francisco; R$5; ⏲10am-5pm) is filled with displays of wealth and splendor. An 80kg silver chandelier dangles over ornate wood carvings covered in gold leaf, and the convent courtyard is paneled

Interior detail of Igreja e Convento São Francisco

LEOKLEEMANN / SHUTTERSTOCK ©

with hand-painted *azulejos* (Portuguese tiles). The complex was finished in 1723.

Museu Afro-Brasileiro

Holding one of Bahia's most important collections, the **Museu Afro-Brasileiro** (☎71 3283-5540; www.facebook.com/museuafro2; Terreiro de Jesus; adult/child R$6/3; ⏲9am-5pm Mon-Fri, 10am-5pm Sat) exhibits wood carvings, baskets, pottery and other artwork and crafts linking Brazilian and African artistic traditions. Don't miss the breathtaking carved wooden panels depicting *orixás* (spirits common in Afro-Brazilian spirituality) by Argentine-born Carybé.

Igreja NS do Rosário dos Pretos

The king of Portugal gave the Irmanidade dos Homens Pretos (Brotherhood of Black Men) the land for the periwinkle-blue **Igreja NS do Rosário dos Pretos** (Largo do Pelourinho; admission by donation; ⏲8am-5pm Mon-Fri, to 7pm Sat) in 1704. Building in their free time, it took these slaves and freed slaves almost 100 years to complete it.

Need to Know

To see what's on while you're in town, log onto Festa da Semana (www.festadasemana.com.br/salvador).

Take a Break

A Cubana (www.acubana.com.br; Portas do Carmo 12; cones R$7-13; ⏲9:30am-10:30pm) is one of Salvador's oldest and best ice-cream shops.

★ Top Tip

The Pelourinho shifts quickly into sketchy areas, so avoid wandering off the beaten path.

Catedral Basílica

The **Catedral Basílica** (Terreiro de Jesus; admission by donation; ⏲9am-5pm Mon-Sat, from 1pm Sun) dates from 1672 and is a marvelous example of Jesuit architecture. The interior is elegant and simple, with marble-covered walls and towering pillars. The sacristy has a beautiful carved jacaranda archway and a painted dome and floor.

Fundação Casa de Jorge Amado

Literary types shouldn't miss a quick visit to the **Fundação Casa de Jorge Amado** (☎71 3321-0070; www.jorgeamado.org.br; Largo do Pelourinho 51; R$5, Wed free; ⏲10am-6pm Mon-Fri, to 4pm Sat), offering an overview of the life of one of Brazil's best-known writers. The museum cafe is a good place to grab a coffee and pastry.

SIGHTS

Casa do Carnaval da Bahia Museum
(☎71 3324-6760; Praça Ramos de Queirós; R$30; ⏰11am-7pm Tue-Sun) The story of Salvador's world-famous Carnaval is told through wonderfully evocative archival video and photographs at this museum which opened in 2018. Even just walking through the museum with its explosions of color and displays of musical instruments and folk-art statues is worth the trip. Downstairs you'll find an excellent gift shop.

Museu de Arqueologia e Etnologia Museum
(Archaeology & Ethnology Museum; ☎71 3283-5533; www.mae.ufba.br; Faculdade de Medicina, Terreiro de Jesus; adult/child R$6/3; ⏰9am-5pm Mon-Fri) Below the Museu Afro-Brasileiro (p77) (one admission ticket gets you into both), the Museu de Arqueologia e Etnologia exhibits indigenous Brazilian pottery, bows and arrows, masks and feather head-pieces. Also tucked between the building's arching stone foundations is 19th-century glass and porcelain found during the excavations for the metro.

exhibits wood carvings, baskets, pottery and other artwork and crafts

Mercado Modelo Market
(Map p73; www.mercadomodelobahia.com.br; Praça Visconde de Cayru; ⏰9am-6pm Mon-Sat, to 2pm Sun) The original 1861 Customs House, where slaves were housed when they arrived in Salvador, was partly destroyed in a fire in 1986. After reconstruction, it was transformed into the Mercado Modelo (p81). The market is a great spot to pick up tourist trinkets, and a couple of cafes out back provide seating with great views of the bay.

Terreiro de Jesus Square
(Praça 15 de Novembro) A colorful intersection of vendors, tourists, capoeiristas and colorful locals, the Terreiro de Jesus is a historic site of religious celebrations, and is ringed by four churches, as well as the 19th-century **Faculdade de Medicina Building**. The plaza feeds into the **Cruzeiro**

Museu Afro-Brasileiro (p77)

de São Francisco, named for the cross in the square's center.

Solar do Unhão Historic Building
(Map p73; ☎71 3117-6139; Av Contorno s/n; ⊙1-6pm Tue-Sun) FREE This well-preserved, 18th-century complex served as a transfer point for sugar shipments: legend says it's haunted by the ghosts of murdered slaves. Today, the building houses the **Museu de Arte Moderna** (MAM; www.jamnomam.com.br/mam; ⊙1-6pm Tue-Sun) FREE, with a changing display of avant-garde exhibits, a hillside **sculpture garden**, and popular Saturday-evening jazz and bossa nova concerts (JAM no MAM (p75) with stunning views over the bay. Take a taxi – the area is known for tourist muggings.

Forte de Santo Antônio da Barra Historic Building
(Map p73; Largo do Farol da Barra s/n) Built in 1698, Bahia's oldest fort is more commonly called the Farol da Barra for the lighthouse (South America's oldest) within its walls. In addition to having superb views, the fort houses an excellent nautical **museum** (Nautical Museum of Bahia; ☎71 3264-3296; www.museunauticodabahia.org.br; adult/student & senior R$15/7.50; ⊙9am-6pm Tue-Sun, daily Jan & Jul), with relics and displays from the days of Portuguese seafaring, plus exhibits on the slave trade.

 COURSES

Classes in *capoeira*, African dance and percussion are easily arranged through guesthouses in the Pelourinho. Generally you can expect to pay anywhere from R$55 to R$120 per hour for a class.

SENAC Cooking
(☎71 3186-4000; www.ba.senac.br; Largo do Pelourinho 13-19; from R$180; ⊙9-11am & noon-4:30 Mon-Fri) A must-see for foodies, SENAC is a Bahian culinary school where both locals and tourists take cooking classes – one course focuses solely on the preparation of popular street foods like *acarajé* (Bahian fritters made of brown beans and dried shrimp fried in palm oil).

 Beach-going in Barra

Praia Porto da Barra, on a horseshoe-shaped stretch of coast, is a small, picturesque beach, that's a great place to be at sunset. The bay's waters are clear and calm, and the people-watching is fantastic. You won't lack for sustenance, with vendors selling everything imaginable.

To the left of the lighthouse, **Praia do Farol da Barra** has a beach break popular with surfers at high tide, and tidal pools popular with children and families at low tide.

Praia Porto da Barra
RUY BARBOSA PINTO / GETTY IMAGES ©

Associação Brasileira de Capoeira Angola Capoeira
(☎71 8824-7869; www.facebook.com/abcangola; Maciel de Baixo 38; prices vary; ⊙classes 6pm Mon & Wed; 👪) This friendly *capoeira* association (known as ABCA) runs classes open to all ages, including children five and older. Be sure to wear comfortable, loose-fitting pants you can move around in.

Associação Artística e Cultural Diáspora Dancing
(Diáspora Art Center; ☎71 3323-0016; Rua das Laranjeiras 44; prices vary; ⊙10am-6pm Mon-Fri) Stop in to inquire about the latest schedule of classes in traditional and contemporary Afro-Brazilian dance, *capoeira* and percussion.

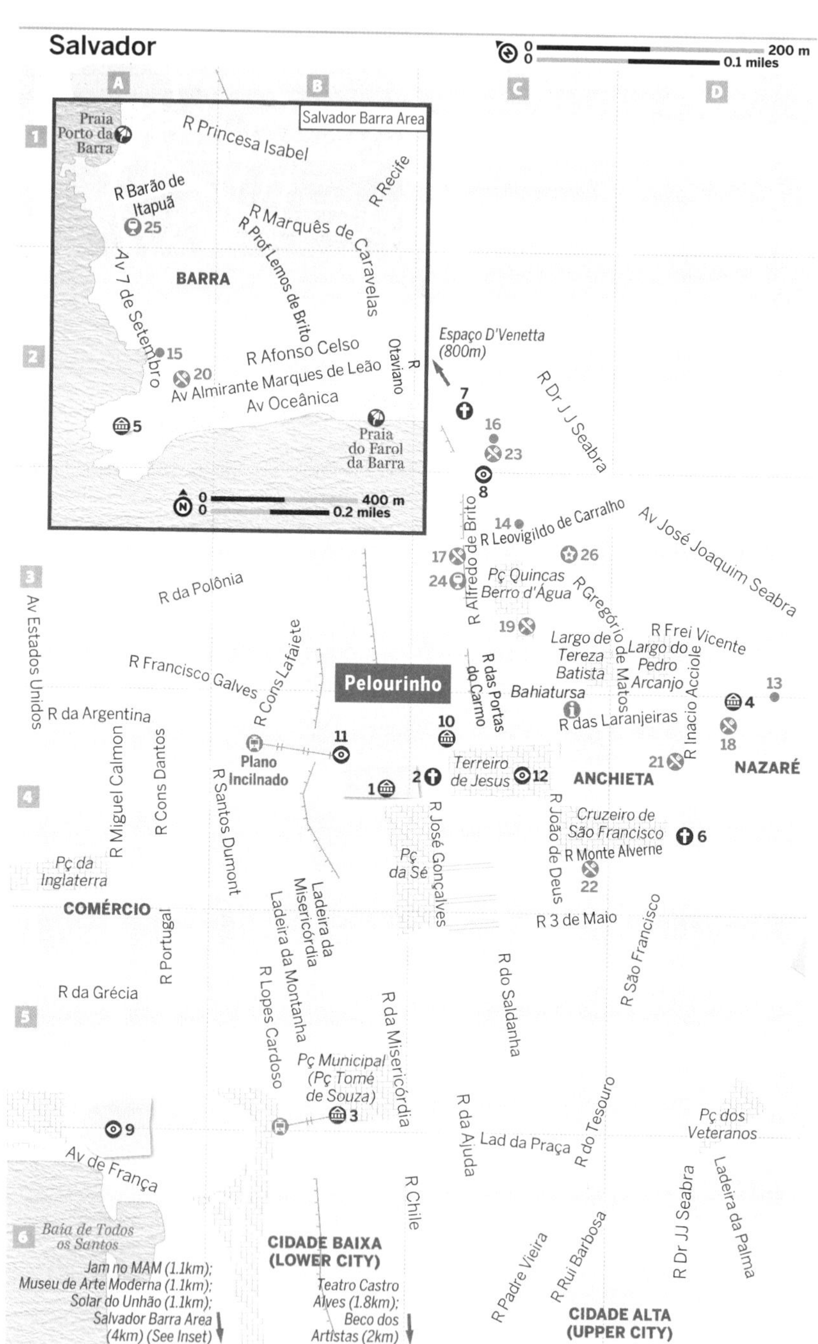

Salvador
200 m
0.1 miles
Salvador Barra Area
Praia Porto da Barra
R Princesa Isabel
R Barão de Itapuã
R Recife
R Marquês de Caravelas
R Prof Lemos de Brito
BARRA
Av 7 de Setembro
R Afonso Celso
R Otaviano
Av Almirante Marques de Leão
Av Oceânica
Praia do Farol da Barra
400 m
0.2 miles
Espaço D'Venetta (800m)
R Dr J J Seabra
R Alfredo de Brito
R Leovigildo de Carralho
Av José Joaquim Seabra
Pç Quincas Berro d'Água
R Gregório de Matos
R da Polônia
Av Estados Unidos
R Francisco Galves
R Cons Lafaiete
Pelourinho
R das Portas do Carmo
Largo de Tereza Batista
Largo do Pedro Arcanjo
R Frei Vicente
R Inacio Acciole
Bahiatursa
R das Laranjeiras
R da Argentina
R Miguel Calmon
R Cons Dantos
Plano Incilnado
R Santos Dumont
Terreiro de Jesus
ANCHIETA
NAZARÉ
R José Gonçalves
R João de Deus
Cruzeiro de São Francisco
R Monte Alverne
Pç da Inglaterra
Pç da Sé
COMÉRCIO
Ladeira da Misericórdia
Ladeira da Montanha
R 3 de Maio
R Portugal
R Lopes Cardoso
R do Saldanha
R São Francisco
R da Grécia
R da Misericórdia
Pç Municipal (Pç Tomé de Souza)
R da Ajuda
Lad da Praça
R do Tesouro
Pç dos Veteranos
Av de França
R Chile
R Dr JJ Seabra
Ladeira da Palma
Baía de Todos os Santos
CIDADE BAIXA (LOWER CITY)
R Padre Vieira
R Rui Barbosa
Jam no MAM (1.1km); Museu de Arte Moderna (1.1km); Solar do Unhão (1.1km); Salvador Barra Area (4km) (See Inset)
Teatro Castro Alves (1.8km); Beco dos Artistas (2km)
CIDADE ALTA (UPPER CITY)

Salvador

Sights

1 Casa do Carnaval da Bahia B4
2 Catedral Basílica C4
3 Elevador Lacerda B5
4 Escola Olodum D4
5 Forte de Santo Antônio da Barra A2
6 Igreja e Convento São Francisco D4
7 Igreja NS do Rosário dos Pretos C2
8 Largo do Pelourinho C3
9 Mercado Modelo A6
10 Museu Afro-Brasileiro C4
Museu de Arqueologia e Etnologia .... (see 10)
Museu Náutico da Bahia .... (see 5)
11 Plano Inclinado Gonçalves B4
12 Terreiro de Jesus C4

Activities, Courses & Tours

13 Associação Artística e Cultural Diaspora D3
14 Associação Brasileira de Capoeira Angola C3
15 Salvador Bus A2
16 SENAC C2

Shopping

Mercado Modelo .... (see 9)

Eating

17 A Cubana C3
18 Bar Zulu D4
19 Dona Chika-ka C3
20 Du Chef Arte e Gastronomia A2
21 Maria Mata Mouro D4
22 O Coliseu C4
Pelô Bistrô .... (see 24)
23 Restaurante do Senac C2

Drinking & Nightlife

24 Casa do Amarelindo Bar C3
25 Pereira A1

Entertainment

26 Balé Folclórico da Bahia C3

TOURS

Salvador Bus — Tours

(☎71 3356-6425; www.salvadorbus.com.br; Av Sete de Setembro s/n; adult/child R$65/50; ⊙9:30am-6:45pm Mon-Sat) If you're short on time, climb aboard the open-air Salvador Bus at Farol da Barra, the Mercado Modelo or a number of other downtown destinations; the hop-on, hop-off sightseeing bus offers multilingual tours.

SHOPPING

Mercado Modelo — Arts & Crafts

(Praça Cayru, Cidade Baixa; ⊙9am-6pm Mon-Sat, to 2pm Sun) In Salvador's unpleasant past the Mercado Modelo (p78) was the site where slaves coming into the city were detained. Now the building houses dozens of tourist-oriented stalls selling local handicrafts, as well as food stalls and restaurants.

EATING

Restaurante do Senac — Buffet $$

(☎71 3324-8101; www.ba.senac.br; Largo do Pelourinho 13; buffet per kg R$50, típico per kg R$51.90; ⊙buffet a quilo 11:30am-3:30pm Mon-Fri, buffet típico 11:30am-3:30pm Mon-Sat; ✎) The best Bahian buffet in town. The cooking school SENAC (p79) spreads a tempting array of regional dishes, including several varieties of seafood, *moqueca* (fish stew), and traditional desserts. The impressive *buffet tipico* (traditional Bahian food) is on the top floor, not to be confused with the more general street-level *buffet a quilo*, which is also good for a quick lunch.

Du Chef Arte e Gastronomia — Seafood $$

(☎71 3042-4433; www.facebook.com/duchefartegastronomia; Afonso Celso 70, Barra; mains R$45-90; ⊙noon-11pm Tue-Thu, to 1am Fri & Sat, to 5pm Sun; ✎) Fresh seafood and upscale plating make the dishes at this swish Barra restaurant pop. You're likely to make the acquaintance of the chef, Lucius Gaudenzi, while you dine on tender shrimp or one of the vegan dishes on the menu.

Dona Chika-ka — Afro-Brazilian $$

(☎71 3321-1712; Rua João Castro Rabelo 10; mains R$30-80; ⊙6-10pm Mon-Sat) Flickering candles lead the way up to a charmingly decorated 2nd-floor dining room, where you can feast on Dona Chika-ka's famous *bobó de camarão* (shrimp chowder) and other

Igreja NS do Bonfim

This famous 18th-century **church** (☎71 3316-2196; www.santuariosenhordobonfim.com; Praça Senhor do Bonfim; ⊙6:30am-6.30pm Mon-Thu & Sat, from 5:30am Fri & Sun), located a few kilometers north of Comércio on the Itapagipe Peninsula, is the source of the *fitas* (colored ribbons) you see everywhere in Salvador, a souvenir of the church and a symbol of Bahia itself. Bonfim's fame derives from its power to effect miraculous cures, making it a popular shrine.

In the Sala dos Milagres (Room of Miracles) devotees leave photos, letters and ex-votos – wax replicas of body parts representing those that were cured or need curing.

Due to Candomblistas' syncretization of Jesus Christ (Nosso Senhor do Bonfim) with Oxalá, their highest deity, Bonfim is their most important church. Huge services are held here on Friday, Oxalá's favorite day of the week.

If you tie a *fita* around your wrist, you are making a commitment that lasts for months. With each of the three knots a wish is made, which will come true by the time the *fita* falls off. Cutting it off is inviting doom.

Check their website for a full schedule of various services and events held daily.

Bahian delights. During quieter months you may find reduced business hours and only the small downstairs dining area open.

Paraíso Tropical Bahian $$$

(☎71 3384-7464; www.restauranteparaisotropical.com.br; Edgar Loureiro 98B, Cabula; mains R$53-98; ⊙noon-10pm Tue-Sat, to 5pm Sun) Far off the beaten path in the residential neighborhood of Cabula, but foodies don't mind the detour to Paraíso Tropical: the classic Brazilian restaurant has long been considered one of Salvador's top choices for beautifully prepared Bahian cuisine with a gourmet twist. Come for a leisurely lunch; expect long waits on weekends.

Maria Mata Mouro Brazilian $$$

(☎71 3321-3929; www.mariamatamouro.com.br; Rua da Ordem Terceira 8; mains R$40-80; ⊙noon-11pm) The picture-perfect garden patio and elegant dining room are fine settings to enjoy one of Pelô's top menus. You'll find Bahian classics, fresh seafood and Portuguese dishes prepared with a gourmet twist, plus a varied wine list and a talented bartender shaking up unique cocktails.

DRINKING & NIGHTLIFE

Casa do Amarelindo Bar Cocktail Bar

(☎71 3266-8550; www.casadoamarelindo.com; Rua das Portas do Carmo 6, Hotel Casa do Amarelindo; ⊙noon-late) The chic tropical-style bar at the lovely **Pelô Bistrô** at Casa do Amarelindo is the ideal spot for a nightcap; better still is the panoramic terrace where a skilled bartender shows up after dark to mix classic cocktails.

Pereira Bar

(☎71 3264-6464; www.pereirarestaurante.com.br; Sete de Setembro 3959, Barra; ⊙noon-4pm & 5pm-midnight Tue-Fri & Sun, noon-4pm & 5:30pm-1am Sat) Up a staircase from the seaside road that curves around the tip of Barra, Pereira is a stylish restaurant and wine bar. Excellent *chope* (draft beer) is on tap and the sunset views over the ocean are beautiful.

Moqueca (fish stew)

Beco dos Artistas Bar

(Artist's Alley; Av Cerqueira Lima 4, Garcia; hours vary) Art mavens and a young, queer-friendly crowd flock to Beco dos Artistas, a small alley with several bars and a nightclub. Take a taxi and enter from Rua Leovigildo Filgueira.

INFORMATION

Bahiatursa The tourism authority is friendly but not very organized. The **Pelourinho office** (71 3321-2463; www.bahiatursa.ba.gov.br; Rua Francisco Muniz Barreto 12, Pelourinho; 8:30am-9pm Mon-Thu, to 10pm Fri-Sun), which has maps and listings of what's happening around town, is your best bet.

GETTING THERE & AWAY

Aeroporto Deputado Luis Eduardo do Magalhães (Praça Gago Coutinho s/n, São Cristóvão; 71 3204-1010) is served by domestic airlines like **GOL** (0300 115-2121; www.voegol.com.br; airport), **LATAM** (1-866-435-9526; www.latam.com), and **Azul** (1-888-587-2985; www.voeazul.com.br). There are several direct flights to/from foreign cities such as Miami or Lisbon via **TAP** (Air Portugal; 1-800-221-7370; www.flytap.com), and Buenos Aires via **Aerolíneas Argentinas** (1-800-333-0276; www.aerolineas.com.ar).

Salvador's **bus station** (Bus Station; 71 3616-8300; www.rodoviariadesalvador.com.br) is 8km east of the city center.

GETTING AROUND

Linking Cidade Alta (the Pelourinho) and Cidade Baixa (Comércio and the ferry terminals) are the **Elevador Lacerda** (71 3322-7049; fare R$0.15; 6am-11pm) and the **Plano Inclinado Gonçalves** (Praça da Sé & Guindaste dos Padres, Comércio; R$0.15; 7am-7pm Mon-Fri, to 1pm Sat).

Public buses crisscross the city; particularly useful to tourists are those that run between Barra and Praça da Sé (R$3.70).The destinations are clearly labeled on the front of the bus.

Taxis can be taken at meter price (legal) or negotiated, but you might not get to choose which. Uber is also available.

BRAZILIAN AMAZON

In this Chapter

Brazilian Amazon

What traveler drawn to the wild places of the planet hasn't imagined a trip to the Amazon, not only to admire the towering trees, secretive wildlife and awesome river, but to enter, in a real sense, the very life spring of the planet?

In fact, the Amazon's quintessential experiences are more sublime than superlative: canoeing through a flooded forest, dozing in a hammock on a boat chugging upriver, waking to the otherworldly cry of howler monkeys. On a river whose size is legendary, it's actually the little things that make it special.

Two Days in the Brazilian Amazon

With limited time, fly into Manaus and head upriver for a couple of nights along the Rio Urubu, the closest you'll get to deep Amazon immersion in this short time frame. There you'll get a chance to see plentiful wildlife on jungle hikes and canoe trips, and to visit local communities.

Four Days in the Brazilian Amazon

Spend day three in Manaus. Browse Amazonian handicrafts at Galeria Amazônica, tour the jaw-dropping Teatro Amazonas and stroll the lush paths of the Jardim Botânico Adolpho Ducke.

On the fourth day, make a half-day trip into the forest with Amazon Tree Climbing, where you can also see the unusual Encontro das Águas.

Previous page: Rio Amazonas
MANTAPHOTO / GETTY IMAGES ©

Belém Map (p95)
Manaus Map (p99)

Arriving in the Brazilian Amazon

The main airport of Manaus, **Aeroporto Internacional Eduardo Gomes** (p101), is located 13km north of the city center, and it has a few international flights, as well as excellent domestic connections.

Belém's **Aeroporto Internacional Val-de-Cans** (p96), located 8km north of the center, is a hub for international, domestic and regional flights.

Where to Stay

The Amazon has everything from five-star city hotels to basic lodges in the remote reaches of the network of rivers. Away from the cities, many places offer packages that include food, accommodations and all activities, as well as transfers from the nearest town. There are many jungle lodges, including the celebrated Pousada Uacari inside the Mamirauá Reserve.

Riverboat at sunset

LUC KOHNEN / SHUTTERSTOCK ©

Riverboat Travel

Rivers are roads in Amazonia, and the slow pace of a boat trip is a uniquely Amazonian experience: you'll be sleeping in a hammock, watching the river, forest and local life glide by.

Great For...

☑ Don't Miss

The view of the bluffs around Monte Alegre on the two-day boat trip between Belém and Santarém.

Life on the Boat

Trips are long and languid, measured in days instead of hours. Much of the time is spent on the boat's upper deck, watching the scenery glide by, knocking back beers, talking and laughing over the ever-blasting music. The middle deck is a place to read, nap in a hammock, or practice Portuguese with your neighbor. Night falls quickly and decisively, and night skies on the river can be spectacular.

Riverboat Realities

For most people a two- to three-day trip is plenty. For all its romantic appeal, riverboat travel can get rather tedious, especially with the constant pounding of the music and engine. The boats typically travel far from shore so there's virtually no chance of

Need to Know

You'll need to bring your own hammock and some rope to attach it.

Take a Break

Be sure to bring your own snacks; food on the boat (rice and beans!) doesn't offer much variety.

★ Top Tip

Get to the boat six to eight hours early to secure a good hammock spot–preferably on the middle deck.

seeing wildlife. Consider taking a boat for one leg, and flying the others; air and boat fares can be surprisingly comparable, and you'll have more time for tours and other activities.

Suggested Itineraries

The two-day boat trip between Belém and Santarém is an interesting one, passing through the tidal zone around Belém, the narrows of Breves, the high bluffs around Monte Alegre and finally the main channel near Santarém. (The Santarém–Manaus leg, by contrast, follows the main channel only.) The Rio Negro, especially the upper regions, has little boat traffic and winds through massive archipelagos. Porto Velho to Manaus, along the Rio Madeira, is another good choice, a scenic backdoor route to the Amazon.

Trip Preparations

Most boats have a few *camarotes* (cabins with two to four bunks and a fan) and suites, with air-con and bathrooms. The advantage is you sleep in a bed instead of a hammock, can lock up your gear, and usually get better food. The disadvantage is you miss out on the camaraderie (and bragging rights) that come from sleeping in a hammock alongside everyone else. If you book a cabin or suite, avoid those on the top deck, where there's blasting music.

Buffet-style meals may or may not be included in the fare. Either way, consider skipping them – you really don't want the runs during a boat trip. Instead, get made-to-order burgers and sandwiches from the kitchen on the upper deck, and pack plenty of food that travels well, such as apples, nuts and energy bars. Don't forget to bring drinking water.

Aerial view of Parque Nacional de Anavilhanas

Jungle Expeditions & Wildlife-Watching

Whether based at a jungle lodge or on a touring riverboat, you can have the experience of a lifetime spying wildlife in the mother of all rainforests. While anything's possible, the most common trip is three to five days with hiking, canoeing, spotting caiman and visiting local villages.

Great For...

☑ Don't Miss

Not-to-be-missed wildlife spotting.

Mamirauá Reserve

The remarkable Mamirauá Sustainable Development Reserve has pristine rainforest, abundant animal life and fairly easy access, located just 1½ hours by boat from Tefé, with its reliable air and boat service. The primary lodge, the **Pousada Uacari** (✆97 3343-4160; www.uakarilodge.com.br; all-inclusive 3/4/7 nights s R$2740/3210/4410, d R$4980/5840/8020; 📶) in the reserve, runs outstanding tours and has comfortable accommodations. It's one of the Amazon's best ecotourism operations.

Parque Nacional de Anavilhanas

Stretching along the Rio Negro for almost 130km and with 400 islands, this national park, centered on the Anavilhanas Archipelago, is one of the most rewarding excursions in the Rio Negro Basin. When water

Squirrel monkey

Need to Know

Manaus (and nearby destinations) serves as the gateway to jungle trips.

Take a Break

Be sure to bring along your favorite snacks, for which you'll be grateful on long hikes.

★ Top Tip

Bring binoculars. Even a small pair makes a big difference in observing wildlife.

levels are low, island beaches appear and camping overnight becomes possible.

The best tours here are run by **Visit Amazônia** (☎92 99114-6038, 92 99215-1648; www.visitamazonia.org; Av Presidente Getulio Vargas) and **Expedição Katerre** (☎92 3365-1644; www.katerre.com; Francisco Cardoso).

Reserva Extrativista Baixo Rio Branco-Jauaperi

This newly minted extractive **reserve** (Xixuaú-Xipariná) has excellent wildlife-watching – if you're here to see the Amazon in its pristine state, this place should be high on your list. The reserve extends north from the Rio Negro and is most easily reached from Novo Airão.

Most tours here are handled by top-notch Visit Amazonia, based in Novo Airão. Other groups offering tours here include Expedição Katerre (p91) and Amazonia Expeditions (p92).

Tropical Tree Climbing

Tours with this warm French–Venezuelan **outfit** (☎92 99245-3669; www.tropicaltreeclimbing.com; Hwy BR-178, Km 144) include garden-fresh meals, hiking through verdant forest and, of course, climbing a tree (or two) – usually a huge *angelim* or *samaúma*. Overnight in comfy guest rooms or even up in a tree!

Tours of one to seven days are available, including dedicated photo safaris. Longer trips include visits to waterfalls and other area sights.

Amazon Eco Adventures

Amazon Eco Adventures (☎92 98831-1011; www.amazonecoadventures.com; 10 de Julho, at Tapajós) is an excellent choice for jungle trips. It offers tours with small groups, comfortable speedboats, its own overnight boat and top guides. You'll go swimming at the meeting of the waters, and activities like visiting indigenous villages don't have a voyeuristic feel.

They also have a lodge up on the Rio Urubu. Although this outfit is pricier than others, it's well worth it.

Swallows & Amazons

This long-established South African–Brazilian **agency** (www.swallowsandamazons tours.com; Ramos Ferreira 922) specializes in riverboat tours, with different boats available for varying levels of comfort. Tours mostly go up the Rio Negro, including to the Anavilhanas Archipelago and Jaú National Park, exploring smaller tributaries along the way, with plenty of hiking, canoeing and fishing.

Amazônia Expeditions

This experienced **operator** (☎92 3671-2731; www.amazoniaexpeditions.com.br; Rua Miguel Ribas 1339) has spent decades leading tour groups as well as prestigious scientific expeditions. It's one of few groups that goes up the Rio Negro to the Reserva Extrativista Baixo Rio Branco-Jauaperi (p91), and guides are professional and knowledgeable about wildlife and botany.

Lo Peix

Tours by **Lo Peix** (☎92 98182-4793; www.lopeix.com; Av Coronel Teixera Puerto, Ponta Negra; per person R$435-1680, 3-12 days) go further up the Rio Negro than other Manaus-based groups and hit places like the Anavilhanas Archipelago, Jaú National Park, prehistoric sites near Airão Velho and

Hiking in the Brazilian Amazon

more, with frequent stops for canoeing, hiking, snorkeling and visiting local communities.

The custom-built boat has small comfortable berths, solar power and up-to-date safety equipment.

Juma Lodge

The deluxe lakefront cabins at **Juma Lodge** (92 3232-2707; www.jumalodge.com; 1 night all-inclusive s R$2245-3265, d R$3326-4838) stand dramatically on 15m stilts, connected by wood walkways, with huge screened windows and private patios. West-facing units can get hot in the late afternoon, but that's when you might be sipping a caipirinha on the lodge's shady deck or in the spacious communal dining area. Tours make use of comfortable motorized canoes, though groups can be large.

★ Did You Know?

The Amazon Basin spans nine countries and three standard time zones. It has an area of more than 7 million sq km, accounting for 40% of the entire South American continent.

GUENTER FISCHER / GETTY IMAGES ©

Amazon Antonio's Lodge

Antonio Gomes has built a splendid **lodge** (92 99961-8314; www.antonio-jungletours.com; Rio Urubu; per person in dm/room with private bathroom incl meals from R$330/375; ❄) on the mosquito-free banks of the Rio Urubu, surrounded by a pristine tract of riverine forest rich in wildlife and tall trees. The rooms are outstanding, especially the chalets with expansive terraces and hammocks. The three-storey observation tower has glorious views, especially at sunset. Activities include fishing, jungle hikes, canoe trips and overnight camping. Combine it with a trip downriver to Antonio's other lodge, **Pousada Cumaru** (per person in dm/d with shared bathroom incl meals R$360/400; P).

Amazon Gero Tours

The effusive **Gero Mesquita** (92 99983-6273, 92 99198-0111; www.amazongerotours.com; Tapajós 27), an all-round good guy, runs a popular lodge in the Juma-Mamori area with comfortable dorms and private rooms, and a cadre of skilled guides. Besides standard tours, Gero arranges multiday treks into untouched forest and organizes 'social sustainability' programs where travelers work on needed community projects.

☑ When to Go

The best time to visit is during the dry season (June to December), when river levels drop and the wildlife-spotting is excellent.

Belém

The eastern gateway to the Amazon region and a destination in its own right, Belém is worth at least a couple of days of your life. It's a rewarding city, with streets and parks shaded by mango trees, the pastel facades of once-decadent mansions now fading in the tropical sun, as well as a number of fascinating museums, pungent markets and decent restaurant-bars.

SIGHTS

Estação das Docas Market

(91 3212-5525; www.estacaodasdocas.com.br; Blvd Castilho França; 9am-1am) An ambitious renovation project converted three down-at-heel riverfront warehouses into a popular gathering spot, with restaurants, bars, shops and even an art-house theater. There are river views and displays about Belém's history, plus a post office and numerous ATMs. Enjoy live music most nights, performed from a moving platform in the rafters, rolling slowly the length of the dining area.

Basílica Santuario de Nazaré Church

(www.basilicadenazare.com.br/site; Praça Justo Chermont; 5:30am-8pm) FREE Rather humdrum from the outside, the Basílica Santuario de Nazaré has a truly spectacular interior. Sink into a cushioned pew and admire the soaring marble columns, brilliant stained-glass windows and ornate wood and tile work in every direction, even the ceiling. The basilica is the focal point of Brazil's largest religious festival, Círio de Nazaré, which draws more than a million worshippers to Belém on the second Sunday in October.

Forte do Presépio Fortress

(Praça Fr Brandão; R$4, free Tue; 10am-6pm Tue-Fri, to 2pm Sat & Sun) The city of Belém was founded in 1616 with the construction of this imposing fort, which was intended to protect Portuguese interests upriver from incursions by the French and Dutch. Today it houses a small but excellent museum, primarily about Pará state's indigenous communities (displays in Portuguese only), and has great river and city views from atop its thick stone walls.

TOURS

Amazon Star Turismo (91 3212-6244; www.amazonstar.com.br; Henrique Gurjão 56; 8am-6pm Mon-Fri, to noon Sat) Organizes day trips around Belém, including birdwatching, nature walks and city tours (per person R$150 to R$300), plus overnight tours combining these options, and multiday packages to Ilha de Marajó.

Valeverde Boating

(91 3218-7333; www.valeverdeturismo.com.br; Estação das Docas) Runs a variety of short tours on the river (per person R$50 to R$175), including sunrise trips and pleasant evening cruises. Valeverde has an office and daily schedule at the pier at Estação das Docas; in most cases you can simply show up.

SHOPPING

Mercado Ver-o-Peso Market

(Av Castilho França; 5am-6pm) This is Belém's best place to browse and shop, whether for long pants, lacquered piranha or anything in between. Pará has gained national attention with *technobrega* music, a defiantly from-the-streets genre whose best collections aren't sold in stores but on amateur CDs in Ver-o-Peso (and on YouTube). Be wary of pickpockets in the early and late hours.

Feira de Artesanato Market

(Praça da República; 7am-3pm Fri-Sun) A large crafts fair that has the city's biggest range of attractive artwork, a lot of which is homemade. It's especially busy on Sundays.

EATING

Rei Do Bacalhau Seafood $

(91 3241-5824; Travessa Campos Sales 216; mains from R$15; 8am-6pm) The 'King of Cod' is a Belém classic, with cheap and cheerful

Belém

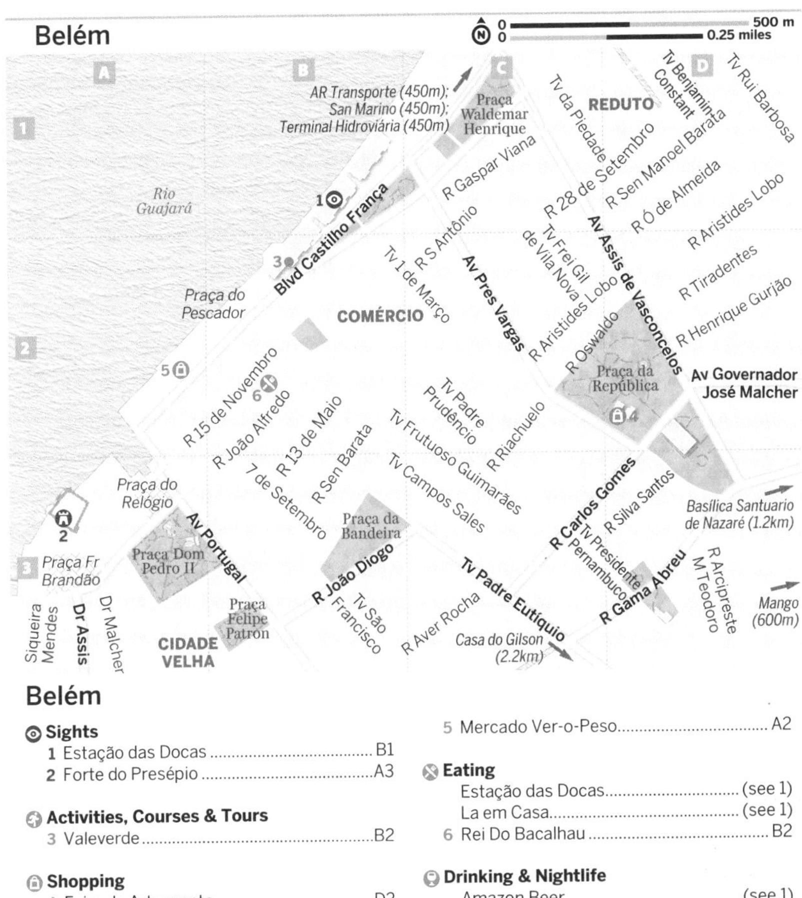

Belém

Sights

1 Estação das Docas B1
2 Forte do Presépio A3

Activities, Courses & Tours

3 Valeverde B2

Shopping

4 Feira de Artesanato D2
5 Mercado Ver-o-Peso A2

Eating

Estação das Docas .... (see 1)
La em Casa .... (see 1)
6 Rei Do Bacalhau B2

Drinking & Nightlife

Amazon Beer .... (see 1)

service and fresh street-food staples straight from the nearby fish market. It's no-frills, which makes us love it all the more.

La em Casa — Brazilian $$

(☎91 3212-5588; www.laemcasa.com; Av Marechal Hermes, Estação das Docas; mains R$28-70, set menu for 1/2 people R$72/120) Around since 1972, La em Casa is an excellent choice for Pará specialties centered around Amazon fish and duck dishes, as well as Brazilian barbecued meats. Try the Pará tasting menu to sample the local flavors; if you snag a riverside table on a warm Amazonian night, you'll love being here even more.

Mango — Cafe $$

(☎91 3199-2731; www.mangoalimentacaosaudavel.com.br; Av Brás de Aguiar 593; mains R$14-45; ⏰11:30am-4pm Tue-Sun & 6-10pm Tue-Sat; 🌿) Wildly popular with Belém's hip young crowd, Mango is devoted to the art of healthy eating, with fab dishes such as duck burger, and grilled mango for dessert. Terrific juices, salads, light quiches and sandwiches round off a fine choice, with plenty of options for vegetarians.

ENTERTAINMENT

Casa do Gilson Live Music

(☎91 3272-7306; www.facebook.com/casadogilson; Travessa Padre Eutíquio 3172; ⏰8pm-3am Fri, from noon Sat & Sun) Come here for Belém's best live music. Opened in 1987, Gilson's attracts crowds with first-rate samba, *choro* (improvised samba-like genre) and other music, and terrific food and atmosphere. It's between ruas Nova and Tambés.

GETTING THERE & AWAY

AIR

Belém's **Aeroporto Internacional Val-de-Cans** (☎91 3210-6000; www.infraero.gov.br), 8km north of the center, is a hub for international, domestic and regional flights. Taxis to the center are R$50.

Belém is worth at least a couple of days of your life.

BOAT

All long-distance boats leave Belém from the centrally located **Terminal Hidroviária** (Av Marechal Hermes). You can purchase tickets from the booths inside the terminal, but an easier and more reliable option is to contact Amazon Star Turismo (p94), whose multilingual staff can book boat tickets over the phone or internet.

AR Transporte (☎91 3224-1225; www.artransporte.com.br) and **San Marino** (☎in Manaus 93 99179-1222; www.facebook.com/Ferryboat.sanmarinoll) offer boat service to Manaus and other points along the way. At last check, boats to Manaus left Wednesday and Saturday, plus every other Tuesday, at 6pm with stops at Monte Alegre (hammock/hammock with air-con/cabin with air-con/cabin with air-con and bathroom R$200/230/750/950, three days), Santarém (R$230/270/800/1000, four days), Parintins (R$330/370/950/1100, five days), and Manaus (R$370/400/1000/1200, six days); cabins rates are for two people. Meals are not included, but you can purchase food on board.

Brazilian dishes, Belém (p94)

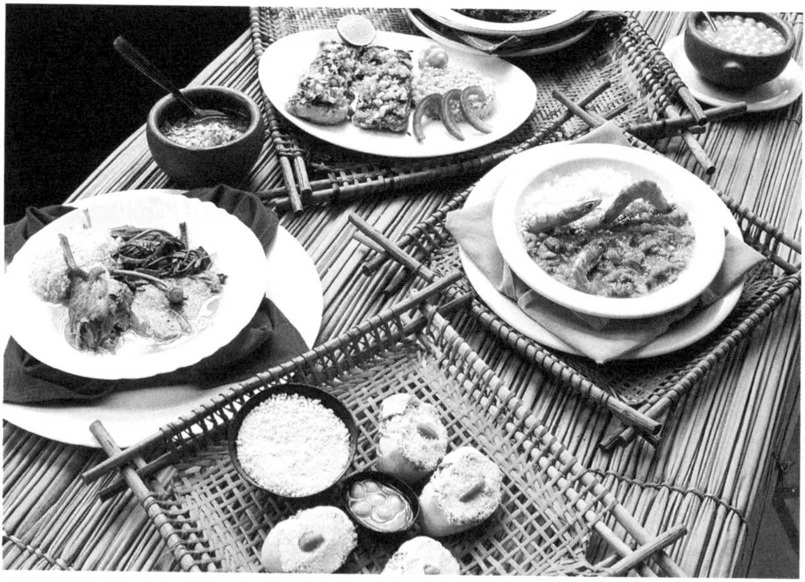

CANNON PHOTOGRAPHY LLC / ALAMY STOCK PHOTO ©

Santarém

Santarém is a terrific destination, a languid riverside town with a breezy waterfront promenade, parks and several good restaurants. More than that, it's a fine gateway to several quintessential Amazon experiences – getting to primary rainforest, in the Floresta Nacional (FLONA) do Tapajós, is much easier here than from Manaus, and Santarém has its very own 'meeting of the waters,' where the Rio Tapajós flows into the Amazon. Not far to the east, Lago Maicá is a gorgeous floodplain rich in birds and other wildlife, including pink dolphins and sloths.

SIGHTS

Lago Maicá Lake

The floodplains east and southeast of Santarém are among the Amazon's most rewarding excursions. Flooded for much of the year, the plains are home to fabulous birdlife (including toucans and macaws), pink dolphins, howler monkeys, sloths and anacondas. The sunrise and sunset views are pure magic and there's a real sense of tranquility out here. Take an overnight boat trip, go canoeing through the flooded forest and relax far from the tourist hordes. Gil Serique (p98) organizes especially enjoyable excursions here.

Praça Mirante do Tapajós Viewpoint

This pleasant oval-shaped plaza and viewpoint has two open-air food stalls and good river views. An observation tower affords an even better view, including of Santarém's own 'meeting of the waters.' Look for a set of stairs just east of Brisa Hotel.

EATING

Quiosque da Praça Street Food $

(Praça Barão de Santarém; from R$8; 7am-1pm & 4-11pm) This small kiosk just west of the center serves the best *tacacá* (local soup with shrimp) we've tasted in Brazil. A late-afternoon bowl of this local favorite will set you up nicely for the night ahead.

Estação das Docas

An ambitious renovation project converted three down-at-heel riverfront warehouses into a popular gathering **spot** (www.estacaodasdocas.com.br; Blvd Castilho França; noon-midnight Sun-Wed, noon-3am Thu-Sat), with restaurants, bars, shops and even an art-house theater. There are river views and displays about Belém's history, plus a post office and ATMs. Enjoy live music most nights, performed from a moving platform in the rafters, rolling slowly the length of the dining area.

Favorite places include Lá em Casa (p95), serving pricey but outstanding regional food, and **Amazon Beer** (91 3212-5400; www.amazonbeer.com.br; Av Marechal Hermes, Estação das Docas; 5pm-1am), with delectable pub grub to accompany its artisanal beer.

Restaurante Piracema Brazilian $$

(93 3522-7461; www.restaurantepiracema.com.br; Av Mendonça Furtado 73; R$25-80; 11am-11:30pm Tue-Sat, to 3pm Sun) Considered by many to be the best restaurant in town, Piracema uses regional ingredients and flavors to create dishes you'll find nowhere else. The specialty is the *peixe á Piracema*, a spherical construction of layered smoked *pirarucú* (a freshwater fish), banana and cheese. It's strange but delicious, and large enough for two.

GETTING THERE & AWAY

Aeroporto de Santarém – Maestro Wilson Fonseca is 14km west of town. It handles flights to/from Manaus and Belém. Buses (R$3.50, 30 minutes) run to the city every half-hour; taxis cost R$60.

The main port, **Docas do Pará**, 2.5km west of the center, has boats to Belém (hammock R$200, double cabin R$600 to R$800, 48 hours) at 10am Friday and every second Sunday, and 11am Monday, which stops at Monte Alegre (hammock R$50, five to seven hours) along the way; to Manaus (hammock R$180, double cabin R$600, 40 to 48 hours) at noon Monday to Wednesday, Friday and Saturday, and at 11am on Thursday.

Alter do Chão

Just a short bus ride from Santarém, Alter do Chão is a cool little town with white-sand river beaches and a laid-back vibe. It's best known for its Ilha do Amor (Island of Love), a picturesque island ringed by a white-sand beach directly in front of town.

But Alter do Chão is much more than a beach town. The lagoon it fronts (Lago Verde) can be explored by canoe or stand-up paddle board. It's also the departure point for boat tours to nearby forest reserves and isolated communities.

ACTIVITIES

Adventure sports are a natural fit for many visitors here. Rewarding options include stand-up paddling (SUP), windsurfing, kayaking, mountain biking and tree climbing (*arbolismo* in Portuguese). Ask at **Mãe Natureza** (☎93 3527-1264, 93 99131-9870; www.maenaturezaecoturismo.com.br; Praça 7 de Setembro; ⏰8:30am-1pm & 4-11pm), **Areia Branca Ecotour** (☎93 3527-1386, 93 99121-5646; www.areiabrancaecotour.com.br; Lago Verde; ⏰8am-noon & 2-7pm Mon-Fri, to 1pm Sat & Sun) or Gil Serique for prices and availability.

TOURS

Gil Serique Ecotour

(☎93 99130-5298; www.gilserique.com; Av Copacabana 45, at PA-457; per person per day US$150) Gil is a true character, a lithe teller of tales and one of the area's top naturalists. Born and raised nearby, Gil's tours are part history, part ecology and part family lore, related with infectious enthusiasm and excellent English. Visits to Lago Maicá (p97), a gorgeous floodplain teeming with birds and other wildlife, are especially memorable. Pricier than others, but worth it.

EATING

Espaço Gastronômico Brazilian $$

(☎93 98401 6144; www.espacoalter.com.br; Lauro Sodré 74; mains R$25-60; ⏰7-11pm; 📶) What a fabulous place! It's made almost entirely from recycled wood and other materials, with a commitment to using local ingredients and indigenous sauces, which might include Brazil nuts, honey and manioc, or ceviche with mango. Upstairs is the place to be, with diaphanous curtains blowing in the sea breeze. Joana is a marvelous host.

GETTING THERE & AWAY

Hourly buses to Alter do Chão depart from Santarém's **bus station** (☎93 3523-4940; Hwy BR-163) (R$3.50, one hour), located 2.5km west of the center.

Manaus

Manaus is the Amazon's largest city, an incongruous urban metropolis in the middle of the jungle and a major port for seafaring vessels that's 1500km from the ocean. The Amazonian rainforest has a population density half that of Mongolia's, but the journey there invariably begins in (or passes through) this gritty, bustling city.

Manaus is no architectural gem, but does have some genuinely rewarding sights. It's also a place to stock up on anything you forgot to pack, make reservations and begin your journey out into the jungle.

SIGHTS

Jardim Botânico Adolpho Ducke Park

(☎92 3582-3188; www.jardimbotanicodemanaus.org; Av Margarita s/n; R$10, incl tower R$30; ⏰8am-noon & 1-4:30pm Tue-Sun, last entry 4pm) FREE Spanning over 100 sq km, this 'garden' is actually the world's largest urban forest. There's a network of five short trails (guides and closed shoes required, two to three hours, free with admission) and an open-air museum that includes rotating exhibits on Amazonian flora and fauna and a spectacular 42-meter-high observation tower. It's busier on weekends and free on Tuesday.

Teatro Amazonas Theater

(☎92 3232-1768; Praça São Sebastião; guided tour R$20; ⏰9:15am-5pm, tours every 30 mins until 4pm) This gorgeous theater was built at the height of the rubber boom, using European designers, decorators and even raw materials. The original driveway was Brazilian, though, made of Amazonian rubber to soften the clatter of late-arriving carriages. The theater's performance schedule

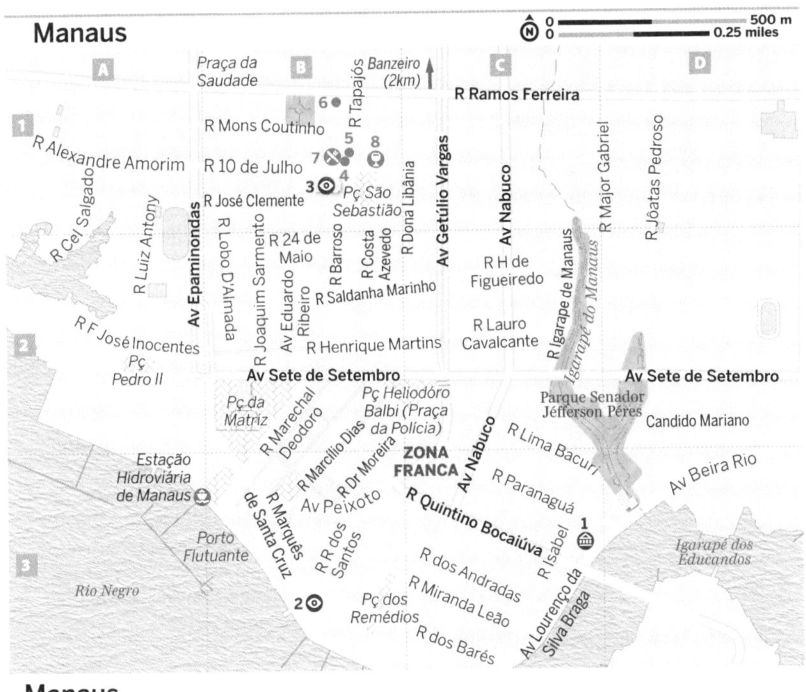

Manaus

Sights

1 Centro Cultural Usina Chaminé C3
2 Mercado Municipal Adolfo Lisboa B3
3 Teatro Amazonas B1

Activities, Courses & Tours

4 Amazon Eco Adventures B1
5 Amazon Gero Tours B1
6 Swallows & Amazons B1

Eating

7 Tacacaria Amazônia B1

Drinking & Nightlife

8 Bar do Armando B1

Floresta Nacional do Tapajós

One of the last and most accessible stretches of primary rainforest in the region, this protected area is the Amazon you always imagined. Behemoth samaúma and other trees, some with trunks too big for even 20 people to stretch their arms around, are a highlight of this 5440-sq-km reserve on the east side of the Rio Tapajós.

Wildlife includes numerous species of birds (king vultures are a highlight), while the forest is also home to elusive cats (including jaguar and ocelot, although they're rarely seen), as well as howler monkeys, squirrel monkeys and capuchins.

The villages of Maguarí, Jamaraquá and São Domingo near the reserve have rustic lodging and forested trails (though it's a 2½-hour hike to reach primary rainforest from the villages). There are some lovely *igarapés* (inlets), too, with good canoeing and possibly animal-spotting when the water is high.

You can get to FLONA by bus from Santarém or boat from Alter do Chão. The recommended guide Gil Serique (p98), whose family once lived in the forest, leads tours (from US$150 per person per day).

Man resting on a samaúma tree
MARIANO VILLAFANE / SHUTTERSTOCK ©

includes an excellent **opera festival** (Festival Amazonas de Ópera; late Apr–early May) in April and May. Hour-long guided tours offer an up-close look at the theater's opulent construction.

Centro Cultural Usina Chaminé — Museum

(92 3633-3026; Av Lourenço da Silva Braga; 8am-2pm Tue-Fri, 9am-1pm Sat) FREE Also known as the Museu dos Cinco Sentidos (Museum of the Five Senses), this innovative museum uses the five senses to evoke and illustrate indigenous and Caboclos life and culture. You can hear recordings of native languages, smell Amazonian spices, admire indigenous folk art and more.

Mercado Municipal Adolfo Lisboa — Market

(92 3232-9210; Rua dos Barés 46; 6am-5pm Mon-Sat, to 7pm Fri, to noon Sun) Manaus' historic city market was inaugurated in 1882, a downscaled replica of Paris' famed Les Halles market. Safe and bustling, the central building has mostly handicraft shops, with wares ranging from predictable kitsch to high quality. A side building houses a working fish market – visit early in morning to see the vast array of Amazonian fish on display. Great little places to eat throughout.

TOURS

Amazon Tree Climbing — Ecotour

(92 8195-8585; www.amazontreeclimbing.com; Caravelle 22a, Tarumã) Yellow-shirted guides lend a youthful vibe to this outfit, whose tours range from half-day trips near Manaus with views of the Meeting of the Waters to all-day excursions that may also include visiting an indigenous village. Getting to the top of the massive trees can be quite challenging physically, but the experience is unforgettable.

EATING

Amazônico Peixaria Regional — Seafood, Brazilian $$

(92 3236-0546; www.amazonico.com.br; Av Darcy Vargas 222; mains R$36-98; noon-3pm & 6:30-11pm Mon-Sat, 11:30am-4pm Sun) However you get your *tambaqui* (perhaps the tastiest of all Amazonian fish) prepared here – stewed, grilled, ribs – the execution is

perfect. They serve all manner of other fish and steak dishes, and fab desserts too. The atmosphere is casual, the service attentive and the cooking top-notch. It will be one of the best meals you'll have in the Amazon.

Tacacaria Amazônia Brazilian $$
(92 99112-3730; www.facebook.com/TacacariaAmazonia; 10 de Julho 503; mains R$20-45; 10:30am-10:30pm Mon-Sat, from 3pm Sun) This bright, appealing place serves a range of local dishes, specializing in *tacacá* (local soup with shrimp) and well-prepared fish from the Amazon, including *tambaqui* and *pirarucú*. English is spoken and they're good at putting an order together without the hard sell.

Banzeiro Brazilian $$$
(92 3234-1621; www.restaurantebanzeiro.com.br; Libertador 102, NS das Gracas; mains R$75-140; 11:30am-3pm & 7-11pm, to 10pm Sun) One of Manaus' top gourmet restaurants, especially for fish. Varieties such as *pirarucú*, *tambaqui* and other Amazonian specialties are served in various preparations, from cheese and banana to parsley and *formigas* (ants). Pricey but truly one of a kind. Online reservations recommended.

DRINKING

Bar do Armando Bar
(92 3232-1195; www.facebook.com/bardoarmando; 10 de Julho 593; 5pm-2am) Near the opera house, this is a traditional rendezvous for Manaus' intellectual and bohemian types, but all sorts of people crowd around the outdoor tables for beers and conversation.

GETTING THERE & AROUND

AIR

Aeroporto Internacional Eduardo Gomes
(92 3652-1210; www4.infraero.gov.br/aeroportos/aeroporto-internacional-de-manaus-eduardo-gomes/; Av Santos Dumont 1350) is located 13km north of the city center. Bus 813 'Aeroporto-Ejecutivo' (R$8) runs every half-hour between the airport and Praça da Matriz in the center of town; taxis charge R$75.

BOAT

There are several terminals. Passenger boats going downstream to Belém depart from the central **Estação Hidroviária de Manaus** (92 3233 7061; www.portodemanaus.com.br; Porto Flutuante) and usually make stops in Santarém and Monte Alegre. To Santarém (36 hours), these depart at 11am Monday to Saturday (hammock/cabin from R$180/8000); boats to Belém (4 days) depart at 11am Wednesday and Friday (hammock/cabin from R$350/R$1100).

Encontro das Águas

Just beyond Manaus, the warm dark Rio Negro pours into the cool creamy Rio Solimões, but because of differences in temperature, speed and density, their waters don't mix, instead flowing side by side for several kilometers. The bi-color phenomenon occurs throughout the Amazon, but nowhere as dramatically as here. Day trips always include a stop here, and many tour operators at least pass by en route to their lodges. Never disappoints.

Waters mixing from Rios Negro and Solimões
MARIANO VILLAFANE / SHUTTERSTOCK ©

THE PANTANAL, BRAZIL

In this Chapter

The Pantanal, Brazil

The Pantanal, one of the most important and fragile ecosystems on the planet, truly shines as a top destination for wildlife-watching. The world's largest wetland, in the heart of the continent, covers some 210,000 sq km. The majority is in Brazil, split between the states of Mato Grosso and Mato Grosso do Sul.

The Pantanal has few people and no towns. Car travel is restricted by the seasons. You can either penetrate the Pantanal from the north, where the Transpantaneira runs deep into the region, or from the south, where Estrada Parque cuts across the wetlands.

Two Days in the Pantanal

Fly into Cuiabá, and head out on a two-day excursion in the northern Pantanal. Look for macaws from lookout towers, spy capybara along the Transpantaneira and go for a jaguar-spotting boat trip near Porto Jofre. Overnight in an eco-minded *fazenda*, like **Pantanal Jaguar Camp** (p108).

Four Days in the Pantanal

On your third day in the region, visit the spectacular red rock formations and shimmering waterfalls of Parque Nacional Chapada dos Guimarães. End the trip with a day taking in the sights of Cuiabá, including the indigenous-focused **Museu Rondon de Etnologia e Arqueologia** (p110). Treat yourself to a memorable meal at **Mahalo** (p110).

Previous page: *Victoria amazonica* (giant water lilies)

Arriving in the Pantanal

Cuiabá is the main gateway to the northern Pantanal. Campo Grande is the principal southern launch point into the Pantanal.

There are direct flights to Cuiabá (p110), Campo Grande (p111) and Corumbá from other Brazilian destinations.

Cuiabá and Campo Grande are easily reached by direct buses from numerous Brazilian cities.

Where to Stay

Pantanal accommodations are divided into roughly three types: *pousadas*, which include all meals and range from simple to top-end; *fazendas*, which are ranch-style hotels that usually have horses and often boats for use; and *pesqueiros*, which cater for anglers and usually have boats and fishing gear for rent.

If you travel independently, you can rent a car and book a stay at various Pantanal lodges.

Jabiru storks

Exploring the Pantanal

The Amazon gets the press coverage, but the Pantanal is a better place to see wildlife. The dense foliage of the Amazon makes it difficult to observe the animals, but in the open marshes of the Pantanal, wildlife is much easier to spot. If you like to see animals in their natural environment, don't miss this place.

Great For...

☑ Don't Miss

Spotting jaguars–the largest big cat in the Americas–from Porto Jofre.

Northern Pantanal

From Cuiabá, the capital of Mato Grosso, small tour operators arrange safaris along the Transpantaneira that include transportation, ranch accommodations on farms, and guides. Tours from Cuiabá tend to be slightly more expensive, but more professional, with smaller groups and better-trained guides than those from Campo Grande.

Transpantaneira

This raised dirt road sectioned by small wooden bridges begins at Poconé and ends 145km south at Porto Jofre. It's a spectacular drive, with plentiful wildlife the whole way. At Porto Jofre, jaguar-spotting boat trips are a major drawcard in the dry season, while great fishing is also a possibility.

Wild jaguar

JAMI TARRIS / GETTY IMAGES ©

Need to Know

Quality tours start from around R$600 per day, including food and lodging.

Take a Break

Before or after a Pantanal trip, indulge in delectable river fish at **Lélis Peixaria** (65 3322-9195; www.lelispeixaria.com.br; Marechal Mascarenhas de Morães 36; rodízio lunch/dinner R$60/90; 11:30am-3pm & 6:30-11pm Mon-Sat, 11:30am-3pm Sun) in Cuiabá.

★ Top Tip

Be prepared: pack sunglasses, binoculars, insect repellent, a hat, sunscreen and a jacket for the early morning chill.

Pantanal Nature

Superb **agency** (65 99925-2265, 65 3322-0203; www.pantanalnature.com.br; Av Historiador Rubens de Mendonça 1856, Cuiabá; 4-day nature tour per person R$4150, jaguar tour R$5800; office hours 7-11:30am & 1:30-5pm Mon-Thu, 8am-noon Fri & Sat) run by Ailton Lara that has a sterling reputation for its professional tours and expert guides. It runs Pantanal nature tours and, in season, jaguar tours from the Pantanal Jaguar Camp (p108) in Porto Jofre.

Ecoverde Tours

This relaxed budget **agency** (65 99638-1614; www.ecoverdetours.com.br; Pedro Celestino 391, Cuiabá; 4-day nature tour s/d R$2400/4000, jaguar tour R$3000/5000) has decades of service and experienced guides. Working with local pousadas toward an ecofriendly approach, Joel Souza can guide you in several languages. He runs nature tours year-round and jaguar-spotting tours from June to October.

Focus Tours

In operation for nearly four decades, this trailblazing ecotourism **operator** (Brazil 31 9134-3833, USA +1 505-216-7780; www.focustours.com) was founded by ecologist Douglas Trent. As well as customizable bird-watching and nature-watching trips, it runs jaguar-watching excursions on the Rio Paraguai and operates a major conservation project.

Southwild

This innovative high-end **operator** (www.southwild.com; 7-day jaguar-spotting packages per person US$5000-7000) has been a pioneer in Pantanal wildlife tourism. It has upmarket packages involving stays at **Southwild Pantanal Lodge** (Fazenda Santa Tereza; www.southwild.com; Transpantaneira, Km 68; d incl full board R$820; ❄ 📶 🏊) 🌿 and **Flotel and Jaguar Suites** (www.southwild.com; Rio Piquirí; 6-night packages per person US$5000-6700; 🕐 Jun-Nov; ❄ @ 📶). Tours cater for serious nature-watchers with on-site biologists.

Araras Eco Lodge

This pioneering **ranch** (☎ 65 3682-2800; www.ararasl odge.com.br; Transpantaneira, Km 32; s/d incl full board & excursions R$1591/2482; ❄ 📶 🏊) 🌿 offers great comfort and luxury in a peaceful setting. There is a treetop tower for bird-watching (hyacinth macaws), while welcoming owners André and Akhila make an immense effort to be sustainable.

Pantanal Jaguar Camp

The **Pantanal Jaguar Camp** (☎ 65 99925-2265; www.pantanaljaguarcamp.com.br; Transpantaneira, Km 145, Porto Jofre; d with meals & excursion R$1035, camping per person R$60, with own tent R$45; ❄ 📶) 🌿 is an intimate, solar-powered wilderness lodge with seven comfortable rooms, camping and an on-site restaurant. This is a great Porto Jofre base for jaguar-seeking boat trips affiliated with Pantanal Nature (p107). Other activities include night safaris and bird-watching.

Southern Pantanal

The southern Pantanal has a fine choice of lodges from backpacker favorites to exclusive eco-havens. Campo Grande is the major launch pad for the southern

Araras Eco Lodge

Pantanal. This is also the best place for budget-friendly trips, with prices starting at around R$500 per day. All accommodations arrange nature-watching trips on both land and water, as well as horseback riding and other Brazilian countryside experiences.

Pousada & Camping Santa Clara

This working **ranch** (☎67 99939-3570; www.pantanalsantaclara.com.br; Estrada Parque, Km 22; 3-day, 2-night package incl full board & excursions camping/dm/s/d R$580/860/1220/1980; ❄📶🏊) is enthusiastically run and has a host of activities (hikes, piranha fishing, night safaris, horseback riding), accommodations to suit all budgets and hearty *pantaneiro* cooking. It is deservedly popular, with compact rooms, a plunge pool and games, plus macaws and peccaries about.

☑ When to Go

It's possible to visit the Pantanal year-round, but it's best to go during the dry season (May to September) as the wildlife converges on the reduced water.

DAVIDCALLAN / GETTY IMAGES ©

Pantanal Discovery

Owner Gil of **Pantanal Discovery** (☎67 99163-3518; www.gilspantanaldiscovery.com.br; Hotel Mohave, Afonso Pena 602, Campo Grande; 3-day, 2-night package hammock/dm/s/d R$1000/1200/1550/2800) is the pick of budget operators in town. He's used to dealing with short notice or tight schedules and has his own transportation.

Pantanal Viagens

A reputable **agency** (☎67 3321-3143; www.pantanalviagens.com.br; Room 9, Old Bus Terminal, Joaquim Nabuco 200, Campo Grande) working with Pousada Passo do Lontra and other Pantanal lodgings. Caters to mid- to high-end budgets and has professional and reliable packages.

Pantanal Jungle Lodge

This boardwalk **lodge** (☎67 3242-1488; www.pantanal-jungle-lodge.com; Estrada Parque, Km 8; 3-day, 2-night package dm/s/d R$910/1380/2310; ❄📶🏊) is a backpacker favorite, thanks to its enviable riverside location and well-organized activities – from canoeing and piranha fishing to night safaris on the river and wildlife-spotting treks. Lodge either in one of the breezy dorms or in a private room with air-conditioning. All have an insect-screened porch to relax in.

★ Bird-Watching

If you are interested in birds, it's worth bringing the *Birds of the Pantanal* field guide, which is on sale at most lodges (R$150).

Cuiabá

A lively place with a vibrant dining scene and some beautiful colonial architecture around its main square, Cuiabá is an excellent starting point for excursions to the Pantanal.

SIGHTS

Museu Rondon de Etnologia e Arqueologia Museum

(MUSEAR; 65 3313-7391; www.museurondonufmt.blogspot.com; Av Fernando Corrêa da Costa 2367; 7:30-11am & 1-5pm Mon-Fri) FREE The small Museu Rondon has exhibits on indigenous culture and is well worth a visit to check out the ornate headdresses and weaponry. The museum is located on the grounds of the Federal University of Mato Grosso (UFMT), behind the swimming pool. To get here, catch a C01 Universitária bus (R$3.85) from Praça Alencastro. Ring ahead to check it's open.

EATING

Mahalo Fusion $$

(65 3028-7700; www.mahalocozinhacriativa.com.br; Presidente Castelo Branco 359; mains from R$45; 11am-2:30pm & 7:30pm-midnight Mon-Sat) Inside a converted mansion, the city's big splurge is one of Brazil's top restaurants, thanks to the efforts of Parisian-trained chef Ariani Malouf. Go for the set weekday lunch (R$55 for two courses) or else choose from the likes of pintado (giant catfish) encrusted with Brazil nuts or a perfectly-seared rack of lamb with sweet potato puree. Dress nicely and book ahead.

GETTING THERE & AWAY

Cuiabá's **international airport** (CGB; 65 3614-2511; Av João Ponce de Arruda, Várzea Grande) is in Várzea Grande, 7km from central Cuiabá.

Cuiabá's **bus station** (Jules Rimet) is 3km north of the center.

Parque Nacional da Chapada dos Guimarães

Picture the scene: red rock buttresses soaring up from a green valley; lines of palm trees marking the location of clear rivers and pools for snorkeling; waterfalls ranging from immense to petite and swimmable; dusty hikes through parched land, observed only by yellow-eyed burrowing desert owls; mysterious caves to explore...

The top-notch **Chapada Explorer** (65 3301-1290; www.chapadaexplorer.com.br; Praça Dom Wunibaldo 57; 8-11am Mon-Sat)  runs excursions to all of the area's attractions in small groups.

SIGHTS

Véu de Noiva Waterfall

(Bridal Veil; 9am-5pm, last entry 4pm) FREE The impressive Véu de Noiva, an 86m free-falling waterfall, provides the park's characteristic postcard moment. A small trail leads to the lookout, perched on top of rocks with the canyon below. This is one of Chapada's most dazzling spots; no guide necessary.

Cidade de Pedra Mountain

(Stone City; www.icmbio.gov.br/parnaguimaraes/guia-do-visitante.html; entry only with authorized guide; 9am-5pm Sun-Fri, from 3pm Sat) FREE Cidade de Pedra provides the region's most transcendent moment. Jagged red sandstone rock formations jut up into the sky from the tops of enormous cliffs that drop down into the vast green valley beneath. You follow the short footpath that skirts the edge of the cliff through scrubland, peering at the abyss below. Morning is the best time to visit, when the sunlight illuminates most of the cliffs. It's 25km northwest of Chapada.

Vale do Rio Claro Snorkeling

(Rio Claro Valley; www.icmbio.gov.br; 8am-5pm, last entry 1pm) A steep scramble takes you to a viewpoint overlooking the lush valley and the razor-thin rock formations of the Crista do Galo (rooster's crest). Then you swim and snorkel in clear, deep, rapid-fed pools in the forest before embarking on a 500m float, following your guide along the twists and turns of the narrow river, the somber underwater world revealing itself beneath you.

 GETTING THERE & AWAY

CMT buses (☎65 3301-2679) leave Cuiabá's bus station for Chapada town (R$17, 1¼ hours, nine daily). Buses will also drop off and pick up at the entrance to Véu de Noiva.

Campo Grande

Campo Grande is a vast, modern metropolis, where high-rises tower above the shopping malls and streets are lined with restaurants.

 SIGHTS

Museu das Culturas Dom Bosco — Museum

(☎67 3326-9788; www.mcdb.org.br; Parque das Nações Indígenas, Av Afonso Pena; R$10; ⏲8am-4:30pm Tue-Sat) Built on the site of a Bororo burial ground, this superb museum is divided into two parts. One is a collection of over 10,000 insects and stuffed flora and fauna, while the other is a visually striking, unmissable introduction to the indigenous people of the Mato Grosso region, with subtly lit underfloor and suspended-glass displays showcasing shaman paraphernalia, weaponry, everyday tools, splendid adornments made of feathers and funerary objects. The enlarged black-and-white photos are almost equally striking.

 EATING

Casa do Peixe — Seafood $$$

(☎67 3382-7121; www.casadopeixe.com.br; Av João Rosa Pires 1030; mains for 2 people R$95, rodízio R$86; ⏲11am-2pm daily, 6-11pm Mon-Sat) This place rightfully deserves its reputation as the best *peixaria* (fish restaurant) in town, with a superior buffet accompanying the hearty mains. The *rodízio* is an awesome way to acquaint yourself with *pintado, pacu* and other fish of the Pantanal, prepared in many sublime ways, while the inclusion of sushi and sashimi pays homage to the city's large Japanese population.

 Circuito das Cachoeiras

The **Circuito das Cachoeiras** (Waterfall Circuit; www.icmbio.gov.br; entry only with authorized guide; ⏲8:30am-5pm, last entry noon) FREE involves a gentle 6.5km hike through a parched red landscape, covered with scrubland and low trees, with six waterfall stops en route; the whole thing takes four to six hours, depending on how easy you want to take it. The first waterfall is the highest, while the others are better for swimming, with deep pools and cascades forming natural Jacuzzis. Entry is free, but you must go with a registered guide.

Andorinhas Waterfall
SERGIOROCHA / SHUTTERSTOCK ©

 GETTING THERE & AWAY

Aeroporto Internacional de Campo Grande (CGR; ☎67 3368-6000; Av Duque de Caxias) is 7km west of town (a R$30 to R$40 taxi ride).

Campo Grande's **bus station** (☎67 3026-6789; Av Gury Marques 1215) is located 6km south of the center on the road to São Paulo.

IGUAZÚ FALLS, BRAZIL & ARGENTINA

In this Chapter

Iguazú Falls, Brazil & Argentina

One of the planet's most awe-inspiring sights, the Iguazú Falls are simply astounding. A visit is a jaw-dropping, visceral experience, and the power and noise of the cascades – a chain of hundreds of waterfalls nearly 3km in length – live forever in the memory. An added benefit is the setting: the falls lie split between Brazil and Argentina in a large expanse of national park, much of it rainforest teeming with unique flora and fauna. The falls are easily reached from either side of the Argentine-Brazilian border.

Two Days in Iguazú Falls

Spend the first day taking in the sweeping views of the waterfalls from the Brazilian side. On day two, cross over to Argentina for a close-up look at the **Garganta del Diablo** (p116), take a boat trip along the river and then visit **Isla San Martín** (p117).

Four Days in Iguazú Falls

Spend day three on the Argentine side of the falls, exploring the rainforest-lined **Sendero Macuco** (p118), where you can spy birds, monkeys and other wildlife, then take a swim at the base of the small waterfall. On day four, head out to **Itaipú Binacional** (p121) for a look at one of the largest dams on the planet.

Previous page: View of Río Iguazú and the Garganta del Diablo (p116) on the left
GCOLES / GETTY IMAGES ©

Visitors at the falls, Argentina

Arriving in Iguazú Falls

Located 9km south of the Argentine side of the falls, **Cataratas del Iguazú International Airport** (www.aa2000.com.ar/iguazu) has flights to Buenos Aires and Cordoba.

On the Brazilian side, **Foz do Iguaçu International Airport** (p121) has flights to major Brazilian cities as well as Lima.

Where to Stay

The towns of Foz do Iguaçu, Brazil, and Puerto Iguazú, Argentina have abundant accommodation options. There are also two high-end hotels near the falls: **Meliá Iguazú** (www.melia.com) in Argentina and **Belmond Hotel das Cataratas** (www.belmond.com) in Brazil.

Visiting the Falls

While the Argentine side, with its variety of trails and boat rides, offers many more opportunities to see individual falls close up, the Brazilian side yields the more panoramic views. You can easily make day trips to both sides of the falls, no matter which side of the border you're on.

Great For...

☑ Don't Miss

The platform overlooking the deafening cascade of the Garganta del Diablo.

Parque Nacional Iguazú, Argentina

On the Argentine side of the falls, this park has loads to offer and involves a fair amount of walking. The spread-out entrance complex ends at a train station, with departures every half-hour to the Cataratas train station, where the waterfall walks begin, and to the Garganta del Diablo. You may prefer to walk: it's only 650m along the Sendero Verde path to the Cataratas station, and a further 2.3km to the Garganta.

Garganta del Diablo

A 1.1km walkway across the placid Río Iguazú leads to one of the planet's most spectacular sights, the 'Devil's Throat.' The lookout platform is perched right over this amazingly powerful, concentrated torrent of water.

Need to Know

Parque Nacional Iguazú (03757-491469; www.iguazuargentina.com; adult foreigners/Mercosur/Argentines AR$600/480/310, child AR$150/120/100; 8am-6pm) , Argentina; **Parque Nacional do Iguaçu** (45 3521-4400; www.cataratasdoiguacu.com.br; Hwy BR-469, Km 18; adult foreigners/Mercosur/Brazilians R$62/49/36, child R$10; 9am-5pm), Brazil.

Take a Break

On the Brazilian side, have a buffet lunch on the terrace at **Restaurante Porto Canoas** (www.cataratasdoiguacu.com.br; Parque Nacional do Iguaçu; buffet R$59.90; noon-4pm).

★ Top Tip

To beat the crowds (and congestion along the narrow gangways), get to the falls by 9am.

From Cataratas train station, train it or walk the 2.3km to the Garganta del Diablo stop. The last train to the Garganta leaves at 4pm and we recommend taking it, as it'll be a somewhat less crowded experience. If you walk, you'll see quite a lot of wildlife around this time of day, too.

Circuito Inferior

This circuit (1400m) descends to the river, passing delightfully close to falls on the way. At the end of the path prepare for a drenching at the hands of Salto Bossetti if you're game. Just short of here, a free launch makes the short crossing to Isla San Martín. At the same junction you can buy tickets for the popular boat rides under the falls.

Circuito Superior

The Circuito Superior (1750m) is entirely level and gives good views of the tops of several cascades and across to more. A recently constructed final section crosses a large swath of the Iguazú river, ending above the powerful Salto San Martín before wending its way back across river islands.

Isla San Martín

From the end of the Circuito Inferior, a free launch takes you across to this island with a trail of its own that gives the closest look at several falls, including Salto San Martín, a huge, furious cauldron of water. When the water is high – and this is the case more often than not – island access is shut off.

Iguazú Jungle Explorer

Offers three adventure **tours** (03757-421696; www.iguazujungle.com). Most popular is the short boat trip leaving from the CircuitoInferior that takes you right under one of the waterfalls for a high-adrenalin soaking (AR$1000), while the Paseo Ecológico (AR$400) is a wildlife-oriented tour in inflatable boats upstream from the falls.

Sendero Macuco

This 3.5km jungle trail leads through dense forest to a nearly hidden waterfall. It's a rare opportunity to explore the park independently. Six interpretive stations explain the flora, including bamboo, palmitos and pioneer plants. The white-bearded manakin and toco toucan live in these parts, as does a troupe of brown capuchin monkeys.

You can swim at the base of the waterfall but take care and don't head out into the river.

Safaris Rainforest

Using knowledgeable guides, this **outfit** (☎03757-491074; www.rainforest.iguazuargentina.com) is the best option for appreciating Parque Nacional Iguazú's flora and fauna. It offers combined driving-walking excursions: the Safari a la Cascada takes you to the Arrechea waterfall (AR$560, 90 minutes); the Safari en la Selva (AR$660, two hours) is better, a trip in a less-touristed part of the park that includes explanations of Guaraní culture.

Parque Nacional do Iguaçu, Brazil

Brazil's section of the falls offers fabulous panoramic views. You can't miss the shiny entrance to Parque Nacional do Iguaçu (p117), which houses bathrooms, ATMs, lockers, souvenir shops, left-luggage

Boat trip to the waterfalls

facilities and a vast parking lot. You can purchase your ticket in advance on the website and pick it up in the preferential line at the ticket windows, or buy from on-site machines (if you have a chip-in-pin card). Once ticketed, you will be directed to board a free double-decker bus, which departs every 10 minutes. In addition to the main event, the park and its environs offers trails, boat trips, whitewater rafting and other nature-focused adventures.

Waterfall Trail & Views

Once you're in the park and ready to visit the falls, take the Parque Nacional do Iguaçu bus to the third stop at Belmond Hotel das Cataratas. Here you can pick up the main waterfall observation trail, Trilha das Cataratas ('Waterfall Trail'), a 1200m trail following the shore of the Iguaçu River, terminating at the stunning Garganta do Diabo.

An elevator heads up to a viewing platform at the top of the falls at Porto Canoas, the last stop of the double-decker buses. Porto Canoas has a gift shop, a couple of snack bars and an excellent buffet restaurant.

★ Did You Know?

Thousands of years before they were 'discovered' by Europeans, the falls were a holy burial place for the Tupi-Guaraní and Paraguas tribes.

JAKUB BARZYCKI / SHUTTERSTOCK ©

Macuco Safari

Under concession from the national park, **Macuco** (☎45 3529-6262; www.macucosafari.com.br; Av das Cataratas, Km 25, Parque Nacional do Iguaçu; boat trip R$215, excursions R$61-515) is the designated adventure operator on the Brazilian side of the falls. The main event is the namesake safari, which involves a wet-and-wild boat ride on rapids and waterfalls, but they also offer trekking, bird-watching, whitewater-rafting and other nature-centric activities. To reach Macuco, get off the double-decker bus at the second stop.

Trilha das Bananeiras

The Bananeiras Trail is a 1.5km walk passing lagoons and observing aquatic wildlife, ending at a jetty where you can take boat rides or silent floating excursions in kayaks down to Porto Canoas. If you plan to do any of these, chat with one of the agents touting them around the park visitor center; they can get you a discount.

Trilha do Poço Preto

A 9km guided hike (get off the bus at the first stop) through the jungle on foot, by bike or on an electric cart. The trail ends at Taquara Island, where you can kayak or take a boat cruise to Porto Canoas. You can also return via the Bananeiras Trail.

★ Wildlife

On the falls trails you'll see large lizards, coatis, monkeys and birds, but you'll see much more on one of the few trails through the dense forest.

Foz do Iguaçu, Brazil

The Brazilian city of Foz do Iguaçu went through a period of frenzied growth during the 18 years that Itaipú Dam was under construction (completed in 1982), when the population increased more than five-fold. These days, it's a fairly average town, but it makes a fine base for exploring the famed waterfalls nearby as well other area attractions such as Itaipú Binacional and Parque das Aves.

SIGHTS

Parque das Aves Bird Sanctuary

(Bird Park; 45 3529-8282; www.parquedasaves.com.br; Av das Cataratas, Km 17.1; R$45; 8:30am-5pm) This 5-hectare bird park, located 300m from the entrance to Parque Nacional do Iguaçu (p117), is home to 800-plus species of birds, including red ibis, bare-throated bellbird and flamingos galore. They live in 8m-high aviaries that are constructed right in the forest, some of which you can walk through. Kids and adults freak out alike. Well worth it.

Enthusiasts can go deeper here with Guaraní forest (R$250) and behind-the-scenes (R$200) experiences.

Marco das Três Fronteiras Viewpoint

(45 3132-4100; www.marcodastresfronteiras.com.br; Av Gen Meira s/n; 2-11pm; adult/child R$22/12) Once little more than an uneventful obelisk, the Parque Nacional do Iguaçu concession folks have now built a small tourist complex around the viewpoint of all three tri-border countries that includes a children's park, a light and water show, cultural shows and a memorial to Álvar Núñez Cabeza de Vaca – the first European to have recorded the existence of the falls around 1540.

ACTIVITIES

In addition to the nature and water-related activities inside Parque Nacional do Iguaçu, Foz offers skydiving (over Itaipú Binacional; R$590) as well as other excursions.

Aguaray Eco Esportes Outdoors

(45 99158-8826; www.aguaray.com.br; Alameda Caete s/n; R$150) Arranges a recommended three-hour excursion on the Rio Iguaçu that involves a nature hike, kayak or stand-up paddle board, and visits to waterfalls.

EATING

Castelo Libanês Middle Eastern $

(45 3526-1218; Vinícius de Moraes 520; mains R$16-60; noon-10pm) Foz's Lebanese community is second in size only to São Paulo's; come here to sample the Middle Eastern cuisine. The bakery does great *esfihas* (open-faced or triangular meat pies); other well-done staples include roast chicken, Lebanese *kafta* (beef kebabs), shawarma and hummus.

Empório com Arte Cafe $$

(Av das Cataratas 569; mains $30-62; 3-11pm Tue-Fri, 2-11pm Sat, 2-10pm Sun;) This *mineiro*-run highlight of the Foz scene ('scene' used loosely) is full of country charm and swarming with town sophisticates gossiping among a potpourri of mostly Minas Gerais art and handicrafts (all for sale). Decent espresso, elaborate mixed-fruit *caipirinhas* made with local *cachaça*, and a few elaborate main courses (eg duck confit in dark-beer reduction) make for rustic-romantic encounters.

DRINKING & NIGHTLIFE

Nightlife is hopping along Av Jorge Schimmelpfeng, where you'll find breezy beer gardens, lively outdoor patio bars and hot-to-trot nightclubs that stay open late. Good outdoor drinking dens include **Rafain Chopp** (www.facebook.com/rafainchopp; Av Jorge Schimmelpfeng 450; 4pm-2am Mon-Thu, from 2pm Fri-Sun;) and **Capitão Bar** (www.capitao.bar; Av Jorge Schimmelpfeng 288; 11:30am-2am;).

Zeppelin Old Bar Live Music

(www.facebook.com/ZeppelinFoz; Raul Mattos 222; 7pm-midnight Tue, 9pm-2am Wed-Sat;) Outstanding bar serving up excellent cocktails and live music that spans the gamut from grunge to reggae. The beautiful people congregate from Thursday onwards.

 GETTING THERE & AWAY

Daily flights link **Foz do Iguaçu/Cataratas International Airport** (IGU; ☎45 3521-4200; Hwy BR-469, Km 16.5) to Lima and several major Brazilian cities.

Bus 120 'Aeroporto/Parque Nacional' runs to the Brazilian side of the waterfalls from Foz do Iguaçu's TTU (p121) bus station every 22 to 30 minutes from 5:25am to midnight (R$3.55).

For Parque Nacional Iguazú on the Argentine side, catch a Puerto Iguazú bus in Foz do Iguaçu (R$5/AR$20, one hour) on **Rua Mem de Sá** (Mem de Sá) across from the local bus terminal or along Av das Cataratas every 30 minutes or so between 7am and 7:15pm (less on Sunday).

Puerto Iguazú, Argentina

At the end of the road in Argentina, Puerto Iguazú sits at the confluence of the Ríos Paraná and Iguazú and looks across to Brazil and Paraguay. There's little feeling of community: everyone is here to see the falls or to make a buck out of them, and planning laws seem nonexistent as hotels go up on every street. Still, it's not unattractive and is quiet and safe, with good transportation connections. There are also many excellent places to stay and eat.

Casa Ecológica de Botellas — Architecture

(http://lacasadebotellas.googlepages.com; RN 12, Km 5; AR$100; 9am-6:30pm) About 300m off the falls road, this fascinating place is well worth a visit. The owners have taken used packaging materials – plastic bottles, juice cartons and the like – to build not only an impressive house, but furnishings and a bunch of original handicrafts that make unusual gifts. The guided visit talks you through their techniques.

Itaipú Binacional

With a capacity of 14 million kilowatts, this binational dam is the world's second-largest hydroelectric power station, and the one that produces the most electricity per year. The impressive structure, at some 8km long and 200m high, is a memorable sight, especially when the river is high and a vast torrent of overflow water cascades down the spillway.

The **visitor center** (☎45 3576-7000; www.turismoitaipu.com.br; Tancredo Neves 6702; 8am-6pm Sun-Thu, to 9pm Fri & Sat) is 12km north of Foz. From here, regular tours (visita panorâmica) depart every 20 minutes between 8:30am to 4:45pm. A variety of other attractions within the complex include a museum, wildlife park and river beaches, and a sunset catamaran tour.

The project was controversial: it plunged Brazil deeply into debt and necessitated the large-scale destruction of rainforest and the displacement of 10,000 people. But it cleanly supplies 75% of Paraguay's energy needs, and 17% of Brazil's.

To get to the Itaipú Dam, catch bus 101 (Vila C Norte-Sohab) or 102 (Vila C Sul-Profilurb), among others (R$3.45, 30 minutes). These leave every 30 minutes from Foz do Iguaçu's **Urban Bus Terminal (TTU)** (Terminal de Transporte Urbano; ☎2105-1385; Av Juscelino Kubitschek 1385).

Full Moon Over the Falls

For five consecutive nights per month, these **guided walks** (03757-491469; www.iguazuargentina.com/en/luna-llena) visit the Garganta del Diablo. There are three departures nightly. The first, at 8pm, offers the spectacle of the inflated rising moon; the last, at 9:30pm, sees the falls better illuminated. The price (AR$1100) includes admission and a drink; dinner is extra (AR$500). Book ahead as numbers are limited.

Extra buses from Puerto Iguazú cater for moonwalkers. If the weather is bad, the tour is postponed to the following night or a refund is offered, so allow some flexibility in your plans.

Güirá Oga Animal Sanctuary

(www.guiraoga.com.ar; RN 12, Km 5; adult/child AR$200/150; 9:30am-6pm, last entry 4:45pm) On the way to the falls, this is an animal hospital and center for rehabilitation of injured wildlife. It also carries out valuable research into the Iguazú forest environment and has a breeding program for endangered species. You get walked around the jungly 20-hectare park by one of the staff, who explains about the birds and animals and the sad stories of how they got there. The visit takes about 90 minutes.

ACTIVITIES & TOURS

Numerous local operators offer day tours to the Brazilian side of the Iguazú Falls, some taking in the Itaipú Dam and Paraguay shopping as well. Many have offices at the bus terminal. At the port, there are various options for boat trips around the junction of the Paraná and Iguazú rivers. Boats leave every 30 minutes during peak periods. Expect to pay around AR$150 for a one-hour cruise in a small boat.

Iguazú Bike Tours Cycling

(03757-15-678220; www.iguazubiketours.com.ar) These guys run anything from gentle jaunts through the nearby forest to long vehicle-supported rides through the lesser-visited corners of Parque Nacional Iguazú.

Iguazú Kayak Kayaking

(03757-549930; www.iguazukayak.com; AR$700) Take a paddle between three countries along the Río Iguazú and down to the Río Paraná on this three-hour, 8km kayaking trip.

Cruceros Iguazú Boating

(03757-421111; www.crucerosiguazu.com; Zona Puerto; 2hr cruise AR$390) Daily two-hour late-afternoon cruises on the Paraná and Iguazú rivers in a large air-conditioned catamaran with a bar and live music on board. You can buy snacks but nothing gourmet.

EATING

Feria Market $

(Feirinha; cnr Av Brasil & Félix de Azara; picadas AR$250-350; 8am-midnight) A really nice place to eat or have a beer is this market in the north of town. It's full of stalls selling Argentine wines, sausages, olives and cheese to visiting Brazilians, and several of them put out *picadas*, grilled meats, other simple regional dishes and cold beer. There's folk music some nights and a good evening atmosphere.

Bocamora Argentine $$

(03757-420550; www.bocamora.com; Av Costanera s/n; mains AR$145-250; noon-11pm Tue-Sun;) A romantic location overlooking two rivers and three nations is reason enough to come to this place just down the hill from the Argentine border marker. It specializes in grilled meats and well-prepared plates of river fish; the food is decent, service is very hospitable and the view is just breathtaking.

La Rueda Argentine $$$

(☎03757-422531; www.larueda1975.com; Av Córdoba 28; mains AR$245-480; ⌚5:30pm-midnight Mon-Tue, from noon Wed-Sun; 📶) A mainstay of upmarket eating in Puerto Iguazú, this culinary heavyweight still packs a punch. The salads are inventive and delicious, as are the imaginative river-fish (mostly pacú and surubí) creations. Meat with a variety of sauce options is reliably good; the homemade pasta is cheaper but doesn't disappoint. Service is good but slow. The wine list has a high flagfall.

DRINKING & NIGHTLIFE

Quita Penas Bar

(☎03757-458223; Av Brasil 120; ⌚6pm-late) A happening open-air bar in the middle of Puerto Iguazú's little nightlife strip, Quita Penas has an elevated deck and a variety of other spaces below. It serves good food and is a fine place to sink some beers and watch the action. Often has live music.

GETTING THERE & AWAY

Aerolíneas Argentinas (☎03757-420168; www.aerolineas.com.ar; Av Victoria Aguirre 295; ⌚8am-noon & 3-7pm Mon-Fri, 8am-1pm Sat) flies from Iguazú to both Buenos Aires airports, Mendoza via Córdoba or Rosario, Salta and El Calafate (via BA). LAN (www.lan.com) and Andes (www.andesonline.com) also fly the Buenos Aires route. **Four Tourist Travel** (☎03757-420681, 03757-422962; www.ftt.tur.ar) runs an airport shuttle for AR$130 per person that meets most flights.

The **bus terminal** (cnr Avs Córdoba & Misiones) has departures for all over the country.

GETTING AROUND

Parque Nacional Iguazú is 20km southeast of Puerto Iguazú. From Puerto Iguazú's bus terminal, buses leave every 20 minutes for the park (AR$75, 40 minutes) between 7:20am and 7:20pm, with return trips between 7:50am and 8pm. The buses make flag stops along the road.

A taxi from town to the park entrance is AR$300 (AR$550 return).

BORDER CROSSING

If traveling by bus, at Brazilian immigration in either direction, most bus drivers won't wait around while you finish visa formalities. Officially, you should get a pass from the driver, get your passport stamped, then wait and reboard the next bus *from the same bus company*.

On the Argentine side, drivers wait, so with luck and patience you can do this for R$5/AR25.

It's important you pay attention as drivers ask if anyone needs to stop at immigration on the Brazilian side – but in Portuguese (or Spanish), if at all. Many travelers miss it and end up with serious immigration hassles later (ie hefty fines).

At Argentine immigration, the bus always stops and usually waits for everyone to be processed. Both borders are open 24 hours but bus service ends around 7:15pm.

Many nationalities, including US citizens, require visas to enter Brazil. It's best to arrange your visa in your home country before coming to South America.

BUENOS AIRES, ARGENTINA

In this Chapter

Buenos Aires, Argentina

Buenos Aires combines faded European grandeur with Latin passion. Sexy and alive, this city gets under your skin. It's also undeniably beautiful, with grand French- and Italian-style palaces, as well as a vibrant street-art scene.

BA's food scene is increasingly dynamic, but for many it's the city's carnivorous pleasures that shine. Parrillas (steakhouses) sit on almost every corner, and make a fine prelude to the city's relentless nightlife. A diverse range of bars, clubs and live-music venues has everything from DJs spinning electronica to live jazz sets, plus plenty of venues for honing those tango moves.

Two Days in Buenos Aires

Spend day one strolling the colonial, cobbled streets of San Telmo. Have dinner and catch a tango show at **El Viejo Almacén** (p130). On day two, explore the gardens and blockbuster museums of Palermo. Have a decadent meat-centric dinner at the *parrilla* **La Carnicería** (p136), followed by cocktails at **Verne** (p149).

Four Days in Buenos Aires

On day three, explore the historic heart of Buenos Aires in and around the **Plaza de Mayo** (p133). Later that night, catch a performance at the iconic Teatro Colón. On the next day, explore Recoleta's famous **cemetery** (p134), have afternoon tea at **L'Orangerie** (p147), and spend the evening enjoying top-notch tango at **Café de los Angelitos** (p128).

Previous page: La Boca (p141)

Campo Argentina de Polo
Estación Ministro Carranza
Parque 3 de Febrero
Estación Saldías
Museo de Arte Latinoamericano de Buenos Aires
Palermo
Palermo Hollywood
Estación Palermo
Palermo Chico
Museo Nacional de Bellas Artes
Aliscafos (Hydrofoils)
0 2 km
0 1 mile
Estación Maritima
Río de la Plata
Recoleta
Av Santa Fe
Palermo Soho
Barrio Norte
Retiro Bus Terminal
Cementerio de la Recoleta
Retiro
Manuel Tienda León
Villa Crespo
Av Scalabrini Ortiz
Gallo
Centro Cultural Kirchner
Av Córdoba
Abasto
Teatro Colón
Laguna de las Gaviolas
Tribunales
Av Corrientes
Av 9 de Julio
Parque Centenario
Once
Estación Once
Juan D Perón
Plaza de Mayo
Reserva Ecológica Costanera Sur
Av Díaz Vélez
Almagro
Av Rivadavia
Caballito
Balvanera
Congreso
Manzana de las Luces
Laguna de los Patos
Av Belgrano
Montserrat
Puerto Madero
Av Acoyte
Av La Plata
Av Jujuy
Av Entre Ríos
Av Independencia
Constitución
San Telmo
San Cristóbal
Av San Juan
Dársena Sur
Internacional Ministro Pistarini (22km)
Av Juan de Garay
Estación Constitución
Boedo
Av Boedo
Av Chiclana
Canal Sur
Barracas
La Boca
Chacabuco Park
Av Caseros
Brandsen
Museo Benito Quinquela Martín
El Caminito
Parque Patricios

Central Buenos Aires Map (p142)
Palermo Map (p146)

Arriving in Buenos Aires

BA's main airport is **Ezeiza airport** (EZE; officially Aeropuerto Internacional Ministro Pistarini). A good way to get downtown is with a shuttle service, such as **Manuel Tienda León** (www.tiendaleon.com).

To catch a taxi, walk past the touts, and you'll see the freestanding city taxi stand, with a blue sign saying **Taxi Ezeiza** (www.taxiezeiza.com.ar). A taxi from the airport to the city center should cost about AR$1290.

Where to Stay

Buenos Aires' hostels range from basic no-frills deals to beautiful, multiperk buildings more luxurious than your standard cheap hotel. Hotels vary from utilitarian to luxurious five-star hotels. Palermo has dozens of boutique hotels; most are pricey but beautiful, with a handful of hip, elegant rooms and decent service. For a quick overview of the pros and cons of BA's diverse neighborhoods, see Where to Stay (p151).

Tango show at El Viejo Alm

Tango in Buenos Aires

Buenos Aires' famous dance is possibly the city's greatest contribution to the world: a steamy strut featuring grand feats of athleticism. You'll find supremely entertaining tango shows as well as milongas (dance salons) and dance schools.

Great For...

☑ Don't Miss

Tango performances at the legendary Esquina Carlos Gardel (p130).

Café de los Angelitos

This **cafe** (Map p142; ☎011-4952-2320; www.cafedelosangelitos.com; Av Rivadavia 2100; show from US$90, show & dinner from US$130; ⏰cafe 8am-midnight; Ⓢ Línea A Congreso) puts on one of the best tango shows in Buenos Aires. The performers dress in top-notch costumes and use interesting props, such as drapes and moving walls. They also dance to modern tunes, including those by local band Bajofondo, and despite a nightclub feel at times – especially due to the lighting – it's all tastefully and creatively done.

El Beso

This small, intimate **dance salon** (Map p142; ☎011-4953-2794; http://elbeso.com.ar; Riobamba 416, 1st fl; Ⓢ Línea B Callao) hosts various different *milongas*; the most popular is Milonga Cachirulo on Tuesdays from 9pm

Need to Know

For discount tickets, show and venue descriptions, and some reviews, check out www.tangotix.com.

Take a Break

A San Telmo gem, **La Poesía** (Map p142; 011-4300-7340; Chile 502; mains AR$57-200; 8am-2am Sun-Thu, to 4am Fri & Sat; S Línea C Independencia) is a vintage 19th-century cafe with good snacks and live music.

★ Top Tip

For a unique outdoor experience, head to the bandstand at the Barrancas de Belgrano, where there's live tango on Saturday and Sunday evenings around 7pm.

to 5am. The Cachirulo attracts some very good dancers – you should be confident of your skills if you plan to take to the floor.

Tango Porteño

Staged in a renovated art-deco theater, this **tango show** (Map p142; 011-4124-9400; www.tangoporteno.com.ar; Cerrito 570; show from US$28, show & dinner from US$120; S Línea D Tribunales) features snippets of old footage interspersed with plenty of athletic (and at times sensual) dancing. There's an interesting blindfold number and the orchestra is excellent. There's a complimentary tango class before the show.

Tango Trips

Tango Trips (011-5235-4923; www.tangotrips.com; tour for 1/2/3 people US$160/190/240) offers private tours to *milongas* with experienced and passionate *tangueros* (tango dancers). Start with a private tango lesson to gain confidence before hitting the salons; if you're not a dancer, just sit back and watch tango danced in its most authentic form.

Salón Canning

Some of BA's finest dancers (no wallflowers here) grace this traditional **venue** (Map p146; 011-15-5738-3850; www.parakultural.com.ar; Av Scalabrini Ortiz 1331; 141, 140, 15) with its great dance floor. Well-known tango company Parakultural stages good events on Monday, Tuesday and Friday, involving orchestras, singers and dance performances; check the website for class times and the milonga musical lineup. Expect big crowds and plenty of tourists.

La Viruta

La Viruta (Map p146; ☎011-4774-6357; www.lavirutatango.com; Armenia 1366; 🚌141, 15, 110) is a popular basement venue in Palermo. Good beginner tango classes are available before the *milongas* – translating into many inexperienced dancers on the floor earlier on – so if you're an expert get here late (after 2am).

Esquina Carlos Gardel

One of the fanciest tango shows in town plays at this impressive 430-seat **theater** (Map p146; ☎011-4867-6363; www.esquinacarlosgardel.com.ar; Carlos Gardel 3200; show from US$96, show & dinner from US$140; S Línea B Carlos Gardel), where Carlos Gardel once hung out. This fine show highlights passionate, top-notch musicians and performers in period costumes, though a modern segment involving a skin suit is cutting-edge, athletic and memorable.

DNI Tango

This excellent **tango school** (Map p146; ☎011-4866-6553; https://dni-tango.com; Bulnes 1101; group class per person AR$130; S Línea B Medrano) offers group and private classes in English and Spanish for all levels. For those starting out, the Saturday afternoon práctica is a friendly place to dance with different partners without the pressure of taking to the floor at a more formal milonga.

El Viejo Almacén

One of BA's longest-running shows (since 1969), this **venue** (Map p142; ☎011-4307-7388; www.viejoalmacen.com; Balcarce 799; show from US$90, show & dinner from US$140; 🚌29, 24, 111) is a charming old building from

Esquina Carlos Gardel

the 1800s. Dinner is served at a multistory restaurant in the main building, then everyone heads across the street to the small theater with an intimate stage, highly athletic dancers and plenty of glitz.

Complejo Tango

For those who wish to not only watch tango but also experience it, there's this classy **venue** (☎011-4941-1119; www.complejotango.com.ar; Av Belgrano 2608; show US$55, dinner & show from US$125; S Línea A Plaza Miserere) in Once. The first hour is a free beginners' tango lesson, which you can follow with a tasty dinner, then an excellent tango show – be warned that performers go around toward the end, picking out audience members to dance with them (usually badly).

Rojo Tango

This sexy performance is the **tango show** (Map p142; ☎011-4952-4111; www.rojotango.com; Martha Salotti 445, Faena Hotel; show US$220, show & dinner US$290; 111, 43, 143) to top all others, though it comes with a hefty price tag. Offering only 100 seats, the Faena's cabaret room is swathed in blood-red curtains and gilded furniture. The show itself loosely follows the history of the tango, starting from its cabaret roots to the modern fusions of Ástor Piazzolla.

La Ventana

This long-running basement **venue** (Map p142; ☎011-4334-1314; www.laventanaweb.com; Balcarce 431; show from US$70, show & dinner from US$120; S Línea E Belgrano) is located in an old converted building with rustic brick walls in San Telmo. The tango show includes a folkloric segment with Andean musicians and a display of *boleadores* (gaucho hunting weapons). There's also a patriotic tribute to Evita, and the dinner offers a wide variety of tasty main dishes – unusual for tango shows.

Maldita Milonga

Held on Wednesday at Buenos Ayres Club, **Maldita Milonga** (Map p142; ☎011-15-2189-7747; www.facebook.com/malditamilonga1; Perú 571, Buenos Ayres Club; class 9pm, milonga 10:30pm Wed; S Línea E Belgrano) is a well-run and popular event, and it's one of the best places to see tango being danced by real couples. The highlight of the night is when the dynamic orchestra El Afronte plays at 11pm; at midnight there's a professional dance demonstration.

☑ What's On

Hoy Milonga (www.hoy-milonga.com) is a useful website listing the day's *milonga* schedule.

WIM WISKERKE / ALAMY STOCK PHOTO ©

Tango Festival

If you're in Buenos Aires in mid- to late August, don't miss the celebrated Tango BA Festival y Mundial (p30).

Plaza de Mayo and Casa R

JEREMY WOODHOUSE / GETTY IMAGES ©

Plaza de Mayo

Plaza de Mayo is the city's political, social and symbolic center. Surrounded by the Casa Rosada, the Cabildo and the city's main cathedral, the plaza has borne witness to many key events from Argentina's turbulent history.

Great For...

☑ Don't Miss

The striking Pirámide de Mayo at the center of the plaza and one of the icons of Buenos Aires.

The City's Historic Heart

When Juan de Garay refounded Buenos Aires in 1580, he laid out the large Plaza del Fuerte (Fortress Plaza) in accordance with Spanish law. Later called the Plaza del Mercado (Market Plaza), then the Plaza de la Victoria (after victories over British invaders in 1806 and 1807), the plaza acquired its present name of Plaza de Mayo after the date Buenos Aires declared independence from Spain: May 25, 1810.

At the center of the plaza is the **Pirámide de Mayo**, a white obelisk built to mark the first anniversary of independence from Spain. Looming on the plaza's northern side is the headquarters of **Banco de la Nación** (Map p142; Bartolomé Mitre 326; S Línea D Catedral), the work of famed architect Alejandro Bustillo. Most other public buildings in this area belong to the late 19th century,

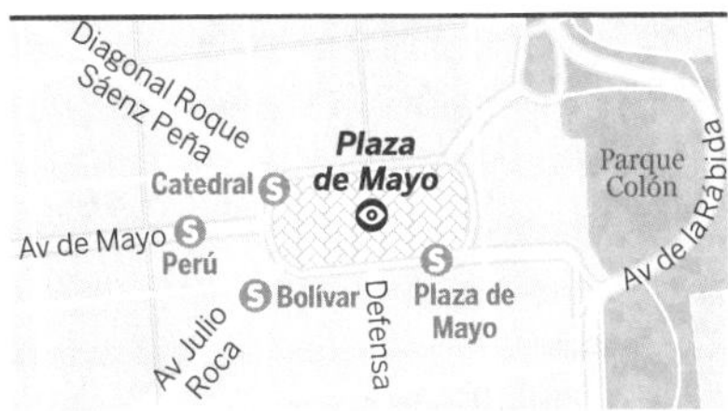

Need to Know

Map p142; cnr Av de Mayo & San Martín; S Línea A Plaza de Mayo

Take a Break

For modern Argentine food washed down with exquisite malbec, head to Aldo's Restoran & Vinoteca (p145).

★ Top Tip

Come on Sunday, when the Feria de San Telmo (p141) stretches all the way along Calle Defensa from Av San Juan to Plaza de Mayo.

when the Av de Mayo first connected the Casa Rosada with the **Plaza del Congreso**, obliterating much of the historic and dignified **Cabildo** (Map p142; ☎011-4342-6729; https://cabildonacional.cultura.gob.ar; Bolívar 65; ⏲10:30am-5pm Tue, Wed & Fri, to 8pm Thu, to 6pm Sat & Sun; S Línea A Perú) FREE in the process.

Madres de Plaza de Mayo

Plaza de Mayo has long been the preferred site of many civil protests; note the unsightly barricades separating the plaza in two, meant to discourage large numbers of *piqueteros* (picketers) from congregating. But these barricades haven't prevented the Madres de la Plaza de Mayo – the mothers of the 'disappeared,' those abducted by the state during the military dictatorship of 1976–1983, from gathering in the plaza every Thursday afternoon at 3:30pm since 1977, and circling the pyramid holding photographs of their missing children. To this day they march on as a reminder of the past – and for other social justice causes.

Casa Rosada

On the eastern side of Plaza de Mayo stands the Casa Rosada, named for its distinctive color. It was from the balcony here that Eva Perón famously addressed the throngs of impassioned supporters packed into Plaza de Mayo. The building houses the Argentine president's offices; the presidential residence is in the suburb of Olivos, north of the center. Free hourlong guided tours are given at weekends and must be booked online in advance; bring ID.

The building occupies the site where colonial riverbank fortifications once stood; today, however, after repeated landfills, the palace stands more than 1km inland. The **Museo Casa Rosada** (Map p142; ☎011-4344-3802; cnr Av Paseo Colón & Hipólito Yrigoyen; ⏲10am-6pm Wed-Sun; S Línea A Plaza de Mayo) FREE is located behind the palace.

Tomb of Rufina Cambacer

MANVMEDIA / SHUTTERSTOCK ©

Cementerio de la Recoleta

Wander for hours in this city of the dead, where countless 'streets' are lined with impressive statues and marble sarcophagi. Peek into the crypts, check out the dusty coffins and try to decipher the history of its inhabitants.

Great For...

☑ Don't Miss

The striking tomb of Evita (Eva Perón), the most visited landmark in the cemetery.

Illustrious Inhabitants

Originally the vegetable garden of the monastery next door, Recoleta cemetery was created in 1822. It covers four city blocks and contains about 4800 mausoleums decorated in many architectural styles, including art nouveau, art deco, classical, Greek, baroque and neo-Gothic. Popular motifs include crosses of all kinds, marble angels, stone wreaths, skulls and crossbones, draped urns, winged hourglasses and the occasional gargoyle. All decorate the final resting places of past presidents, military heroes, influential politicians, famous writers and other very noteworthy personages.

The most impressive tomb is not Evita's, though it's certainly the most visited. Get a good map and look for other sarcophagi; interesting stories, odd facts and myths abound. Also note the cemetery's rough

Need to Know

Map p142; ☎0800-444-2363; visitasguiadasrecoleta@buenosaires.gob.ar; Junín 1760; ⏱7am-5:30pm; Ⓢ Línea H Las Heras; FREE

Take a Break

Go for a meal at the traditional neighborhood restaurant Rodi Bar (p147), which serves classic Argentine fare.

★ Top Tip

For an overlook of the cemetery, head to the cloisters museum at the Basílica de Nuestra Señora del Pilar.

edges – the cobwebs and detritus inside many of the tombs, the vegetation growing out of cracks, the feral cats prowling the premises. All add to the charm.

Tours

Free tours are offered in Spanish at 11am and 2pm from Tuesday to Sunday and at 11am and 3pm on Saturday and Sunday (weather permitting). For a great map and information, order Robert Wright's PDF guide (www.recoletacemetery.com); touts also sell maps at the entrance.

Basílica de Nuestra Señora del Pilar

A short stroll from the cemetery is this gleaming white **colonial church** (Map p142; ☎011-4806-2209; www.basilicadelpilar.org.ar; Junín 1904; museum adult/child AR$25/free; ⏱museum 10:30am-6pm Mon-Sat, 2:30-6pm Sun; Ⓢ Línea H Las Heras), built by Franciscans in 1732. Its centerpiece is a Peruvian altar adorned with silver from Argentina's northwest. Inside, head to the left to visit the small but historic cloisters museum; it's home to religious vestments, paintings, writings and interesting artifacts, and there are good views of Recoleta cemetery.

On the left-hand side of the courtyard as you enter the church, look for a ceramic tiled artwork depicting Buenos Aires as it was in 1794, back when the church stood in open countryside outside the town.

Centro Cultural Recoleta

Before or after visiting the cemetery, be sure to head to the nearby **Centro Cultural Recoleta** (Map p142; ☎011-4803-1040; www.centroculturalrecoleta.org; Junín 1930; Ⓢ Línea H Las Heras) FREE. Part of the original Franciscan convent and alongside its namesake church and cemetery, this excellent cultural center houses a variety of facilities, including art galleries, exhibition halls and a cinema.

Don Julio

Parrillas

Argentines have perfected the art of grilling beef on the asado (barbecue). Succulent char-grilled meats, matched with rich red wines, are served up in hallowed* parrillas *(steakhouses) all across the city.

Great For...

☑ Don't Miss

A sizzling plate of *bife de chorizo* (sirloin), a popular thick and juicy cut.

Don Julio

Classy service and a great wine list add an upscale bent to this traditional – and very popular – corner **steak house** (Map p146; ☎011-4832-6058; www.parrilladonjulio.com.ar; Guatemala 4691; mains AR$296-657; ⏰noon-4pm & 7:30pm-1am; S Línea D Plaza Italia). The *bife de chorizo* (sirloin steak) is the main attraction here, but the baked goat cheese provolone, *bondiola de cerdo* (pork shoulder) and gourmet salads are a treat as well, and portions are large. Reserve ahead.

La Carnicería

The menu at this modern **parrilla** (Map p146; ☎011-2071-7199; www.facebook.com/xlacarniceriax; Thames 2317; mains AR$360-380; ⏰8pm-midnight Tue-Fri, 1-3:30pm & 8pm-midnight Sat & Sun; S Línea D Plaza Italia) is limited, but everything on it is spectacular,

Chimichurri (herb sauce)

ILDI PAPP / SHUTTERSTOCK ©

Need to Know

Parrillas are generally open daily from noon to 3:30pm for lunch and 8pm to midnight or 1am for dinner.

Take a Break

For dining in a hurry, stop by the *parrilla* **Lo de Freddy** (Map p142; Bolívar 950; choripanes AR$50, vaciopanes AR$100; 1:30-5:30pm & 8-11:30pm Mon-Fri, 1-11:30pm Sat & Sun; 29) for delectable *choripanes* (sausage sandwiches).

Don't Miss

Chimichurri, a tasty sauce made with olive oil, garlic and parsley. It adds a tantalizing spiciness.

from the crispy *provoleta* (barbecued cheese), to the homemade chorizo and morcilla, to the tenderloin and rib cuts. This is a place for serious meat lovers who won't be put off by the butcher-themed decor. Portions are huge. Reserve ahead.

La Cabrera

La Cabrera (Map p146; 011-4832-5754; www.lacabrera.com.ar; José Antonio Cabrera 5099; mains AR$388-562; 12:30-4:30pm & 8:30pm-midnight Sun-Thu, to 1am Fri & Sat; 140, 34) is hugely popular for grilling up some of BA's most sublime meats, so soft they can be cut with a spoon. Steaks weigh in at 400g or 800g and arrive with many little complimentary side dishes. Come at 7pm for happy hour, when everything is 40% off – arrive early to score a table; reservations are taken from 8:30pm only.

La Boca

The same family has been running **El Obrero** (011-4362-9912; Agustín R Caffarena 64; mains AR$175-360; noon-4pm & 8pm-midnight Mon-Sat; 130, 168, 29) since 1954, and a number of famous people have passed through over the years, including Bono and Robert Duvall (check out the photos on the walls). You'll also see old Boca Juniors jerseys, antique furniture, old tile floors and chalkboards showing the day's specials and standard parrilla fare. Take a taxi.

Parrilla Tour

On this foodie **tour** (011-15-4048-5964; www.parrillatour.com; per person US$85; Palermo tour noon Tue, Fri & Sat, San Telmo tour noon Mon & Wed), you'll meet your knowledgeable guide at a restaurant for a *choripán*, then an empanada. You'll finish at a local *parrilla*.

Walking Tour: Historical Saunter

This stroll through the attractive neighborhood of San Telmo takes in art, history and a fabulous covered market.

Start El Zanjón de Granados
Distance 1.5km
Duration 2½ hours

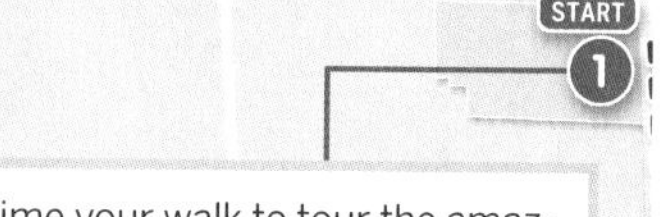

1 Time your walk to tour the amazing tunnels and brick archways of **El Zanjón de Granados** (Map p142; www.elzanjon.com.ar), which formed the foundations of BA's oldest homes.

Classic Photo: Dome of the famous Mercado de San Telmo

3 Stroll through the covered **Mercado de San Telmo** (Map p142), which has been running since 1897.

5 Stop to have a look at the patios and rooms of the 19th-century **Pasaje de la Defensa** (Map p142), a microcosm of San Telmo's history.

6 The **Museo de Arte Moderno de Buenos Aires** (Map p142; www.museodeartemoderno.buenosaires.gob.ar) offers cutting-edge exhibitions, along with works by well-known Argentine artists.

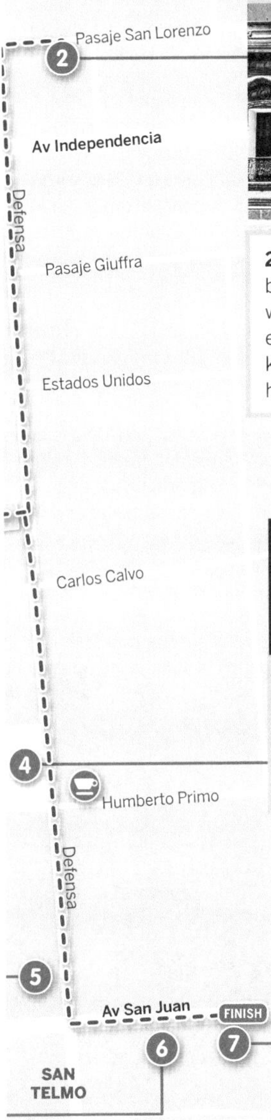
0 100 m
0 0.05 miles
Pasaje San Lorenzo
2
Av Independencia
Defensa
Pasaje Giuffra
Estados Unidos
Carlos Calvo
4
Humberto Primo
Defensa
5
Av San Juan
FINISH
6
7
SAN TELMO

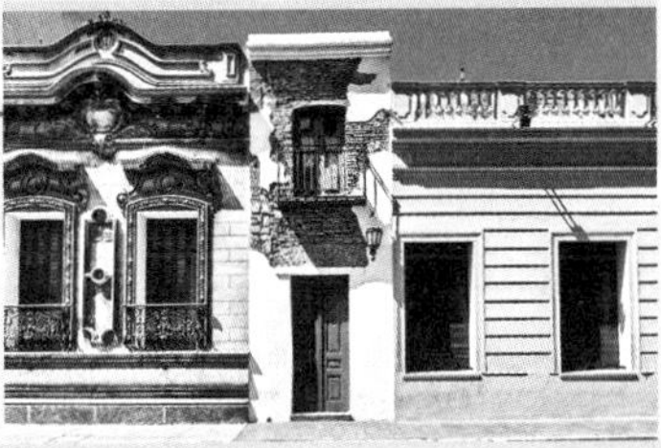

2 The decaying white-stucco-and-brick **Casa Mínima**, barely 2m wide at San Lorenzo 380, is a good example of the narrow-lot style known as *casa chorizo* (sausage house).

Take a Break...

Bar Plaza Dorrego (Map p142) is an atmospheric spot for snacking and people-watching.

4 The heart of the barrio is **Plaza Dorrego** (Map p142). On Sunday the lively **Feria de San Telmo** (p141) sets up in the plaza and surrounding streets.

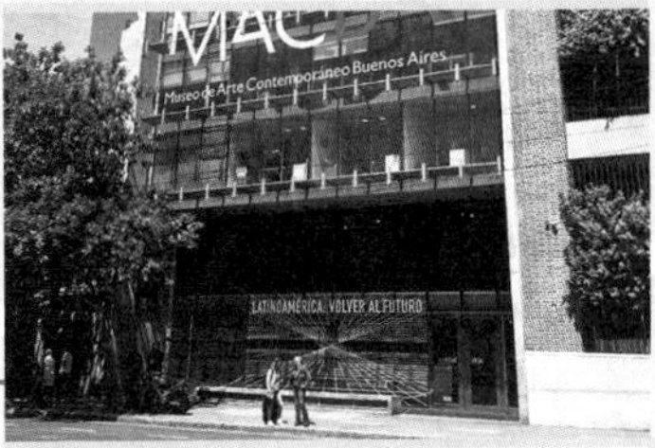
Museo de Arte Contemporáneo Buenos Aires
LATINOAMÉRICA: VOLVER AL FUTURO

7 The **Museo de Arte Contemporáneo Buenos Aires** (Map p142; www.macba.com.ar) is great for abstract art.

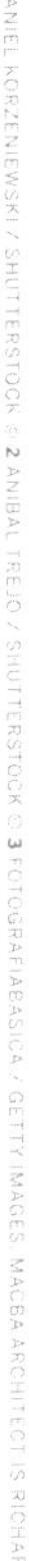

SIGHTS

City Center

Centro Cultural Kirchner — Cultural Center

(Map p142; ☎0800-333-9300; www.culturalkirchner.gob.ar; Sarmiento 151; ⊙1-8pm Wed-Sun; S Línea B Alem) FREE It was former president Néstor Kirchner who, in 2005, first proposed turning the abandoned former central post office into a cultural center. He died in 2010 before the project was completed, and the breathtaking cultural center was named in his honor. Within the vast beaux-arts structure – which stands eight stories tall and takes up an entire city block – are multiple art galleries, events spaces and auditoriums. The highlight, however, is the Ballena Azul, a concert hall with world-class acoustics that seats 1800.

Within the vast beaux-arts structure are multiple art galleries, events spaces and auditoriums.

Manzana de las Luces — Notable Building

(Block of Enlightenment; Map p142; ☎011-4342-6973; Perú 222; ⊙10am-7:30pm Mon-Fri, 2-8pm Sat & Sun; S Línea E Bolívar) FREE In colonial times, the Manzana de las Luces was Buenos Aires' most important center of culture and learning, and today the block still symbolizes education and enlightenment. Two of the five original buildings remain; Jesuit defensive tunnels were discovered in 1912. Free tours in Spanish are given at 2pm from Monday to Friday, but you can go inside and see the main patio area without taking a tour.

Teatro Colón — Theater

(Map p142; ☎011-4378-7100; www.teatrocolon.org.ar; Tucumán 1171, Cerrito 628; tours AR$500-600; ⊙tours 9am-5pm; S Línea D Tribunales) This impressive seven-story building is one of BA's most prominent landmarks. It's the city's main performing-arts venue and a world-class forum for opera, ballet and classical music, with astounding acoustics. Occupying an entire city block, the Colón can seat 2500 spectators and provide standing

Centro Cultural Kirchner

room for another 500. The theater's real beauty lies on the inside, so if you can't get hold of tickets to a performance, take one of the frequent 50-minute backstage tours to view the stunning interior.

La Boca

El Caminito Street

(Map p127; Av Don Pedro de Mendoza, near Del Valle Iberlucea; 33, 64, 29, 168, 53) FREE La Boca's most famous street and 'open-air' museum is a magnet for visitors, who come to see its brightly painted houses and snap photographs of the figures of Juan and Eva Perón, Che Guevara and soccer legend Diego Maradona, who wave down from balconies. (Expect to pay a few pesos to take pictures of tango dancers or pose with props.) Sure, it could be called a tourist trap, but don't let that put you off.

Museo Benito Quinquela Martín Museum

(Map p127; 011-4301-1080; www.buenosaires.gob.ar/museoquinquelamartin; Av Don Pedro de Mendoza 1835; AR$40; 10am-6pm Tue-Fri, 11:15am-6pm Sat & Sun; 33, 64, 29) Once the home and studio of painter Benito Quinquela Martín (1890–1977), this fine-arts museum exhibits his works and those of other Argentine artists. Quinquela Martín used silhouettes of laboring men, smokestacks and water reflections as recurring themes, and painted with broad, rough brushstrokes and dark colors. Don't miss the colorful tiles of his former kitchen and bathroom, his hand-painted piano and the sculptures on the rooftop terraces; the top tier has awesome views of the port.

Palermo

Museo de Arte Latinoamericano de Buenos Aires Museum

(MALBA; Map p146; 011-4808-6500; www.malba.org.ar; Av Figueroa Alcorta 3415; adult/student Thu-Mon AR$140/70, Wed AR$70/free; noon-8pm Thu-Mon, to 9pm Wed; 102, 130, 124) Sparkling inside its glass walls, this airy modern art museum is one of BA's most impressive. It displays the fine collection of Latin American art of millionaire and philanthropist Eduardo Costantini, including works by Argentines Xul Solar and Antonio Berni, as well as pieces by Mexicans Diego Rivera and Frida Kahlo. The temporary exhibitions here are usually world class so it's worth checking what's currently on offer. A cinema screens art-house films.

Feria de San Telmo

On Sundays, San Telmo's **main drag** (Map p142; Defensa; 10am-6pm Sun; 10, 22, 29, 45, 86) is closed to traffic and the street is a sea of both locals and tourists browsing craft stalls, waiting at vendors' carts for freshly squeezed orange juice, poking through the antique glass ornaments on display on Plaza Dorrego, and listening to street performances by myriad music groups. Runs from Avenida San Juan to Plaza de Mayo. It's a tight and crowded scene, so be prepared to bump into people and watch your bag carefully.

Street performers

TERRY CARTER/LONELY PLANET ©

Museo Nacional de Bellas Artes Museum

(Map p142; 011-5288-9900; www.mnba.gob.ar; Av del Libertador 1473; 11am-8pm Tue-Fri, 10am-8pm Sat & Sun; 130, 92, 63) FREE This is Argentina's most important fine art museum and contains many key works by Benito Quinquela Martín, Xul Solar, Eduardo Sívori and other Argentine artists, including a whole room of works by Antonio Berni. There are also pieces by European masters such as Cézanne, Degas, Picasso, Rembrandt, Toulouse-Lautrec and Van Gogh.

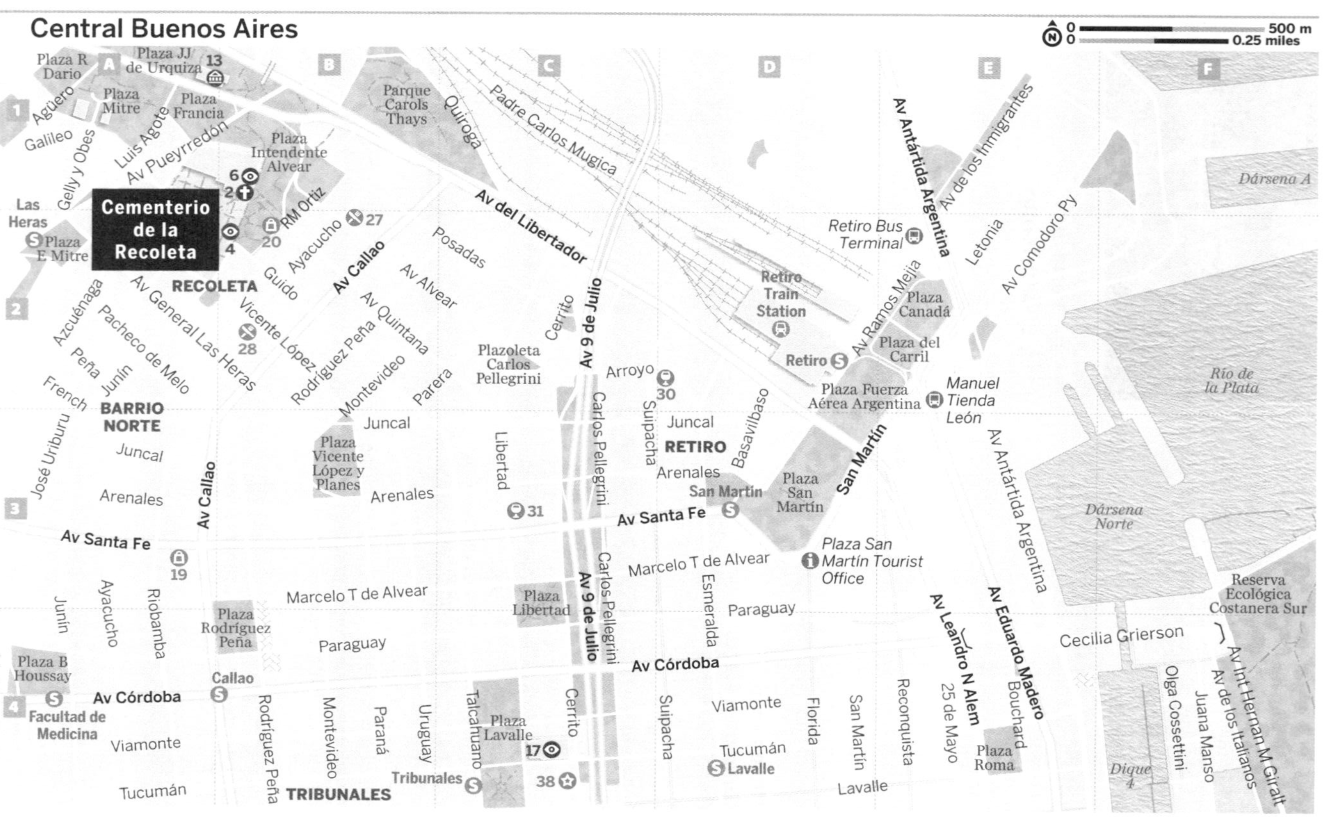
Central Buenos Aires
500 m
0.25 miles
Cementerio de la Recoleta
Río de la Plata
Dársena A
Dársena Norte
Dique 4
Reserva Ecológica Costanera Sur
Av Int Hernan M Giralt
Av de los Italianos
Juana Manso
Olga Cossettini
Cecilia Grierson
Av Antártida Argentina
Av Eduardo Madero
Bouchard
Plaza Roma
Av Leandro N Alem
25 de Mayo
Reconquista
San Martín
Florida
Lavalle
Av Comodoro Py
Av de los Inmigrantes
Letonia
Manuel Tienda León
Retiro Bus Terminal
Plaza Canadá
Plaza del Carril
Av Ramos Mejía
Plaza Fuerza Aérea Argentina
Retiro
Retiro Train Station
Plaza San Martín
Plaza San Martín Tourist Office
Basavilbaso
Paraguay
Marcelo T de Alvear
Esmeralda
Viamonte
Tucumán
Lavalle
RETIRO
Juncal
Arenales
San Martín
Av Santa Fe
Suipacha
Arroyo
30
Av Córdoba
Carlos Pellegrini
Av 9 de Julio
Cerrito
Padre Carlos Mugica
Av del Libertador
Plazoleta Carlos Pellegrini
Libertad
31
Plaza Libertad
17
38
Plaza Lavalle
Talcahuano
Quiroga
Parque Carols Thays
Posadas
Av Alvear
Parera
Uruguay
Tribunales
Av Quintana
Montevideo
Paraná
27
Av Callao
Ayacucho
Rodríguez Peña
Plaza Vicente López y Planes
TRIBUNALES
Plaza Intendente Alvear
RM Ortiz
20
Guido
Vicente López
28
6
2
4
RECOLETA
Plaza JJ de Urquiza
13
Plaza Francia
Av Pueyrredón
Luis Agote
Av General Las Heras
Plaza Rodríguez Peña
Callao
19
Riobamba
Pacheco de Melo
BARRIO NORTE
Plaza Mitre
Plaza R Darío
Agüero
Galileo
Gelly y Obes
Plaza E Mitre
Las Heras
Azcuénaga
Peña
Junín
French
José Uriburu
Ayacucho
Plaza B Houssay
Facultad de Medicina
A
B
C
D
E
F
1
2
3
4

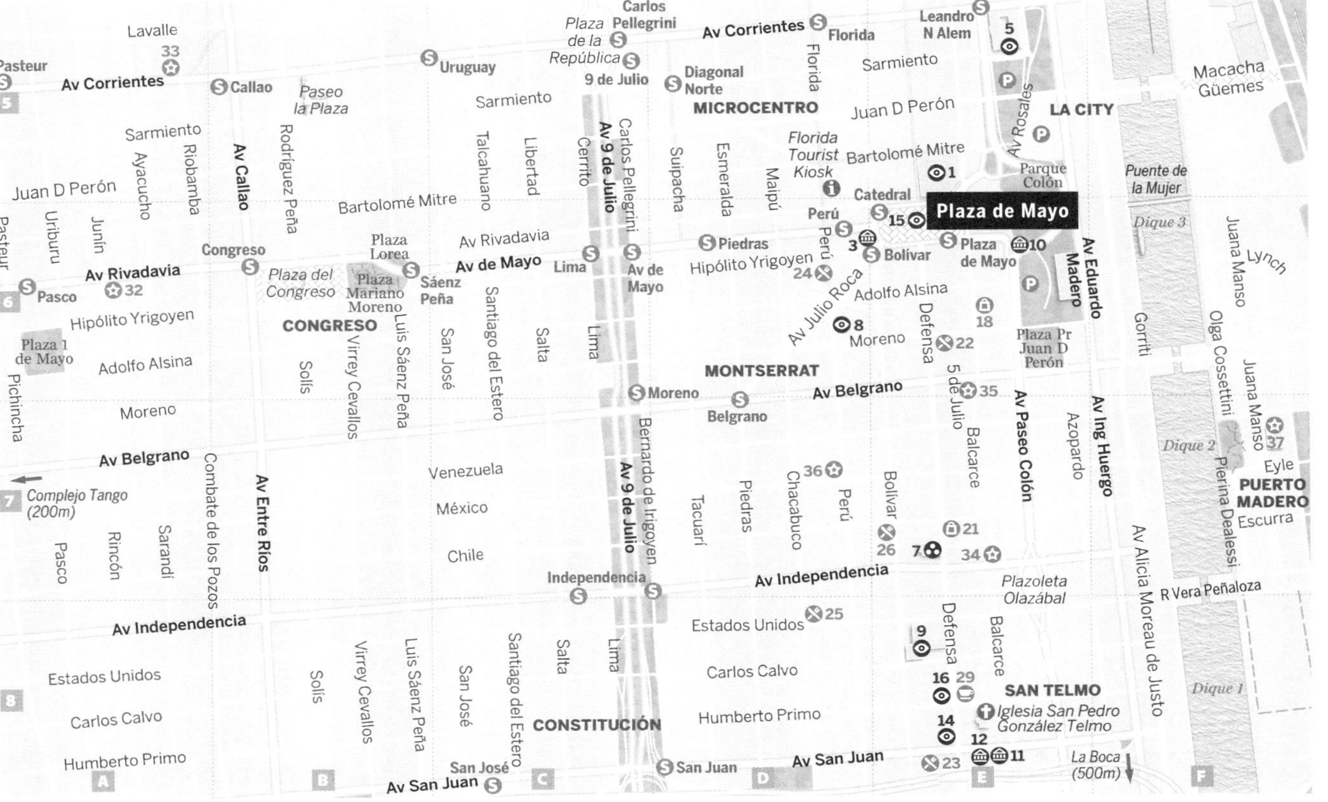
Plaza de Mayo
LA CITY
MICROCENTRO
MONTSERRAT
CONGRESO
SAN TELMO
CONSTITUCIÓN
PUERTO MADERO
Macacha Güemes
Lynch
Juana Manso
Olga Cossettini
Eyle
Escurra
Pierina Dealessi
R Vera Peñaloza
Dique 1
Dique 2
Dique 3
Puente de la Mujer
Gorriti
Av Alicia Moreau de Justo
Av Eduardo Madero
Av Ing Huergo
Azopardo
Av Paseo Colón
Balcarce
Defensa
Bolívar
Perú
Chacabuco
Piedras
Tacuarí
Bernardo de Irigoyen
Av 9 de Julio
Lima
Salta
Santiago del Estero
San José
Luis Sáenz Peña
Virrey Cevallos
Solís
Av Entre Ríos
Combate de los Pozos
Sarandí
Rincón
Pasco
Pichincha
Av Rosales
Parque Colón
Plaza Pr Juan D Perón
Plaza de Mayo
Leandro N Alem
Sarmiento
Juan D Perón
Bartolomé Mitre
Catedral
Bolívar
Perú
Florida
Florida Tourist Kiosk
Maipú
Esmeralda
Suipacha
Carlos Pellegrini
Cerrito
Libertad
Talcahuano
Uruguay
Av Corrientes
Diagonal Norte
Plaza de la República
9 de Julio
Piedras
Hipólito Yrigoyen
Adolfo Alsina
Moreno
Av Julio A Roca
5 de Julio
Av Belgrano
Belgrano
Av de Mayo
Av Rivadavia
Plaza Lorea
Plaza Mariano Moreno
Sáenz Peña
Plaza del Congreso
Venezuela
México
Chile
Av Independencia
Independencia
Plazoleta Olazábal
Estados Unidos
Carlos Calvo
Humberto Primo
Av San Juan
San Juan
San José
Iglesia San Pedro González Telmo
La Boca (500m)
Paseo la Plaza
Rodríguez Peña
Av Callao
Callao
Congreso
Riobamba
Ayacucho
Junín
Uriburu
Pasteur
Lavalle
Pasco
Plaza 1 de Mayo
Complejo Tango (200m)
A
B
C
D
E
F
1
2
3
4
5
6
7
8
9
10
11
12
14
15
16
18
21
22
23
24
25
26
29
32
33
34
35
36
37

Central Buenos Aires

Sights
1 Banco de la Nación E5
2 Basílica de Nuestra Señora del Pilar B1
3 Cabildo D6
4 Cementerio de la Recoleta B2
5 Centro Cultural Kirchner E5
6 Centro Cultural Recoleta B1
7 El Zanjón de Granados E7
Feria de San Telmo .... (see 16)
8 Manzana de las Luces D6
9 Mercado de San Telmo E8
10 Museo Casa Rosada E6
11 Museo de Arte Contemporáneo Buenos Aires E8
12 Museo de Arte Moderno de Buenos Aires E8
13 Museo Nacional de Bellas Artes A1
14 Pasaje de la Defensa E8
15 Plaza de Mayo E6
16 Plaza Dorrego E8
17 Teatro Colón C4

Shopping
18 Arte y Esperanza E6
19 El Ateneo Grand Splendid A3
20 Feria Artesenal Plaza Francia B2
21 Materia Urbana E7

Eating
22 Aldo's Restoran & Vinoteca E6
23 Café San Juan E8
24 D'Oro D6
25 El Refuerzo Bar Almacen D8
26 La Poesia E7
Lo de Freddy .... (see 9)
27 L'Orangerie B2
28 Rodi Bar B2

Drinking & Nightlife
29 Bar Plaza Dorrego E8
30 Florería Atlántico D2
31 Gran Bar Danzón C3

Entertainment
32 Café de los Angelitos A6
33 El Beso A5
34 El Viejo Almacén E7
35 La Ventana E6
36 Maldita Milonga D7
37 Rojo Tango F7
38 Tango Porteño C4

Parque 3 de Febrero Park

(Map p146; cnr Avs del Libertador & de la Infanta Isabel; 10, 34, 130) Also known as Bosques de Palermo (Palermo Woods), this sweeping open parkland abounds with small lakes and pretty gazebos. Stands rent bikes and in-line skates, and joggers and power walkers circle the ponds – if you don't have the energy to join them, lie back under a tree and people-watch. There's also a monument to literary greats called El Jardín de los Poetas (the Garden of Poets), and the exquisite Rosedal (rose garden).

SHOPPING

Arte y Esperanza Arts & Crafts

(Map p142; 011-4343-1455; www.arteyesperanza.com.ar; Balcarce 234; 10am-6pm Mon-Fri; S Línea A Plaza de Mayo) This store sells fair-trade, handmade products that include many made by Argentina's indigenous craftspeople. Shop for silver jewelry, pottery, ceramics, textiles, *mate* gourds, baskets, woven bags, wood utensils and animal masks.

Materia Urbana Arts & Crafts

(Map p142; 011-4361-5265; www.materiaurbana.com; Defensa 702; 11am-7pm Wed-Fri, from 2pm Sat & Tue, 11am-6pm Sun; 29) This innovative design shop shows the work of over 100 local artists; cool finds include leather animal organizers, retro tote bags, plastic *mate* sets and jewelry made from metal, wood and leather.

El Ateneo Grand Splendid Books

(Map p142; 011-4813-6052; www.yenny-elateneo.com/local/grand-splendid; Av Santa Fe 1860; 9am-10pm Mon-Thu, to midnight Fri & Sat, noon-10pm Sun; S Línea D Callao) This glorious bookstore in a converted theater continues to flourish in the age of the Kindle. The Grand Splendid theater opened in 1919 and was converted into a bookstore in 2000. Most of the seating was replaced with bookshelves, but the original features have been preserved, including the beautiful painted cupola and balconies.

Feria Artesanal Plaza Francia — Market

(Map p142; www.feriaplazafrancia.com; Plaza Intendente de Alvear; 11am-8pm Sat & Sun; S Línea H Las Heras) Recoleta's popular artisan fair has dozens of booths and a range of creative, homemade goods. Hippies, mimes and tourists mingle. It's at its biggest on weekends, though there are usually a few stalls open during the week. Despite its name, the market is located just outside the Cementerio de la Recoleta in Plaza Intendente de Alvear.

Elementos Argentinos — Homewares

(Map p146; 011-4832-6299; www.elementos argentinos.com.ar; Gurruchaga 1881; 11am-7pm Tue-Sat; S Línea D Plaza Italia) The high-quality carpets, rugs and blankets sold here are hand-dyed, hand-woven on a loom, and fair trade; the owners work with cooperatives and NGOs to help the communities in northwestern Argentina where the textiles are produced. Larger items can be shipped home, or pick up a super-soft llama-wool blanket to squeeze into your suitcase.

EATING

City Center

D'Oro — Italian $$

(Map p142; 011-4342-6959; Perú 159; mains AR$190-300; noon-4pm Mon-Fri; S Línea E Bolívar) This tiny, popular lunch spot is a serious Italian wine bar and restaurant to rival others in more gastronomically famous neighborhoods. Come for thin, crispy, oven-baked pizzas, mushroom risotto, fettuccine with shellfish and garlic-topped focaccia.

Aldo's Restoran & Vinoteca — Argentine $$$

(Map p142; 011-4334-2380; www.aldosvino teca.com; Moreno 372; mains AR$360-490; noon-midnight Sun-Thu, to 1am Fri, 7pm-1am Sat; S Línea A Plaza de Mayo) This restaurant and wine shop is an upscale eatery serving a small but tasty menu of meat, seafood and pasta dishes, all amid walls lined with wine. Look out for wine tastings held on Tuesday evenings, or ask your server to recommend one of the nearly 600 bottles in stock.

El Ateneo Grand Splendid

FABRIZIO348 / SHUTTERSTOCK ©

Palermo

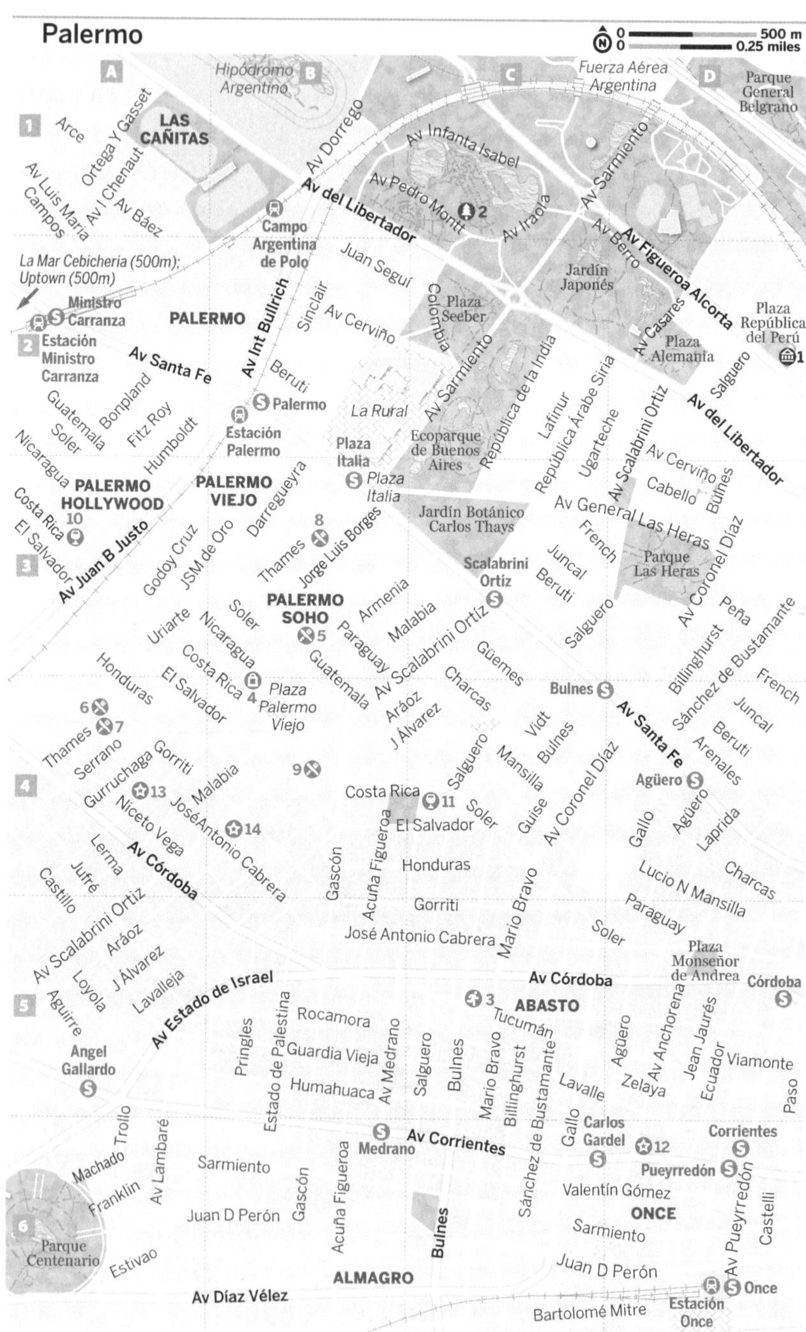
0 500 m
0 0.25 miles
A
B
C
D
1
2
3
4
5
6
Hipódromo Argentino
Fuerza Aérea Argentina
Parque General Belgrano
LAS CAÑITAS
Arce
Ortega Y Gasset
Av I Chenaut
Av Luis María Campos
Av Báez
Av Dorrego
Av Infanta Isabel
Av Sarmiento
Av Pedro Montt
2
Av Iraola
Av del Libertador
Campo Argentina de Polo
Av Berro
Av Figueroa Alcorta
Jardín Japonés
Juan Seguí
La Mar Cebichería (500m);
Uptown (500m)
Ministro Carranza
Estación Ministro Carranza
PALERMO
Av Int Bullrich
Sinclair
Av Cerviño
Colombia
Plaza Seeber
Av Casares
Plaza Alemania
Plaza República del Perú
1
Av Santa Fe
Beruti
Palermo
Estación Palermo
La Rural
Av Sarmiento
República de la India
Lafinur
República Árabe Siria
Ugarteche
Av Scalabrini Ortiz
Salguero
Av del Libertador
Guatemala
Bonpland
Fitz Roy
Humboldt
Soler
Nicaragua
Plaza Italia
Ecoparque de Buenos Aires
Av Cerviño
Cabello
Bulnes
PALERMO HOLLYWOOD
PALERMO VIEJO
Darregueyra
Plaza Italia
Av General Las Heras
Jardín Botánico Carlos Thays
French
Av Coronel Díaz
Costa Rica
10
El Salvador
Av Juan B Justo
Godoy Cruz
JSM de Oro
Thames
8
Jorge Luis Borges
Scalabrini Ortiz
Juncal
Beruti
Parque Las Heras
Armenia
PALERMO SOHO
5
Soler
Uriarte
Nicaragua
Malabia
Av Scalabrini Ortiz
Salguero
Peña
Billinghurst
Sánchez de Bustamante
Paraguay
Güemes
Honduras
Costa Rica
El Salvador
4
Plaza Palermo Viejo
Guatemala
Charcas
Bulnes
Av Santa Fe
French
Juncal
Áráoz
J Álvarez
6
7
Thames
Serrano
Gurruchaga
Gorriti
Vidt
Bulnes
Mansilla
Salguero
Beruti
Arenales
9
Agüero
Malabia
13
Niceto Vega
JoséAntonio Cabrera
Costa Rica
11
El Salvador
Soler
Guise
Av Coronel Díaz
Gallo
Agüero
Laprida
14
Av Córdoba
Lerma
Jufré
Castillo
Gascón
Acuña Figueroa
Honduras
Gorriti
Mario Bravo
Lucio N Mansilla
Charcas
Paraguay
Soler
José Antonio Cabrera
Av Scalabrini Ortiz
Áráoz
J Álvarez
Loyola
Lavalleja
Aguirre
Av Estado de Israel
Plaza Monseñor de Andrea
Córdoba
Av Córdoba
3
ABASTO
Tucumán
Rocamora
Pringles
Estado de Palestina
Guardia Vieja
Humahuaca
Av Medrano
Salguero
Bulnes
Mario Bravo
Billinghurst
Sánchez de Bustamante
Lavalle
Agüero
Zelaya
Av Anchorena
Jean Jaurés
Ecuador
Viamonte
Paso
Angel Gallardo
Trollo
Machado
Av Lambaré
Franklin
Sarmiento
Medrano
Av Corrientes
Gallo
Carlos Gardel
12
Corrientes
Pueyrredón
Juan D Perón
Gascón
Acuña Figueroa
Bulnes
Valentín Gómez
ONCE
Av Pueyrredón
Castelli
Parque Centenario
Estivao
Sarmiento
ALMAGRO
Juan D Perón
Av Díaz Vélez
Bartolomé Mitre
Estación Once
Once

Palermo

Sights

1 Museo de Arte Latinoamericano de Buenos Aires D2
2 Parque 3 de Febrero C1

Activities, Courses & Tours

3 DNI Tango C5

Shopping

4 Elementos Argentinos B4

Eating

5 Don Julio B3
6 Il Matterello A4
7 La Cabrera A4
8 La Carnicería B3
9 Proper B4

Drinking & Nightlife

10 On Tap A3
11 Verne C4

Entertainment

12 Esquina Carlos Gardel D6
13 La Viruta A4
14 Salón Canning B4

La Boca

Il Matterello — Italian $$

(☎011-4307-0529; Martín Rodríguez 517; mains AR$200-260; ⏰12:30-3pm & 8:30pm-midnight Tue-Sat, 12:30-3pm Sun; 🚌29, 53, 152) This Genovese trattoria serves up some of the best pasta in town, including perfectly al dente *tagliatelle alla rúcola* (tagliatelle with arugula), and *tortelli bianchi con burro foso al aglio* (pasta pillows stuffed with chard and Parmesan in a burned garlic sauce). For dessert there's a great tiramisu. Take a taxi here at night. Also in **Palermo** (Map p146; ☎011-4831-8493; Thames 1490; mains AR$230-290; ⏰noon-4pm & 8pm-1am Tue-Sun; 🚌140, 39).

Recoleta & Barrio Norte

Rodi Bar — Argentine $$

(Map p142; ☎011-4801-5230; Vicente López 1900; mains AR$200-450; ⏰8am-1am Mon-Sat; 📶; S Línea H Las Heras) A great option for well-priced, unpretentious food in upscale Recoleta. This traditional neighborhood restaurant with a fine old-world atmosphere and extensive menu offers something for everyone, from inexpensive combo plates to relatively unusual dishes such as marinated beef tongue.

L'Orangerie — French $$$

(Map p142; ☎011-4808-2949; Alvear Palace Hotel, Av Alvear 1891; full tea Mon-Fri AR$450, Sat & Sun $490; ⏰afternoon tea 4:30-7pm Mon-Sat, 5-7pm Sun; 🚌130, 92, 63) Afternoon tea at the Alvear Palace Hotel's beautiful, flower-filled Orangerie is a classic Recoleta experience for a special occasion. The formal tea, served from 4:30pm (from 5pm on Sunday), offers an endless array of exquisite cakes, sandwiches and pastries as well as a selection of loose-leaf teas and background piano music.

Palermo

La Mar Cebicheria — Peruvian $$$

(☎011-4776-5543; http://lamarcebicheria.com.ar; Arévalo 2024; mains AR$320-520; ⏰8pm-midnight Mon, 12:30pm-midnight Tue-Thu & Sun, to 12:30am Fri & Sat; 📶; S Línea D Ministro Carranza) For lovers of fresh fish, this upmarket Peruvian *cebichería* is a welcome addition to the meat-dominated BA food scene. The team at La Mar travel across

Proper Eating

Bringing new life to the BA food scene, the young chefs behind **Proper** (Map p146; ☎011-4831-0027; www.properbsas.com.ar; Aráoz 1676; small plates AR$85-320; ⏰8pm-midnight Tue-Sat; 📶; 🚌111, 160, 141) pack flavor into seasonal produce cooked in a wood-fired oven at their roughly finished restaurant in a former car-repair shop. Order several small plates to share and delight in dishes such as perfectly cooked lamb chops or sweet potato with Patagonian blue cheese, fried almonds and kale.

Argentina to source their ingredients, and the quality of the fish is evident in the eating. The menu is lengthy, with a choice of Peruvian dishes, and there's plenty of outdoor seating.

San Telmo

Café San Juan International $$$

(Map p142; ☎011-4300-1112; www.facebook.com/CafeSanJuanrestaurant; Av San Juan 450; mains AR$300-390; ⏰12:30-4pm & 8pm-midnight Sun & Tue-Thu, to 1am Fri & Sat; Ⓢ Línea C San Juan) Having studied in Milan, Paris and Barcelona, TV-chef Leandro Cristóbal now runs the kitchen at this renowned San Telmo bistro. Start with fabulous tapas, then delve into the grilled Spanish octopus (AR$1100), *molleja* (sweetbreads) cannelloni and amazing pork *bondiola* (deliciously tender after nine hours' roasting). Reserve ahead for lunch and dinner.

El Refuerzo Bar Almacen Argentine $$$

(Map p142; ☎011-4361-3013; www.facebook.com/elrefuerzobaralmacen; Chacabuco 872; mains AR$230-450; ⏰10am-2am Tue-Sun; Ⓢ Línea C Independencia) The small dining room fills up quickly at this *almacén*-style restaurant. There's an excellent wine list to match the menu of top-notch dishes written on blackboards on the walls – think cured meats, cheeses, homemade pastas and bistro-style casseroles. It's a casual, friendly place that's popular with locals.

DRINKING & NIGHTLIFE

Florería Atlántico Cocktail Bar

(Map p142; ☎011-4313-6093; http://floreriaatlantico.com.ar; Arroyo 872; ⏰7pm-2am Mon-Wed, to 2:30am Thu, to 4am Fri, 8pm-4am Sat, 8pm-2am Sun) This basement speakeasy is located within a flower shop, which adds an air of mystery and is likely a key reason for its success. Hipsters, artists, chefs, businesspeople and foreigners all flock here for the excellent cocktails, both classic and creative, accompanied by delicious tapas.

Uptown Bar

(☎011-2101-4897; www.uptownba.com; Arévalo 2030; ⏰8:30pm-2am Tue & Wed, to 3am Thu-Sat; Ⓢ Línea D Ministro Carranza) Descend the

From left: Florería Atlántico; L'Orangerie (p147); Usina del Arte

MICHAEL THOMAS / ALAMY STOCK PHOTO ©

KRZYSZTOF DYDYNSKI / LONELY PLANET ©

graffiti-strewn stairwell and step aboard the carriage of an actual New York subway train to reach BA's hottest bar, a cavernous underground space with DJs and dancing, and a smaller, cozier room styled as a pharmacy. It's a popular place, so call ahead to put your name on the guest list.

Verne Cocktail Bar

(Map p146; 011-4822-0980; http://vernecocktailclub.com; Av Medrano 1475; 9pm-2am Sun-Tue, 8pm-2am Wed, 8pm-3am Thu, 8pm-4am Fri, 9pm-4am Sat; 160, 15) This upscale yet casual bar has a vague Jules Verne theme. Cocktails are the house specialty, whipped up by one of BA's best bartenders, Fede Cuco. A few tables, some cushy sofas and an airy outdoor patio offer a variety of seating options, but plant yourself at the bar to watch the mixologists work their magic.

Gran Bar Danzón Bar

(Map p142; 011-4811-1108; www.granbardanzon.com.ar; Libertad 1161; 7pm-2am Mon-Fri, from 8pm Sat & Sun; S Línea D Tribunales) Upscale restaurant-wine bar with a good selection of wines by the glass as well as fresh fruit cocktails, exotic martinis and Euro- and Asian-inspired dinner selections. It's very popular, so come early and snag a good seat on a sofa.

On Tap Craft Beer

(Map p146; 011-4771-5424; www.ontap.com.ar; Costa Rica 5527; 5pm-midnight Mon-Wed & Sun, to 1am Thu-Sat) This popular pub has 20 Argentine microbrews on tap, including IPAs, pilsners, stouts, wheat porters and honey beers. It's more of a place to enjoy beers than to hang out – there's only counter seating and a communal table, though a few burgers and other pub food are available. Bring a growler for refills; happy hour runs from 5pm to 8:30pm.

ENTERTAINMENT

Usina del Arte Concert Venue

(www.buenosaires.gob.ar/usinadelarte; Agustín R Caffarena 1; 130, 86, 8) FREE This former power station has been transformed into a spectacular concert venue in an effort to regenerate a somewhat sketchy area of La Boca. It's a gorgeous red-brick building complete with scenic clock tower, and the

BERNARDO GALMARINI / ALAMY STOCK PHOTO ©

La Bombonera Stadium

Seeing Boca Juniors play at **La Bombonera** (☎011-5777-1200; www.bocajuniors.com.ar; Brandsen 805; 🚌29, 53, 152) is one of the world's top spectator sports experiences, especially if the game happens to be the 'superclasico' derby match against River. Tickets are hard to come by – it's best to go via an agent like LandingPadBA (http://landingpadba.com). You can see the stadium during a visit to the Museo de la Pasión Boquense.

SUNSINGER / SHUTTERSTOCK ©

two concert halls have top-notch acoustics. Nearly all the art exhibitions, concerts and dance performances here are free; check the website for upcoming events.

INFORMATION

There are several tourist offices and kiosks in Buenos Aires. Staff speak English and can provide maps and information about free guided walks and other activities.

Ezeiza airport (☎011- 4480-0224; Terminal A arrivals, 1st fl, Ezeiza Airport; ⏰8:15am-7:15pm)

Florida (Map p142; cnr Florida & Roque Sáenz Peña; ⏰9am-6pm; Ⓢ Línea D Catedral)

La Boca (https://turismo.buenosaires.gob.ar; Av Don Pedro de Mendoza 1901; ⏰9am-6pm; 📶; 🚌33, 64, 29)

Plaza San Martín (Map p142; cnr Av Florida & Marcelo T de Alvear; ⏰9am-6pm; Ⓢ Línea C San Martín)

GETTING THERE & AWAY

AIR

Most international flights arrive at Buenos Aires' Aeropuerto Internacional Ministro Pistarini (p401), about 35km south of the Center. Ezeiza is a modern airport with ATMs, restaurants, a pharmacy and duty-free shops.

BUS

Buenos Aires' modern **Retiro bus terminal** (Retiro; Map p142; ☎011-4310-0700; www.retiro.com.ar; Av Antártida Argentina; Ⓢ Línea C Retiro) has buses to practically anywhere in Argentina and departures are fairly frequent to the most popular destinations.

GETTING AROUND

BA's public transportation is efficient. Use Como Llego (http://comollego.ba.gob.ar), the city government website, to plot your journey, or download the free app.

Bus The city has hundreds of bus lines that can take you within a few blocks of any destination.

Subte BA's underground, or subway, is not difficult to figure out. It's a quick way to get around – though it gets hot and very crowded during rush hour.

Taxi Black-and-yellow street taxis are ubiquitous and generally fine.

Where to Stay

You'll find a wide range of places to rest your head here, from hostels to boutique hotels, guesthouses, rental apartments and international five-star hotels. Just remember to book ahead – or pay in cash – for the best deals.

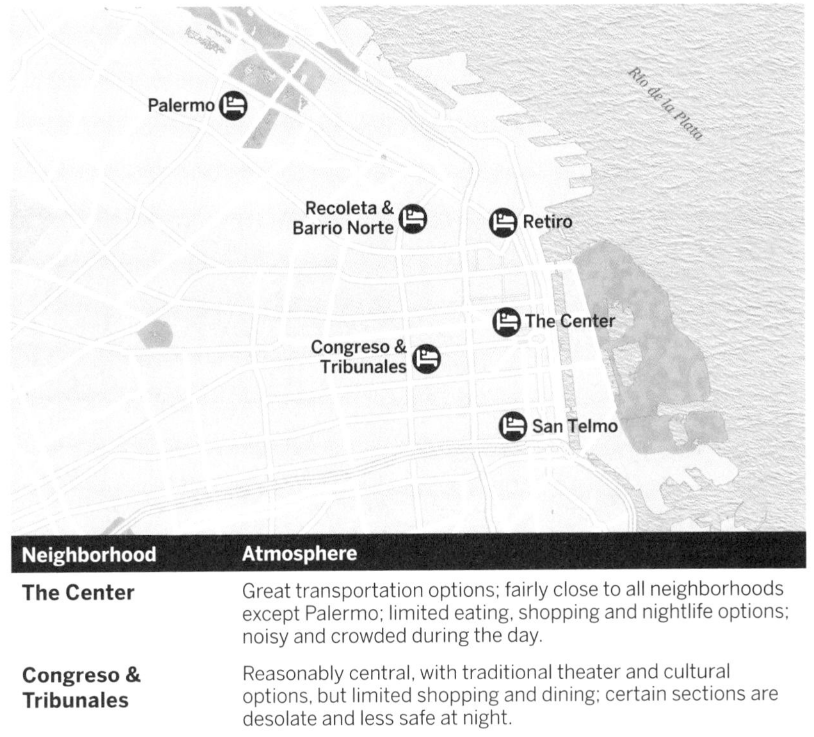

Neighborhood	Atmosphere
The Center	Great transportation options; fairly close to all neighborhoods except Palermo; limited eating, shopping and nightlife options; noisy and crowded during the day.
Congreso & Tribunales	Reasonably central, with traditional theater and cultural options, but limited shopping and dining; certain sections are desolate and less safe at night.
San Telmo	Endearing traditional atmosphere, reasonable shopping and nightlife, a good range of restaurants and many decent hostels; far from Palermo; some areas can be edgy at night; public transportation is somewhat limited.
Retiro	Beautiful upscale neighborhood within walking distance of Recoleta and the Center; convenient for public transportation; very expensive; limited accommodations options; not many affordable restaurants or shops.
Recoleta & Barrio Norte	Buenos Aires' most upscale neighborhood; gorgeous architecture, good transportation options and fairly safe; most accommodations, restaurants and shopping are very expensive.
Palermo	Many boutique hotels to choose from; the city's widest range of interesting restaurants; great shopping and nightlife; a bit of a trek to the Center and San Telmo; might be too touristy for some.

SOUTHERN PATAGONIA, ARGENTINA

In this Chapter

Southern Patagonia, Argentina

On South America's southern frontier, nature grows wild, barren and beautiful. Spaces are large, as are the silences that fill them. For the newly arrived, such emptiness can be as impressive as the sight of Patagonia's jagged peaks, pristine rivers and dusty backwater oases. In its enormous scale, Patagonia offers a wealth of potential experiences and landscapes.

Though now mostly paved, lonely RN 40 remains the iconic highway that stirred affection in personalities as disparate as Butch Cassidy and Bruce Chatwin. On the eastern seaboard, paved RN 3 shoots south, connecting oil boomtowns with ancient petrified forests, Welsh settlements and the incredible Península Valdés.

Two Days in Southern Patagonia

Spend day one taking in the magnificent sight of Glaciar Perito Moreno on a cruise with **Southern Spirit** (p157) or on a horseback riding excursion with **Cabalgatas del Glaciar** (p157). In the evening have a memorable meal at **Pura Vida** (p163) in El Calafate. On day two, head out on a four-hour hike with **Glaciar Sur** (p161).

Four Days in Southern Patagonia

On your third day set out on a scenic full-day hike in the Fitz Roy Range: the **Laguna de Los Tres** (p158) trek is spectacular if you're fit. On day four, go rock-climbing with **Patagonia Mágica** (p164). At trip's end treat yourself to a massage at **Spa Yaten** (p164).

Previous page: Glaciar Perito Moreno (p156)
AILTONSZA / SHUTTERSTOCK ©

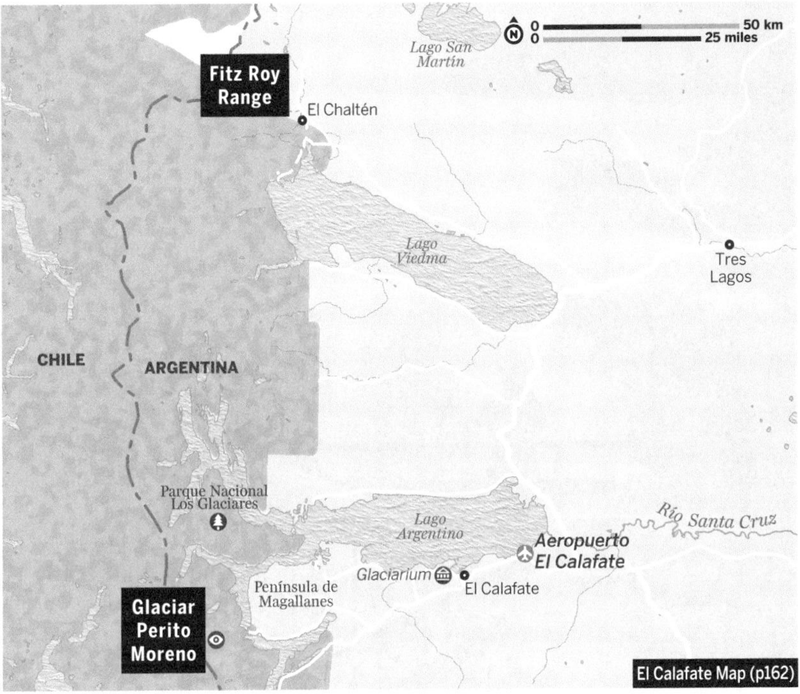

Fitz Roy Range
El Chaltén
Lago San Martín
0 50 km
0 25 miles
Lago Viedma
Tres Lagos
CHILE
ARGENTINA
Parque Nacional Los Glaciares
Lago Argentino
Río Santa Cruz
Aeropuerto El Calafate
Glaciarium
El Calafate
Península de Magallanes
Glaciar Perito Moreno
El Calafate Map (p162)

Arriving in Southern Patagonia

The modern **Aeropuerto El Calafate** (www.aeropuertoelcalafate.com/en/) is 23km east of town and has flights to Buenos, Bariloche and other destinations.

El Chaltén is 220km from El Calafate via smooth paved roads. Car hire is available in El Calafate; or you can take a bus (AR$600, 3½ hours, three daily in summer).

Where to Stay

For visiting the Glaciar Perito Moreno, the village of El Calafate has ample lodging options. The town of El Chaltén, near the Fitz Roy Range, likewise offers abundant lodging for all price points. Wherever you stay, book well ahead. If you bring a sturdy tent, however, there's always space in the campgrounds.

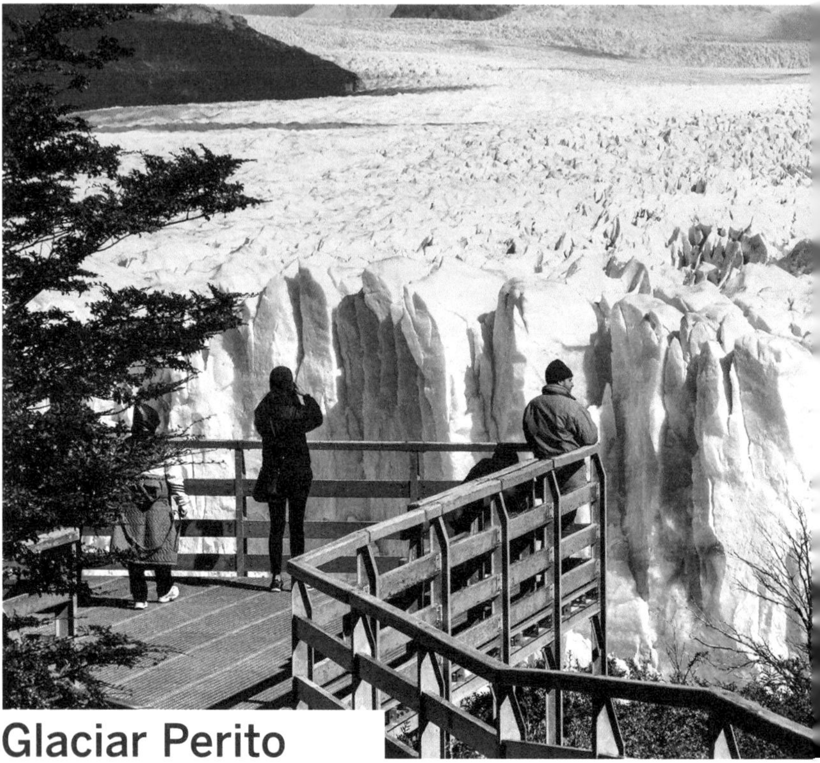

AGE FOTOSTOCK / ALAMY STOCK PHOTO ©

Glaciar Perito Moreno

Among the Earth's most dynamic and accessible ice fields, Glaciar Perito Moreno is the stunning centerpiece of the southern sector of Parque Nacional Los Glaciares.

Great For...

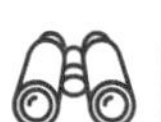

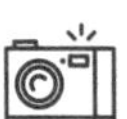

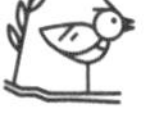

☑ Don't Miss

The sight (and sound!) of huge icebergs calving into the Iceberg Channel.

The Experience

The glacier measures 30km long, 5km wide and 60m high, but what makes it exceptional in the world of ice is its constant advance – up to 2m per day, causing building-sized icebergs to calve from its face.

Glaciar Perito Moreno is as much an auditory as a visual experience when huge icebergs calve and collapse into the Canal de los Témpanos (Iceberg Channel). This natural-born tourist attraction at Península de Magallanes is close enough to guarantee great views, but far enough away to be safe.

Vantage Points

A series of steel catwalks (almost 4000m total) and vantage points allow visitors to see, hear and photograph the glacier. Sun hits its face in the morning and the glacier's appearance changes as the day progresses

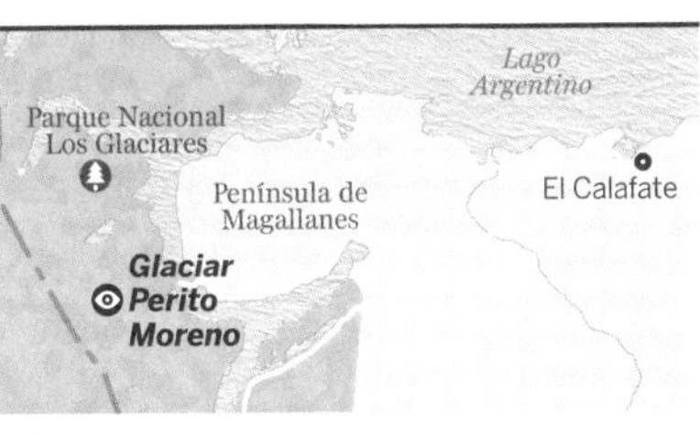

Need to Know

Glaciar Perito Moreno is inside **Parque Nacional Los Glaciares** (www.parquesnacionales.gob.ar/areas-protegidas/region-patagonia-austral/pn-los-glaciares; adult/child AR$600/150; 8am-6pm Sep-Easter, 9am-4pm Apr-Aug).

Take a Break

There are no restaurants on-site. Bring a picnic from the nearby town of El Calafate.

★ Top Tip

Visit late in the afternoon on sunny days for the most dramatic ice cracking.

and shadows shift. A closed *refugio* with glass walls allows for glacier viewing in bad weather.

Cruises

Excursions by boat allow you to sense the magnitude of Glaciar Perito Moreno, still from a safe distance.

Southern Spirit (02902-491582; www.southernspiritfte.com.ar; Libertador 1319, El Calafate; 1hr cruise AR$1800; 9am-1pm & 4-8pm) has one- to three-hour cruises on Lago Argentino in southern Parque Nacional Los Glaciares to see Glaciar Perito Moreno. An active alternative includes hiking.

Solo Patagonia (02902-491115; www.solopatagonia.com; Libertador 867, El Calafate; 9am-12:30pm & 4-8pm) offers the Ríos de Hielo Express (AR$1350) from Puerto Punta Bandera, visiting Glaciar Upsala, Glaciar Spegazzini and Glaciar Perito Moreno. Weather may alter the route.

Mar Patag (02902-492118; www.crucerosmarpatag.com; Libertador 1319, El Calafate; day cruise AR$2550; 7am-9pm) has luxury cruises with a chef serving gourmet meals. The day trip leaves from the private port of La Soledad and visits Glaciar Upsala, with a four-course meal served on board. The two-day cruise (from US$1050 per person) leaves five times a month and also visits the Glaciares Mayo and Perito Moreno.

Cabalgatas del Glaciar

Cabalgatas del Glaciar (02902-495447; www.cabalgatasdelglaciar.com; full day AR$2250) runs one-day and multiday riding or trekking trips with glacier panoramas to Lago Roca and Paso Zamora on the Chilean border. Tours include transfer from El Calafate and a steak lunch.

Cerro Fitz Roy

Hiking the Fitz Roy Range

The Fitz Roy Range – with its rugged wilderness and shark-tooth summits – is the de facto trekking and climbing capital of Argentina. Numerous well-marked trails offer spectacular scenery.

Great For...

☑ Don't Miss

The view of the wildly beautiful glacial Laguna de los Tres.

Laguna de Los Tres

This hike to a high alpine tarn provides one of the most photogenic spots in Parque Nacional Los Glaciares. It's somewhat strenuous (10km and four hours one way) and best for those in good physical shape. Exercise extra caution in foul weather as trails are very steep.

Laguna Torre

Views of the stunning rock needle of Cerro Torre are the highlight of this 18km round-trip hike. If you have good weather – ie little wind – and clear skies, make this hike (three hours one way) a priority, since the toothy Cerro Torre is the most difficult local peak to see on normal blustery days.

Hiking in Parque Nacional Los Glaciares

Loma del Pliegue Tumbado & Laguna Toro

Heading southwest from El Chaltén's Park Ranger Office, this trail (10km and four to five hours one way) skirts the eastern face of Loma del Pliegue Tumbado going toward Río Túnel, then cuts west and heads to Laguna Toro. It's less crowded than the main routes. The hike is gentle, but prepare for strong winds and carry extra water.

Piedra del Fraile

This 16km round-trip (three hours one way) follows the Valle Río Eléctrico. There are some stream crossings with sturdy tree trunks to cross on and one bridge crossing; all are well-marked. From Hostería El Pilar walk 1km northeast on the main road to hit the signposted trailhead for Piedra del Fraile, near a big iron bridge.

Need to Know

The Fitz Roy Range is in the northern swath of the Parque Nacional Los Glaciares (p157).

Take a Break

After a long hike, treat yourself to a pint and comfort fare at **La Cervecería** (02962-493109; Av San Martín 320; mains AR$100-190; noon-midnight).

★ Top Tip

Before heading out on hikes, stop by El Chaltén's Park Ranger Office for updated trail conditions.

Guided Trips

Many companies offer multiday treks, guided climbs and kayaking trips.

Fitzroy Expediciones (Adventure Patagonia; 02962-436110; www.fitzroyexpediciones.com.ar; Av San Martín 56, El Chaltén; 9am-1pm & 2-8pm) runs trekking excursions, ice trekking on Glaciar Cagliero, kayaking and a five-day itinerary that includes trekking in the Fitz Roy and Cerro Torre area. Note that Fitzroy Expediciones does accept credit cards.

Chaltén Mountain Guides (02962-493329; www.chaltenmountainguides.com; Río de las Vueltas 212, El Chaltén) do ice-field traversing, trekking and mountaineering. Rates decrease significantly with group size. The office is in the Kaulem hotel.

The **Casa de Guías** (02962-493118; www.casadeguias.com.ar; Lago del Desierto 470, El Chaltén; 10am-1pm & 4:30-9pm) is friendly and professional, with English-speaking guides certified by the Argentine Association of Mountain Guides (AAGM). It specializes in small groups.

El Calafate

Named for the berry that, once eaten, guarantees your return to Patagonia, El Calafate hooks you with another irresistible attraction: Glaciar Perito Moreno, 80km away in Parque Nacional Los Glaciares. This magnificent must-see has converted once-quaint El Calafate into a chic fur-trimmed destination. With a range of traveler services, it's still a fun place to be.

SIGHTS

Reserva Natural Laguna Nimez — Wildlife Reserve

(AR$150; daylight hours) Reserva Natural Laguna Nimez is a prime avian habitat alongside the lakeshore north of El Calafate, with a self-guided trail and staffed Casa Verde information hut with binoculars rental. It's a great place to spot flamingos – but watching birds from El Calafate's shoreline on Lago Argentino can be just as good.

Centro de Interpretación Historico — Museum

(02902-497799; www.museocalafate.com.ar; Brown & Bonarelli; AR$170; 10am-8pm Sep-May, 11am-5pm Jun-Aug) Small but informative, with a skeleton mold of *Austroraptor cabazai* (found nearby) and Patagonian history displays. The friendly host invites museum-goers for a post-tour *mate* (a bitter ritual tea).

TOURS

Some 40 travel agencies arrange excursions to Glaciar Perito Moreno and other local attractions, including fossil beds and stays at regional *estancias,* where you can hike, ride horses and relax. Tour prices for Glaciar Perito Moreno don't include the park entrance fee. Ask agents and other travelers about added benefits, such as extra stops, boat trips, binoculars or multilingual guides.

...the glacier is as much an auditory as a visual experience...

Kayaking near Glaciar Perito Moreno (p156)

Glaciar Sur Adventure

(☎02902-495050; www.glaciarsur.com; 9 de Julio 57; per person US$250; ⊙10am-8pm) Get glacier-stunned *and* skip the crowds with these recommended day tours to the unexplored end of Parque Nacional Los Glaciares. Small groups drive to Lago Roca with an expert multilingual guide to view Glaciar Frías. The adventure option features a four-hour hike; the culture option includes a traditional *asado* (barbecue grill) and off-hour visits to Glaciar Perito Moreno.

Trips run October through April, weather permitting.

Hielo y Aventura Outdoors, Cruise

(☎02902-492094, 02902-492205; www.hieloyaventura.com; Libertador 935) Hielo y Aventura's conventional cruise Safari Nautico (AR$500, one hour) tours Brazo Rico, Lago Argentino and the south side of Canal de los Témpanos. Catamarans crammed with up to 130 passengers leave hourly between 10:30am and 4:30pm from Puerto Bajo de las Sombras. During busy periods buy tickets in advance for afternoon departures.

To hike on Glaciar Perito Moreno, try minitrekking (AR$2700, under two hours on ice), or the longer and more demanding Big Ice (AR$5200, four hours on ice). Both involve a quick boat ride from Puerto Bajo de las Sombras, a walk through lenga forests, a chat on glaciology and then an ice walk using crampons. Children under eight are not allowed; reserve ahead and bring your own food. Don't forget rain gear: it's often snowing around the glacier and you might quickly become wet and cold on the boat deck. Transfers cost extra (AR$1000).

Chaltén Travel Tours

(☎02902-492212; www.chaltentravel.com; Libertador 1174; ⊙9am-9pm) Recommended tours to Glaciar Perito Moreno, stopping for wildlife-viewing (binoculars provided); also specializes in RN 40 trips. It outsources some excursions to **Always Glaciers** (☎02902-493861; www.alwaysglaciers.com; Libertador 924).

Glaciarium: The World of Ice

Unique and exciting, this gorgeous **museum** (Map p155; ☎02902-497912; www.glaciarium.com; adult/child AR$480/200; ⊙9am-8pm Sep-May, 11am-8pm Jun-Aug) illuminates the world of ice. Displays and bilingual films show how glaciers form, along with documentaries on continental ice expeditions and stark meditations on climate change. Adults suit up in furry capes for the *bar de hielo* (AR$240 including drink), a blue-lit below-zero club serving vodka or fernet and cola in ice glasses.

The gift shop sells handmade and sustainable gifts crafted by Argentine artisans. Glaciarium also hosts international cinema events. It's 6km from Calafate toward Parque Nacional Los Glaciares. To get here, take the free hourly shuttle from 1 de Mayo between Av Libertador and Roca.

MICHELE FALZONE / GETTY IMAGES ©

EATING

Olivia Cafe $

(☎02902-488038; 9 de Julio 187; snacks AR$90-180; ⊙11am-8pm Mon-Sat, 2-8pm Sun; 📶) This adorable coffee shop does *croque monsieurs* (grilled ham and cheese), fresh donuts and espresso drinks in a loungy pastel setting. It also uses whole-bean Colombian coffee. Want to take the chill off? Try the cheese scones served hot with cream.

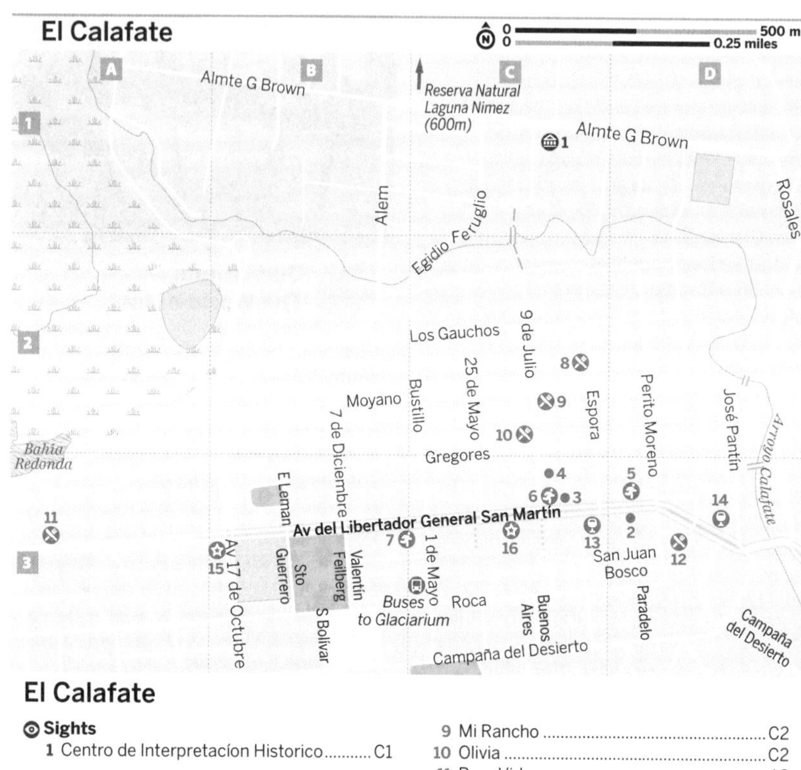

El Calafate

Sights

1 Centro de Interpretacíon Historico C1

Activities, Courses & Tours

2 Always Glaciers D3
3 Chaltén Travel C3
4 Glaciar Sur C3
5 Hielo y Aventura D3
Mar Patag .... (see 7)
6 Solo Patagonia SA C3
7 Southern Spirit B3

Eating

8 Buenos Cruces C2
9 Mi Rancho C2
10 Olivia C2
11 Pura Vida A3
12 Viva la Pepa D3

Drinking & Nightlife

13 Borges y Alvarez Libro-Bar C3
14 La Zorra D3

Entertainment

15 Don Diego de la Noche B3
16 La Toldería C3

Viva la Pepa Cafe $

(☎02902-491880; Amado 833; mains AR$125-390; ⏰11am-11pm Mon-Sat) Decked out in children's drawings, this cheerful cafe specializes in crepes but also offers great sandwiches with homemade bread (try the chicken with apple and blue cheese), fresh juice and gourds of *mate*.

Buenos Cruces Argentine $$

(☎02902-492698; www.facebook.com/BuenosCrucesRestaurante; Espora 237; mains AR$150-310; ⏰12:30-3pm & 7-11pm Mon-Sat; 👪) This dynamic family-run enterprise brings a twist to Argentine classics. Start with a warm beet salad with balsamic reduction. The nut-crusted trout is both enormous and satisfying, as is the guanaco meatloaf or the baked ravioli crisped at the edge and bubbling with Roquefort cheese. The service is excellent and there's a play area for children.

Pura Vida Argentine $$
(02902-493356; Libertador 1876; mains AR$130-290; 7:30-11:30pm Thu-Tue;) Featuring the rare treat of Argentine home cooking, this offbeat, low-lit eatery is a must. Its longtime owners are usually found cooking up buttery spiced chicken potpies and filling wine glasses. For vegetarians, brown rice and wok veggies or salads are satisfying. Servings are huge. Don't skip the decadent chocolate brownie with ice cream and warm berry sauce. Reserve ahead.

Mi Rancho Argentine $$$
(02902-490540; Moyano 1089; mains AR$180-310; noon-3:30pm & 8pm-midnight) Inspired and intimate, Mi Rancho serves up oversized osso buco, delicious braided pastas stuffed with king crab, divine salads and sweetbreads with wilted spinach on toast. For dessert, chocolate fondant or passion-fruit semifreddo are both worth the calorie hit, and more. Located in a tiny brick pioneer house with space for few.

DRINKING & NIGHTLIFE

La Zorra Microbrewery
(02902-490444; www.facebook.com/cervezalazorra; Av San Martín s/n; 6pm-2am Tue-Sun) Long, skinny tables fill with both locals and travelers to quaff what we consider to be the best artisan beer in Patagonia, La Zorra. The smoked porter and double IPA do not disappoint. There's also pub fare such as fries and sausages.

Borges y Alvarez Libro-Bar Bar
(Libertador 1015; noon-9pm Mon-Thu, 3pm-midnight Fri & Sat;) Upstairs in the gnome village shopping complex, this hip bookstore-bar serves coffee, artisan beers and pricey cocktails. Peruse the oversized photography books on Patagonian wildlife or bring your laptop and take advantage of the free wi-fi. There's also 2nd-story deck seating.

La Vinería

Transplanted from Alaska, this tiny, congenial **wine bar** (02962-493301; Lago del Desierto 265; 2:30pm-3am Oct-Apr) offers a long Argentine wine list accompanied by 70 craft-beer options and standout appetizers. With 50 wines sold by the glass and an entire gin menu, enthusiasts might be tempted to sabotage their next day on the trail.

AFRICA STUDIO / SHUTTERSTOCK ©

La Toldería Live Music
(02902-491443; www.facebook.com/LaTolderia; Libertador 1177; noon-4am Mon-Thu, to 6am Fri-Sun) This petite storefront opens its doors to dancing and live acts at night; it's probably the best spot to try if you're feeling boisterous.

Don Diego de la Noche Live Music
(Libertador 1603; 8pm-late) This perennial favorite serves dinner and features live music such as tango, guitar and *folklórica* (folk music).

El Chaltén

This colorful village overlooks the stunning northern sector of Parque Nacional Los Glaciares. Every summer thousands of trekkers explore the world-class trails that start right here.

SIGHTS & ACTIVITIES

Capilla de los Escaladores Chapel

A simple chapel of Austrian design memorializes the many climbers who have lost their lives to the precarious peaks since 1953.

Spa Yaten Health & Fitness

(☎02962-493394; spayaten@gmail.com; Av San Martín 36; 1hr massage AR$1750; ⊙10am-10pm) Spa Yaten has showers, robes and slippers, so sore hikers can come straight here off the trail. There are various therapies, massage, dry sauna and Jacuzzi tubs in a communal room. Reserve massages in advance.

TOURS

El Relincho Horseback Riding

(☎02962-493007, in El Calafate 02902-491961; www.elrelinchopatagonia.com.ar; Av San Martín 505) Outfitter El Relincho takes riders to the pretty valley of Río de las Vueltas (three hours) and also offers more challenging rides up the Vizcacha hill followed by a barbecue on a traditional ranch. Cabin-style accommodations are also available through the company.

Zona Austral Tours

(☎02902-489755; http://zonaaustralturismo.com; Av MM de Güemes 173; half-day/full-day tour US$15.50/20) Offers sea kayaking and the Glaciar Vespignani tour at Lago del Desierto.

Patagonia Mágica Outdoors

(☎02962-486261; www.patagoniamagica.com; Fonrouge s/n) The friendly Patagonia Mágica runs one-day rock-climbing workshops for beginners on the natural rock-climbing walls near El Chaltén. Experienced climbers can go on expeditions with certified guides.

SHOPPING

Chalteños Chocolate

(Av San Martín 249; ⊙10am-1pm & 4-9pm) Bring home Chalteños' handmade *alfajores* filled with *dulce de leche* or homemade jams and your loved ones will forgive all your wanderings.

...this colorful village overlooks the stunning northern sector of Parque Nacional Los Glaciares.

Outdoor cafe in El Chaltén (p163)

Viento Oeste Books
(☎02962-493200; Av San Martín 898; ⏰10am-11pm) Sells books, maps and souvenirs and also rents a wide range of camping equipment, as do several other sundries shops around town.

EATING

Cúrcuma Vegan **$$**
(☎02902-485656; Av Rojo 219; mains AR$320-380; ⏰10am-10pm; ✍) With an avid following, this vegan, gluten-free cafe does mostly takeout, from adzuki-bean burgers to whole-wheat pizzas, stuffed eggplant with couscous and arugula. Salads, coconut-milk risottos and smoothies are as rare as endangered species in Patagonia – take advantage. Hikers can reserve a lunch box a day in advance.

Maffía Italian **$$**
(Av San Martín 107; mains AR$180-360; ⏰11am-11pm) Bring your appetite. In a gingerbread house, this pasta specialist makes delicious stuffed *panzottis* and *sorrentinos*, with creative fillings like trout, eggplant and basil or fondue. There are also homemade soups and garden salads. Service is professional and friendly. For dessert, the oversize homemade flan delivers.

Estepa Argentine **$$**
(☎02962-493069; cnr Cerro Solo & Av Antonio Rojo; mains AR$120-350; ⏰11:30am-2pm & 6-11pm) Local favorite Estepa cooks up consistent, flavorful dishes such as lamb with calafate sauce, trout ravioli or spinach crepes. Portions are small but artfully presented, with veggies that hail from the on-site greenhouse. For a shoestring dinner, consider its rotisserie takeout service.

La Tapera Argentine **$$$**
(☎02962-493195; Antonio Rojo 74; mains AR$260-330; ⏰noon-3pm & 6:30-11pm Oct-Apr) With tender steak in balsamic-reduction sauce, ultra-fresh trout from Lago del Desierto and red-wine glasses as big as your head, it's hard to go wrong at Chipo's place, reminiscent of a log cabin with an open fireplace. Vegetarian options invite less enthusiasm – best to try elsewhere. Otherwise, service is snappy, portions generous and there are wonderful wine options.

DRINKING

La Chocolatería Cafe
(☎02962-493008; Lago del Desierto 105; ⏰11am-9pm Mon-Fri, 9am-9pm Sat & Sun Nov-Mar) This irresistible chocolate factory tells the story of local climbing legends on the walls. It makes for an intimate evening out, with options ranging from spirit-spiked hot cocoa to wine and fondue. Chocolate and coffee drinks are AR$90.

Laguna los Tres Bar
(Trevisán 42; ⏰6pm-2am) For a dose of rock or reggae with ping-pong on the side, this disheveled bar will do nicely. There's live music on weekends; check the Facebook page for events.

SANTIAGO, CHILE

In this Chapter

Santiago, Chile

Surprising, cosmopolitan, energetic, sophisticated and worldly, Santiago is a city of syncopated cultural currents, madhouse parties, expansive museums and top-flight restaurants.

It's a wonderful place for strolling, and each neighborhood has its unique flavor and tone. Head out for the day to take in the museums, grand architecture and pedestrian malls of the Centro, before an afternoon picnic in one of the gorgeous hillside parks that punctuate the city's landscape. Nightlife takes off in the sidewalk eateries, cafes and beer halls of Barrios Brasil, Lastarria and Bellavista.

Two Days in Santiago

Start off at the iconic **Museo Chileno de Arte Precolombino** (p176), then delve into Chile's dark past at the **Museo de la Memoria y los Derechos Humanos** (p180). Have a long and lazy dinner at **Peumayen** (p183).

Start day two at Pablo Neruda's house, **La Chascona** (p177), then take in great views atop **Cerro San Cristóbal** (p171). That night catch a show at **Centro Gabriela Mistral** (p177).

Four Days in Santiago

Spend your third day touring the Maipo Valley vineyards. Have a picnic lunch at **Viña Santa Rita** (p173) and make your own blend at **Viña de Martino** (p173).

Get active on day four in the Cajón del Maipo. Go rafting with **Rutavertical** (p174) or take a scenic walk in the **Monumento Natural El Morado** (p174). Afterwards soak in the rejuvenating **Termas Valle de Colina** (p175).

Previous page: Plaza de Armas and the Catedral Metropolitana de Santiago
EMPERORCOSAR / SHUTTERSTOCK ©

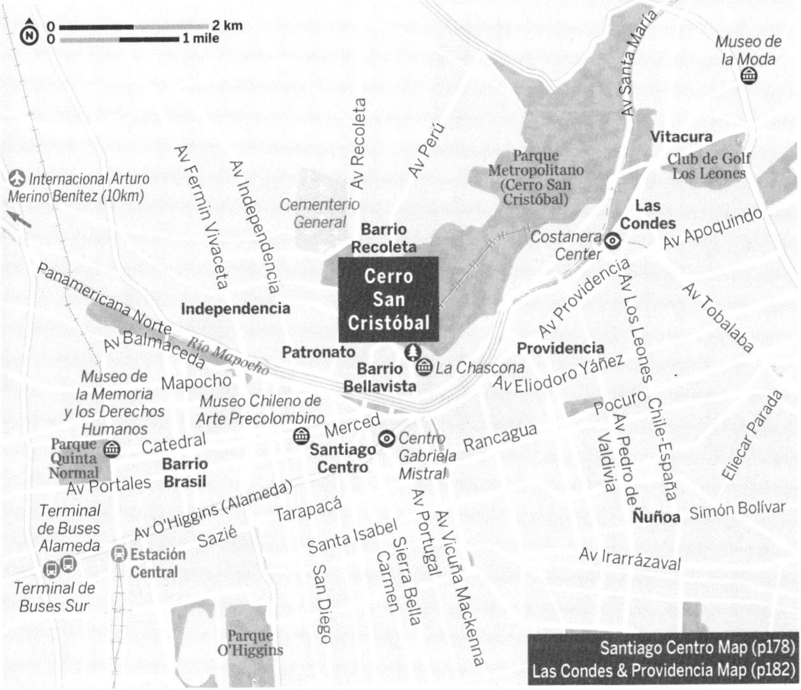

Santiago Centro Map (p178)
Las Condes & Providencia Map (p182)

Arriving in Santiago

Aeropuerto Internacional Arturo Merino Benítez (Santiago; p402) Centropuerto and Turbus Aeropuerto run buses to the city center (40 minutes). A taxi to Centro costs CH$18,000; Transvip runs shared shuttles (from CH$7000).

Terminal de Buses Sur The city's main bus station is connected to the metro at the Universidad de Santiago station. From here, take trains east on Línea 1 to reach the Centro.

Where to Stay

Santiago's unique neighborhoods provide the backdrop for your stay. For easy access to museums and restaurants, consider the Centro, budget-friendly Barrio Brasil or nightlife districts like classy Barrio Lastarria and raucous Bellavista. For fancier digs and sophisticated dining – but limited access to most major sights – head to leafy Providencia, trendy Barrio Italia or well-heeled Las Condes.

Teleféricos (cable cars) and views of Santiago

TIFONIMAGES / GETTY IMAGES ©

Cerro San Cristóbal

The best views over Santiago are from the peaks and viewpoints of the Parque Metropolitano, better known as Cerro San Cristóbal. At 722 hectares, the park is Santiago's largest green space.

Great For...

☑ Don't Miss

The marvelous view from the *teleférico* as you ascend to the hilltop.

Virgen de la Inmaculada Concepción

A snowy white 14m-high statue of the Virgin of the Immaculate Conception towers atop the *cumbre* (summit) at the Bellavista end of the park. The benches at its feet are the outdoor church where Pope John Paul II said Mass in 1984.

Skybound Journey

A funicular carries you between different landscaped sections on one side, while a *teleférico* (cable car) swoops you away on the other.

To go by foot you can take a steep switchbacked dirt trail from the Plaza Caupolicán. This is also the start of the **funicular** (http://funicularsantiago.cl; Barrio Bellavista; adult/child 1-way from CH$1500/1000,

Virgen de la Inmaculada Concepción

JOPSTOCK / GETTY IMAGES ©

Need to Know

Map p178; www.parquemet.cl; Pio Nono 450; funicular adult/child 1-way from CH$1500/1000; funicular 10am-6:45pm Tue-Sun, 1-6:45pm Mon; ; M Baquedano

Take a Break

Enjoy a drink and a snack with unrivaled views from Terraza Bellavista.

★ Top Tip

The park has entrances in both Bellavista and Providencia neighborhoods.

round-trip from CH$2000/1500; 10am-6:45pm Tue-Sun, 1-6:45pm Mon; M Baquedano), and the site of a tourist info kiosk. Alternatively, enter the park from Pedro de Valdivia and board the **teleférico** (www.parquemet.cl; Parque Metropolitano; weekdays/weekends 1-way' CH$1910/2290; 10am-7pm Tue-Sun; M Baquedano).

Family Fun

Other attractions on the hillside include the **Zoológico Nacional** (National Zoo; Map p178; 2-2730-1368; www.parquemet.cl/zoologico-nacional; Parque Metropolitano; adult/child CH$3000/1500; 10am-5pm Tue-Sun; M Baquedano); the Jardín Botánico Mapulemu, a botanical garden; the child-oriented Plaza de Juegos Infantiles Gabriela Mistral, featuring attractive wooden playground equipment and an interactive water fountain; and two huge public swimming pools, the **Piscina Tupahue** (2-2730-1331; Cerro San Cristóbal s/n, Parque Metropolitano; adult/child CH$6000/3500; 10am-6:30pm Tue-Sun Nov-Mar; M Baquedano) and **Piscina Antilén** (Map p182; 2-2730-1331; Cerro San Cristóbal s/n, Parque Metropolitano; adult/child CH$7500/4000; 10am-6:30pm Tue-Sun Nov-Mar; M Baquedano). The small but perfectly landscaped Jardín Japonés (Japanese Garden) is just above the Pedro de Valdivia entrance.

Terraza Bellavista

Near the top of the funicular is the **Terraza Bellavista** (Map p178; Parque Metropolitano; M Baquedano), where there are a few snack stands and extraordinary views across the city.

Viña Cousiño Macul

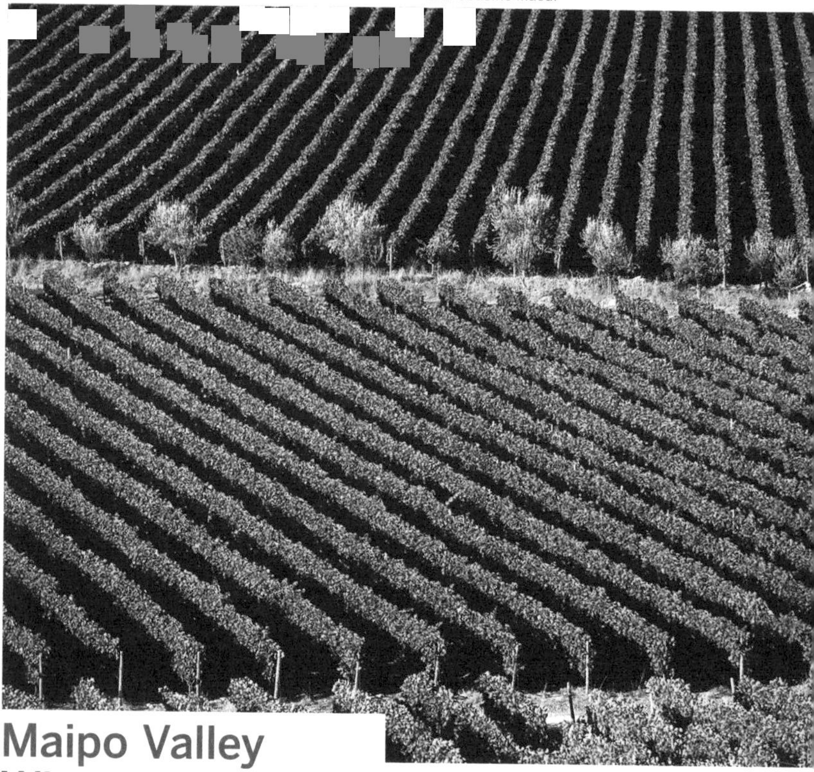

Maipo Valley Wineries

When you've had your fill of Santiago's museums and plazas, head south of the city center to check out the gorgeous vineyards of the Maipo Valley, home to some outstanding big-bodied reds.

Great For...

☑ Don't Miss

The chance to blend your own wine at Viña de Martino.

Organized Tours

You can go it alone as many wineries are within 1½ hours of the city center on public transportation. But if you'd like to hit the wine circuit with a knowledgeable guide, try the specialized tours at **Uncorked Wine Tours** (2-2981-6242; www.uncorked.cl; full-day tour US$195). An English-speaking guide will take you to three wineries, and a lovely lunch is included.

Also recommended is the winery bike tour with **La Bicicleta Verde** (Map p178; 2-2570-9939; https://labicicletaverde.com; Loreto 6, Barrio Recoleta; bike tours from CH$25,000, rentals half-/full-day from CH$5000/9000; M Bellas Artes).

Enotour (Map p182; 2-2481-4081; www.enotourchile.com; Luis Thayer Ojeda 0130, Oficina 1204, Providencia; tours from CH$37,000; M Tobalaba) is another curated wine-tour

TINAFIELDS / GETTY IMAGES ©

Need to Know

If you plan on visiting two or more wineries, you're better off renting a car.

Take a Break

Viña Santa Rita (2-2362-2520; www.santarita.com; Camino Padre Hurtado 0695, Alto Jahuel; tours CH$14,000-40,000; tours 10am-5pm Tue-Sun) has its own on-site restaurant, and can also prepare picnic baskets.

★ Top Tip

Book your Viña Santa Rita bike or wine trip through **Turistik** (Map p178; 2-2820-1000; https://turistik.com; Municipal Tourist Office, Plaza de Armas s/n, Centro; day pass from CH$23,000; 10am-6pm Mon-Fri; M Plaza de Armas).

outfit. Most wine tours require advance reservations.

Viña Santa Rita

Famous for the premium Casa Real Cabernet, Santa Rita offers bike and wine trips, as well as picnics, tastings and tours of its stunning winery. There's also a jaw-dropping pre-Columbian art collection on display at the on-site Museo Andino, with pottery, textiles and gold Incan jewelry.

Viña Cousiño Macul

A historic **winery** (2-2351-4100; www.cousinomacul.com; Av Quilín 7100, Peñalolen; tours CH$14,000-24,000; English-language tours 11am, 12:15pm, 3pm & 4:15pm Mon-Fri, 10:15am & 11:30am Sat) set in Santiago's urban sprawl. Most of the vineyards are now at Buin, but tours take in the production process and underground *bodega*, built in 1872. La Bicicleta Verde runs frequent bike and wine tours here.

Viña Undurraga

The subterranean *bodegas* at **Undurraga** (2-2372-2850; www.undurraga.cl; Camino a Melipilla, Km34, Talagante; tours from CH$12,000; tours at 10:15am, noon & 3:30pm daily) date from 1885. Come for tours or to try wines by the glass.

Viña de Martino

Reserve ahead for personalized tours and tastings in a Tuscan-style **manor** (2-2577-8037; www.demartino.cl; Manuel Rodríguez 229, Isla de Maipo; tastings from CH$14,000, tours from CH$17,500; 9am-1:30pm & 3-6pm Mon-Fri, 10:30am-1pm Sat), including one where you can blend your own wine. Note: you will need a car to visit this winery.

Termas Valle de Colina

Cajón del Maipo Outdoor Activities

Rich greenery lines the steep, rocky walls of this stunning gorge of the Río Maipo. It's popular on weekends with Santiaguinos, who come here to camp, hike, climb, cycle, raft and ski.

Great For...

☑ Don't Miss

Abundant bird species, foxes and rodents, and the endangered Chilean iguana at Reserva Nacional Río Clarillo.

Rafting

Rutavertical Rafting (cell 9-9435-3143; www.rutavertical.cl; Camino al Volcán 19635, San José de Maipo; trips CH$17,000; daily departures at 11am, 2pm & 4:30pm) has one-hour rafting trips led by enthusiastic multilingual guides that take in some lovely gorges before ending up back in San José de Maipo. Allot about 2½ hours in total for the briefing, outfitting and drive upriver to the starting point. Helmets, wetsuits and lifejackets are provided, and there are lockers to store your belongings.

Monumento Natural El Morado

At Baños Morales you'll find the entrance to **Monumento Natural El Morado** (www.conaf.cl/parques/monumento-natural-el-morado; adult/child CH$5000/2500; must enter 8:30am-1pm & leave by 6pm Oct-Apr, enter

Cascada de las Animas

8:30am-12:30pm & leave by 5:30pm May-Sep), a small national park. From the banks of sparkling Laguna El Morado there are fabulous views of Glaciar San Francisco and the 5000m summit of Cerro El Morado. It takes about two hours to reach the lake on the well-marked 6km trail from the Conaf post.

Reserva Nacional Río Clarillo

A mix of Andean forest and scrubland make up this hilly, 100-sq-km **nature reserve** (www.conaf.cl/parques/reserva-nacional-rio-clarillo; Camino a Reserva Nacional Río Clarillo s/n, Pirque; adult/child CH$6000/3000; ⌚8:30am-6pm) in a scenic tributary canyon of the Cajón del Maipo, 18km southeast of Pirque.

Two short, clearly labeled trails start near the Conaf rangers office, 300m after the entrance: Quebrada Jorquera takes about half an hour; Aliwen Mahuida takes

Need to Know

The Cajón del Maipo starts 25km southeast of Santiago, though it's about 100km to Termas Valle de Colina.

Take a Break

Pizzería y Cervecería Jauría (www.cervezajauria.cl; Bernardo O'Higgins 18; pizzas CH$9000; ⌚5pm-midnight Fri, 1:30pm-1am Sat, 1:30pm to 8pm Sun) serves creative pizzas and satisfying IPAs.

★ Top Tip

November to March is peak rafting season as glacier meltwater brings Class III or IV rapids to the Río Maipo.

1½ hours. The rangers give advice on longer hikes along the river, but plan on starting early as camping is not allowed here.

Cascada de las Animas

Organized activities are the only way to visit this private nature **reserve** (☎2-2861-1303; www.cascadadelasanimas.cl; Camino al Volcan 31087), which takes its name from a stunning waterfall reached by the shortest walk offered (CH$7000); there are also guided half-day hikes into the hills (CH$12,000) and rafting trips (CH$18,000). Horseback riding is the real specialty, however – indeed, the reserve is also a working ranch.

Termas Valle de Colina

At **Termas Valle de Colina** (☎2-2985-2609; www.termasvalledecolina.com; entrance incl camping adult/child CH$8000/4000), scolding hot pools of milky blue water overlook a stark Andean valley. There's a well-organized camping ground with showers, but be sure to bring food and supplies.

SIGHTS

Centro

Museo Chileno de Arte Precolombino Museum

(Chilean Museum of Pre-Columbian Art; Map p178; 2-2928-1500; www.precolombino.cl; Bandera 361, Centro; CH$6000; 10am-6pm Tue-Sun; M Plaza de Armas) Exquisite pottery from most major pre-Columbian cultures is the backbone of Santiago's best museum, the Museo Chileno de Arte Precolombino. As well as dozens of intricately molded anthropomorphic vessels, star exhibits include hefty Maya stone columns, towering Mapuche totems and a fascinating Andean textile display.

Barrio París-Londres Area

(Map p178; cnr París & Londres; M Universidad de Chile) This pocket-sized neighborhood developed on the grounds of the Franciscan convent of Iglesia de San Francisco is made up of two intersecting cobblestone streets, París and Londres, which are lined by graceful European-style town houses built in the 1920s. Look for the memorial at **Londres 38** (Map p178; www.londres38.cl; Barrio Paris-Londres; 10am-1pm & 3-6pm Tue-Fri, 10am-2pm Sat; M Universidad de Chile) FREE, a building that served as a torture center during Augusto Pinochet's government.

...star exhibits include hefty Maya stone columns, towering Mapuche totems...

Centro Cultural Palacio La Moneda Arts Center

(Map p178; 2-2355-6500; www.ccplm.cl; Plaza de la Ciudadanía 26, Centro; exhibitions from CH$3000; 9am-9pm, exhibitions to 7:30pm; ; M La Moneda) Underground art takes on a new meaning in one of Santiago's newer cultural spaces: the Centro Cultural Palacio La Moneda beneath Plaza de la Ciudadanía. A glass-slab roof floods the vaultlike space with natural light, and ramps wind down through the central atrium past the Cineteca Nacional, a state-run art-house movie theater, to two large temporary exhibition spaces that house some of the biggest touring shows to visit Santiago.

Museo Chileno de Arte Precolombino

Barrio Lastarria & Barrio Bellas Artes

Centro Gabriela Mistral Arts Center

(GAM; Map p178; ☎2-2566-5500; www.gam.cl; Av O'Higgins 227, Barrio Lastarria; ⏰plazas 8am-10pm, exhibition spaces 10am-9pm Tue-Sat, from 11am Sun; Ⓜ Universidad Católica) FREE This striking cultural and performing-arts center – named for Chilean poet Gabriela Mistral, the first Latin American woman to win the Nobel Prize in Literature – is an exciting addition to Santiago's art scene, with concerts and performances most days. Drop by to check out the rotating art exhibits on the bottom floor, the iconic architecture that vaults and cantilevers on the inside and looks like a giant rusty cheese grater from the street, the little plazas, murals, cafes and more.

Cerro Santa Lucía Park

(Map p178; entrances cnr Av O'Higgins & Santa Lucía, cnr Santa Lucía & Subercaseaux, Bellas Artes; ⏰9am-6:30pm Mar-Sep, to 8pm Oct-Feb; Ⓜ Santa Lucía) FREE Take a break from the chaos of the Centro with an afternoon stroll through this lovingly manicured park. It was just a rocky hill until 19th-century mayor Benjamín Vicuña Mackenna had it transformed into one of the city's most memorable green spaces.

Museo Nacional de Bellas Artes Museum

(National Museum of Fine Art; Map p178; ☎2-2499-1600; www.mnba.cl; José Miguel de la Barra 650, Barrio Bellas Artes; ⏰10am-6:45pm Tue-Sun; Ⓜ Bellas Artes) FREE This fine art museum is housed in the stately neoclassical Palacio de Bellas Artes, built as part of Chile's centenary celebrations in 1910. The museum features an excellent permanent collection of Chilean art. There are free guided tours starting at 10:30am daily (except January and February, when they begin at noon).

Museo de Artes Visuales Museum

(MAVI, Visual Arts Museum; Map p178; ☎2-2664-9337; www.mavi.cl; Lastarria 307, Plaza Mulato Gil de Castro, Barrio Lastarria; CH$1000, Sun free;

Parque Bicentenario

This gorgeous urban **oasis** (Bicentennial Park; Map p182; Bicentenario 3236, Vitacura; Ⓜ Tobalaba) was created, as the name suggests, in celebration of the Chilean bicentennial. In addition to more than 4000 trees, a peaceful location alongside the Río Mapocho and access to city bike paths, the park features inviting chaise lounges and sun umbrellas, plus state-of-the-art playground equipment for kids.

It's a quick taxi ride from the Tobalaba metro station, or hop on bus 405 and get off at Av Alonso de Córdova (three blocks east of the park).

⏰11am-7pm Tue-Sun; Ⓜ Universidad Católica) Exposed concrete, stripped wood and glass are the materials local architect Cristián Undurraga chose for the stunningly simple Museo de Artes Visuales. The contents of the four open-plan galleries are as impressive as the building: top-notch modern engravings, sculptures, paintings and photography form the regularly changing temporary exhibitions.

Bellavista

La Chascona Historic Building

(Map p178; ☎2-2777-8741; www.fundacionneruda.org; Fernando Márquez de La Plata 0192, Barrio Bellavista; adult/student CH$7000/2500; ⏰10am-7pm Tue-Sun Jan & Feb, to 6pm Tue-Sun Mar-Dec; Ⓜ Baquedano) When poet Pablo Neruda needed a secret hideaway to spend

Santiago Centro

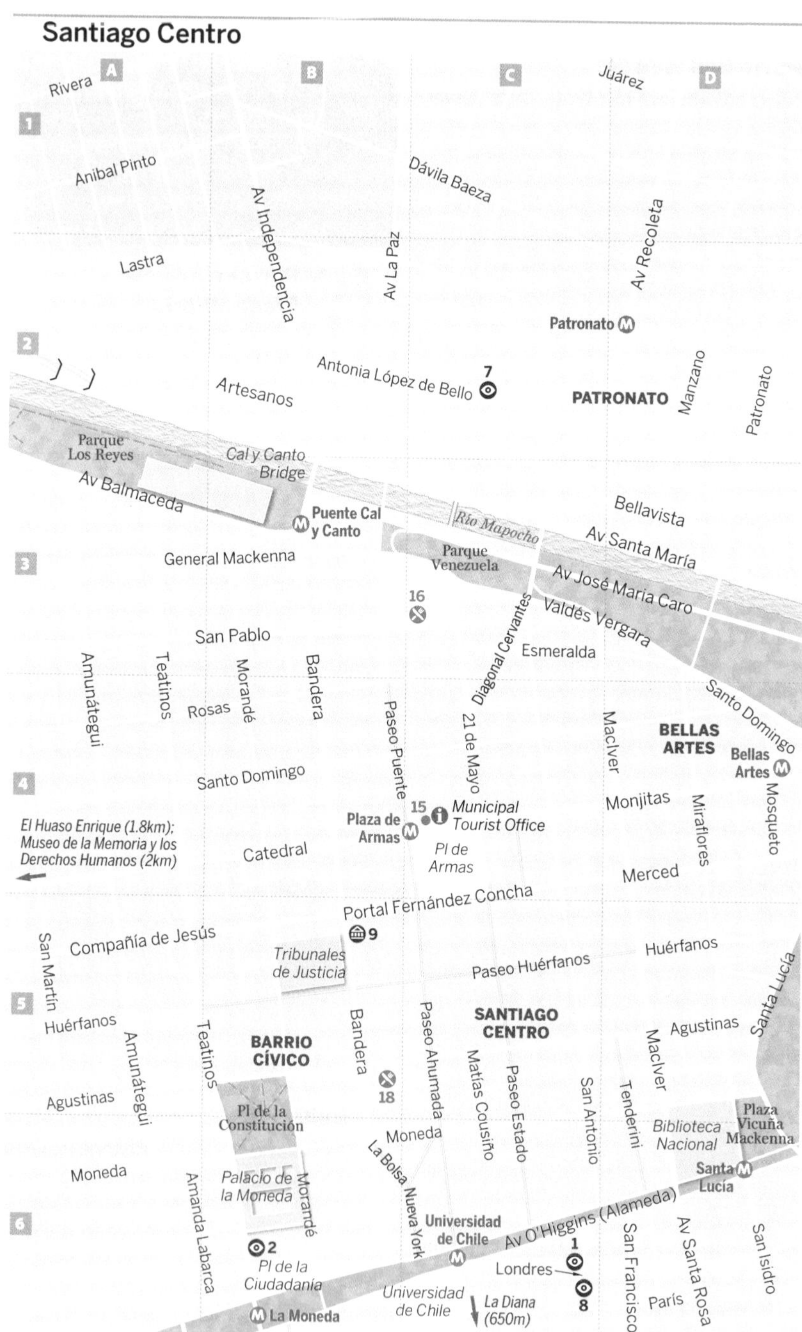

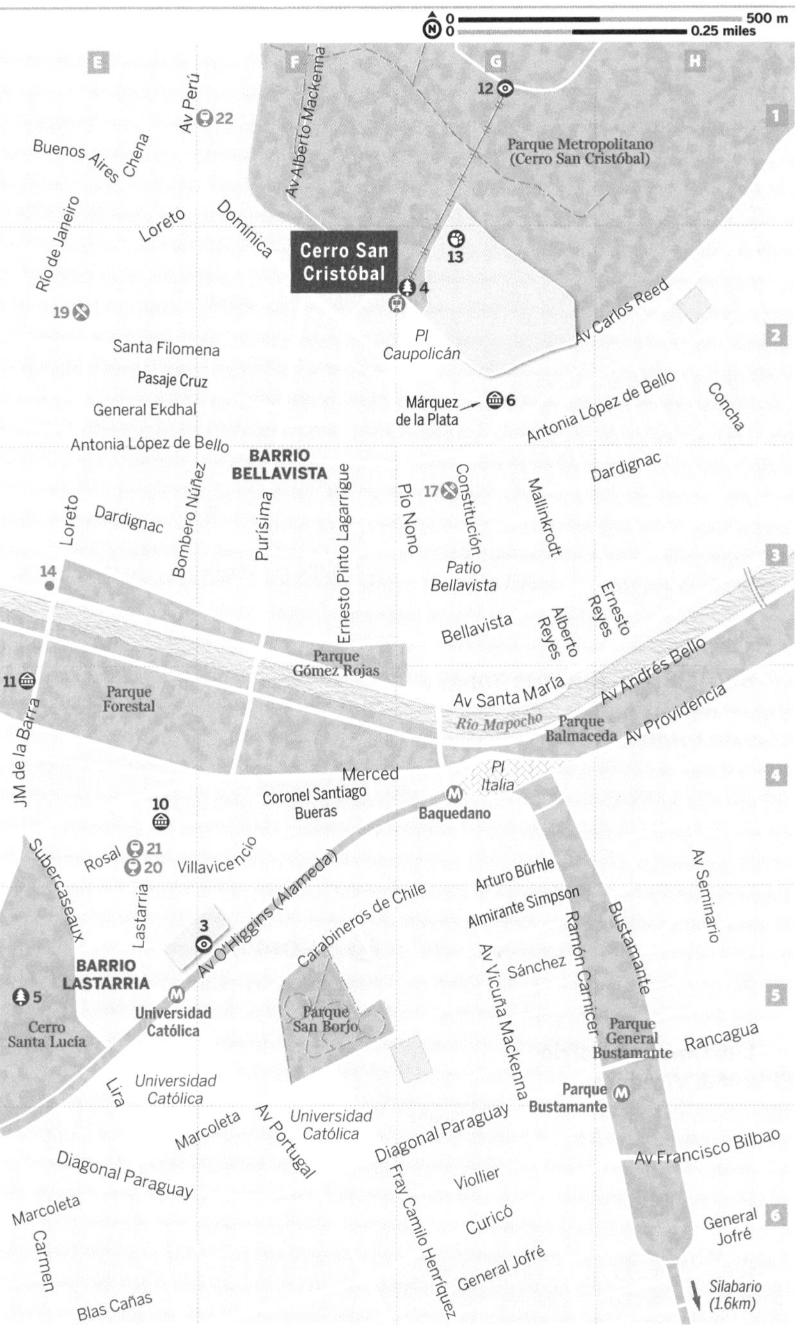
0 500 m
0 0.25 miles
E
F
G
H
1
2
3
4
5
6
Parque Metropolitano (Cerro San Cristóbal)
Cerro San Cristóbal
12
13
4
22
19
17
6
14
11
10
21
20
3
5
Av Perú
Buenos Aires
Chena
Av Alberto Mackenna
Río de Janeiro
Loreto
Domínica
Av Carlos Reed
Pl Caupolicán
Santa Filomena
Pasaje Cruz
General Ekdhal
Antonia López de Bello
Márquez de la Plata
Antonia López de Bello
Concha
BARRIO BELLAVISTA
Dardignac
Loreto
Dardignac
Bombero Núñez
Purísima
Ernesto Pinto Lagarrigue
Pío Nono
Constitución
Mallinkrodt
Patio Bellavista
Ernesto Reyes
Alberto Reyes
Bellavista
Parque Gómez Rojas
Parque Forestal
JM de la Barra
Av Santa María
Av Andrés Bello
Río Mapocho
Parque Balmaceda
Av Providencia
Pl Italia
Merced
Coronel Santiago Bueras
Baquedano
Subercaseaux
Rosal
Villavicencio
Av O'Higgins (Alameda)
Lastarria
Carabineros de Chile
Arturo Bürhle
Almirante Simpson
Av Seminario
Av Vicuña Mackenna
Sánchez
Ramón Carnicer
Bustamante
BARRIO LASTARRIA
Universidad Católica
Cerro Santa Lucía
Parque San Borja
Parque General Bustamante
Rancagua
Lira
Universidad Católica
Parque Bustamante
Marcoleta
Av Portugal
Universidad Católica
Diagonal Paraguay
Av Francisco Bilbao
Diagonal Paraguay
Fray Camilo Henríquez
Viollier
Marcoleta
Curicó
General Jofré
Carmen
General Jofré
Blas Cañas
Silabario (1.6km)

Santiago Centro

Sights

1	Barrio París-Londres	C6
2	Centro Cultural Palacio La Moneda	B6
3	Centro Gabriela Mistral	F5
4	Cerro San Cristóbal	G2
5	Cerro Santa Lucía	E5
6	La Chascona	G2
7	La Vega Central	C2
8	Londres 38	C6
9	Museo Chileno de Arte Precolombino	B5
10	Museo de Artes Visuales	E4
11	Museo Nacional de Bellas Artes	E4
12	Terraza Bellavista	G1
13	Zoológico Nacional	G2

Activities, Courses & Tours

14	La Bicicleta Verde	E3
15	Turistik	C4

Shopping

	Artesanías de Chile	(see 2)

Eating

16	Mercado Central	C3
17	Peumayen	G3
18	Salvador Cocina y Café	B5
19	Vietnam Discovery	E2

Drinking & Nightlife

20	Bocanáriz	E4
21	Chipe Libre	E4
22	Restobar KY	F1

time with his mistress Matilde Urrutia, he built La Chascona, the name loosely translated as 'Messy Hair' and inspired by her unruly curls. Neruda, of course, was a great lover of the sea, so the dining room is modeled on a ship's cabin and the living room on a lighthouse.

Barrio Brasil & Barrio Yungay

Museo de la Memoria y los Derechos Humanos — Museum

(Museum of Memory & Human Rights; Map p169; ☎2-2597-9600; www.museodelamemoria.cl; Matucana 501, Barrio Yungay; 10am-8pm Tue-Sun Jan & Feb, to 6pm Tue-Sun Mar-Dec; M Quinta Normal) FREE Opened in 2010, this striking museum isn't for the faint of heart: the exhibits expose the terrifying human rights violations and large-scale 'disappearances' that took place under Chile's military government between 1973 and 1990.

Las Condes, Barrio El Golf & Vitacura

Museo de la Moda — Museum

(Museum of Fashion; Map p169; ☎2-2219-3623; www.museodelamoda.cl; Av Vitacura 4562, Vitacura; adult/student & senior/child CH$3000/1500/free; 10am-6pm Tue-Fri, 11am-7pm Sat & Sun; M Escuela Militar) This slick, privately operated fashion museum comprises a vast and exquisite permanent collection of Western clothing – 20th-century designers are particularly well represented.

Costanera Center — Notable Building

(Map p182; ☎2-2916-9226; www.costanera center.cl; Av Andrés Bello 2425, Providencia; 10am-10pm; M Tobalaba) The four skyscrapers that make up Costanera Center include **Gran Torre Santiago**, the tallest building in Latin America (300m). The complex also contains offices, a high-end hotel and the largest shopping mall in South America. Head to **Sky Costanera** (Map p182; www.skycostanera.cl; adult/child CH$15,000/10,000; 10am-10pm; M Tobalaba) for panoramic views from the top of Gran Torre.

SHOPPING

Artesanías de Chile — Arts & Crafts

(Map p178; ☎2-2697-2784; www.artesaniasde chile.cl; Plaza de la Ciudadanía 26, Centro Cultural Palacio La Moneda, Centro; 9:30am-7:30pm Mon-Fri, 10:30am-7pm Sat & Sun; M La Moneda) Not only do this foundation's jewelry, wood carvings, ceramics and naturally dyed textiles sell at reasonable prices, most of what you pay goes directly to the artisans who made them. Look for other locations at Los Dominicos and the airport, as well as towns throughout Chile.

Pueblito Los Dominicos Arts & Crafts
(Los Dominicos Handicraft Village; www.plosdominicos.cl; Av Apoquindo 9085, Las Condes; 10:30am-7pm Tue-Sun; M Los Dominicos) The best place in Santiago to buy quality gifts that were actually made in Chile. This mock village houses dozens of small stores, art galleries and traditional cafes. Look for lapis lazuli jewelry, Andean textiles, carved wooden bowls and ceramics with indigenous motifs.

Galería Drugstore Fashion & Accessories
(Map p182; www.drugstore.cl; Av Providencia 2124, Providencia; shops 11am-8pm Mon-Fri, to 6:30pm Sat; M Los Leones) Head to this cool three-story independent shopping center for clothes no one back home will have – it has tiny boutiques of several up-and-coming designers, arty bookstores and cafes.

EATING

Mercado Central Seafood $
(Central Market; Map p178; www.mercadocentral.cl; cnr 21 de Mayo & San Pablo, Centro; food stands & restaurants 9am-5pm Mon-Fri, 7am-3:30pm Sat & Sun; M Puente Cal y Canto) Santiago's wrought-iron fish market is a classic for seafood lunches (and hangover-curing fish stews like the tomato- and potato-based *caldillo de congrio*, Pablo Neruda's favorite). Skip the touristy restaurants in the middle and head for one of the tiny low-key stalls around the market's periphery.

Salvador Cocina y Café Chilean $$
(Map p178; www.facebook.com/SalvadorCocinaYCafe; Bombero Ossa 1059, Centro; mains CH$7700; 8am-8:30pm Mon-Fri; M Universidad de Chile) This no-frills two-story lunch spot packs a surprising punch with market-focused menus that change daily and highlight unsung dishes (and exotic meats) from the Chilean countryside. Chef Rolando Ortega won Chile's coveted chef of the year award in 2015 and the tables have been packed ever since.

Santiago's wrought-iron fish market is a classic for seafood lunches...

Paila marina (seafood soup), Mercado Central

Las Condes & Providencia

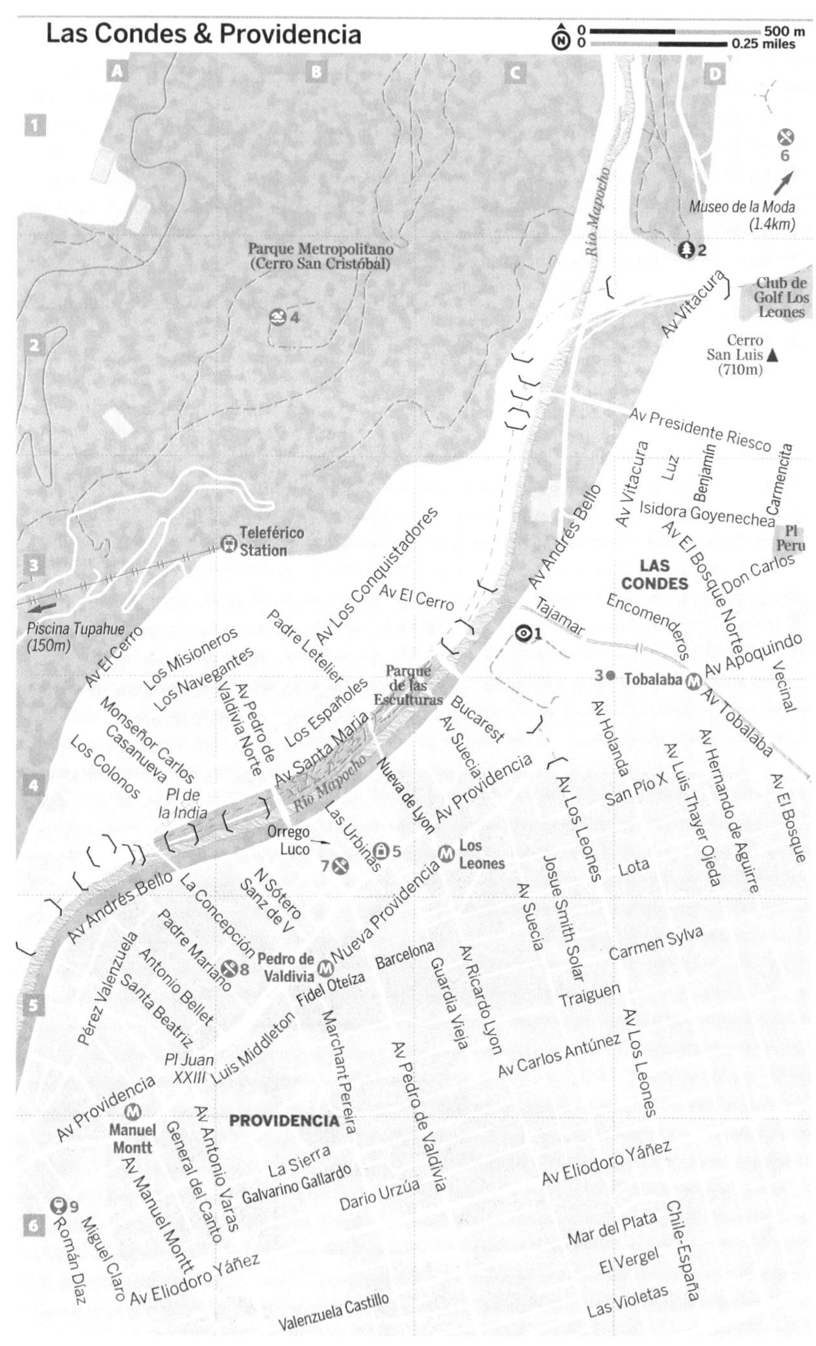

Las Condes & Providencia

La Diana Chilean $$
(2-2632-8823; www.ladiana.cl; Arturo Prat 435, Centro; mains CH$6000-8500; 1pm-12:30am Tue-Sat, to 6:30pm Sun; M Universidad de Chile) Attached to a children's arcade of the same name and built within the walls of an old monastery, La Diana defies easy description. Its ceilings are adorned with as many potted plants as chandeliers, its tables are a mishmash of found furnishings, and its menu is as notable for grilled seafood as it is for seafood-packed pizzas.

Silabario Chilean $$
(2-2502-5429; www.facebook.com/Silabarioficial; Lincoyan 920, Barrio Italia; mains CH$6000-9500; 7-11:30pm Tue-Fri, 1-4:30pm & 7pm-midnight Sat, 1-4:30pm Sun; M Irarrázaval) Tucked away in an old home just south of Barrio Italia's main drag, this intimate restaurant re-envisions staples from the Chilean countryside as gourmet dishes. From northern quinoa salads to hearty Mapuche stews from the south, each culinary journey ends with a complimentary homemade *bajativo* (digestif).

Holm Cafe $$
(Map p182; cell 9-4227-4411; https://holmcomidafeliz.cl; Padre Mariano 125, Providencia; meals CH$5000-7500; 9am-10pm Mon-Fri, 10am-4pm Sat & Sun; ; M Pedro de Valdivia) Santiaguinos flock to this homey Providencia cafe each weekend for the best brunches in town. Fresh-baked breads and jams, yogurt and granola or scrambled eggs with crispy bacon are but a few of the offerings. Salads, sandwiches and fresh fruit juices round out the midweek fare.

El Huerto Cafe $$
(Map p182; 2-2231-4443; www.elhuerto.cl; Orrego Luco 054, Providencia; mains CH$6000-8000; noon-11pm Mon-Sat, 12:30-4:30pm Sun; ; M Pedro de Valdivia) This earthy restaurant's healthy, vegetarian fare is a big hit with both hip young things and ladies who lunch. Come for seaweed ceviches, fresh fruit juices, quinoa salads and wonderfully rich desserts.

Peumayen Chilean $$$
(Map p178; www.peumayenchile.cl; Constitución 134, Barrio Bellavista; tasting menu CH$12,500; 1-3pm & 7pm-midnight Tue-Sat, 1-4pm Sun; M Baquedano) Without a doubt one of the most unusual culinary experiences in Chile,

El Huaso Enrique

Going strong in Barrio Yungay for almost 60 years, **El Huaso Enrique** (2-2681-5257; www.elhuasoenrique.cl; Maipú 462, Barrio Yungay; cover CH$2500-3000; 7pm-2am Wed-Sun; M Quinta Normal) is the best place to see Chileans performing their national dance, *la cueca*. You can watch proud locals hit the dance floor while you feast on hearty regional dishes like *pastel de choclo* (a casserole-like dish consisting of baked corn, meat and onions). The place comes alive on weekends with live music. If you really want to get into the spirit, El Huaso Enrique also offers *cueca* lessons; check out the website for details.

Barrio Recoleta

Bustling Korean eateries and Middle Eastern takeout counters, a happening marketplace overflowing with ripe fruit, a colorful jumble of street vendors, an achingly hip cocktail lounge – this burgeoning barrio just west of Bellavista is a slight detour off the beaten path. Here are a few spots you shouldn't miss.

Restobar KY (Map p178; 2-2777-7245; www.restobarky.cl; Av Perú 631, Barrio Recoleta; 8pm-2am Tue-Sat; Cerro Blanco) Set in a rambling old house, this stunning cocktail bar is a mix of glowing Chinese lanterns, antique chandeliers, carved wooden furnishings and vibrant artwork.

La Vega Central (Map p178; www.lavega.cl; cnr Nueva Rengifo & Antonia López de Bello, Barrio Recoleta; 6am-6pm Mon-Sat, 7am-2pm Sun; Patronato) Raspberries, quinces, figs, peaches, persimmons, custard apples…if it grows in Chile you'll find it at this buzzing market.

Vietnam Discovery (Map p178; 2-2737-2037; www.vietnamdiscovery.cl; Loreto 324, Barrio Recoleta; mains CH$7000-11,000; 1pm-midnight Mon-Sat, to 4pm Sun; ; Patronato) Run by a hip French-Vietnamese couple, this lavishly designed eatery serves creative Thai and Vietnamese dishes. Book ahead, using the online form, or you'll never see the inside.

La Vega Central
JEREMYRICHARDS / SHUTTERSTOCK ©

this upstart is innovating Chilean cuisine by looking back to the culinary roots of the Mapuche, Rapa Nui and Atacameños.

Boragó Chilean $$$

(Map p182; 2-2953-8893; www.borago.cl; Av Nueva Costanera 3467, Vitacura; tasting menu from CH$50,000; 7-11:15pm Mon-Sat) Chef Rodolfo Guzman earned a coveted spot among the World's 50 Best Restaurants by elevating Chilean cuisine to new heights at this Vitacura restaurant, whose minimalist design forces you to focus on the food. The multicourse tasting menus, which include little-known endemic ingredients, sweep you away on an unforgettable culinary adventure from the Atacama to Patagonia. Reserve well in advance.

DRINKING & NIGHTLIFE

Bocanáriz Wine Bar

(Map p178; 2-2638-9893; www.bocanariz.cl; Lastarria 276, Barrio Lastarria; 12:30pm-midnight Mon-Sat, 7-11:30pm Sun; Bellas Artes) You won't find a better wine list anywhere in Chile than at this homey restobar whose servers are trained sommeliers. Try creative wine flights (themed by region or style) or sample several top bottles by the glass. There are also meat and cheese plates, as well as hearty Chilean dishes (mains CH$8000 to CH$12,000). Reservations recommended.

Chipe Libre Cocktail Bar

(Map p178; 2-2664-0584; Lastarria 282, Barrio Lastarria; 12:30pm-12:30am Mon-Wed, to 1am Thu-Sat; Bellas Artes) Learn about the big sour over *pisco* – and who made it first – at the only bar in Santiago dedicated to the South American brandy. There are as many *piscos* from Peru as Chile on the menu and you can try them in flights of three or within an array of flavored sours. Reserve ahead for tables on the interior patio.

Santo Remedio Cocktail Bar

(Map p182; www.santoremedio.cl; Román Díaz 152, Providencia; 1-3:30pm & 6pm-2am Mon-Fri, 6pm-2am Sat; Manuel Montt) Strictly speaking, this low-lit and spectacularly funky old house is a restaurant, and an aphrodisiacal one at that. But it's the bar action people really come for: powerful, well-mixed

Plaza de Armas metro station

cocktails and regular live DJs keep the 20- and 30-something crowds happy.

 INFORMATION

Municipal Tourist Office (Map p178; www.santiagocapital.cl; Plaza de Armas s/n, Centro; 9am-6pm Mon-Fri, to 4pm Sat & Sun; M Plaza de Armas) Well-meaning but under-resourced staff provide basic maps and information. There's also a small gallery and a shop with Chilean products.

 GETTING THERE & AWAY

AIR

Chile's main air hub for both national and domestic flights is Aeropuerto Internacional Arturo Merino Benítez (p402), 16km west of central Santiago.

BUS

Bus services leave from four different terminals, though you'll find countrywide services at these terminals:

Terminal de Buses Sur (Terminal Santiago; Av O'Higgins 3850, Barrio Estación Central; M Universidad de Santiago) Santiago's largest terminal (aka Terminal Santiago) serves destinations south of Santiago as well as a few northbound buses, and many international services.

Terminal de Buses Alameda (cnr Av O'Higgins & Jotabeche, Barrio Estación Central; M Universidad de Santiago) Next door to Terminal de Buses Sur, buses here run to destinations all over Chile.

 GETTING AROUND

The city's ever-expanding **metro** (www.metro.cl; per ride from CH$630; 6am-11pm Mon-Fri, from 6:30am Sat, from 8am Sun) is a clean and efficient way of getting about. Services on its six interlinking lines are frequent, but often painfully crowded.

THE LAKES DISTRICT, CHILE

In this Chapter

The Lakes District, Chile

The Lakes District – named 'Los Lagos' for its myriad glacial lakes that dot a countryside otherwise characterized by looming, snowcapped volcanoes, otherworldly national parks and serene lakeside villages – is one of Chile's most picturesque regions. Outdoor adventurers congregate around pretty Puerto Varas, the region's most touristy town and the jumping-off point for most of the area's attractions. Go horseback riding or rock climbing in the Río Cochamó Valley, linger around Lagos Llanquihue, Puyehue or Todos los Santos, or flashpack through any number of impressive national parks.

Two Days in the Lakes District

Start off with a whitewater rafting adventure on Río Petrohué with **Al Sur** (p191). In the evening enjoy a first-rate meal and microbrews in Puerto Varas.

On day two, hit the trails on a memorable mountain-bike ride that takes in volcanic scenery and lake views with **La Comarca Puelo Adventure** (p191).

Four Days in the Lakes District

On days three and four, make a trip to the Huilliche Communities on the Osorno Coast. Spend the first night in the picturesque **Altos de Pichi Mallay** (p195) in San Juan de la Costa, then head to gorgeous Caleta Cóndor for outdoor adventures (and a memorable homestay) with **Caleta Cóndor Expediciones** (p195).

Previous page: Puerto Varas (p197) with views of Lago Llanquihue and Volcán Osorno

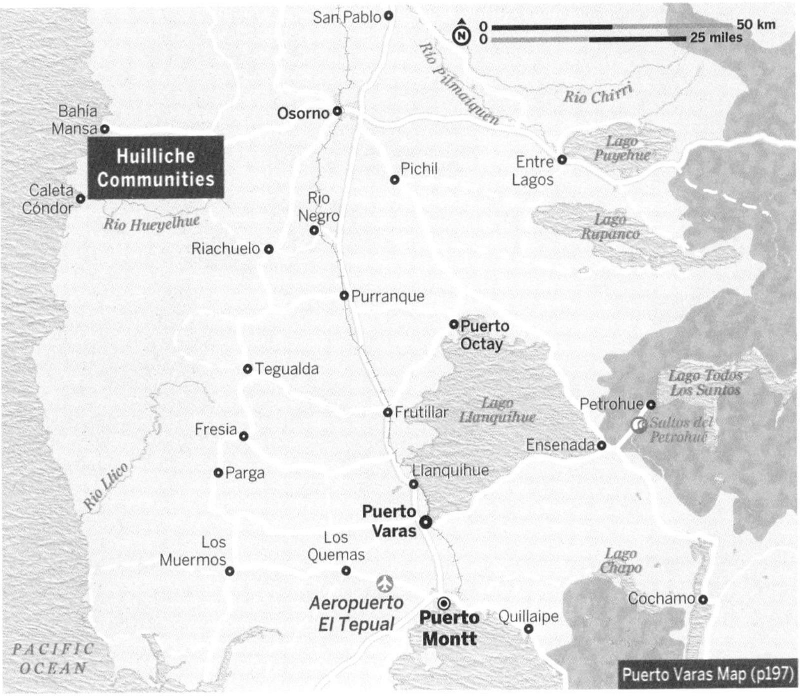

Puerto Varas Map (p197)

Arriving in the Lakes District

Puerto Montt's **Aeropuerto El Tepual** (www.aeropuertoeltepual.cl), located 22km southwest of Puerto Varas, is Sur Chico's busiest airport and its main gateway for those arriving by air.

Puerto Montt's **bus terminal** (www.terminalpm.cl) is also the region's busiest and biggest, serving major Chilean cities. The city also has a seaport for destinations deeper into Patagonia.

Where to Stay

With such an abundance of gorgeous lakes, one might expect lakeside accommodations to be the main event in Los Lagos, but there are plenty more options from which to choose. Puerto Varas leads the way – from excellent hostels to high-design boutique hotels, there is something for everyone in PV. Elsewhere you'll find family-run guesthouses, adventure-centric camping and *cabañas*.

Kayaking on Futaleufú River

Adrenalin Activities

You'll find adventure aplenty in Chile's stunning Lakes District. You can go rafting, kayaking, mountain biking, volcano trekking, horseback riding and skiing amid some of the country's most majestic scenery.

Great For...

☑ Don't Miss

Whitewater rafting Class III and IV rapids on the Río Petrohué.

Climbing Volcanoes

Summiting Osorno or Calbuco volcanoes on a tour runs CH$200,000 for one person, but it drops to CH$180,000 per person thereafter and includes transport, all meals, overnight in a mountain retreat, all technical equipment, insurance and bilingual guide. No experience is necessary.

Moyca Expediciones (☎cell 9-7790-5679; www.facebook.com/moycaexpediciones; San José 192, oficina 203; ⏰10am-2pm & 3-7pm, shorter hr winter) is the go-to outfitter in Puerto Varas, but the three companies that climb all share the same 10 or so guides. Independent climbers must obtain **Conaf** (☎65-248-6115; www.conaf.cl; Ochagavía 458; ⏰9am-1pm & 2:30-5:45pm Mon-Thu, to 4:30pm Fri) permission, but this is not recommended unless you are a highly trained technical mountaineer.

Hiker in Puerto Montt

BENJAMIN WU / EYEEM / GETTY IMAGES ©

Need to Know

Puerto Varas is the region's most touristy town and the jumping-off point for many adventures.

Take a Break

After a day of adventure, kick back with a microbrew at Chester Beer Brewing Company (p199).

★ Top Tip

Be sure to bring a waterproof and windproof jacket, and bring ample layers for cooler weather.

Mountain Biking

La Comarca Puelo Adventure (cell 9-9799-1920; www.pueloadventure.cl; Av Vicente Pérez Rosales 1621) specializes in dramatic and custom-tailored adventure trips to less-explored areas of the Río Puelo Valley, Río Cochamó Valley and beyond. Highlights include extensive mountain-bike and road-cycling holidays in Chile and Argentina (including an epic 12-day single-track ride from Bariloche to Puerto Varas); beer-sluggin' and biking; and a wine-and-cheese excursion to the 900m viewpoint at Arco Iris in La Junta.

The Bike & Beer tour is a good-fun 30km bike ride along the lake, culminating in craft-brew tasting at Chester Beer (p199). Groups are never more than 12 strong and everyone here is dedicated to giving travelers a unique off-the-beaten-path experience. Also rents road bikes, full-suspension mountain bikes and e-bikes.

Rafting & Kayaking

Al Sur (65-223-2300; www.alsurexpeditions.com; cnr Aconcagua & Imperial) specializes in rafting – with an exclusive base camp on the banks of the Río Petrohué – and also does high-end, multiday kayaking trips within the fjords of Parque Pumalín, all with a heavy focus on environmental NGOs. Also inquire about their epic one-month Top to Bottom trip, a trekking, rafting, fishing and driving tour from San Pedro de Atacama to Torres del Paine.

Ko'Kayak (65-223-3004; www.kokayak.cl; San Pedro 311; 8:30am-7pm) is another long-standing favorite for half-day rafting trips, as well as one-and two-day sea kayaking trips.

Yak Expediciones (cell 9-8332-0574; www.yakexpediciones.cl) is a fan favorite for both short and multiday sea-kayaking trips on Lago Todos Los Santos, Reloncaví fjord and beyond.

Other Adventures

A bit of a renegade cowboy, guide-of-all-trades **Guillermo Duarte** (cell 9-7952-4279; www.facebook.com/guillermoduartetravel) can get you on the trails, horseback, up the volcano or on cross-country skies, but where he really excels is with bespoke tours – no adventure is too outrageous. Prices run around CH$160,000 per day for his services plus vehicle – the itinerary is left to your wildest dreams. Spanish, English, French and Portuguese spoken.

OpenTravel (☎65-226-0524; www.opentravel.cl) offers off-the-beaten-path trekking and horseback riding to remote areas in northern Patagonia and across the Andes to Argentina, including remote Argentine-French retreats on Isla Las Bandurrias in Lago Las Rocas and multiday horseback-riding/cultural-farmstay trips between Argentina and Chile.

Trekking

Co-run by a young, enthusiastic climber from Osorno, **Patagonia Expeditions** (☎cell 9-9104-8061; www.anticura.com; Ruta Internacional 215, Km90) operates the concession on Centro Turístico Anticura. Short hikes – trail fee CH$1000 – from the visitors center include Salto de Princesa, Salto del Indio – where, according to legend, a lone Mapuche hid to escape *encomienda* (colonial labor system) service in a nearby Spanish gold mine – and Repucura, which ends back up on Ruta 215 (buses come careening down the highway; walk on the opposite side).

There's also a 4km steep hike up to a lookout point.

Excursions from here include climbing Volcán Casablanca (1960m; CH$40,000); Volcán Puyehue (2240m; CH$55,000, or CH$90,000 along with the 2011 Puyehue eruption crater), nocturnal waterfall visits and multiday treks. A restaurant serves three meals a day (CH$5000 to CH$9000).

Río Petrohué and Volcán Osorno in the background

Saltos del Petrohué

Six kilometers southwest of Petrohué, the **Saltos del Petrohué** (www.conaf.cl/parques/parque-nacional-vicente-perez-rosales; adult/child Chilean CH$2000/1000, foreigner CH$4000/2000; ⏰9am-6pm) is a rushing, frothing waterfall raging through a narrow volcanic rock canyon carved by lava. Anyone wondering why the rafting trips don't start from the lake will find the answer here, although experienced kayakers have been known to take it on. Parking is CH$1000.

An excellent new visitors center houses a cafe and handicrafts shops. Try to arrive in the sweet spot between 9am and 9:15am before the TurisTour day-tour bus unloads the masses.

☑ When to Go

Hiking and aquatic sports are best from December to March, while June to mid-October is the skiing season.

MONA F / GETTY IMAGES ©

Skiing

If you come from mid-June to mid-October, you can hit the ski slopes! The **Centro de Esquí Antillanca** (☎64-261-2070; www.antillanca.cl; Ruta U-485; lift tickets CH$35,000, full rentals adult/child CH$33,000/22,000) has five surface lifts and 460m of vertical drop. The resort includes a pricey hotel (two buildings, Hotel Eduardo Meyer and Refugio Carlos) open year-round with typical ski-resort trimmings. There is a full-service restaurant at the resort's lodge (mains CH$6000 to CH$12,000).

Further south, the **Centro de Ski y Montaña Volcán Osorno** (☎cell 9-9158-7337; www.volcanosorno.com; Ruta V-555, Km12, Volcán Osorno; half-/full-day lift tickets CH$20,000/26,000; ⏰10am-5:30pm) has two lifts for skiing and sightseeing and has recently undergone an expansion of its restaurant and rental shop. It has ski and snowboard rentals (full packages CH$20,000) and food services on the mountain year-round. There's also a tubing park – fun for kids and adults alike (from CH$15,000).

Expanded summer options include taking the ski lift up for impossibly scenic views at 1420m (CH$12,000) or 1670m (CH$16,000). You can descend a little faster via zip lines (CH$12,000).

Stand-up Paddling

Stand-up paddle boarding (SUP) enthusiast Eduardo offers sunset excursions on Laguna Escondida, advanced trips on the Río Petrohué, an eight-day paddling extravaganza through the Río Puelo Valley, SUP surf trips on the coast), classes, yoga retreats and rentals.

★ Bariloche Bound

You can make an adventurous crossing by buses and boats from Puerto Varas to Bariloche, Argentina, with Cruce Andino (www.cruceandino.com).

Maicolpué on Osorno's cc

Visiting Huilliche Communities

Along Osorno's gorgeous coast, you can immerse yourself in indigenous Huilliche communities. On multiday treks, you can take in stunning beaches and Valdivian forest treks, while lodging in rural homestays.

Great For...

☑ Don't Miss

A trekking, kayaking or horseback riding adventure with Caleta Cóndor Expediciones (p195).

San Juan de la Costa

In San Juan de la Costa, a series of five magnificent *caletas* (coves) – Pucatrihue, Maicolpué, Bahía Mansa, Manzano and Tril-Tril are the jumping off point for Caleta Cóndor.

Popular hikes include the 10km round-trip jaunt from Maicolpué to Playa Tril-Tril (also reachable by car) and, from Pucatrihue, a 16km round-trip to Caleta Manzano (reachable within 1km, by 4WD only). Boat trips (CH$10,000 per person, minimum three) to visit a penguin colony are also offered. At sunset, surfers even hit the waves in Maicolpué.

Caleta Cóndor

Caleta Cóndor, part of the protected indigenous zone of Territorio Mapa Lahual, is an impossibly gorgeous bay almost completely

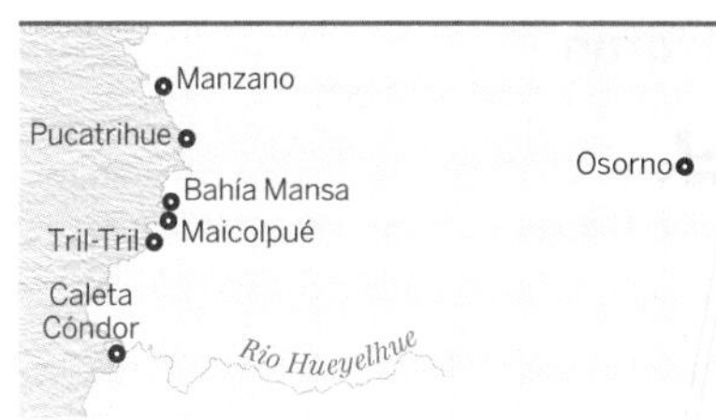

Need to Know

The easiest way to get to Caleta Cóndor is via two-hour boat ride from Bahía Mansa.

Take a Break

Enjoy scrumptious seafood with bay views from the outdoor patio at **Glorymar** (cell 9-8299-8587; Costanera Bahía Mansa s/n, Bahía Mansa; mains CH$5900-12,900; 10am-9pm, to 8pm Sun, shorter hr winter).

★ Top Tip

If arriving by boat, be sure to take preventatives for seasickness!

off the grid. If the weather is clear, arriving here is miraculous. As you enter via the scenic and translucent Río Cholguaco from the Pacific, you are greeted with idyllic moss-strewn riverbanks, horses and seabirds, and hillsides peppered with arrayán trees, with a small community (20 or so families – all running on solar power) living in this piece of paradise. It all culminates at the river's end on a sublime ocean beach.

Caleta Cóndor Expediciones

Besides gawking at scenery, kayaking, diving, trekking, and horseback riding are the main activities in Caleta Cóndor. Locally owned and operated **Caleta Cóndor Expediciones** (cell 9-9773-6383; www.caletacondorexpediciones.cl) is the go-to agency to set things up and connect travelers with providers.

Rural Homestays

Perched high above Maicolpué beach in Maicolpué Río Sur, the **Altos de Pichi Mallay** (64-255-4165; raicesrestaurant1@gmail.com; Maicolpué Río Sur camino a Tril Tril, Maicolpué Río Sur; campsites/r per person CH$5000/25,000; P) is family-run paradise with 12 cozy guest rooms, most with panoramic sea views. There's also a six-person, wood-fired hot tub nestled in the forest with a jaw-dropping ocean view.

Imagine free-range horses, sheep and cows grazing in front of one of South America's most perfect Pacific beaches and you have an idea what's in the front yard of the purpose-built **Hostal Caleta Cóndor** (9-9382-4035; www.caletacondorexpediciones.cl; Caleta Cóndor; r per person without bathroom incl breakfast CH$18,000, meals CH$5000). Sleeps 13.

Osorno

Osorno is a bustling place and the commercial engine for the surrounding agricultural zone. Though it's an important transportation hub on the route between Puerto Montt and Santiago and the Huilliche communities of the Osorno coast, most visitors spend little time here, though Osorno now harbors a handful of cool cafes, good restaurants and quality brewpubs.

EATING

Mercado Municipal Chilean $
(cnr Prat & Errázuriz; 6am-9pm) Large and modern Mercado Municipal has an array of *cocinerías* (lunch stalls) serving good and inexpensive food.

Café Central Cafe $
(O'Higgins 610; sandwiches CH$1950-6500; 8am-midnight Mon-Sat, noon-10pm Sun) This bi-level plaza hot spot is more or less a Chilean diner, crowded for its decent coffee, colossal burgers, ridiculous sandwiches and hot dogs *completísimo* (sauerkraut, avocado, mayo). There's also a counter – convenient for solo travelers.

Parque Nacional Vicente Pérez Rosales

In this park of celestial lakes and soaring volcanoes, **Lago Todos Los Santos** and **Volcán Osorno** may be the standouts, but they're actually just part of a crowd. One lake leads to the next and volcanoes dominate the skyline on all sides of this storied pass through the Andes range. The needlepoint of **Volcán Puntiagudo** (2493m) lurks to the north and craggy **Monte Tronador** (3491m) marks the Argentine border to the east.

Established in 1926, the 2510-sq-km Pérez Rosales was Chile's first national park. Get park info and pick up maps from **Conaf's visitors center** (65-221-2036; www.conaf.cl; Laguna Verde; 8:30am-5:30pm Sun-Thu, to 4:30pm Fri).

Panca Peruvian $$
(64-223-2924; Rodríguez 1905; mains CH$5500-12,000; 12:30-3pm & 8-11:30pm Mon-Sat, 12:30-3:30pm Sun;) You'll be as surprised as we were about how authentic the classic Peruvian dishes at this hip newcomer are, considering the Peruvian side of this Chilean-Peruvian partnership handles the finances, not the food. Spicy ceviche, *chaufa* (Peruvian-Chinese fried rice), *ají de gallina* (spicy creamed chicken), *lomo saltado* (marinated steak) – it's all pretty perfect.

El Galpón Steak $$$
(64-223-4098; www.hotelwaeger.cl; Cochrane 816; steaks CH$13,000-18,500; 12:30-3pm & 7:30-11pm Mon-Sat;) Tucked away around the side of Hotel Waeger, you'll find dark flooring and a rustic, barnyard vibe (old-school metallic buckets as lampshades) complementing the main event: perfectly grilled steaks for devout carnivores, on a *parrilla* piled high with wood, like a fireplace. The fillets are superthick and the potent pisco sours often outrun the wine.

DRINKING & NIGHTLIFE

Cervecería Artesanal Armin Schmid Microbrewery
(cell 9-8294-1818; Ruta 215, Km12; beer CH$2300-3300, pizzas CH$8100; 1:30-10:30pm Tue-Sat) If you're within 100km of Osorno and a beer lover, you'll want to readjust your itinerary to visit this improvised temple of suds. It's the south's most interesting craft brewery, located 12km outside of Osorno on Ruta 215 toward Entre Lagos and the border with Argentina.

Gallardía Gastropub
(www.facebook.com/gallardia.sg; O'Higgins 1270; 6pm-1am Mon, 1pm-1am Tue-Sat, 1-6pm Sun;) Occupying a traditional Osorno residence, Gallardía is a rooster-adorned enclave for craft beers (Kross, along with Belgian, Dutch, Spanish and German selections), cocktails made with Patagonia's very own hipster craft spirit Trä·kál (born in Osorno; CH$5000) and a battery of slang-named gourmet sandwiches that

hit the spot when buzzed (CH$5000 to CH$7300). It's where the cool kids go.

Taberna Pirata Bar

(www.facebook.com/tabernapirata; MacKenna 1873; 6pm-3am Mon-Sat;) The quirkily themed Pirata is vaguely divey and catering to bohemian locals in the know. It's the city's best for craft beer, with 10 taps flowing in summer (weekends only otherwise), which are a mix of house brews and Chilean micro/nanobrews from Valdivia and Puerto Varas (along with a West Coast USA–heavy bottle list).

Puerto Varas

Two menacing, snowcapped volcanoes, Osorno and Calbuco, stand sentinel over picturesque Puerto Varas and its scenic Lago Llanquihue like soldiers of adventure, allowing only those on a high-octane quest to pass. Just 23km from Puerto Montt but worlds apart in charm, scenery and options for the traveler, Puerto Varas is the region's destination for outdoor adventure sports.

Puerto Varas

Activities, Courses & Tours

1 Al Sur C3
2 Ko'Kayak B2
3 Moyca Expediciones B2

Shopping

4 Fundación Artesanías de Chile B3

Eating

5 Costumbrista B2
6 El Humedal B1

Drinking & Nightlife

7 Caffé El Barista B2

SIGHTS

Paseo Patrimonial — Architecture

Many notable constructions in town are private houses from the early 20th century. Grab a city map at the tourist office to follow the **Paseo Patrimonial**, a walking tour of historic homes listed as Monumentos Nacionales. Several of these houses serve as *hospedajes*, including the 1941–42 **Casa Schwerter** (Del Carmen 873), the 1930 **Casa Hitschfeld** (Prat 107) and the 1930 **Casa Wetzel** (O'Higgins 608).

SHOPPING

Fundación Artesanías de Chile — Arts & Crafts

(www.artesaniasdechile.cl; Del Salvador 109; 9am-9pm Mon-Sat, 10:30am-7pm Sun) A not-for-profit foundation offering beautiful Mapuche textiles as well as high-quality jewelry and ceramics from all over southern Chile.

EATING

Costumbrista — Chilean $

(cell 9-6237-2801; Del Salvador 547B; mains CH$5000-6000; 1-4pm & 7-9:30pm Mon-Sat;) This little, unassuming Chiloé-inspired eatery is Puerto Varas' secret gourmet *cocinería* (kitchen). It's a two-man, eight-table show among aqua clapboard walls with a limited menu of fish and heartier dishes – a perfect pork chop, osso buco, a beautiful salmon or *meluza* (hake) – and is executed with skill and results that completely outshine its extraordinary-value price range.

La Gringa — American $

(Imperial 605; mains CH$4800-11,900; 8am-11pm Mon-Fri, 9am-11pm Sat;) Evoking the rainy-day cafes of the American Pacific Northwest, this charming spot run by an adorable Seattleite dishes up scrumptious house-produced bread and pastries, hearty sandwiches (such as pulled pork with cabbage) and refreshing main courses (barbecue baby back ribs with spicy austral-pepper mash) along with standout CH$7300 *menús* (fixed-price menus; 1pm to 4pm except February).

From left: Chilean blankets and ponchos; Enchiladas; Brewing espresso; Río Cochamó Valley

HOLGER LEUE / GETTY IMAGES ©

El Humedal Fusion $$

(☎65-223-6382; www.humedal.cl; Turismo 145; mains CH$7000-11,000; ⏰12:30-11pm Tue-Sat, to 5pm Sun; 📶) In an adorable and cozy home perched on a hilltop over town, El Humedal (oddly, it means 'Wetland') serves up one of the best lunches in Puerto Varas with its interpretations of Asian curries and stir-fries, Mexican enchiladas and burritos, ramen bowls, and fish and chips, among others. Desserts are scrumptious as well.

DRINKING & NIGHTLIFE

Chester Beer Brewing Company Microbrewery

(www.chesterbeer.cl; Línea Nueva 93, Campo Molino Viejo; pints CH$2500; ⏰10am-5pm Mon-Fri, noon-7pm Sat) American nanobrewer 'Chester' (real name Derek Way) has been at it since 2006, long before 'craft' was a thing in Chile. His rustic but epic countryside brewery – fashioned from shipping containers – is a true makeshift beervana, with four taps dedicated to experimental one-offs and all of his staples in bottles (IPA, summer ale, APA and stout).

Caffé El Barista Cafe

(www.elbarista.cl; Martínez 211; coffee CH$1400-3200; ⏰8am-1am Mon-Thu, to 2am Fri & Sat, noon-1pm Sun, shorter hours winter; 📶) This stylish Italian-style coffeehouse serves Sur Chico's best espresso from its La Marzocco machine, and draws a healthy breakfast and lunch crowd for cast-iron eggs, excellent CH$6800 *menús del día* and a selection of tasty sandwiches. As night falls, it morphs into a fine spot for a drink as well.

Cochamó

The Chilote-style, alerce-shingled **Iglesia Parroquial María Inmaculada** stands picturesque and proud against a backdrop of milky-blue water along the road to Cochamó, forming one of the most stunning spots throughout the region and the gateway to the upper Río Cochamó Valley. In addition to its made-over *costanera*, some vibrant new accommodation choices are now vying for your attention, doing their best to graduate Cochamó to more than just the spot where you put your kayaks in the water on a day trip from Puerto Varas.

RARANO / SHUTTERSTOCK ©

MANON VAN GOETHEM / SHUTTERSTOCK ©

EATING

El Faro Chilean $

(Costanera s/n; mains CH$3700-8000; ⌚9am-10pm, shorter hr winter) Probably your best bet for a decent home-cooked meal in Cochamó, El Faro does ceviches, fresh fish such as *merluza* (hake) and congrio (conger eel) a number of ways, and other seafood delights. It's right on the water, so views are expectedly dramatic.

Frutillar

Frutillar, right up the coastline of Lago Llanquihue from Puerto Varas, has an attractive pier, a long lakeside beach and quaint German architecture, with a soundtrack provided by buff-necked ibises, who cackle from rooftops all over town. Though it can at times feel touristy, Frutillar remains a serene spot that makes for a pleasant alternative to staying in busier Puerto Varas.

...with a soundtrack provided by buff-necked ibises, who cackle from rooftops...

SIGHTS

Museo Histórico Alemán Museum

(www.museosaustral.cl; cnr Pérez Rosales & Prat; CH$2500; ⌚9am-5:30pm) The Museo Histórico Colonial Alemán was built with assistance from Germany and is managed by the Universidad Austral. It features nearly perfect reconstructions of a water-powered mill, a blacksmith's house and a farmhouse and belfry set among manicured gardens. It is considered the best museum on German colonialism in the region.

SHOPPING

Vipa & Co. Food, Cosmetics

(www.vipaonline.cl; Av Philippi 989; ⌚11am-7:50pm) A great shop for picking up artisanal foodstuff and biodegradable cosmetics, including high-quality brands such as Melí (spices, salsas and mustards) and Agua de Patagonia (soaps, shampoos, aromatherapy).

Frutillar Pier

YURI BANICHIVICH / GETTY IMAGES ©

 EATING

Lavanda Casa de Té Teahouse $$

(cell 9-9458-0804; www.lavandacasadete.cl; Camino a Quebrada Honda, Km1.5; menú CH$15,000; 1-8pm Dec-Mar) On a lavender farm just outside town, this is a lakeside favorite for tea, gourmet lavender products and farm-fresh lunches. Make a reservation for afternoon tea (CH$9800) or a lingering lunch. Minimum consumption is CH$6000.

Se Cocina Chilean $$$

(cell 9-8972-8195; www.secocina.cl; Camino a Quebrada Honda, Km2; mains CH$10,500, 3-course meal CH$21,200; 1-3pm & 8-10:30pm Tue-Sun Jan-Feb, closed Mon & Tue Dec-Mar) Se Cocina is hit or miss, but even when it misses, this beautiful 1850s farmstead 2km from Frutillar is one of the most interesting foodie destinations on the lake. The daily changing menu marries Nueva Chilena cuisine with a modern atmosphere housed inside a historically protected farm.

Puerto Octay

Cute and quaint, Puerto Octay (ock-*tie*) isn't heavily visited, but it's actually one of the more charming towns on Lago Llanquihue. The tranquil streets, perched on a hillside above the lake, yield interesting 1800s German-settler architectural treasures around every turn, making for a nice tour of historic homes and buildings and giving the town a supremely sedate and picturesque colonial air. It is the oldest town on the lake settled by Germans, and, of course, it has a requisite **Oktoberfest** (www.oktoberfestpuertooctay.cl).

 SIGHTS

Museo de Puerto Octay Museum

(Independencia 591, 2nd fl; CH$1000; 10am-1pm & 3-5pm) A small but well-done museum inside the historic 1920 Casa Niklitschek telling the story of Puerto Octay via antiques.

Teatro del Lago

This amazing 12-years-in-the-making, US$25-million world-class **performing-arts center** (Teatro del Lago; 65-242-2900; www.teatrodellago.cl; Av Philippi 1000; box office 10am-6pm) opened in 2010, and has single-handedly put Frutillar on the global cultural map. The striking copper-roofed structure is a thing of beauty in itself, flanked against the lake with postcard views of four volcanoes. Daily 45-minute tours start at noon throughout the year (CH$4500).

Inside, it houses a state-of-the-art 1178-seat concert hall – acoustically insured by beautiful beechwood walls – and a second 278-seat amphitheater, as well as a pizzeria and lakeside cafe. It currently hosts a wealth of cultural events, including the music festival, and attracts internationally known orchestras and artists in all genres.

Alfresco dining at Teatro del Lago

 EATING

Rancho Espantapájaros Chilean $$$

(65-233-0049; www.espantapajaros.cl; Quilanto, Camino Puerto Octay–Frutillar Km5; buffet CH$17,000, sandwiches CH$3500-6500; noon-10pm Jan-Feb, noon-8pm Mar, noon-5:30pm Mon-Thu, to 10pm Fri & Sat, to 7:30pm Sun Apr-Nov;) The most famous restaurant on the lake is 6km outside Puerto Octay on the road to Frutillar. It packs in the crowds for the main attraction, succulent *jabalí* (wild boar, fatty but fantastic) cooked on 3.5m spits across a giant *fogón* behind the buffet.

TORRES DEL PAINE, CHILE

In this Chapter

Torres del Paine, Chile

Soaring almost vertically above the Patagonian steppe, the granite pillars of Torres del Paine (Towers of Paine) dominate the landscape of South America's finest national park. Part of Unesco's Biosphere Reserve system since 1978, this 1810-sq-km park is, however, much more than its one greatest hit. Its landscapes range from teal and azure lakes to emerald forests, roaring rivers and that one big, radiant blue glacier. Guanacos roam the vast open steppe, while Andean condors soar alongside looming peaks.

Two Days in Parque Nacional Torres del Paine

On the first day, set out early for a rewarding day hike along the Río Pingo up to a lookout with views of Glaciar Zapata. For your second day, admire the amazing scenery while kayaking on the iceberg dotted Lago Grey on an excursion with **Big Foot Patagonia** (p208).

Four Days in Parque Nacional Torres del Paine

On day three, head off for some uncommon adventures–either ice trekking on Glaciar Grey or horseback riding along Laguna Azul.

On day four take in a bit of rural life (including herding-dog and sheep-shearing demonstrations) at **Estancia La Península** (p210). In the evening treat yourself to a Chilean feast at **Singular Restaurant** (p211).

Previous page: Mirador Las Torres, Parque Nacional Torres del Paine

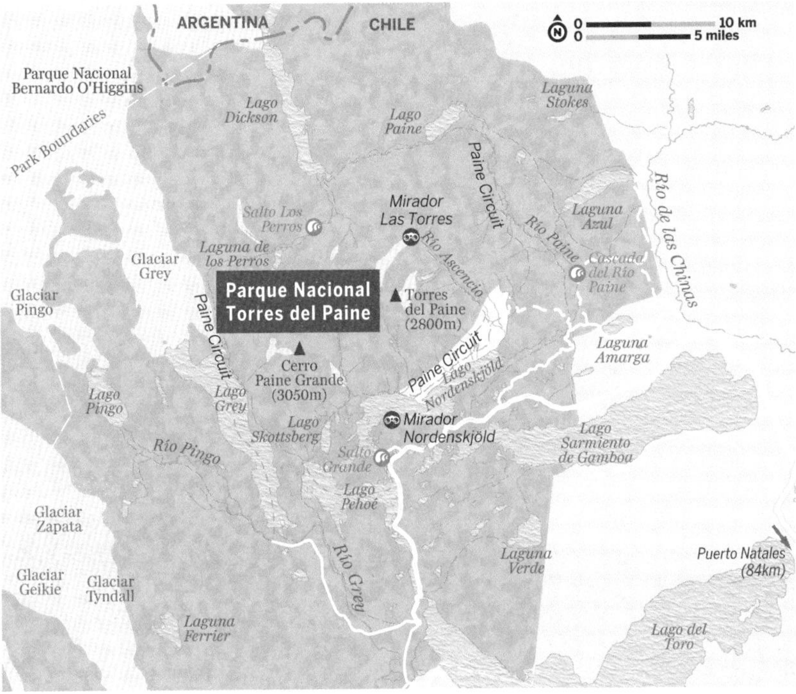

ARGENTINA
CHILE
0 10 km
0 5 miles
Parque Nacional
Bernardo O'Higgins
Park Boundaries
Lago
Dickson
Lago
Paine
Laguna
Stokes
Paine Circuit
Río de las Chinas
Salto Los
Perros
Mirador
Las Torres
Río Paine
Laguna
Azul
Laguna de
los Perros
Río Ascencio
Cascada
del Río
Paine
Glaciar
Grey
Parque Nacional
Torres del Paine
Torres
del Paine
(2800m)
Glaciar
Pingo
Paine Circuit
Laguna
Amarga
Cerro
Paine Grande
(3050m)
Paine Circuit
Lago
Nordenskjöld
Lago
Pingo
Lago
Grey
Mirador
Nordenskjöld
Lago
Skottsberg
Lago
Sarmiento
de Gamboa
Río Pingo
Salto
Grande
Lago
Pehoé
Glaciar
Zapata
Río Grey
Laguna
Verde
Puerto Natales
(84km)
Glaciar
Geikie
Glaciar
Tyndall
Laguna
Ferrier
Lago del
Toro

Arriving in Parque Nacional Torres del Paine

Most visitors access the region by road via Punta Arenas (300km south of Torres del Paine), though there are some flights into Puerto Natales (60km south of Torres del Paine). There's frequent bus service between Parque Nacional Torres del Paine and Puerto Natales, but for more remote locations visitors may need a rental car. High-end lodgings provide transfers.

Where to Stay

Forget roughing it. You can hike the whole 'W' while sleeping in beds, eating hot meals, taking showers and toasting your day with a pisco sour. Among the lodging options are campsites, dormitory-style *refugios* (trailside cabins with four to eight bunks per room), *domos* (yurt-like 'domes') and high-end hotels. Reservations are essential.

Guanacos in Parque Nacional Torres del Paine

EKATERINA POKROVSKY / SHUTTERSTOCK ©

Hiking the Parque Nacional Torres del Paine

Torres del Paine's 2800m granite peaks inspire a mass pilgrimage of hikers from around the world. Most go for the Paine Circuit or the 'W' to soak in these classic panoramas.

Great For...

☑ Don't Miss

The remarkable view over the jagged landscape from the **Mirador Las Torres**.

The 'W'

Hiking west to east provides superior views of Los Cuernos, especially between Lago Pehoé and Valle Francés. Most hikers take the catamaran across Lago Pehoé and head to Mountain Lodge Paine Grande. Going in this direction, the hike is roughly 71km in total. It's also possible to take a cruise from Hotel Lago Grey to Refugio Grey to avoid some backtracking.

In clear weather the 10km stretch between Valle Francés to Los Cuernos is magnificent. The route runs from 3050m Cerro Paine Grande in the west to the lower but still spectacular Torres del Paine and Los Cuernos to the east, with glaciers hugging the trail.

Hiker near Salto Grande waterfall (p208)

SHARPTOYOU / SHUTTERSTOCK ©

ℹ Need to Know

www.parquetorresdelpaine.cl; high/low season CH$21,000/11,000

✕ Take a Break

Meal plans are available at *refugios*, though high demand means not all last-minute requests can be satisfied.

★ Top Tip

Weather can present four seasons in a day, with sudden rainstorms and knock-down gusts like a hearty Patagonian handshake.

The Paine Circuit

For solitude, stellar views and bragging rights over your compadres doing the 'W,' this longer trek is the way to go. This loop takes in the 'W,' plus the backside between Refugio Grey and Refugio Las Torres; the total distance is roughly 112km. The landscape is desolate yet beautiful. **Paso John Gardner** (the most extreme part of the trek) sometimes offers knee-deep mud and snow.

Other Overnight Hikes

From Guardería Lago Grey, a four-hour trail follows Río Pingo to Conaf's Camping Zapata, from where hikes (another 1½ to two hours) continue to a lookout with impressive views of **Glaciar Zapata** and **Lago Pingo**. Because of ongoing studies of wildlife and fossil beds, hiking in this pristine area is authorized only for groups traveling with a Conaf-approved guide.

From Guardería Laguna Amarga a four-hour hike leads to **Laguna Azul**. The camping area on the northeastern shore closed after a wildfire; check with Conaf about its current status. After another two-hour hike north the trail reaches **Lago Paine**. Accessibility to meet up with the Paine Circuit trail near the other side of the lake is made impossible by the river.

From the Administración, the three-hour hike to Hostería Pehoé is an easy, mainly flat trail with great views. For more solitude and bird-watching, a four-hour hike branches east after crossing Río Paine, zigzags up the skirt of the Sierra del Toro to access a string of lakes, ending with **Laguna Verde**. There is no camping, but those inclined could splurge for a night at Hostería Mirador del Payne.

Day Hikes

Walk from Guardería Pudeto, on the main park highway, to **Salto Grande**, a powerful waterfall between Lago Nordenskjöld and Lago Pehoé. Another easy hour's walk leads to **Mirador Nordenskjöld**, an overlook with superb views of the lake and mountains.

For a more challenging day hike with tranquility and gorgeous scenery, try the four-hour trek to **Lago Paine**; its northern shore is only accessible from Laguna Azul.

Kayaking & Boating

Big Foot Patagonia (61-241-4611; www.bigfootpatagonia.com; kayaking CH$66,000, ice hike CH$105,000; Oct-Apr) leads 2½-hour tours of the iceberg-strewn Lago Grey several times daily in summer; this is a great way to get up close to glaciers. A more demanding five-hour tour (CH$160,000) starts at Río Pingo to paddle the river toward Glaciar Grey, surrounded by icebergs, ending at Río Serrano.

From October through April, catamaran *Grey III* does **Navegación Glaciar Grey** (Glaciar Grey Cruise; 61-271-2100; www.lagogrey.com; adult/child round-trip CH$80,000/40,000, one-way CH$70,000/35,000; Oct-Apr), a three-hour cruise to take in the massive glacier up close, with a stop to let hikers on and off. In high season there are four daily departures; the last two do glacier viewing before stopping at the trail for passengers.

Family-oriented floating trips that take rafts down the mild Río Serrano are run by **Fantástico Sur** (61-261-4184; www.fantasticosur.com; Esmeralda 661; 9am-1pm & 3-6pm Mon-Fri).

Horseback Riding

Baqueano Zamora (61-261-3530; www.baqueanozamora.cl; Baquedano 534; 10am-1pm & 3-7pm) runs excursions to Laguna Azul, Valle Francés, Dickson glacier and more remote locations, with one-day and multiday options.

Kayaking on Lago Grey

Hotel Las Torres (☎61-261-7450; www.lastorres.com; booking address Magallanes 960, Punta Arenas; s/d incl breakfast from US$382/437; ⊙Jul-May; 📶) 🍃 offers full-day horseback-riding trips around Lago Nordenskjöld and beyond.

Ice Trekking

A fun walk through a sculpted landscape of ice, and you don't need experience to go. Antares' Big Foot Patagonia is the sole company with a park concession for ice hikes on Glaciar Grey, using the Conaf house (former Refugio Grey) as a starting point. The five-hour excursion is available from October to April, in high season three times per day.

ℹ Reserving Ahead

Park regulations require hikers doing the Circuit or the 'W' to reserve all lodgings ahead; this includes both *refugios* and camping.

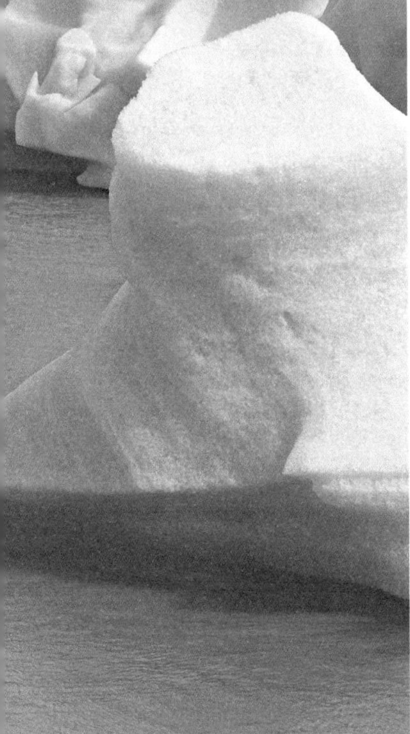

MARCO SIMONI / GETTY IMAGES ©

Wildlife

The park is home to flocks of ostrich-like rhea (known locally as the ñandú), Andean condor, flamingo and many other bird species. Its star success in conservation is undoubtedly the guanaco, which grazes the open steppes where pumas cannot approach undetected. After more than a decade of effective protection from poachers, these large, growing herds don't even flinch when humans or vehicles approach. The puma population is also growing, and huemul (an endangered Andean deer) have been spotted in Valle Francés.

Tours

Tour operators in Puerto Natales offer guided treks, which include all meals and accommodations at *refugios* (rustic shelters) or hotels. Per person rates decrease significantly in groups.

Guided day trips on minibuses from Puerto Natales are possible, but allow only a glimpse of what the park has to offer.

Patagonia Bagual (☎cell 9-5325-1266; http://patagoniabagual.cl; Laguna Azul; CH$135,000) takes hikers into the most pristine part of Torres del Paine to hike cross country to observe wild horses. Nothing about it is a canned experience. Guides are experienced and multilingual. Includes 4WD transfer but park entrance is not included.

Hotel Las Torres (☎61-271-0050; www.lastorres.com; Estancia Cerro Paine) controls the eastern area of the park and runs day and multiday tours with hiking and horseback riding; see the activities desk at the hotel for information if you are already in the park.

★ Beating the Crowds

Most hikers go up to the Torres around 8am and down at 4pm. With full summer light, you can beat the crowds by starting a couple of hours earlier or later.

Puerto Natales

A formerly modest fishing port on Seno Última Esperanza, Puerto Natales has blossomed into a Gore-Tex mecca. The gateway to Parque Nacional Torres del Paine, this town feeds off tourism, an all-you-can-eat feast with unwavering demand. Boutique beers and wine tastings have overtaken tea time, and gear shops have replaced the yarn sellers. While there are growing services that cater to international tastes, there's appeal in Natales' corrugated-tin houses strung shoulder to shoulder and cozy granny-style lodgings.

SIGHTS

Museo Histórico Museum

(☎61-241-1263; Bulnes 285; CH$1000; ⏰8am-7pm Mon-Fri, 10am-1pm & 3-7pm Sat & Sun, reduced hours May-Nov) Worth a quick visit, this is a crash course in local history, with archaeological artifacts, a Yaghan canoe, Tehuelche bolas (throwing weapon) and historical photos.

ACTIVITIES

Estancia La Península Outdoors

(☎cell 9-6303-6497; www.estanciaspatagonia.com; Península Antonio Varas; day tour CH$130,000) Run by a family with pioneer roots in the region, this classic *estancia* across the water offers day visits that include hiking or riding, herding-dog and sheep-shearing demonstrations and an awesome barbecue lunch of spit-roasted lamb. There are also excellent multiday hiking options with a remote feel. The meeting place is the dock at **Singular Hotel**.

Antares/Big Foot Patagonia Adventure

(☎61-241-4611; www.antarespatagonia.com; Costanera 161, Av Pedro Montt; Lago Grey kayaking CH$66,000) Specializing in Torres del Paine, Antares can facilitate climbing permits and made-to-order trips. Its sister company Big Foot has the park concession for Lago Grey activities, including Glacier Grey ice-trekking and kayak trips, with a base in the park.

Chile Nativo Adventure

(☎61-241-1835, cell 9-9078-9168; www.chilenativo.cl; Eberhard 230, 2nd fl) Links visitors with local gauchos, organizes photo safaris and can competently plan your tailor-made dream adventures.

Mirador Dorotea Hiking

(Ruta 9; CH$5000) A day hike through a lenga forest on private land to splendid views of Puerto Natales and the glacial valley. Less than 10km from Natales. Dorotea is the large rocky outcrop just off Ruta 9.

Turismo 21 de Mayo Tours

(☎61-261-4420; www.turismo21demayo.com; Eberhard 560; ⏰8am-10pm Oct-Mar) Organizes day-trip cruises and treks to the Balmaceda and Serrano glaciers (CH$90,000) and horseback riding on Cerro Dorotea (CH$30,000), just outside Puerto Natales.

Mandala Andino Spa

(☎cell 9-9930-2997; mandalaandino@yahoo.com; Bulnes 301; massages from CH$25,000; ⏰10am-9pm Nov-Mar) A recommended full-service wellness center with spot-on massages, tub soaks and various pampering treatments, including cannabis-oil massages.

Patagom Lila Yoga

(☎cell 9-6140-7857; www.yogapatagomlila.com; Galvarino 345) Wonderful yoga teacher Susanne offers classes in English, German and Spanish in both a downtown house and a spectacular rural dome with views of the Seno Última Esperanza, where you will also find permaculture courses, yoga vacations and Thai and singing bowl massages. She also brings alternative therapies into the local community.

SHOPPING

Oneaco Sports & Outdoors

(cnr Eberhard & Magallanes; ⏰10am-9pm Mon-Sat, 11am-2pm & 4-8:30pm Sun) Down jackets, hiking boots and mountain equipment from international brands are sold here. Ticket prices may be double those back home, but for those waiting on lost luggage it's a lifesaver.

Wine & Market Wine

(☎61-269-1138; www.wmpatagonia.cl; Magallanes 46; tasting CH$20,000; ⏰10am-10pm Mon-Sat) Picnickers should pop in here for a range of tasty gourmet products from all over Chile, and a great wine and craft-beer selection. If your trip doesn't take you to wine country, it's well worth attending one of its daily tastings, with a sommelier presenting four classic wines.

EATING

La Guanaca Pizza $$

(☎61-241-3245; Magallanes 167; mains CH$5000-16,000; ⏰12:30-10pm Mon-Sat; ✎) From crisp oven-fired pizzas to crepes and marinated mushroom appetizers, this homespun restaurant delivers warming and satisfying meals. Oversized salads, like the quinoa with roasted vegetables, are abundant and varied. There's craft beer and several wines to choose from.

La Aldea Mediterranean $$

(☎cell 9-6141-4027; www.aldearestaurant.cl; Barros Arana 132; mains CH$8000-16,000; ⏰7-11pm Wed-Mon) Chef Pato changes the offerings daily, but the focus is fresh and Mediterranean, with a nod to local ingredients. Think grilled clams, lamb tagine and quinoa dishes with an elegant presentation. Don't skip the decadent *tres leches* (three milks) cake for dessert.

Santolla Seafood $$$

(☎61-241-3493; Magallanes 77; mains CH$15,000-22,000; ⏰7-11pm Mon-Sat) For worthwhile upscale seafood, look no further than this cozy container restaurant attended by the owner. Feast on gorgeous salads and local king crab prepared several ways; we liked it with *merken* (smoked chili), white wine and parsley. Nonseafood eaters have options such as steak or rabbit in black-truffle sauce.

Singular Restaurant Chilean $$$

(☎61-272-2030; Puerto Bories; mains CH$12,000-18,000; ⏰8am-11pm) The perfect port in a storm, part supper club of yore, part modern bistro, with exquisite food and attentive service. Leather sofas and polished wood meet bare beams and stark views of the sound. Chef Hernan Vaso reinvigorates local ingredients: the freshest ceviche, tender lamb medallions and lovely salads come with original sides and fine Chilean wines. Vegetarian options excel.

DRINKING

Last Hope Distillery

(☎cell 9-7201-8585; www.lasthopedistillery.com; Esmeralda 882; ⏰5pm-2am Wed-Sun Dec-Mar, 8pm-2am Sat & Sun Apr-Nov) Two Australians on vacation tossed in their day jobs to distill whiskey and gin at the end of the world. With bonhomie to spare, their bar caters to locals and travelers alike, with a rotating menu of gorgeous cocktails. The signature drink is a calafate berry gin and tonic. It's tiny and the overflow waits outside – wear your down jacket.

Baguales Microbrewery

(www.cervezabaguales.cl; Bories 430; ⏰6pm-2:30am Mon-Sat; 📶) Climber friends started this microbrewery as a noble quest for quality suds and the beer (crafted on-site) does not disappoint. A 2nd-floor addition seeks to meet the heavy demand. The gringo-style bar food is just so-so.

ENTERTAINMENT

Centro Cultural Galpon Patagonia Cultural Center

(http://galponpatagonia.cl; Pedro Montt 16; ⏰10am-1pm & 3-7pm Tue-Sun) This cultural center and teahouse occupies a revamped 1920 warehouse with exposed beams and worn floorboards. Features art exhibits, theater, dance and music.

THE ATACAMA DESERT, CHILE

In this Chapter

The Atacama Desert, Chile

The Atacama is home to northern Chile's most spectacular scenery. Amid a parched, untrammeled landscape, you'll find vast salt flats, russet-colored lunar-like ridges and topaz lakes sparkling against a backdrop of soaring mountain peaks. The region is also home to the ruins of pre-Columbian peoples, as well as gurgling geyser fields, towering sand dunes (ideal for sandboarding) and some of the clearest night skies on the planet. Given the great variety on offer, you could easily spend a week in the area and still not see everything.

Two Days in the Atacama Desert

On the first day head to the **Valle de la Muerte** (p216) for a walk amid the Mars-like scenery or to sandboard down massive dunes. Later, watch the sunset over the spectacular **Valle de la Luna** (p217).

On day two rise early for the trip to the bubbling **El Tatio Geysers** (p217). In the evening, treat yourself to dinner at **Baltinache** (p221).

Four Days in the Atacama Desert

Visit pre-Columbian ruins on a guided visit to **Aldea de Tulor** (p219). Later, soak in the **Termas de Puritama** (p218). At night go stargazing with **Una Noche con las Estrellas** (p221).

In the morning, check out the salt lake of **Laguna Cejar** (p217), then spy flamingos at **Laguna Chaxa** (p218). In the afternoon, take a walk with **Tours 4 Tips** (p220) followed by craft shopping around town.

Previous page: Valle de la Luna (p217)

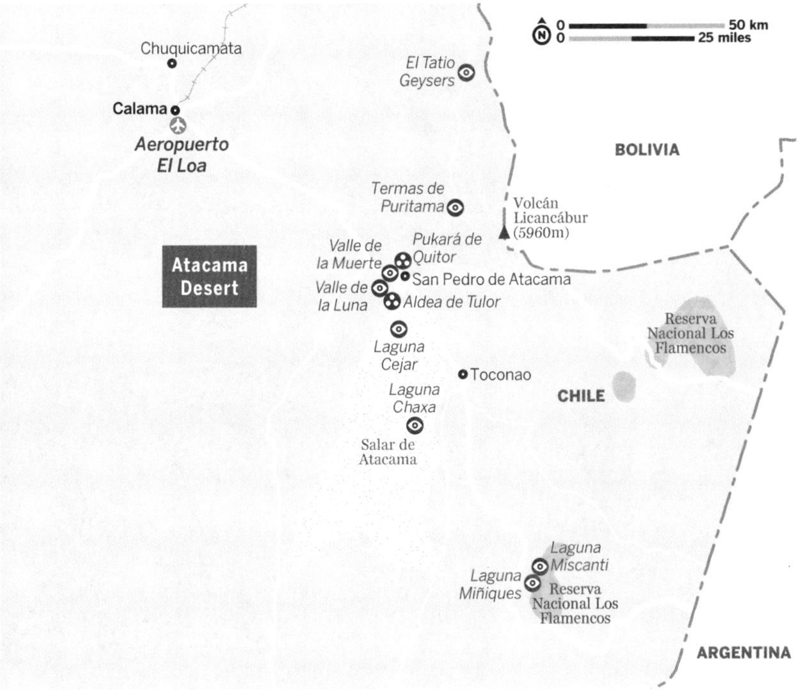

0 50 km
0 25 miles
Chuquicamata
Calama
Aeropuerto El Loa
El Tatio Geysers
BOLIVIA
Termas de Puritama
Volcán Licancábur (5960m)
Atacama Desert
Valle de la Muerte
Pukará de Quitor
San Pedro de Atacama
Valle de la Luna
Aldea de Tulor
Reserva Nacional Los Flamencos
Laguna Cejar
Toconao
Laguna Chaxa
CHILE
Salar de Atacama
Laguna Miscanti
Laguna Miñiques
Reserva Nacional Los Flamencos
ARGENTINA

Arriving in the Atacama Desert

The nearest airport, Aeropuerto El Loa, is 100km northwest of San Pedro de Atacama and has daily flights to Santiago. Several agencies offer transfer services to/from Calama airport including **Tour Magic** (www.tourmagic.cl; CH$8000 per person, 1½ hours).

San Pedro's bus terminal is 1km southeast of the plaza, with regular departures to Calama where you can connect to all major destinations in Chile.

Where to Stay

The village of San Pedro de Atacama is the obvious base for exploring the desert attractions nearby. You'll find a dizzying number of accommodations, particularly hostels. Midrange hotels are in short supply at this backpackers' haven, but many budget hostels have midrange rooms. Top-end hotels have sprouted around San Pedro, though many are outside the center.

Valle de la Muerte

IGNACIO PALACIOS / GETTY IMAGES ©

Visiting the Desert

Just outside the small village of San Pedro there are intriguing archaeological ruins, steaming geyser fields and stunning landscapes. One of the big must-see attractions is here: the Valle de la Muerte, with its otherworldly scenery and a big dune that's perfect for sandboarding.

Great For...

☑ Don't Miss

Seeing the myriad desert colors come to life while the sun sets over the Valle de la Luna (p217).

Valle de la Muerte

Around 3.5km west of San Pedro, this striking **valley** (Map p215; off Ruta 23; CH$3000; 9am-8pm) should figure high on any itinerary to the region, with jagged rocks, a towering sand dune and dramatic viewpoints of the distant cordillera. The name Valle de la Muerte (Death Valley) is actually a linguistic distortion of Valle de Marte (Mars Valley), which more accurately represents its red rock features and otherworldly beauty.

Tour groups typically come in the afternoon before heading over to the nearby Valle de la Luna for sunset. It's an easy bike ride (or long walk) here, and also accessible by your own vehicle. The tall sand dune is a prime destination for sandboarding, with outfits like **Sandboard San Pedro** (cell 9-8135-1675; www.sandboardsanpedro.com; Caracoles 362-H) offering both morning and afternoon excursions.

El Tatio Geysers

IGNACIO PALACIOS / GETTY IMAGES ©

Need to Know

You can visit all of the sights on guided tours from San Pedro de Atacama.

Take a Break

After a day in the desert, refresh with artisanal ice cream at Babalú (p220).

★ Top Tip

Be sure to pack a jacket for those chilly desert nights.

El Tatio Geysers

One of the must-see sights of Atacama is this sputtering **geyser field** (Map p215; 95km north of town; CH$10,000; 6am-6pm), located at an altitude of more than 4300m, some 90km north of San Pedro de Atacama. Fringed by rolling peaks, the landscape churns with bubbling pools and steaming columns wafting into the air. Tiny eruptions from more than 60 gurgling geysers pierce the alpine calm. Tours here typically depart at 4am or 5am to arrive in time for sunrise, which is the most dramatic time to see Tatio.

Valle de la Luna

This **valley** (Map p215; CH$3000; 9am-6pm) owes its name to the striking lunar-like landscape, which is located in the Cordillera de la Sal. Over the eons, its chiseled rock formations have been carved by the desert winds, leaving behind a handful of caverns. See the desert don its surrealist cloak as you stand atop a giant sand dune, with the sun slipping below the horizon and multicolored hues bathing the sands, all with a backdrop of distant volcanoes and the rippling Cordillera de la Sal.

Laguna Cejar

San Pedro has its own mini version of the Dead Sea, a mere 22km south of the village. This topaz-colored **lake** (Map p215; CH$10,000-15,000; 9am-5pm) allows you to float effortlessly because of its high salt content – a fine place to contemplate the mountainous horizon. Cejar is just one of three lakes here; the other two (Laguna Piedra and Laguna Baltinache) do not allow bathing, though you can often see flamingos feeding here.

Laguna Chaxa

The jagged crust of the **Salar de Atacama** looks for all the world like God went crazy with a stippling brush. But in the midst of these rough lifeless crystals is an oasis of activity: the pungent **Laguna Chaxa** (Map p215; CH$2500; ⌚8am-8pm), about 25km southwest of Toconao and 65km from San Pedro, the Reserva Nacional Los Flamencos' most easily accessible flamingo-breeding site.

Three of the five known species (James, Chilean and Andean) can be spotted at this salt lake, as well as plovers, coots and ducks: bring zoom lenses and snappy reflexes. Sunrise is feeding time for the birds, though the park doesn't open until 8am. It's also gorgeous at sunset.

Lagunas Miscanti & Miñiques

Shimmery high-altitude lakes dot the altiplano and make for worthwhile excursions from San Pedro. The glittery-blue sweet-water lakes, **Miñiques** (Map p215; incl entrance to Laguna Miscanti CH$3000; ⌚9am-6pm) and **Miscanti** (Map p215; incl entrance to Laguna Miñiques CH$3000; ⌚9am-6pm) are watched over by snow-touched volcanoes. The smaller Laguna Miñiques is the largest breeding site for the horned coot on the western side of the Andes, and visitors are kept at bay when the birds are breeding.

Termas de Puritama

These idyllic volcanic hot **springs** (Map p215; https://termasdepuritama.cl; adult/child CH$19,500/9100; ⌚9:30am-5:15pm) puddle together in a box canyon, about 30km northeast of San Pedro en route to

Andean flamingos, Laguna Chaxa

El Tatio. Their temperature is about 33°C (91°F), and there are several falls, pools and changing rooms on-site. Few tours stop here because of the hefty admission charged, but taxis will take you or you can drive yourself. The springs are a 20-minute walk from the parking lot.

Bring food, water and sunblock. Go early in the day to beat the crowds. Prices are cheaper Monday to Friday after 2pm.

Pukará de Quitor

Dominating a curvaceous promontory over the Río San Pedro, this crumbling 12th-century **pukará** (Map p215; CH$3000; 8:30am-7pm; fort) was one of the last bastions against Pedro de Valdivia and the Spanish in northern Chile. The indigenous forces fought bravely, but were overcome and many were promptly beheaded. About 100 defensive enclosures hug the slopes here, like big stone bird's nests. The hilltop commands an impressive view of the oasis.

The fort is just 3.5km northwest of San Pedro, and easily accessible on foot, by bike or by vehicle. Note that the *mirador* (lookout) closes at 6pm.

★ Did You Know?

The Atacama Desert is one of the driest regions on earth; some areas have not seen rainfall for over 400 years.

DELPIXART / GETTY IMAGES ©

Aldea de Tulor

Circular adobe structures huddle together like muddy bubblewrap in the ruins of **Tulor** (Map p215; CH$3000; 9am-7pm), the oldest excavated village in the region. It's an interesting diversion 11km southwest of San Pedro. You can get there by your own vehicle, driving along sandy tracks, or by riding a mountain bike. However, you'll get more out of the experience if you go on a good guided tour.

If you go alone, there's often a Spanish-speaking guide on hand who can fill in some of the historical details (included with admission).

Trekking & Biking

Around San Pedro rise immense volcanoes, a few of them active, and begging to be climbed. If climbing isn't your cup of tea, consider a more active trekking or biking trip to the usual suspects in the area, such as Valle de la Luna. Bikes are available for rent at several agencies and hotels in San Pedro, for about CH$6000 per day; try **Km O** (Caracoles 282B; half-/full day CH$3500/6000; 9am-9pm).

☑ Uyuni Connection

From San Pedro de Atacama, several agencies, including **Cordillera Traveler** (55-320-5028; www.cordilleratraveller.com; Tocopilla 429-B; 9am-9pm), run multiday trips to the surreal Salar de Uyuni (p240) in Bolivia.

San Pedro de Atacama

It is said that the high quantities of quartz and copper in the region give its people positive energy, and the good vibes of northern Chile's number-one tourist draw, San Pedro de Atacama, are sky high. The village itself is small and compact, with almost everything of interest within easy strolling distance of the plaza. Many buildings now have street numbers, although many still do without.

SIGHTS

Iglesia San Pedro Church

(Le Paige s/n) FREE The recently restored Iglesia San Pedro is a delightful little colonial church built with indigenous or artisanal materials: chunky adobe walls and roof, a ceiling made from *cardón* (cactus wood) resembling shriveled tire tracks and, in lieu of nails, hefty leather straps. The church dates from the 17th century, though its present walls were built in 1745, and the bell tower was added in 1890.

ACTIVITIES

Tours 4 Tips Walking

(www.tours4tips.com; Plaza de Armas; tours 10am & 3pm) For a deeper understanding of San Pedro, take an edifying stroll with this friendly outfit. On two-hour walks around the village and its outskirts, enthusiastic guides relate fascinating episodes from San Pedro's past, touching on indigenous beliefs and symbols, desert plants and hallucinogens, and even a bit of celestial mythology. Tours are offered in Spanish and English.

Rancho La Herradura Horseback Riding

(55-285-1956; www.atacamahorseadventure.com; Tocopilla 406; 9am-8pm) Sightseeing from the saddle is available from several places, including Rancho La Herradura. Tours vary from two hours for CH$23,000 to epic 10-day treks with camping in the desert. English-, German- and French-speaking guides are available.

Vulcano Expediciones Adventure

(cell 9-5333-6021; www.vulcanochile.com; Caracoles 317; 10am-8pm Tue-Sun) Runs treks to volcanoes and mountains, including day climbs to Sairecabur (5971m, CH$110,000), Lascar (5592m, CH$85,000) and Tocco (5604m, CH$670,000). Two-day climbs take in Licancábur (CH$250,000) and other mountains. It can also hook you up with motorbike tours offered by On Safari.

Desert Adventure Tours

(cell 9-9779-7211; www.desertadventure.cl; cnr Caracoles & Tocopilla; 9:30am-9pm) Has the full spectrum of tours and bilingual guides. Unique offerings include an ethnocultural 'Ancestral Caravan' tour that features two hours of llama trekking along routes used by Atacameños in centuries past (CH$25,000).

On Safari Tours

(cell 9-7215-3254; www.onsafariatacama.com; 4hr motorbike tour CH$170,000) Offers motorbike, all-terrain-vehicle (ATV), 4WD, mountain-biking and mountaineering tours in the Atacama region and further afield. Other offerings include tours with an emphasis on photography, bird-watching or astronomy.

SHOPPING

Shaded Paseo Artesanal, a poker-straight alley squeezing north from the plaza, is the place to hunt down novel *cardón* carvings, llama and alpaca woolens and other curious trinkets. More artisanal outlets are strewn throughout town.

For something unique, visit the handicraft shops by the bus terminal. You'll find beautifully crafted copper jewelry, one-of-a-kind alpaca clothing, handworked leather and other gear.

EATING

Babalú Ice Cream $

(Caracoles 140; ice creams CH$1900-3900; 10am-10pm) One of several ice-cream shops on the main street, Babalú serves up rich flavors you won't find at home. Try ice creams made from desert fruits like *chañar* or *algarrobo*, and sample *pisco* sour, *hoja de coca* (coca leaf) and delightful surprises such as quinoa. You can't go wrong.

Franchuteria Bakery $

(www.lafranchuteria.com; Le Paige 527; croissants CH$1100-2500; ⏲7am-8:30pm) About 500m east of the plaza, you'll find San Pedro's best bakery. Run by a talented young Frenchman, Franchuteria has beautifully baked goods, including perfect baguettes with rare combinations of fillings like fig and Roquefort cheese, or goat's cheese and oregano, and buttery-rich croissants – also available stuffed with unusual things like *manjar* (*dulce de leche*).

Las Delicias de Carmen Chilean $$

(www.lasdeliciasdecarmen.cl; Calama 370; lunch specials CH$4000-7000, mains CH$8000-14,000; ⏲8:30am-10:30pm;) Great breakfasts, delicious cakes and empanadas, brick-oven pizzas (choose your own toppings) and different dishes daily are churned out at this light-flooded restaurant with leafy views. Daily specials – such as *cazuela* (stew) or carrot-ginger soup – and a filling *menú del día* (three-course lunch) always bring in the crowds.

La Casona Chilean $$

(☎55-285-1337; Caracoles 195; mains CH$9000-14,000; ⏲noon-midnight Wed-Mon;) A high-ceilinged dining room with dark wood paneling and an adobe fireplace in the middle, classic La Casona serves up sizzling *parrilladas* (mix of grilled meats) and Chilean staples such as *pastel de choclo* (maize casserole). There's a long list of Chilean wines and a small patio for alfresco lunches.

Adobe International $$$

(☎55-285-1132; Caracoles 211; mains CH$11,000-14,000; ⏲11am-1am;) Popular with travelers for its studied rusticity, rock-art decor, bench-like seating and smoky fire in the alfresco dining room. Adobe serves tasty but pricey dishes such as mushroom quinoa risotto or lamb with tabouli and hummus; it's also a good spot for a drink.

Stargazing in the Atacama

Climatic conditions in the Atacama Desert make it an ideal location for stargazing. This is not only thanks to cloudless desert nights, but also the predictable winds that blow steadily in from the Pacific Ocean, causing minimal turbulence – a crucial requirement for observatories to achieve optimal image quality.

If all that whets your appetite for astronomy, consider taking a 'Tour of the Night Sky' from San Pedro, where there's a range of astronomical tours available, including with reputable outfits like **San Pedro de Atacama Celestial Explorations** (☎55-256-6278; www.spaceobs.com; Caracoles 400-2; 2½hr tours CH$25,000; ⏲11am-9pm Dec-Mar, to 7pm Apr-Nov) and **Una Noche con las Estrellas** (☎cell 9-5272-2201; www.unanocheconlasestrellas.cl; Calama 440; astronomy tour CH$20,000; ⏲10am-11pm).

The Milky Way above the Atacama Desert

Baltinache Chilean $$$

(☎cell 9-3191-4225; Atienza; 3-course menu CH$15,000; ⏲1-4pm & 7:30-10pm) A short walk south from busy Caracoles, Baltinache has some of San Pedro's best cuisine. Thick adobe walls hung with geoglyph-inspired artwork and flickering candles set the scene at this elegantly understated gem. The menu changes by night and features high-quality local products like river trout, vegetable soup with grated goat's cheese, rabbit and desserts made from desert fruits.

LA PAZ, BOLIVIA

In this Chapter

La Paz, Bolivia

La Paz is a mad carnival of jostling pedestrians, honking, diesel-spewing minivans, street marches and cavalcades of vendors that seems to reinvent itself at every turn – a jaw-dropping subway in the sky brings you from the heights of El Alto to the depths of Zona Sur in the blink of an eye.

Beneath the blinding altiplano sun, sharp-suited business people flank machine-gun-toting bank guards and balaclava-camouflaged shoeshine boys. Lung-busting inclines terminate in peaceful plazas. This maze of contradictions, where cobblestones hit concrete, and Gothic spires vie with glassine hotels, will amaze all who enter.

Two Days in La Paz

Stroll the cobblestone streets around Calle Jaén, home to the wonderful **Calle Jaén Museums** (p232), then visit the fascinating **Mercado de las Brujas** (p227). Dine that evening in award-winning **Gustu** (p237).

On the second day, hop aboard **Mi Teleférico** (p233) up to El Alto for memorable views. Have dinner in upmarket **Sopocachi** (p233) then catch traditional music at a *peña* (p237).

Four Days in La Paz

On your third day, take a day trip out of La Paz to **Tiwanaku** (p228) to explore pre-Columbian ruins. Then browse for crafts at **Walisuma** (p236).

On your fourth day, head out for some adventure, on an adrenaline-fueled ride with **Gravity Assisted Mountain Biking** (p233). In the evening check out La Paz' cocktail scene at the speakeasy-style **La Costilla de Adán** (p239).

Previous page: Bolivian woman on Calle Jaén (p232)

Central La Paz Map (p234)
Sopocachi Map (p238)

Arriving in La Paz

Minibus 212 runs frequently between **El Alto International Airport** (p239) and Plaza Isabel la Católica between around 7am and 8pm (B$3.80). Look for the sign that says 'Minibus Cotranstur' just outside arrivals. Heading into town from the airport, this service will drop you anywhere along El Prado.

Radio taxis charge around B$70 to the centre.

Where to Stay

The area around the Mercado de las Brujas (Witches' Market; between Illampu, Av Mariscal Santa Cruz and Sagárnaga) is a true travelers' ghetto. To be closer to a wider array of restaurants and a bar or two, consider Sopocachi. For more upmarket luxury, look along the lower Prado and further south in the Zona Sur.

Street market in La Paz

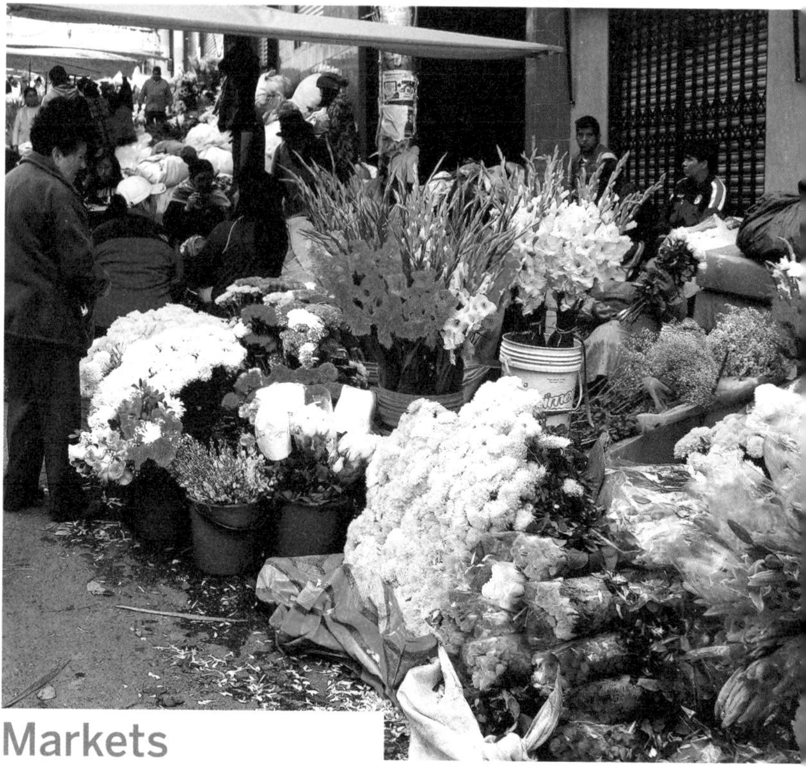

JOSEMAR FRANCO / SHUTTERSTOCK ©

Markets

La Paz' frenetic markets are easily the highlight of any trip, where modern commerce and culture collide in a wonderful riot of honks, shouts and smells.

Great For...

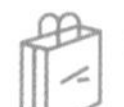

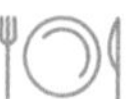

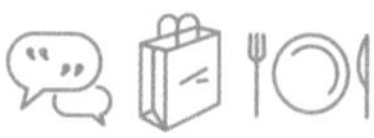

☑ Don't Miss

The strange charms, herbs and amulets of the Mercado de las Brujas (p227).

Mercado Negro

The narrow cobblestone streets off Max Paredes – the **Mercado Negro** (Black Market; Map p234; ⏰6am-8pm) – are a good place to start the market experience. Especially interesting are the sections near Graneros ('designer' clothes), Tumusla and Isaac Tamayo (everything and anything), and between Santa Cruz and Sagárnaga (tools and building materials). The best place for electronics is along Eloy Salmón. Be especially careful when wandering around this part of town: it's notorious for light fingers. It's best to take a taxi here at night.

Mercado Lanza

North of Plaza San Francisco, on Calle Figueroa, the **Mercado Lanza** (Map p234; Rosario; snacks B$5-25; ⏰6am-8pm) is one of La Paz' main food markets. It sells all

Souvenirs on display, Mercado de las Brujas

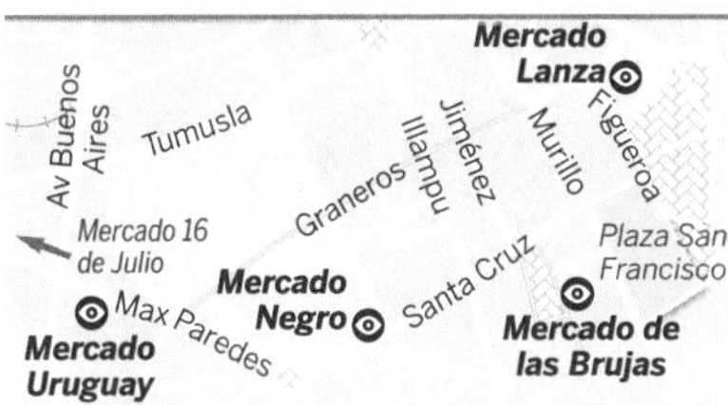

Need to Know

You'll find open-air markets all across town, though the Rosario neighborhood has a notable concentration.

Take a Break

Mercado Camacho (Map p234; cnr Av Camacho & Bueno, Casco Viejo; snacks B$5-25; 7am-9pm Mon-Fri, to 6pm Sat & Sun) makes an ideal lunch stop with stands selling empanadas, fruit juices and chorizo sandwiches.

★ Top Tip

Every day is a de facto market day in La Paz, but Saturdays are particularly fun.

manner of fruits, vegetables, juices, dairy products, breads and canned foods, and there are numerous stalls where you can pick up a sandwich, soup, *salteña* (filled pastry shells), empanada or full meal. It also houses the splendid **Flower Market**.

Mercado de las Brujas

The famed **Mercado de las Brujas** (Witches' Market; La Hechicería; Map p234) is chock-a-block with stores selling mysterious potions for lovemaking, llama fetuses and Aymará good-luck charms, including frogs. Artisan stores in the area sell *oriente* wood carvings and ceramics, and Potosí silver. Others deal in rugs, wall hangings, woven belts and pouches. Amid the lovely weavings and other items of exquisite craftsmanship, you'll find plenty of tourist kitsch, an art form unto itself: Inca-themed ashtrays, fake Tiwanaku figurines, costume jewelry and mass-produced woolens.

Mercado 16 de Julio

To visit the biggest market in Bolivia – some say it's the largest in South America – you'll need to hop in a cable car and head up to El Alto, where each Thursday and Sunday the massive **Mercado 16 de Julio** (El Alto; 6am-3pm Thu & Sun) completely absorbs dozens of city blocks. You can buy everything from new cars to animals, textiles and firearms. For the most part, however, it's a colossal flea market, the likes of which you won't soon forget.

Mercado Uruguay

On the far side of El Prado, **Mercado Uruguay** (Map p234; off Max Paredes, Rosario; snacks B$5-25; 7am-8pm) is purely the domain of adventurous eaters after tiny *ispi* fish from Lake Titicaca or stews made with unidentifiable offal.

Carved face on the wall of Templete Semisubterráneo (p230)

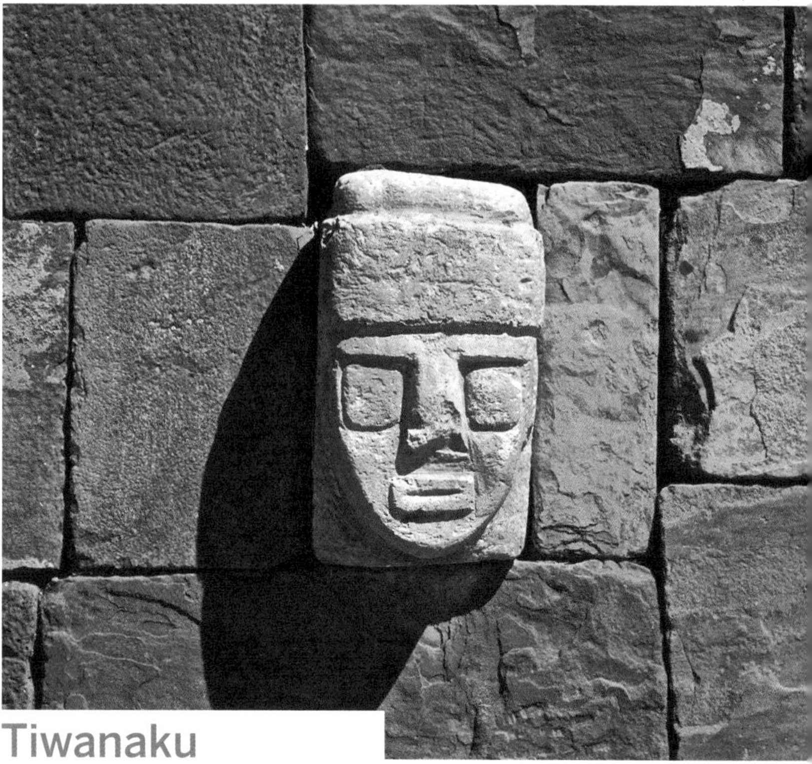

Tiwanaku

The ruins of Tiwanaku make for a good day trip from La Paz for those who want to view a few carved monoliths, archways and arcades, and two decent museums. History buffs will love diving into the myths and mysteries of this lost civilization.

Great For...

☑ Don't Miss

The many carved faces along the walls of the Templete Semisubterráneo (p230).

Museo Cerámico

Near the ticket office, this gallery showcases a small collection of the ceramics found at the site, as well as a ceremonially deformed cranium and artifacts from the Chiripa and Wankarani cultures.

Museo Lítico Monumental

The star of the show at this Tiwanaku museum is the massive 8m Monolito Bennett Pachamama, rescued in 2002 from its former smoggy home at the outdoor Templete Semisubterráneo in La Paz. You'll also find a basic collection of other monoliths and artifacts dug up on-site here. Labeling is in Spanish.

Much of the collection is currently mothballed, as the roof of the relatively new museum is already collapsing.

Monolith

SL-PHOTOGRAPHY / SHUTTERSTOCK ©

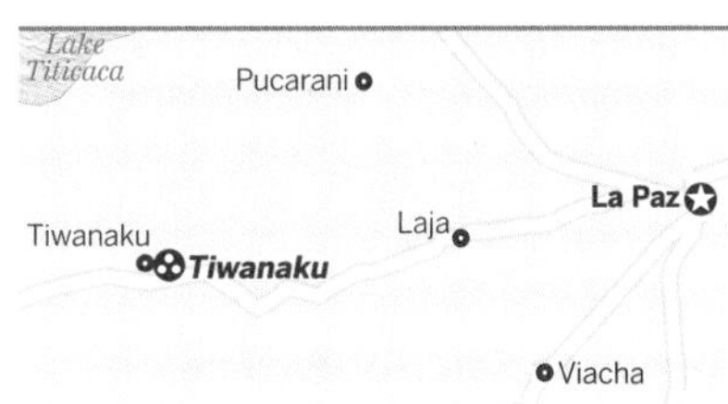

Megaphones

At the entrance to the Tiwanaku site there are two stone blocks that can be used as megaphones. Entertain yourself for a minute or two with this interesting pre-Columbian, pre-iPod technology.

Akapana Pyramid

Climb the hill up to Tiwanaku's most outstanding structure, the partially excavated Akapana pyramid, which was built on an existing geological formation. At its base this roughly square, 16m hill covers a surface area of about 200 sq meters. In the center of its flat summit is an oval-shaped sunken area, which some sources attribute to early, haphazard, Spanish excavation. The presence of a stone drain in the center, however, has led some archaeologists to believe it was used for water storage.

Need to Know

Ticket Office (Av Puma Punku s/n; B$100; tickets 9am-4pm, site 9am-5pm)

Take a Break

Restaurante Cabaña del Puma (Av Puma Punku s/n; almuerzo B$25; 9am-6pm) serves decent Bolivian fare next to the ruin entrance.

★ Top Tip

Guided **tours** (7724-9572; walipini.tiwanacu@gmail.com; Av Ferrocarril s/n; tour for up to 6 people in Spanish/English/French B$150/180/180) are available in English, French and Spanish, and are highly recommended.

Recent findings include craniums, assumed to be war trophies, suggesting the pyramid may have been a ceremonial temple. Others think it was used for the study of astronomy.

Kalasasaya

North of the Akapana Pyramid is Kalasasaya, a partially reconstructed 130m-by-120m ritual-platform compound with walls constructed of huge blocks of red sandstone and andesite. The blocks are precisely fitted to form a platform base 3m high. Monolithic uprights flank the massive entrance steps up to the restored portico of the enclosure, beyond which is an interior courtyard and the ruins of priests' quarters. Note the size of the top stair – a massive single block.

The Monolito Ponce monolith, with his turban (no doubt covering up his deformed cranium), mask, ceremonial vase and walking stick, sits at the center of the first platform. Some say the stick and the vase are symbolic of the dualism of Andean culture (nature versus nurture).

Other stairways lead to secondary platforms, where there are other monoliths including the famous El Fraile (priest).

Templete Semisubterráneo

East of the main entrance to Kalasasaya, a stairway leads down into the Templete Semisubterráneo, an acoustic, red-sandstone pit structure measuring 26m by 28m, with a rectangular sunken courtyard and walls adorned with 175 crudely carved stone faces. In the 1960s archaeologists tried to rebuild these and used cement between the stones.

Putuni

West of Kalasasaya is a 55m-by-60m rectangular area known as **Putuni** (Palacio de los Sarcófagos, Palace of the Sarcophagi). It is surrounded by double walls and you can see the foundations of several tombs. About 90% of the artifacts collected by amateur enthusiast Fritz Buck in the early 20th century from these tombs are found in La Paz' Museo de Metales Preciosos (p232).

Puerta del Sol

At the far northwest corner of Kalasasaya is Tiwanaku's best-known structure, the 10-ton **Puerta del Sol** (Gateway of the Sun). This megalithic gateway was carved from a single block of andesite, and archaeologists assume that it was associated with the sun deity. The surface of this fine-grained, gray

Celebration of Aymará New Year

volcanic rock is ornamented with low-relief designs on one side and a row of four deep niches on the other.

The gateway was most likely originally located in the center of Kalasasaya Platform and was used as a calendar, with the sun striking specific figures on the solstice and equinox.

There's a smaller, similar gateway carved with zoomorphic designs near the western end of the site that is informally known as the Puerta de la Luna.

★ Tours From La Paz

Diana Tours (Map p234; www.diana-tours.com) and **Vicuña Travel** (Map p234; ☎228-0140; http://vicuna-travel.com) have round-trip guided trips to Tiwanaku from La Paz, leaving daily at 8:30am and returning around 4pm.

WIN-INITIATIVE / GETTY IMAGES ©

Kantatayita

The heap of rubble at the eastern end of the Tiwanaku site is known as Kantatayita. Archaeologists are still trying to deduce some sort of meaningful plan from these well-carved slabs; one elaborately decorated lintel and some larger stone blocks bearing intriguing geometric designs are the only available clues.

Puma Punku

Across the railway line southwest of the Tiwanaku site, you'll see the excavation site of **Puma Punku** (Gateway of the Puma). In this temple area megaliths weighing more than 130 tons have been discovered. Like Kalasasaya and Akapana, there is evidence that Puma Punku was begun with one type of material and finished with another; part was constructed of enormous sandstone blocks and, during a later phase of construction, notched and jointed basalt blocks were added.

Note also, in the distance of the site's northern boundary, the *sukakollo,* a highly sophisticated system of terraced irrigation.

Aymará New Year

The biggest celebration of the year happens during the **Aymará New Year** (Machaq Mara; ⏲Mar 21, Jun 21, Sep 21). Locals don colorful ceremonial dress and visitors are invited to join the party, drink *singani* (distilled grape liquor), chew coca and dance until dawn at celebrations that take place on fall and spring equinox, when the rays of the rising sun shine through the temple entrance on the eastern side of Kalasasaya. The big event happens on June 21, when as many as 5000 people, including a large contingent of New Agers, arrive from all over the world. Artisans hold crafts fairs to coincide with the annual celebrations.

★ Did You Know?

Nobody knows why Tiwanaku's population disappeared by 1200, though most archaeologists point to climate change as the likely cause of the civilization's rapid decline.

SIGHTS

Calle Jaén Museums Museum

(Map p234; Calle Jaén, Casco Viejo; 4 museums B$20; 9am-12:30pm & 3-7pm Tue-Fri, 9am-1pm Sat & Sun) La Paz's best-preserved colonial street is home to four small museums. They are all clustered together and can generally be bundled into one visit. Buy tickets at the **Museo Costumbrista** (Map p234; cnr Jaén & Sucre; 9am-12:30pm & 3-7pm Tue-Fri, 9am-1pm Sat & Sun) and continue to the **Museo de Metales Preciosos** (Museum of Precious Metals; Map p234; Jaén 777; 9am-12:30pm & 3-7pm Tue-Fri, 9am-1pm Sat & Sun), **Museo del Litoral** (Museo de la Guerra del Pacífico; Map p234; Jaén 798; 9am-12:30pm & 3-7pm Tue-Fri, 9am-1pm Sat & Sun) and **Casa de Murillo** (Map p234; Jaén 790; 9am-12:30pm & 3-7pm Tue-Fri, 9am-1pm Sat & Sun).

Museo de Etnografía y Folklore Museum

(Ethnography & Folklore Museum; Map p234; 240-8640; www.musef.org.bo; cnr Ingavi & Sanjinés, Casco Viejo; B$20, with photography B$40; 9am-12:30pm & 3-7pm Mon-Fri, 9am-4:30 Sat, 9am-12:30pm Sun) Anthropology buffs should check out this museum, one of the city's best. The building, itself a real treasure, was constructed in 1720 and was once the home of the Marqués de Villaverde. Highlights include an awe-inspiring collection of ritualistic masks and an exhibition of stunning weavings from around the country. A guided tour is available by calling ahead.

Museo Nacional del Arte Museum

(National Art Museum; Map p234; www.facebook.com/museonacionaldeartebolivia; cnr Comercio & Socabaya, Casco Viejo; B$20; 9:30am-12:30pm & 3-7pm Tue-Fri, 10am-5:30pm Sat, 10am-1:30pm Sun) This colonial building was constructed in 1775 of pink sandstone and has been restored to its original grandeur, in *mestizo* (mixed) baroque and Andino baroque styles. In the center of a huge courtyard, surrounded by three stories of pillared corridors, there is a lovely alabaster fountain. The various levels are dedicated to different eras, with an emphasis on religious themes.

Mountain biking on Yungas Road

Catedral Metropolitana Cathedral
(Map p234; Plaza Murillo, Casco Viejo) Although it's a relatively recent addition to La Paz's religious structures, the 1835 cathedral is impressive – mostly because it is built on a steep hillside. The main entrance is 12m higher than its base on Calle Potosí. The cathedral's sheer immensity, with its high dome, hulking columns, thick stone walls and high ceilings, is overpowering, but the altar is relatively simple.

Iglesia de San Francisco Church
(Map p234; Plaza San Francisco, Rosario) The hewed stone basilica of San Francisco was founded in 1548 by Fray Francisco de los Ángeles. The original structure collapsed under heavy snowfall around 1610, but it was rebuilt between 1743 and 1772. The second building is made of stone quarried at nearby Viacha. The facade is decorated with carvings of natural themes such as *chirimoyas* (custard apples), pine cones and tropical birds.

Sopocachi Area
(Map p238) Sopocachi has some of La Paz' best restaurants and nightspots. You can spend a few hours people-watching on **Plaza Eduardo Avaroa**, before hoofing up to the wonderful views from **Montículo Park**.

Mi Teleférico

At 30km-long and growing, **Mi Teleférico** (Aerial Cable Car System; www.miteleferico.bo; ticket B$3, plus B$2 per line transfer; 6am-11pm Mon-Sat, 7am-9pm Sun) is easily the world's longest aerial cable-car system. Riders can hop between lines for an additional B$2 per segment (pay in advance), creating endless combinations of ways to travel across the city. One popular trip takes you from the Zona Sur to El Alto via the yellow and green lines.

The thrill of riding above La Paz' swirling traffic and deep canyons is undeniably cool. There's more than enough time to cruise down from the center to the Zona Sur for lunch or dinner, and back. Not for the faint of heart.

SAIKO3P / GETTY IMAGES ©

TOURS

La Paz on Foot Ecotour
(Map p238; cell 7154-3918; www.lapazonfoot.com; Av Ecuador 2022, Sopocachi; 10:30am-6:30pm Mon-Fri) This tip-top operation, run by the passionate English-speaking ecologist Stephen Taranto, offers a range of activities, including walks in and around La Paz, Apolobamba, the Yungas, Chulumani, Madidi and Titicaca. The interactive La Paz urban treks (half-day or full-day, fee depending on group size) venture from the heights of El Alto to the depths of the historic center.

Gravity Assisted Mountain Biking Mountain Biking
(Map p234; 231-0218, cell 7721-9634; www.gravitybolivia.com; Linares 940, Rosario; 9am-7pm Mon-Fri, 10am-3pm Sat, 2-6pm Sun) This knowledgeable, highly regarded and professional outfit has an excellent reputation among travelers and tip-top Kona downhill bikes. Their Dangerous Road Trip (B$850 per person) ends with hot showers, an all-you-can-eat buffet and an optional tour of the **Senda Verde animal refuge** (www.sendaverde.org; Yolosa; B$100, bear visit extra B$20; 10am-4pm).

Climbing South America Climbing
(Map p234; cell 7190-3534; www.climbingsouthamerica.com; Linares 940, 2nd fl, Rosario; 9am-6:30pm Mon-Fri, 10am-3pm Sat) A reputable English-speaking operator for climbing, mountaineering and trekking

Central La Paz

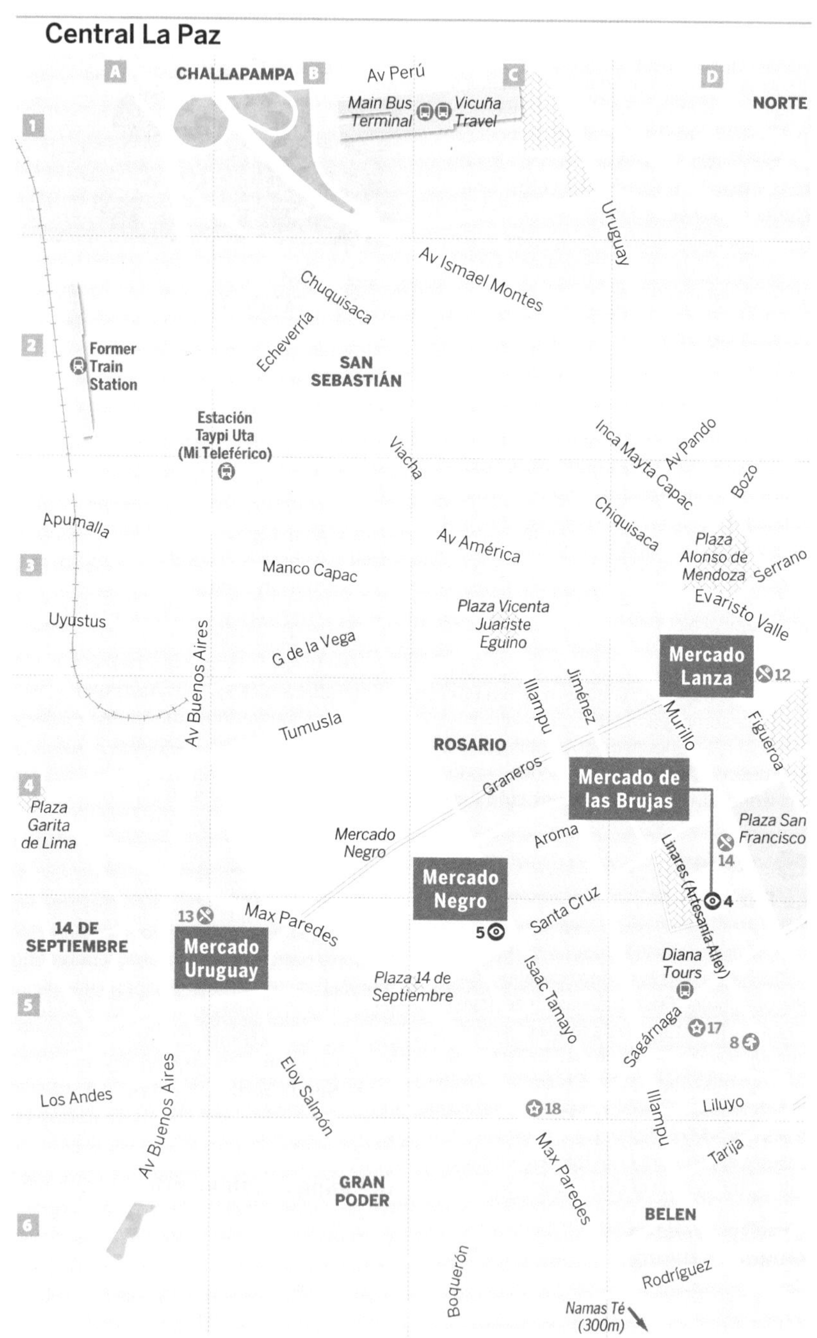

400 m
0.2 miles
E
F
G
H
1
2
3
4
5
6
VILLA PABÓN
Pisaqua
Estación Apacheta (Mi Teleférico)
Humahuaca
Junín
Av Armentia
Pisaqua
Alto de la Alianza
1
9
Jaén
16
Indaburo
Pichincha
CASCO VIEJO
Catacora
Montes
Ingavi
Genaro Sanjinés
Yanacocha
Sucre
SAN JUAN
Plaza Pérez Velasco
Junín
6
Comercio
Bolívar
Av Mariscal Santa Cruz
Indaburo
Plaza Pedro D Murillo
Potosí
7
2
Ballivián
3
Socabaya
Comercio
Ayacucho
Colón
Av Saavedra
Loayza
10
Obispo Cárdenas
Cochabamba
15
Mercado
Illimani
Tarija
SANTA BÁRBARA
Bueno
Murillo
Estación San José (Mi Teleférico)
Av Camacho
Oruro
Juan de la Riva
Almirante Grau
Av 16 de Julio (El Prado)
Estación Prado (Mi Teleférico)
Velasco
Parque Urbano Central
Tourist Information
11
Av Simón Bolívar
Plaza Venezuela
Río Choqueyapu

Central La Paz

Sights
1 Calle Jaén Museums E2
Casa de Murillo .... (see 1)
2 Catedral Metropolitana F4
3 Iglesia de San Francisco E4
4 Mercado de las Brujas D5
5 Mercado Negro C5
Museo Costumbrista Juan de Vargas .... (see 1)
6 Museo de Etnografía y Folklore F4
Museo de Metales Preciosos .... (see 1)
Museo del Litoral .... (see 1)
7 Museo Nacional del Arte F4

Activities, Courses & Tours
Climbing South America .... (see 8)
8 Gravity Assisted Mountain Biking D5
9 HanaqPacha Travel E3

Eating
10 Ali Pacha G5
11 Mercado Camacho G6
12 Mercado Lanza D3
13 Mercado Uruguay A5
14 Popular Cocina Boliviana D4

Drinking & Nightlife
15 Hb Bronze Coffeebar H5

Entertainment
16 Jallalla E3
17 Peña Huari D5
18 Peña Jamuy C5

in the nearby mountains. Also sells great topography and trekking maps.

HanaqPacha Travel Tours
(Map p234; cell 6980-3602; www.hanaqpachatravel.com; Jaén 765, Casco Viejo; 9am-6:30pm) Runs recommended daily tours to El Alto (B$140) to step inside the prismatic *cholets* of Aymará architect Freddy Mamani. Also has a daily Tastes of Bolivia tour (B$140) to learn about typical food. Uyuni, Tiwanaku and Rurrenabaque are the focus of longer tours.

SHOPPING

Walisuma Arts & Crafts
(www.facebook.com/walisuma.org; Aliaga 1231, San Miguel; 10am-8pm Mon-Fri, to 7pm Sat) For a one-of-a-kind souvenir head to Walisuma, which works with 59 Bolivian artisans. Star items include gorgeous (and ultrasoft) alpaca and vicuña textiles made with natural dyes. There are also quinoa soaps, flavored Uyuni salts and designer sweaters. Prices match the quality.

EATING

Namas Té Vegetarian $
(www.namastebolivia.com; Zoilo Flores 1334, San Pedro; mains B$12-30; 8:30am-7pm Mon-Fri, to 4pm Sat;) Tea lovers take note: the tea menu at this lovable lime-green veggie restaurant is a staggering four pages long! There's also plenty of quinoa in all forms (falafel, soup, tabbouleh salad) and even a raved-about tofu pad thai. Smoothies, juices and sandwiches round out the well-priced menu.

Los Qñapés Bolivian $
(www.facebook.com/losqnapes; René Moreno 1283, San Miguel; snacks B$6-15; 3:30-10pm) Snack on Bolivian favorites like *cuñapé* (a cheesy yuca bread), *humitas* (a steamed corn pie) and *masacos* (plantains or yucca mashed with meat or cheese) at this always-busy cafe. All of the ingredients are organic and come from within the country.

Popular Cocina Boliviana Bolivian $$
(Map p234; www.facebook.com/popularlapazbolivia; Murillo 826, Rosario; 3-course lunch B$50; 12:30-2:30pm Mon-Sat) The concept of waiting in line for a restaurant doesn't exist in La Paz, but that's exactly what you'll need to do to get into Popular. Seasonal three-course menus put a gourmet spin on the city's humble lunch spots. Ingredients come fresh from the market and the plates are true works of art. Did we mention that it's ridiculously affordable?

MagicK Cafe Cultural International $$
(Map p238; www.cafemagick.com; Presbítero Medina 2526, Sopocachi; mains B$30-55; ⌚4-11:30pm Tue-Sat;) This funky pescatarian restaurant serves up fig-and-blue-cheese pizza, quinoa tabbouleh and pasta with smoked trout in a lovingly converted Sopocachi home. Vegan and gluten-free options abound, as do good tunes and chill vibes.

Toga Asian $$
(Map p238; ☎mobile 7650-4643; Av Sánchez Lima 2235, Sopocachi; 4-course meal B$35; ⌚10am-11pm Mon-Sat) There's no fixed menu here so you'll have to put your trust in chef Rubén Gruñeiro as he takes you on a four-course culinary journey mixing Asian flavors with Bolivian produce. With just four tables and an open kitchen, it's an incredibly intimate experience.

Ali Pacha Vegetarian $$$
(Map p234; ☎220-2366; www.alipacha.com; Colón 1306, Casco Viejo; 3/5/7 courses B$100/150/200; ⌚noon-3pm Tue-Sat & 7-10pm Wed-Sat;) Locals thought it absurd on so many levels to open a high-end vegetarian restaurant with degustation menus in La Paz's downtrodden Casco Viejo neighborhood. And it is absurd. Fantastically so! Even carnivores will swoon over the creative plant-based creations and herbaceous cocktails. You're guaranteed to taste the flavors of Bolivia like never before.

Gustu Bolivian $$$
(☎211-7491; www.gustu.bo; Calle 10 No 300, Calacoto; almuerzo B$95, dinner tasting menu B$430-560, à la carte mains B$95-130; ⌚noon-3pm & 6:30-11pm; P) Credited with sparking La Paz' culinary renaissance, and launched by the Danish culinary entrepreneur Claus Meyer (of Noma fame), this groundbreaking restaurant works to both rescue and showcase underutilized Bolivian ingredients. It's located in a gorgeous building rich with Andean textiles and offers everything from Andean grains to caiman from the Amazon. Even the wine pairings come from within Bolivia.

Bolivian Peñas

Typical of La Paz (and most of Bolivia) are folk-music venues known as *peñas*. These present traditional Andean music, rendered on *zampoñas* (pan flutes), *quenas* (cane flute) and *charangos* (ukulele-style instrument), as well as guitar shows and song recitals. Most shows happen on Friday and Saturday nights, starting at 9pm or 10pm and running into the wee hours.

Jallalla (Map p234; Indaburo 710, cnr Jaén, Casco Viejo; cover incl cocktail B$30-70; ⌚9pm-1am Tue, Thu, Fri & Sat) Just above the Mamani Mamani Gallery, this is one art-filled *peña* you won't want to miss. The top-tier live music goes nicely with authentic Bolivian tapas and creative cocktails.

Peña Huari (Map p234; ☎231-6225; Sagárnaga 339, Rosario; cover B$105; ⌚show 8pm) The city's best-known *peña* draws tourists and Bolivian business-people. The attached restaurant specializes in Bolivian fare.

Peña Jamuy (Map p234; ☎cell 7676-7817; www.facebook.com/jamuybolivia; Max Paredes, near Sagárnaga, Rosario; cover B$25-50; ⌚9pm-7am Fri & Sat) Locals flock to this fun two-story Andean-themed venue. It hosts all-night ragers each weekend.

Dancers at Peña Huari

Sopocachi

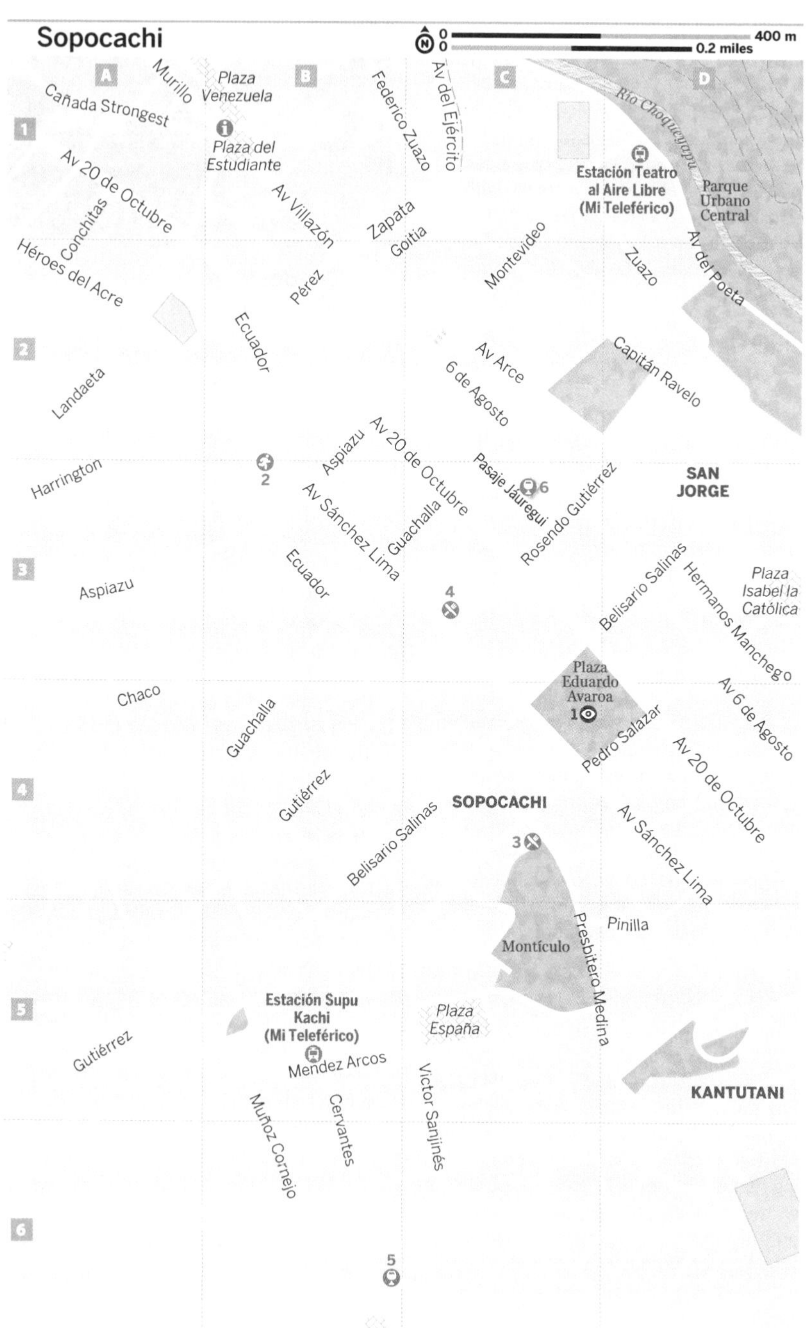
0
400 m
0
0.2 miles
A
B
C
D
1
2
3
4
5
6
Murillo
Plaza Venezuela
Cañada Strongest
Plaza del Estudiante
Federico Zuazo
Av del Ejército
Río Choqueyapu
Estación Teatro al Aire Libre (Mi Teleférico)
Parque Urbano Central
Av 20 de Octubre
Conchitas
Héroes del Acre
Av Villazón
Zapata
Goitia
Pérez
Montevideo
Zuazo
Av del Poeta
Ecuador
Landaeta
Av Arce
6 de Agosto
Capitán Ravelo
Harrington
2
Aspiazu
Av 20 de Octubre
Pasaje Jáuregui
6
Rosendo Gutiérrez
SAN JORGE
Av Sánchez Lima
Guachalla
Ecuador
Aspiazu
4
Belisario Salinas
Hermanos Manchego
Plaza Isabel la Católica
Plaza Eduardo Avaroa
1
Chaco
Guachalla
Pedro Salazar
Av 6 de Agosto
Av 20 de Octubre
Gutiérrez
SOPOCACHI
Belisario Salinas
3
Av Sánchez Lima
Pinilla
Montículo
Presbitero Medina
Estación Supu Kachi (Mi Teleférico)
Plaza España
Gutiérrez
Mendez Arcos
Victor Sanjinés
KANTUTANI
Muñoz Cornejo
Cervantes
5

Sopocachi

Sights
1 Sopocachi C4

Activities, Courses & Tours
2 La Paz on Foot B3

Eating
3 MagicK Cafe Cultural C4
4 Toga C3

Drinking & Nightlife
5 La Costilla de Adán B6
6 Reineke Fuchs C3

DRINKING & NIGHTLIFE

Hb Bronze Coffeebar Coffee
(Map p234; http://hb-bronze.com; Plaza Tomás Frías 1570, Casco Viejo; 8:30am-midnight Mon-Sat, 1-9pm Sun;) Sleek, earthy and architecturally inspiring – coffee shops don't get much cooler than Hb Bronze! This sorely needed addition to the Casco Viejo neighborhood offers the strongest brews in the city, and it doubles as a bar by night with 100% Bolivian cocktails, beers and wines. The food is equally memorable.

La Costilla de Adán Cocktail Bar
(Map p238; cell 7207-4518; Armaza 2974, Sopocachi; 9pm-4am Wed-Sat) Take a dive down the rabbit hole into the mind of owner Roberto Cazola at this supremely surreal speakeasy. Prepare yourself for hundreds of creepy dolls, a dozen hanging bicycles and a night full of wonder next to the roaring fire. There's no sign out front. Simply ring the bell, wait, and let the magic begin.

Reineke Fuchs Beer Hall
(Map p238; www.reinekefuchs.com; Pasaje Jáuregui 2241, Sopocachi; noon-3pm & 7pm-late Mon-Fri, 7pm-late Sat) This woodsy Sopocachi *brewhaus* features imported German beers, *schnappsladen* and hearty sausage-based fare. They also make their own Pilsner, dunkel and amber ales, based on centuries-old Deutsch traditions – heady concoctions, indeed.

INFORMATION

Tourist Information (Map p234; cnr Av Mariscal Santa Cruz & Colombia, Prado; 8:30am-7pm Mon-Fri) Stop by to grab some maps and get detailed information. English is spoken by some staff.

Tourist Information (Map p238; www.facebook.com/Gamlpturismo; Plaza del Estudiante, Prado; 8:30am-7pm Mon-Fri) Maps, flyers and some English-speaking staff.

GETTING THERE & AWAY

AIR

El Alto International Airport (LPB; Héroes Km 7, El Alto) is 10km via toll road from the city center on the altiplano. At 4062m, it's the world's highest international airport.

BUS

La Paz has three bus terminals/bus areas. You can use the **main bus terminal** (Terminal de Buses; Map p234; cnr Avs Perú & Uruguay, Challapampa) for most national and international destinations.

GETTING AROUND

MICRO & MINIBUS

La Paz' buses charge from B$2 per trip. Look for your destination on a signboard posted in the front window.

TAXI & RIDE SHARE

Radio taxis (with roof bubbles advertising their telephone numbers) are recommended.

A newer solution to safe taxis is to use the **Easy Taxi app** (www.easytaxi.com/bo, in Spanish). **Uber** (www.uber.com) is also available in La Paz.

SALAR DE UYUNI, BOLIVIA

In this Chapter

Salar de Uyuni, Bolivia

An evocative and eerie sight, the world's largest salt flat measures 12,106 sq km and sits at 3653m (11,984ft). When the surface is dry, the salar is a pure white expanse of the greatest nothing imaginable – just blue sky, white ground and you. When there's a little water, the surface perfectly reflects the clouds and the blue altiplano sky, and the horizon disappears. If you're driving across the surface at such times, the effect is surreal; it's hard to believe that you're not flying through the clouds.

Two Days in Salar de Uyuni

On day one, check out the locomotive graveyard of the **Cementerio de Trenes** (p248). Then head to Colchani village to learn about salt extraction. End the day with a sunset at **Isla Incahuasi** (p244).

On day two continue south through the Desierto de Siloli, stopping at the strange **Árbol de Piedra** (p246) and flamingo-studded **Laguna Colorada** (p246).

Four Days in Salar de Uyuni

Rise early for a sunrise visit to the **Sol de Mañana** (p247) geyser field, then soak in the mineral-rich waters of **Termas de Polques** (p247). Later photograph the striking Desierto de Dalí and emerald-hued **Laguna Verde** (p247).

On day four make a day trip from Uyuni up to the semi-ghost town of **Pulacayo** (p249). In the evening dine at first-rate **Tika** (p248).

Previous page: Salar de Uyuni
SARA WINTER / SHUTTERSTOCK ©

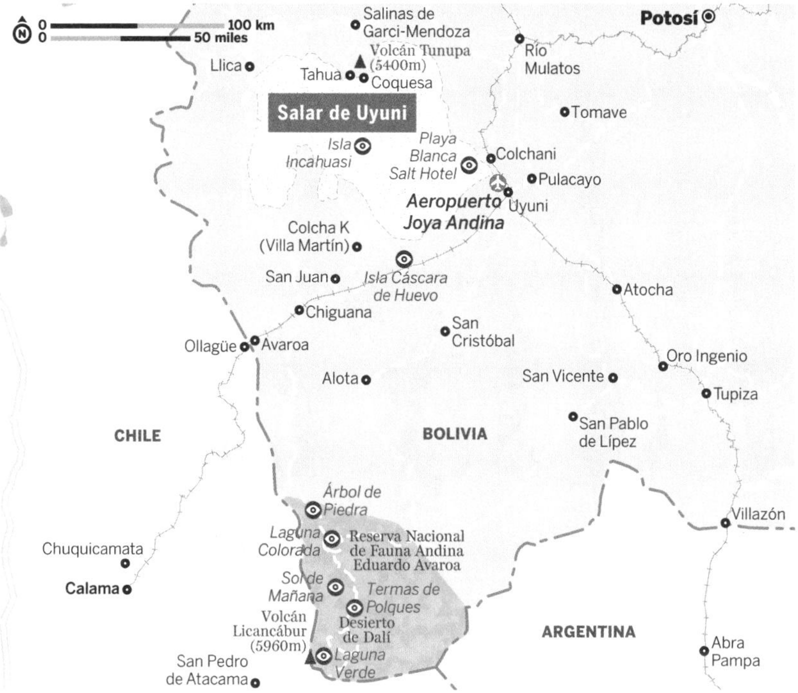

Arriving in Salar de Uyuni

Aeropuerto Joya Andina is 1km north of the town of Uyuni. **Amaszonas** (www.amaszonas.com) and **Boliviana de Aviación** (www.boa.bo) operate two flights a day to La Paz (from B$700, one hour).

The safest, most comfortable ground transport from La Paz is with **Todo Turismo** (www.todoturismo.bo), which runs a heated bus service.

Where to Stay

When you're on a salt flat, what better place to spend the night than in a salt hotel? The simple salt hotels in Coquesa, Chuvica and San Juan are nearly identical, with salt floors, furniture and walls, and common dining rooms where you can eat dinner (and shiver). There are also more luxurious salt hotels just outside of Uyuni.

Flag Monuments

Visiting the Salt Flats

Bolivia's most awe-inspiring site is the blindingly white Salar de Uyuni, a vast (12,106 sq km) salt flat that sits at an elevation of 3653m (11,984ft). Tours here also take in surreal rock formations, otherworldly lakes (that are home to several flamingo species) and bizarre desert landscapes.

Great For...

Need to Know

Tours to Salar de Uyuni cost B$800 to B$1200 for three days at a standard agency, and B$1200 to B$1500 at a high-end operation.

Isla Incahuasi

One of the highlights of a Salar de Uyuni tour is a hike around the spectacular **Isla Incahuasi** (Map p243), otherwise known as Inkawasi. It's located in the heart of the *salar*, 80km west of Colchani. This hilly outpost is covered in Trichocereus cactus and surrounded by a flat white sea of hexagonal salt tiles.

It was once a remarkably lonely, otherworldly place but since the advent of *salar* tours it receives large numbers of visitors every day. Nonetheless, it's still a beautiful sight if you forget the crowds.

You have to pay an entry fee to climb the hill (B$30), and tour groups clamber over the hiking trails chasing the perfect photo of cacti and salt. It's a 15-minute walk to the top of the island, with a trail that loops back, but it's worth it. Note that during the

Bolivian cacti

GALYNA ANDRUSHKO / SHUTTERSTOCK ©

★ **Top Tip**

Bring several liters of water, snacks, a headlamp, sunscreen, sunglasses, a hat, warm clothes, a camera, and a plastic dinosaur (for photos, of course).

Take a Break

There are simple restaurants in the villages of Colchani, Coquesa and Chuvica on the edge of the *salar.*

wet season when the *salar* is flooded, the island is inaccessible.

Playa Blanca Salt Hotel

Although the **salt hotel** (Map p243) is now closed to overnight visitors, you can still check out the salt sculptures inside and the Dakar Rally and Flag Monuments outside (add your flag if you've brought one). Find your own isolated piece of salt desert to enjoy and take out your props – it's here that plastic dinosaurs come out, as photographers play with the bizarre perspective caused by the bright blue skies and superflat landscape. Many tour groups stop for lunch here.

Colchani

Located right on the edge of Salar de Uyuni, Colchani is the easiest place to access the great salt flat and the place to go if you just want a glimpse of the *salar*. Most salt-flat tours stop here to visit the souvenir stalls and small salt museum, which is built from salt and contains salt sculptures (admission is free). Colchani is 22km north of Uyuni; buses to Oruro pass the village (B$5, 40 minutes).

The families here make their living from salt extraction as part of a cooperative; you can see small pyramids of salt draining on the *salar*, close to the village.

Isla Cáscara de Huevo

The small **'Eggshell Island'** (Map p243) was named for the broken shells of birds' eggs that litter it. It's located near the southern end of Salar de Uyuni and is visited mainly for the strange patterns of salt crystallization in the area, some of which resemble roses. However, due to nearby lithium mines and restricted access to the surrounding area, Cáscara de Huevo is no longer included on tour itineraries.

Coquesa

At the village of Coquesa on the northern edge of the *salar*, take time to explore the ruined ancient villages and burial grounds nearby. Ceramic, gold and copper artifacts, and articles of clothing have been discovered at some of the sites, indicating the presence of an advanced but little-known culture. The **Museo Coquesa** (per 4WD B$20; hours vary) houses a collection of mummies and ceramics.

Unfortunately, the sites' remoteness has left the sites vulnerable to amateur treasure hunters who have plundered several items of archaeological value.

Coquesa is also the starting point for climbs up **Volcán Tunupa**. Local guides charge B$500 to take you up.

Árbol de Piedra

This much-photographed, 5m-tall **rock** (Map p243) in Desierto Siloli resembles a tree. Most tours stop here on the way to Laguna Colorada.

Laguna Colorada

Laguna Colorada (Map p243; 4278m) is a rusty-burnt-orange-hued lake that covers approximately 60 sq km and reaches a depth of just 80cm. The rich red coloration on the lake is derived from algae and plankton that thrive in the mineral-rich water, and the shoreline is fringed with brilliant white deposits of sodium, magnesium, borax and gypsum. More apparent are the flamingos that breed here; all three South American species are present.

The lake sediments are rich in diatoms (tiny microfossils used in the production of fertilizer, paint, toothpaste and plastics, and as a filtering agent for oil, pharmaceuticals, aviation fuel, beer and wine). The clear air is bitterly cold and winter nighttime temperatures can drop below –20°C.

Árbol de Piedra

Sol de Mañana

Most tour groups wake at dawn to visit the large geyser field dubbed **Sol de Mañana** (Map p243). This 4850m-high geyser basin has bubbling mud pots, hellish fumaroles and a thick and nauseating aroma of sulfur fumes. Approach the site cautiously; any damp or cracked earth is potentially dangerous and cave-ins do occur, sometimes causing serious burns.

Desierto de Dalí

Where the route splits about 20km south of Sol de Mañana, the more scenic left fork climbs up and over a 5000m pass, then up a hillside dotted with enormous rocks, which look like they were meticulously placed by the surrealist master Salvador Dalí.

☑ Don't Miss

Hiking amid the strange salt formations and cacti on the top of Isla Incahuasi (p244).

BOTOND HORVATH / SHUTTERSTOCK ©

Termas de Polques

At the foot of Cerro Polques lies **Termas de Polques** (Map p243; B$6), a small 29.4°C hot-spring pool, and an absolute paradise after the chilly *salar* nights. Although the mineral-rich waters are not boiling by any means, they're suitable for bathing and are thought to relieve the symptoms of arthritis and rheumatism.

Laguna Verde

The stunning blue-green **Laguna Verde** (Map p243; 4400m) is tucked into the southwestern corner of Bolivian territory, 52km south of Sol de Mañana. The incredible green color comes from high concentrations of lead, sulfur, arsenic and calcium carbonates. Most tours visit this in the morning, but it's at its most dramatic during the afternoon when incessant icy winds have whipped the water into a brilliant green-and-white froth.

This surface agitation, combined with the high mineral content, means that it can remain liquid at temperatures as low as −21.2°C. Behind the lake rises the cone of Volcán Licancabur (5960m), whose summit is said to have once sheltered an ancient Inca crypt.

Volcán Licancabur

Though not included on the standard tours, there is plenty of scope for hiring your own driver and climbing some volcanoes.

The most frequently climbed is Volcán Licancabur (5960m); it takes about eight hours to climb to the summit and two to get down. Several Uyuni and Tupiza agencies can include a guided climb of the volcano in a Southwest Circuit route, adding an extra day to the trip.

The climb can be done comfortably (if you can handle the altitude) in one day. As the volcano is sacred to the locals, the guides usually perform a ritual for Pachamama, asking the earth goddess for her permission to climb.

Uyuni

Standing in defiance of the desert-like landscape that surrounds it, Uyuni occupies a desolate corner of southwestern Bolivia. Mention Uyuni to a Bolivian and they will whistle and emphasize *harto frío* (extreme cold). Yet despite the icy conditions, the town has a cheerful buzz about it, with hundreds of travelers passing through every week to kick off their tour of Salar de Uyuni or the Southwest Circuit.

SIGHTS

Cementerio de Trenes Historic Site

(Train Cemetery) FREE The only real attraction in Uyuni, Cementerio de Trenes is a rusty collection of historic steam locomotives and rail cars dating back to the 19th century, when there was a rail-car factory here. Today they sit decaying in the yards about 3km southwest of the modern-day station along Av Ferroviaria. They're fun to climb on, and it's a nice walk from town to keep you warm. Most tours visit the train cemetery as a first or last stop on the three-day *salar* circuit.

TOURS

Quechua Connection Tour

(693-3923; www.quechuaconnection4wd.com; cnr Bolívar & Cabrera; 7:30am-noon & 3-8pm) This company offers salt-flat tours with English-speaking guides. Its best sellers are tours that include the chance to cycle 3km across the salt flats.

Salty Desert Aventours Tour

(7237-0444; www.saltydesert-uyuni.com; Av Ferroviaria, btwn Av Arce & Bolívar; 10am-12:30pm & 2:30-7:30pm) This operator gets good reviews. Tours with an English-speaking guide are available for an extra cost.

Hidalgo Tours Tours

(693-2989; www.salardeuyuni.net; Av Potosí 113, Hotel Jardines de Uyuni; 7am-7:30pm) This upscale agency offers high-end, private tours with accommodations at luxury salt hotels.

Andes Salt Expeditions Tour

(591 7241 4748; www.andes-salt-uyuni.com.bo; Av Ferroviaria 56) This agency offers a range of tours at various price points. Its founder, ex-miner Raul Braulio Mamani, worked as the guide for *The Devil's Miner* documentary, a 2005 film about two brothers working in mines near Potosí.

Cordillera Tours Tours

(693-3304; www.cordilleratraveller.com; Av Ferroviaria 314; 7:30-11am & 1:30-7pm) Offers the usual salt-flat tours as well as transfers to Chile (from B$350 per person).

SHOPPING

Market Market

(Av Potosí; Sun & Thu) The big market day in Uyuni is Thursday when Av Potosí gets taken over by stalls selling anything from arts and crafts to television sets; Sunday is a smaller market day.

EATING

Mercado Campesino Market $

(Avaroa, cnr Av Potosí; meals B$5-10; 6am-noon) For quick eats, cheap meals are on offer at the market's *comedor* (dining hall) and nearby street-food stalls.

Tika Bolivian $$

(693-2989; www.tikarestaurante.com.bo; Av Potosí 113; mains B$40-92; 4-10pm;) Tika's chic, modern dining room is an appealing setting to sample contemporary takes on traditional Bolivian dishes, such as *charque lipeño* (sun-dried llama meat with potatoes, cheese and corn) and *k'alaphurka*, a gurgling corn soup served with a hot volcanic stone.

Minuteman Revolutionary Pizza Pizza $$

(693-3186; Av Ferroviaria 60; mains B$55-65; 8-10am & 5-9pm) This convivial spot inside **Toñito Hotel** is run by Chris from Boston and his Bolivian wife Sussy, and is a travelers' favorite. Sample the best pizzas in town as well as tasty gourmet salads. It's also a cozy spot for a beer, glass of Tarija wine or a hearty breakfast (B$20 to B$50).

Lithium Club Bolivian $$$

(693-3399; Av Potosí 24; mains B$70-120; 10:30am-10pm Mon-Sat, 4-10pm Sun) This upper-end choice has international takes on traditional Bolivian dishes like *charque de llama* (llama jerky) and *pailita de llama* (llama stew), bringing together authentic flavor combinations with a smidgen of European styling.

DRINKING & NIGHTLIFE

Extreme Fun Pub Pub

(La Llamita; Sucre 23; 2:30pm-1am) For a night of extreme fun head to Uyuni's top drinking spot. The extensive cocktail list features concoctions such as Sexy Llama Bitch and Sensual Llama's Navel, as well as hot cocktails to warm you up on cold nights. There are salt floors, drinking games, friendly service and beautiful *salar* photos. Guitars are on hand for impromptu music sessions.

INFORMATION

Infotur (693-3666; cnr Avs Potosí & Arce; 8am-noon & 2:30-6:30pm Mon-Fri) Well stocked with leaflets on Uyuni and the rest of Bolivia. At the time of research, the office was located in the bus terminal while the office on Avenida Arce was being renovated.

Office of Reserva Nacional de Fauna Andina Eduardo Avaroa (REA; 693-2225; www.boliviarea.com; cnr Colón & Avaroa; 9am-6pm Mon-Fri) Administrative office for the park in Uyuni. You can buy your park entry (B$150) here if going on your own.

GETTING THERE & AWAY

AIR

The quickest way to get to Uyuni is by flying direct from La Paz to Aeropuerto Joya Andina, 1km north of town.

Ghostly Pulacayo

At this virtual ghost **town** (B$10), brilliantly colored rocks rise beside the road and a mineral-rich stream reveals streaks of blue, yellow, red and green. The silver mines north of the village closed in 1959 and today only a few hundred hardy souls remain.

Also worth seeing here is the mansion of the 22nd president of Bolivia, Aniceto Arce Ruíz. Nearby is a collection of decaying steam locomotives that were originally imported to transport ore. They include Bolivia's first steam engine, El Chiripa, and the train that was robbed by legendary bandits Butch Cassidy and the Sundance Kid, including a wooden rail car that bears the bullet holes from the attack.

Take any bus to Potosí and ask to be dropped off at Pulacayo (B$5, 30 minutes) or book a tour. There is a fee of B$10 to enter the village.

BUS

Uyuni's gleaming new **bus terminal** (Avaroa) has a choice of companies to most destinations, so ask around to get the best price, time and service.

Potosí buses leave hourly; for Sucre it's easiest to head to Potosí and change there.

TRAIN

Uyuni has a modern, well-organized **train station** (693-2153; www.fca.com.bo; Av Ferroviaria s/n). Trains take you north to Oruro and south to Villazón. Seats often sell out, so buy your ticket several days in advance or get an agency to do it for you.

LAKE TITICACA, PERU

In this Chapter

Lake Titicaca, Peru

In Andean belief, Titicaca is the birthplace of the sun. In addition, it's the largest lake in South America and the highest navigable body of water in the world. Enthralling and in many ways singular, the shimmering deep-blue Lake Titicaca is the longtime home of highland cultures steeped in the old ways. Pre-Inca Pukara, Tiwanaku and Collas all left a mark on the landscape.

Today, the region is a mix of crumbling cathedrals, desolate altiplano and checkerboard fields backed by high Andean peaks. In this world, ancient holidays are marked with riotous celebrations where elaborately costumed processions and brass bands start a frenzy that lasts for days.

Lake Titicaca in Two Days

Spend the day exploring the extraordinary floating **Islas Uros** (p254). Overnight in the excellent homestay of **Cristina Suaña** (p255) on Isla Khantati.

On day two visit the impressive funerary towers of **Sillustani** (p256), keeping an eye out for abundant birdlife in the area. In the evening, return to Puno for a fantastic Peruvian meal at **Mojsa** (p261).

Lake Titicaca in Four Days

Head to traditional **Isla Taquile** (p258). Climb the island's many steps, admire the fine stonework and shop for locally made crafts.

On day four, explore the sights of Puno. See pre-Columbian artifacts at **Museo Carlos Dreyer** (p260), learn about coca and traditional dress at the **Museo de la Coca y Costumbres** (p260) and dine at **La Table del Inca** (p261).

Previous page: Peruvian women on Islas Uros (p254)

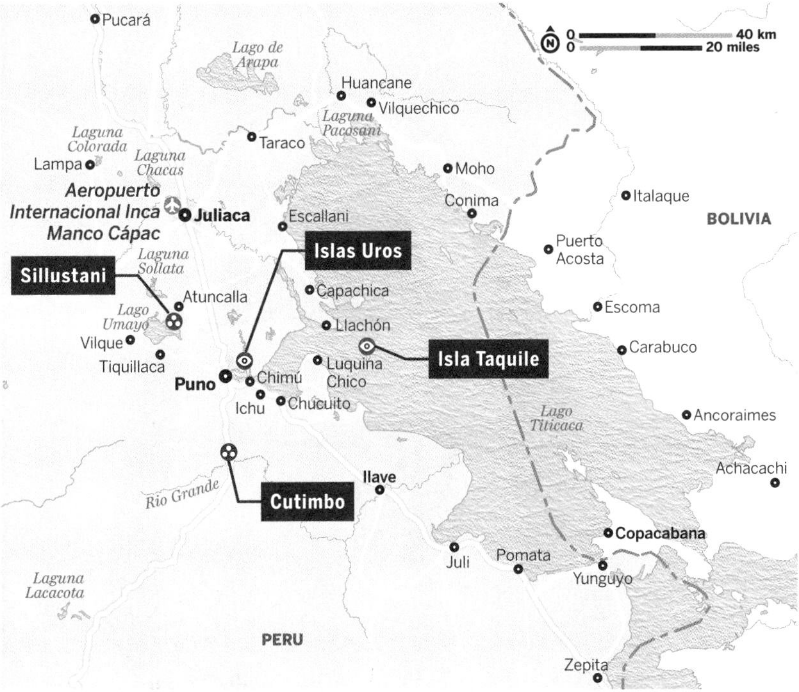

Arriving in Lake Titicaca

Aeropuerto Internacional Inca Manco Cápac The region's only airport is one hour from Puno, the gateway to Titicaca.

Bus & Car Overland crossings from the southeast side of the lake are usually through Copacabana in Bolivia to the border post at Yunguyo.

Where to Stay

In Puno, pedestrianised Calle Lima between Parque Pino and Plaza de Armas is the most active and safest street. Staying anywhere within three blocks of here is the most convenient and secure. Calle Lima and Jirón Arequipa can suffer from nighttime bar or traffic noise, so try to avoid street-facing rooms.

There are homestays on many of the islands, which include the option of a home-cooked meal while staying with a local family.

Sculpture and boat mad

AKUGASAHAGY / SHUTTERSTOCK ©

Islas Uros

These extraordinary floating islands are Lake Titicaca's top attraction. Their uniqueness is due to their construction, created entirely with the buoyant totora reeds that grow abundantly in the shallows of the lake.

Great For...

☑ Don't Miss

A taste test of the reeds, which resemble sugarcane without any sweetness.

The lives of the Uros people are interwoven with these reeds. Partially edible (tasting like nonsweet sugarcane), the reeds are also used to build homes, boats and crafts. The islands are constructed from many layers of the *totora*, which are constantly replenished from the top as they rot from the bottom, so the ground is always soft and springy.

Some islands also have elaborately designed versions of traditional tightly bundled reed boats on hand and other whimsical reed creations, such as archways and even swing sets. Be prepared to pay for a boat ride (S10) or to take photographs.

Intermarriage with the Aymará-speaking indigenous people has seen the demise of the pure-blooded Uros, who nowadays all speak Aymará. Always a small tribe, the Uros began their unusual floating existence

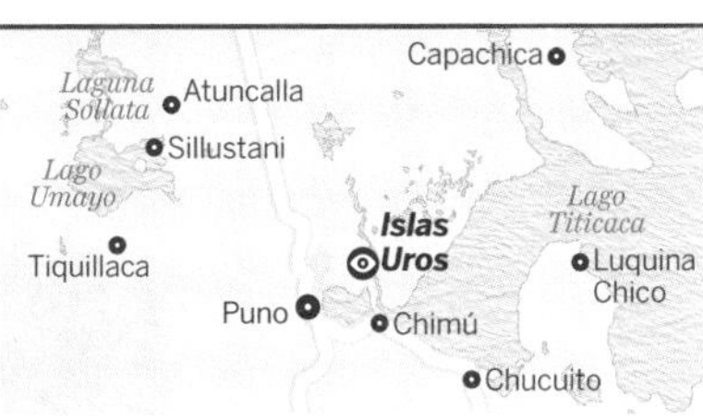

Need to Know

Boat tours take you to the islands, 7km east of Puno.

Take a Break

Snacks and drinks are sold by island inhabitants, but there are no restaurants.

★ Top Tip

Handicrafts sold on the islands are an important livelihood for inhabitants, who sometimes see little tour money.

centuries ago in an effort to isolate themselves from the aggressive Collas and Incas.

The popularity of the islands has led to aggressive commercialization in some cases. The most traditional reed islands are located further from Puno through a maze of small channels, only visited by private boat. Islanders there continue to live in a relatively traditional fashion and prefer not to be photographed.

Homestays

There are now more than a handful of upmarket homestays on Islas Uros, ranging from elegant huts to luxury rooms with floor-to-ceiling windows to maximize lake views. Check if boat transfer and any cultural activities are included in rates.

An outstanding option is staying in the reed huts of Isla Khantati with effervescent **Cristina Suaña** (951-472-355, 951-695-121; uroskhantati@hotmail.com; Isla Khantati; per person full board S180), an Uros native who has built a number of impeccable semi-traditional huts (with solar power, outhouses and shady decks), which occupy half the tiny island. The hyper-relaxed pace means a visit here is not ideal for those with little time on their hands. The tariff is steep but includes top-notch accommodations, three meals, fishing and ample cultural activity.

Getting There & Away

Getting to the Uros is easy – there's no need to go with an organized tour, though you'll miss out on the guides' history lesson. Ferries leave from the port for Uros (return trip S10) at least once an hour from 6am to 4pm. The community-owned ferry service visits two islands, on a rotation basis. Ferries to Taquile and Amantaní can also drop you off in the Uros.

Chullpas, Sillustani

Chullpas

The ancient Colla people who once dominated the Lake Titicaca area buried their nobility in imposing chullpas (funerary towers), which can be seen scattered widely around the hilltops of the region.

Great For...

☑ Don't Miss

Lago Umayo (partially encircling Sillustani), home to a wide variety of plants and Andean waterbirds.

The Colla people were a warlike, Aymará-speaking tribe, who later became the southeastern group of the Incas. Their *chullpas* housed the remains of complete family groups, along with plenty of food and belongings for their journey into the next world. Their only opening was a small hole facing east, just large enough for a person to crawl through, which would be sealed immediately after a burial. Nowadays, nothing remains of the burials, but the *chullpas* are well preserved.

Sillustani

The most impressive towers are at **Sillustani** (adult/child S15/2), where the tallest reaches a height of 12m. The afternoon light is the best for photography, though the site can get busy at this time.

Prehistoric Inca ruin, Cutimbo

RAFAL CICHAWA / SHUTTERSTOCK ©

Need to Know

Sillustani tours leave at 2:30pm daily (from S30; taxi S80); Cutimbo tours cost from US$59 (taxi S30).

Take a Break

Tours often include visiting local families and eating boiled potato dipped in *arcilla* (edible clay).

★ Top Tip

A *turismo vivencia* (homestay) means you can help your host family with farming and visit lesser-known archaeological sites.

The walls of the towers are made from massive coursed blocks reminiscent of Inca stonework, but are considered to be even more complicated. Carved but unplaced blocks, and a ramp used to raise them, are among the site's points of interest, and you can also see the makeshift quarry. A few of the blocks are decorated, including a well-known carving of a lizard on one of the *chullpas* closest to the parking lot.

Sillustani is partially encircled by the sparkling Lago Umayo (3890m), which is home to a wide variety of plants and Andean waterbirds, plus a small island with vicuñas (threatened, wild relatives of alpacas). Bird-watchers take note: this is one of the best sites in the area.

Tours to Sillustani leave Puno at around 2:30pm daily and cost from S30.

Cutimbo

Just over 20km from Puno, this dramatic site has an extraordinary position upon a table-topped volcanic hill surrounded by a fertile plain. Its modest number of well-preserved *chullpas*, built by the Colla, Lupaca and Inca cultures, come in both square and cylindrical shapes. You can still see the ramps used to build them. Look closely and you'll find several monkeys, pumas and snakes carved into the structures. Go in a group and keep an eye out for muggers.

Combis (minibuses) en route to Laraqueri (S3, 30 minutes) leave from the Terminal Zonal in Puno.

The view from Isla Taquile

NEALE COUSLAND / SHUTTERSTOCK ©

Isla Taquile

In the strong island sunlight, the deep, red-colored soil of Taquile contrasts with the intense blue of the lake and the glistening backdrop of Bolivia's snowy Cordillera Real.

Great For...

☑ Don't Miss

Fiesta de San Diego – a celebration with dancing and music from July 25 until early August.

Inhabited for thousands of years, Isla Taquile is a tiny 7-sq-km island with a population of about 2000 people. Taquile's lovely scenery is reminiscent of the Mediterranean, with several hills that boast Inca terracing on their sides and small ruins on top.

Taquile's People

Quechua-speaking islanders are distinct from most of the surrounding Aymará-speaking island communities and maintain a strong sense of group identity. They rarely marry non-Taquile people.

Handicrafts

Taquile has a fascinating tradition of handicrafts, and the islanders' creations are made according to a system of deeply ingrained social customs. Men wear tightly woven woolen hats that resemble floppy

Woman weaving on Isla Taquile

HADYNYAH / GETTY IMAGES ©

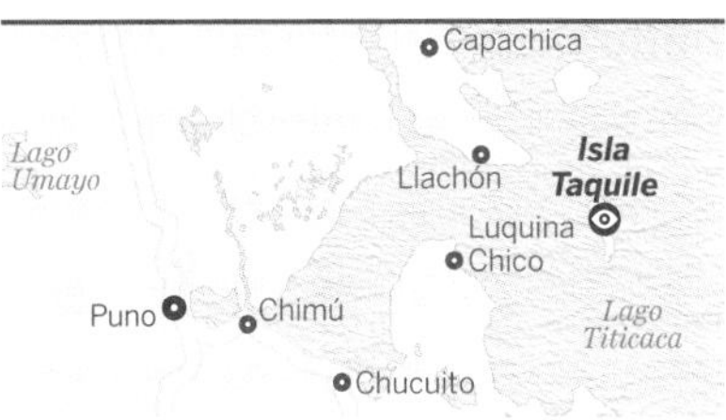

Need to Know

Ferries (round-trip S25; island admission S5) leave from the Puno port for Taquile from 7:35am.

Take a Break

Consider eating in the Restaurante Comunál, Taquile's only community-run food outlet.

★ Top Tip

There are no roads or streetlights, so bring a flashlight for an overnight stay.

nightcaps, which they knit themselves – only men knit, learning from the age of eight. These hats are closely bound up with social symbolism: men wear red hats if they are married and red-and-white hats if they are single, and different colors can denote a man's current or past social position.

Taquile women weave thick, colorful waistbands for their husbands, which are worn with roughly spun white shirts and thick, calf-length black pants. Women wear eye-catching outfits comprising multilayered skirts and delicately embroidered blouses. These fine garments are considered some of the most well-made traditional clothes in Peru, and can be bought in the cooperative store on the island's main plaza.

Visiting

Visitors are free to wander around, explore the ruins and enjoy the tranquility. The island is a wonderful place to catch a sunset and gaze at the moon, which looks twice as bright in the crystalline air, rising over the breathtaking peaks of the Cordillera Real.

A stairway of more than 500 steps leads from the dock to the center of the island. The climb takes a breathless 20 minutes if you're acclimatized – more if you're not.

Make sure you already have lots of small bills in local currency, as change is limited and there's nowhere to exchange dollars. You may want to bring extra money to buy some of the exquisite crafts sold in the cooperative store.

The *hospedajes* (small, family-owned inns) on Taquile offer basic accommodation for around S20 a night. Meals are additional (S10 to S15 for breakfast, S20 for lunch). Options range from a room in a family house to small guesthouses. As the community rotates visitors to lodgings, there is little room for choosing.

Puno

With a regal plaza, concrete block buildings and crumbling bricks that blend into the hills, Puno has its share of both grit and cheer. It serves as the jumping-off point for Lake Titicaca and is a convenient stop for those traveling between Cuzco and La Paz. But it may just capture your heart with its own rackety charm.

SIGHTS

Casa del Corregidor Historic Building

(051-35-1921; www.casadelcorregidor.pe; Deustua 576; 9am-9pm Mon-Sat) FREE An attraction in its own right, this 17th-century house is one of Puno's oldest residences. The former community center now houses a small fair-trade arts-and-crafts store and a cafe.

Museo Carlos Dreyer Museum

(Conde de Lemos 289; admission with English-speaking guide S15; 9am-7pm Mon-Fri, to 1pm Sat) This small museum houses a fascinating collection of Puno-related archaeological artifacts and art from pre-Inca, Inca, colonial and Republic periods. Upstairs there are three mummies and a full-scale fiberglass *chullpa* (funerary tower). It's around the corner from Casa del Corregidor. Guides tend to leave an hour before closing.

Museo de la Coca y Costumbres Museum

(Museum of Coca and Customs; 051-977-0360; www.museodelacoca.com; Ilave 581; admission S10; 9am-7pm Mon-Sat, 3-7pm Sun) Tiny and quirky, this museum offers lots of interesting information – historical, medicinal, cultural – about the coca plant and its many uses. Presentation isn't that interesting, though: reams of text (in English only) are stuck to the wall and interspersed with photographs and old Coca-Cola ads. The display of traditional costumes is what makes a visit here worthwhile.

Though the relation between traditional dress and coca is unfathomable, it's a boon for making sense of the costumes worn in street parades.

TOURS

Edgar Adventures Cultural

(051-35-3444; www.edgaradventures.com; Lima 328; office 7am-8pm) Longtime agency with positive community involvement. More unusual activities include kayaking on Lake Titicaca and visiting remote areas.

All Ways Travel Cultural

(051-35-3979; www.titicacaperu.com; Deustua 576, 2nd fl) Offers both classic and 'nontourist' tours of Islas Uros and Taquile, Sillustani and rural communities in Llachón. They aim to be socially conscious.

Transturin Boat

(051-35-2771; www.transturin.com; Ayacucho 148; 2-day tour US$181; departures 6:30am) There are no passenger ferries across Lake Titicaca from Puno to Bolivia, but you can get to La Paz via the lake in one or two days on high-class catamaran tours with Transturin, visiting Isla del Sol and other sights along the way.

SHOPPING

Feria Arts & Crafts

(Av Costanera, Puno port; 7am-5pm) This craft market sells llama toys, rugs, alpaca sweaters, masks from Puno's La Virgen de la Candelaria festival and other handicrafts you'll see elsewhere in town and on the islands, but at prices more open to haggling. The dozens of nearly identical stalls are at the port entrance, at the end of Av Del Puerto.

EATING

Pushka Peruvian $

(Grau 338; mains S8-15 ménus S8;) It's hard to imagine that just a couple blocks from Puno's busy tourist street there is a large beer-garden-style restaurant. Yet here it is, with play equipment for kids, astroturf and excellent-value *menús* (set meals) of Peruvian dishes. The food is of the same quality you'll find back on Calle Lima, but without the frills.

Mojsa Peruvian $$

(☎051-36-3182; Lima 635; mains S22-30; ⊙noon-9.30pm; ᯤ✎) The go-to place for locals and travelers alike, Mojsa overlooks the plaza and lives up to its name, which is Aymará for 'delicious.' It has a thoughtful range of Peruvian and international food, including innovative trout dishes and a design-your-own salad option. All meals start with fresh bread and a bowl of local olives. In the evening crisp brick-oven pizzas are on offer.

La Table del Inca Fusion $$

(☎994-659-357; www.fb.me/latabledelinca; Ancash 239; mains S26-40, 3 courses with wine S80; ⊙noon-2pm & 6-9.30pm Mon-Thu, 6-9.30pm Sat & Sun; ᯤ) If you need a reason to dress up, this fusion restaurant, a little away from the noise, shows off paintings by local artists on its walls, with colorful plating. Peruvian dishes like *lomo saltado* (stir-fried beef with potatoes and chili) hold their own against Euro-Peruvian twists such as quinoa risotto, alpaca carpaccio with *huacatay* (a local aromatic herb) and French desserts.

Tulipans Pizza $$

(☎051-35-1796; Lima 394; mains S15-30, menús S20; ⊙10am-10pm; ᯤ) Highly recommended for its yummy sandwiches, big plates of meat and piled-high vegetables, this cozy spot is warmed by the pizza oven in the corner. It also has a selection of South American wines. The courtyard patio is attractive for warm days – whenever those happen! Pizzas are only available at night. Tulipans is inside La Casona Parodi.

La Casona Peruvian $$

(☎051-35-1108; http://lacasona-restaurant.com; Lima 423, 2nd fl; mains S22-45; ⊙noon-9.30pm) A solid choice for upscale *criollo* (spicy Peruvian fare with Spanish and African influences) and international food, even if portions are on the small side. Trout comes bathed in garlic or chili sauce. There's also pasta, salad and soup.

Exploring Ichu

Ten kilometers out of Puno, this rural community, spread across a gorgeous green valley, is home to little-known Inca ruins – Centro Ceremonial Tunuhuire. It has superb views, so it's a great place for a hike.

Leave the Panamericana at Ichu's second exit (after the service station) and head inland past the house marked 'Villa Lago 1960.' Walk 2km, bearing left at the junction, aiming for the two small, terraced hills you can see in the left of the valley. Bear left at a second junction (you'll pass the school if you miss it), and the road will take you between the two hills. Turn left again and head straight up the first one. Fifteen minutes of stiff climbing brings you to the top, where you'll be rewarded with the remains of a multilayered temple complex, and breathtaking 360-degree views.

This can be done as an easy half-day trip from Puno, arranged by private tour. Take plenty of water and food as there's no store.

DRINKING

Kamizaraky Rock Pub Pub

(Grau 158; ⊙5pm-midnight) With a classic-rock soundtrack, grungy cool bartenders, cocktails, pizzas and liquor-infused coffee drinks essential for staying warm during Puno's bone-chilling nights, this may be a hard place to leave.

CUZCO & THE SACRED VALLEY, PERU

In this Chapter

Cuzco & the Sacred Valley, Peru

For the Incas, Cuzco was the belly button of the world. A visit to this city and its nearby ruins tumbles you back into the cosmic realm of ancient Andean culture – knocked down and fused with the colonial imprint of Spanish conquest, only to be repackaged as a thriving tourist center. The capital of Cuzco is only the gateway. Beyond lies the Sacred Valley, Andean countryside dotted with villages, high-altitude hamlets and ruins linked by trail and railway tracks to the continent's biggest draw – Machu Picchu.

Two Days in Cuzco & the Sacred Valley

Spend two full days exploring the city of Cuzco. On day one visit the **Museo Machu Picchu** (p275) and **Qorikancha** (p274) and enjoy decadent Andean fare at **Chicha** (p278).

On day two, browse the wares at the **Mercado San Pedro** (p275) and the **Center for Traditional Textiles of Cuzco** (p275). Take the **Marcelo Batata Cooking Class** (p275) and hear some live music at **Centro Qosqo de Arte Nativo** (p279).

Four Days in Cuzco & the Sacred Valley

Head out early for a trip to the impressive **Pisac Ruins** (p268). Take a taxi to the top, then make the walk down to Pisac for a visit to the famed **Mercado de Artesanía** (p280).

On day four, catch a bus to ancient, cobbled Ollantaytambo and hike through the spectacular **ruins** (p270) above town. End the day with a meal at **El Albergue Restaurante** (p281).

Previous page: Agricultural terraces, the Sacred Valley

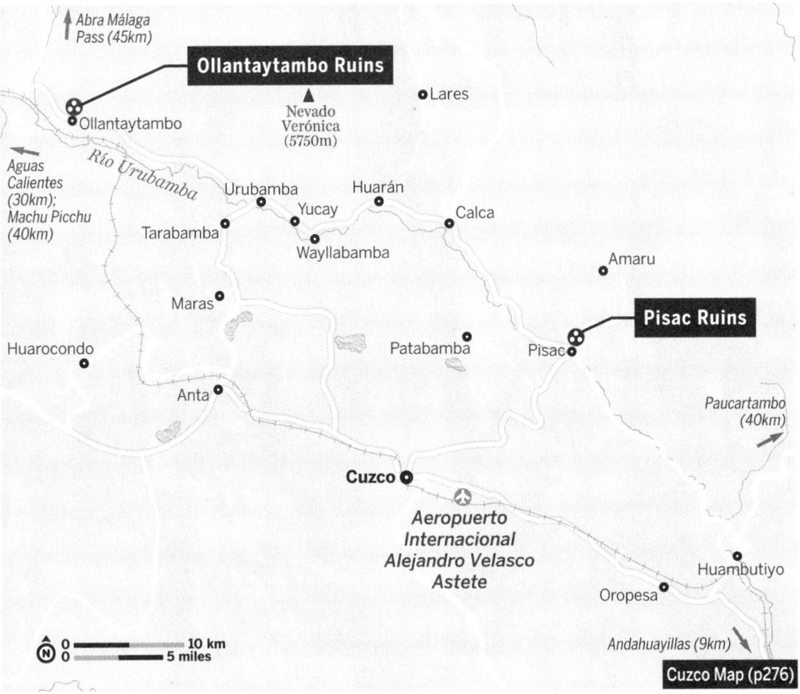

Abra Málaga Pass (45km)
Ollantaytambo Ruins
Nevado Verónica (5750m)
Lares
Ollantaytambo
Aguas Calientes (30km); Machu Picchu (40km)
Río Urubamba
Urubamba
Huarán
Yucay
Calca
Tarabamba
Wayllabamba
Amaru
Maras
Pisac Ruins
Huarocondo
Patabamba
Pisac
Anta
Paucartambo (40km)
Cuzco
Aeropuerto Internacional Alejandro Velasco Astete
Huambutiyo
Oropesa
0 10 km
0 5 miles
Andahuaylillas (9km)
Cuzco Map (p276)

Arriving in Cuzco & the Sacred Valley

Cuzco's **Aeropuerto Internacional Alejandro Velasco Astete** (p279), 6km south of the center, receives national and international flights. The *combi* lines Imperial and C4M (S0.80, 20 minutes) run from just outside the airport to Av El Sol. An official radio taxi from within the airport costs S40.

Where to Stay

The region offers a range of lodging options from hostels to luxury hotels. Cuzco has hundreds of lodgings of all types and prices, with some of Peru's highest room rates. Booking ahead is recommended in high season (June to August). Rural areas may have lodging without adequate heating – ask ahead if you're concerned.

Inti Raymi festival

Festivals & Events

Cuzco and the surrounding highlands celebrate many lively fiestas and holidays. Between them they provide riveting manifestations of both Andean and Catholic culture.

Great For...

☑ Don't Miss

June's Inti Raymi, the drawcard festival of Cuzco.

El Señor de los Temblores

This procession through the Plaza de Armas takes place on Holy Monday, the Monday before Easter. It dates to the earthquake of 1650. El Señor de los Temblores' crucifix of the savior (now charred with soot) is considered the patron saint of Cuzco, responsible for saving the city from further earthquake damage.

Crucifix Vigil

On May 2–3, a Crucifix Vigil is held on all hillsides with crosses atop them.

Corpus Christi

Held on the ninth Thursday after Easter, Corpus Christi usually occurs in early June and features fantastic religious processions and celebrations in the cathedral.

Need to Know

National holidays and local festivals are the most crowded times – book accommodations well ahead.

Take a Break

Feasts are integral to most festivals in Cuzco, so expect plentiful, delicious street food.

★ Top Tip

Book a seat for the Inti Raymi ceremony (though it can be more fun to stand with the locals).

The Q'oyoriti Pilgrimage

Incredibly elaborate costumes, days of dancing, repetitive brass-band music, fireworks and sprinklings of holy water: welcome to one of Peru's lesser known, but most intense, festivals, Q'oyoriti (Star of the Snow).

Held at the foot of Ausangate the Tuesday before Corpus Christi, in late May or early June, this is a dizzy, delirious spectacle, yet no alcohol is involved or even allowed. Offenders are whipped by anonymous men dressed as *ukukus* (mountain spirits) with white masks that hide their features.

At 6384m, Ausangate is the Cuzco department's highest mountain and the most important *apu* (sacred deity) in the area. The subject of countless legends, it's the *pakarina* (mythical place of sacred origin) of llamas and alpacas, and controls their health and fertility.

Q'oyoriti is a pilgrimage – the only way in is by trekking three or more hours up a cold mountain, arriving around dawn. The sight of a solid, endless line of people quietly wending their way up or down the track and disappearing around a bend in the mountain is unforgettable, as is Q'oyoriti's eerie, otherworldly feel.

Many *cuzqueños* (inhabitants of Cuzco) believe that if you attend Q'oyoriti three times, you'll get your heart's desire.

Inti Raymi

Cuzco's most important festival, the 'Festival of the Sun' is held on June 24. Visitors from throughout Peru and the world join the whole city celebrating in the streets with dancing and parades. The festival culminates in a re-enactment of the Inca winter-solstice festival at Sacsaywamán. Despite its commercialization, it's still worth seeing the pageantry in the city and at Sacsaywamán.

Pisac Ruins

A truly awesome site with relatively few tourists, this hilltop Inca citadel lies high above the village on a triangular plateau with a plunging gorge on either side.

Great For...

☑ Don't Miss

Taking a taxi up to the ruins and walking the 4km back to town.

Terracing

The most impressive feature is the agricultural terracing, which sweeps around the south and east flanks of the mountain in huge and graceful curves, almost entirely unbroken by steps (which require greater maintenance and promote erosion). Instead, the terracing is joined by diagonal flights of stairs made of flagstones set into the terrace walls. On the terraces, the Incas could grow food crops that would feed much of the mountaintop city; many terraces are still planted today. Above the terraces are cliff-hugging footpaths, watched over by caracara falcons and well defended by massive stone doorways, steep stairs and a short tunnel carved out of the rock.

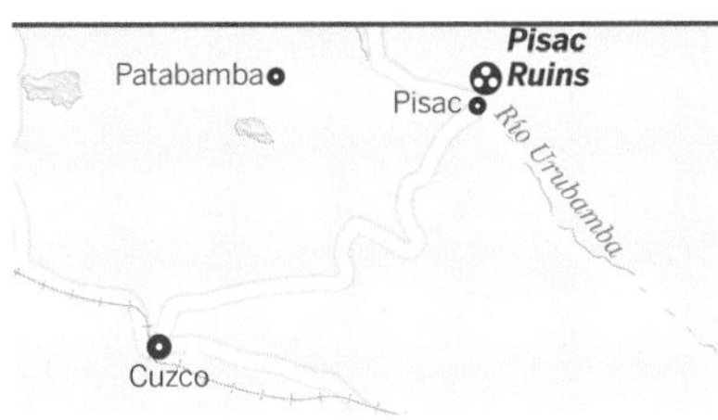

Need to Know

boleto turístico adult/student S130/70; 7am-6pm

Take a Break

Vendors sell drinks and snacks at the top.

★ Top Tip

Note that organized tours, while often informative, are more rushed than private tours.

Temples

This dominating site guards not only the Urubamba Valley below, but also a pass leading into the jungle to the northeast. Topping the terraces is the site's ceremonial center, with an *intihuatana* (literally 'hitching post of the sun'; an Inca astronomical tool), several working water channels, and some painstakingly neat masonry in the well-preserved temples.

A path leads up the hillside to a series of ceremonial baths and around to the military area. Looking across the Kitamayo Gorge from the back of the site, you'll also see hundreds of holes honeycombing the cliff wall. These are Inca tombs that were plundered by *huaqueros* (grave robbers), and are now completely off-limits to tourists.

No one knows the exact date of construction, but it was likely built no earlier than the early 15th century because no pre-Inca elements have been found. It probably served as a defensive outpost at the southern end of the valley, though some archaeologists believe it may have been constructed to celebrate victory over the Cuyos, a group living north of the Sacred Valley.

Hiking

At the time of writing, the trail starting above the west side of the church in town was closed. Check for updates in Pisac. When it's open, it's a two-hour climb and 1½ hours return. Worthwhile but grueling, it's good training for the Inca Trail! The footpath has many crisscrossing trails, but if you aim toward the terracing, you won't get lost. To the west, or the left of the hill as you climb up on the footpath, is the Río Kitamayo Gorge; to the east, or right, is the Río Chongo Valley.

Inca storehouses, Ollantaytambo

Ollantaytambo Ruins

Both fortress and temple, these spectacular Inca ruins rise above Ollantaytambo, making a splendid half-day trip.

Great For...

☑ Don't Miss

Hiring a local guide is worthwhile to demonstrate how to turn on the faucet of the royal baths.

Inca Victory

The huge, steep terraces that guard Ollantaytambo's spectacular Inca ruins mark one of the few places where the Spanish conquistadores lost a major battle.

The rebellious Manco Inca had retreated to this fortress after his defeat at Sacsaywamán. In 1536, Hernando Pizarro, Francisco's younger half-brother, led a force of 70 cavalrymen to Ollantaytambo, supported by large numbers of indigenous and Spanish foot soldiers, in an attempt to capture Manco Inca.

The conquistadores, showered with arrows, spears and boulders from atop the steep terracing, were unable to climb to the fortress. In a brilliant move, Manco Inca flooded the plain below the fortress through previously prepared channels. With Spaniards' horses bogged down in

Need to Know

boleto turístico adult/student S130/70; 7am-5pm

Take a Break

There are bars and local restaurants just around the corner from the ruins.

★ Top Tip

The *boleto turístico* tourist card, used for admission, is valid for 10 days and for 16 other sites across the region.

the water, Pizarro ordered a hasty retreat, chased down by thousands of Manco Inca's victorious soldiers.

Yet the Inca victory would be short lived. Spanish forces soon returned with a quadrupled cavalry force and Manco fled to his jungle stronghold in Vilcabamba.

Construction

Though Ollantaytambo was a highly effective fortress, it also served as a temple. A finely worked ceremonial center is at the top of the terracing. Some extremely well-built walls were under construction at the time of the conquest and have never been completed. The stone was quarried from the mountainside 6km away, high above the opposite bank of the Río Urubamba. Transporting the huge stone blocks to the site was a stupendous feat. The Incas moved the blocks across the river by carting them to the riverside and then diverting the entire river channel around them.

Hiking & Views

The 6km hike to the Inca quarry on the opposite side of the river is a good walk from Ollantaytambo. The trail starts from the Inca bridge by the entrance to the village. It takes a few hours to reach the site, passing several abandoned blocks known as *piedras cansadas* – tired stones.

Looking back towards Ollantaytambo, you can see the enigmatic optical illusion of a pyramid in the fields and walls in front of the fortress. A few scholars believe this marks the place where the legend says the original Incas first emerged from the earth.

Walking Tour: Central Cuzco

At every turn, Cuzco's architecture exhibits the collision of the city's Inca and colonial past. There are refreshments everywhere, and small supermarkets near Plaza de Armas.

Start Plaza de Armas
Distance 4km
Duration 3 hours

2 As you pass through **Plaza Regocijo**, there's a beautiful building on your left; the former hotel houses restaurants and chic boutiques.

3 Calle Garcilaso is named for the Inca chronicler Garcilaso de la Vega, whose childhood home now houses the **Museo Histórico Regional** (Map p276; 8am-5pm).

4 On Sundays, Quechua-speaking countryfolk meet in **Plaza San Francisco**. Drop in to the **Iglesia San Francisco** (Map p276; 9am-6pm).

5 If it's open, peek inside the **Iglesia y Convento de Santa Clara** (Map p276). Its mirrors were used in colonial times to entice curious indigenous people inside.

Take a Break...
Order a juice from one of the many stalls at **Mercado San Pedro** (p275).

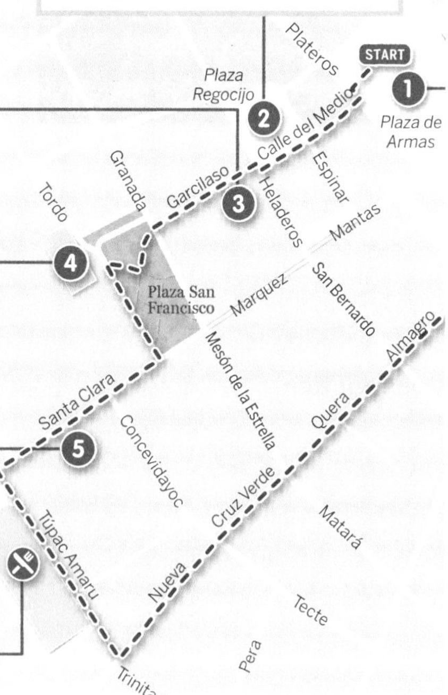

10 Last, forge uphill to **Sacsaywamán**.

Classic Photo: Bohemian-style Plaza San Blas

9 From **Plaza San Blas**, Cuzco's bohemian HQ, head along **Tandapata** for the classic cobblestone experience.

1 Start from the stunning **Plaza de Armas** (Map p276).

8 The **Museo de Arte Religioso** (Map p276; ⌚8am-6pm) is housed in the former palace of the sixth Inca, Roca. Its wall on Hatunrumiyoc is home to the **12-sided stone**.

7 The east wall of **Loreto**, a walkway with Inca walls on both sides, is one of the best and oldest in Cuzco, belonging to the Acllahuasi (House of the Chosen Women). Post-conquest, it became part of the **Iglesia y Monasterio de Santa Catalina** (Map p276).

6 The **Palacio de Justicia** is a big white building with llamas mowing the back garden.

Cuzco

SIGHTS

Cusco Planetarium Museum

(☎974-877-776, 084-23-1710; www.planetariumcusco.com; Carr Sacsayhuamán, Km 2; per person with transport S75; ⏱presentations 6pm) An excellent way to explore the fascinating Inca cosmovision. They defined constellations of darkness as well as light, used astronomy to predict weather patterns, and designed Cuzco's main streets to align with constellations at key moments. After an indoor presentation in English and Spanish there's high-powered telescope viewings outside. Reservations are essential; price varies with group size, and includes pickup and drop-off. The planetarium van picks up visitors at 5:40pm from Plaza Regocijo.

Museo de Arte Precolombino Museum

(Map p276; ☎084-23-3210; www.map.museolarco.org/museo.html; Plazoleta Nazarenas 231; S20; ⏱8am-10pm) Inside a Spanish colonial mansion with an Inca ceremonial courtyard, this dramatically curated pre-Columbian art museum showcases a stunningly varied, if selectively small, collection of archaeological artifacts previously buried in the vast storerooms of Lima's Museo Larco. Dating from between 1250 BC and AD 1532, the artifacts show off the artistic and cultural achievements of many of Peru's ancient cultures, with exhibits labeled in Spanish, English and French.

La Catedral Church

(Map p276; Plaza de Armas; adult/student S25/12.50; ⏱10am-5:45pm) A squatter on the site of Viracocha Inca's palace, the cathedral was built using blocks pilfered from the nearby Inca site of Sacsaywamán. Its construction started in 1559 and took almost a century. It is joined by the 1536 **Iglesia del Triunfo** (Map p276; Triunfo s/n) to its right and the 1733 **Iglesia de Jesús María** to the left.

Qorikancha Ruins

(Map p276; ☎084-24-9176; Plazoleta Santo Domingo; admission S15 or boleto turístico; ⏱8:30am-5:30pm Mon-Sat, 2-5pm Sun) If you

La Catedral

AHIMARIE / GETTY IMAGES ©

visit only one Cuzco site, make it these Inca ruins forming the base of the colonial church and convent of Santo Domingo. Once the richest temple in the Inca empire, all that remains today is the masterful stonework. The temple was built in the mid-15th century during the reign of the 10th Inca, Túpac Yupanqui. Postconquest, Francisco Pizarro gave it to his brother Juan who bequeathed it to the Dominicans, in whose possession it remains.

COURSES

Marcelo Batata Cooking Class — Cooking

(Map p276; ☎984-384-520; www.cuzcodining.com; Calle Palacio 135; 4hr course S297; ⏰2pm) If you've fallen for Peruvian cooking, this four-hour course is a worthwhile foray. A fully stocked market pantry demystifies the flavors of the region and the kitchen setup is comfortable. Includes appetizers, a pisco tasting and a main course. In English, Spanish or Portuguese. Accommodates vegetarians, and there's a private-course option.

TOURS

Alpaca Expeditions — Hiking

(Map p276; ☎084-25-4278; www.alpacaexpeditions.com; Heladeros 157, piso 2 No 24; ⏰9am-7:30pm Mon-Fri, 4:30-7:30pm Sat & Sun) A popular outfitter for the Inca Trail, Sacred Valley treks, Salkantay and Choquequirao, this is one of the few companies to prioritize hiring female guides and porters. Also uses portable bathrooms, plants trees and participates in trail cleanup.

Apus Peru — Hiking

(Map p276; ☎084-23-2691; www.apus-peru.com; Cuichipunco 366; ⏰9am-1pm & 3-7pm Mon-Sat) A recommended outfitter for the Inca Trail and others, also offering conventional tours. Responsible and popular with travelers. The company joins the Choquequirao trek with the Inca Trail for a total of nine days of spectacular scenery and an ever-more-impressive parade of Inca ruins, culminating in Machu Picchu.

Museo Machu Picchu

This newish **museum** (Casa Concha; Map p276; ☎084-25-5535; Santa Catalina Ancha 320; adult/child S20/10; ⏰8am-7pm Mon-Fri, 9am-5pm Sat) exhibits 360 pieces from Machu Picchu taken by Hiram Bingham's expeditions and recently returned by Yale University, including lithic and metals, ceramics and bones. The collection shows the astounding array of fine handicrafts and ceramics acquired from throughout the vast Incan empire. There's also good background on the Bingham expeditions with informative documentaries (subtitled). Signs are in English and Spanish.

SHOPPING

Center for Traditional Textiles of Cuzco — Arts & Crafts

(Map p276; ☎84-228-117; Av El Sol 603; ⏰7:30am-8pm) This nonprofit organization, founded in 1996, promotes the survival of traditional weaving. You may be able to catch a shop-floor demonstration illustrating different weaving techniques in all their finger-twisting complexity. Products for sale are high end.

Mercado San Pedro — Market

(Map p276; Plazoleta San Pedro; ⏰6am-7pm) Cuzco's central market is a must-see. Pig heads for *caldo* (soup), frogs (to enhance sexual performance), vats of fruit juice, roast *lechón* (suckling pig) and tamales are just a few of the foods on offer. Around the edges are typical clothes, spells, incense and other random products to keep you entertained for hours.

EATING

Monkey Cafe — Cafe $

(Map p276; ☎084-59-5838; Tandapata 300; mains S15-20; ⏰8am-8pm Wed-Mon) Cuzco's finest coffee shop is shoehorned into a tiny locale at the top of San Blas hill. All espresso

Cuzco
0
200 m
0
0.1 miles
A
B
C
D
E
F
1
2
3
4
Cusco Planetarium (1km)
Pumacurco
Choquechaca
Tandapata
19
Tres Cruces (Kiskapata)
Arco
Ese
Atocsaycuchi
Angelitos
Saphi
Amargura
Ladrillos
20
Pasñapakana
Kiskapata
Iris
Suecia
Coricalle
Tecsecocha
Resbalosa
Huaynapata
Purgatorio
Palacio
Qanchipata
Carmen Alto
Plazoleta
6
7 Culebras
Tambo de Montero
Tigre
Ataúd
Plazoleta Nazarenas
Cuesta San Blas
Plaza San Blas
Tandapata
Procuradores
Plaza del Tricentenario
Tucumán
Carmen Bajo
22
iPerú
Peru Rail
18
Hatunrumiyoc
Huarancalqui
Meloc
Siete Cuartones
Santa Teresa
24
Inca Rail
17
7
5
1
Alabado
Plateros
Plaza
Triunfo (Sunturwasi)
Herrajes
Ruinas
Chihuampata
10
Plaza de Armas
Nueva Alta
Teatro
San Juan de Dios
Plaza Regocijo
Recoleta

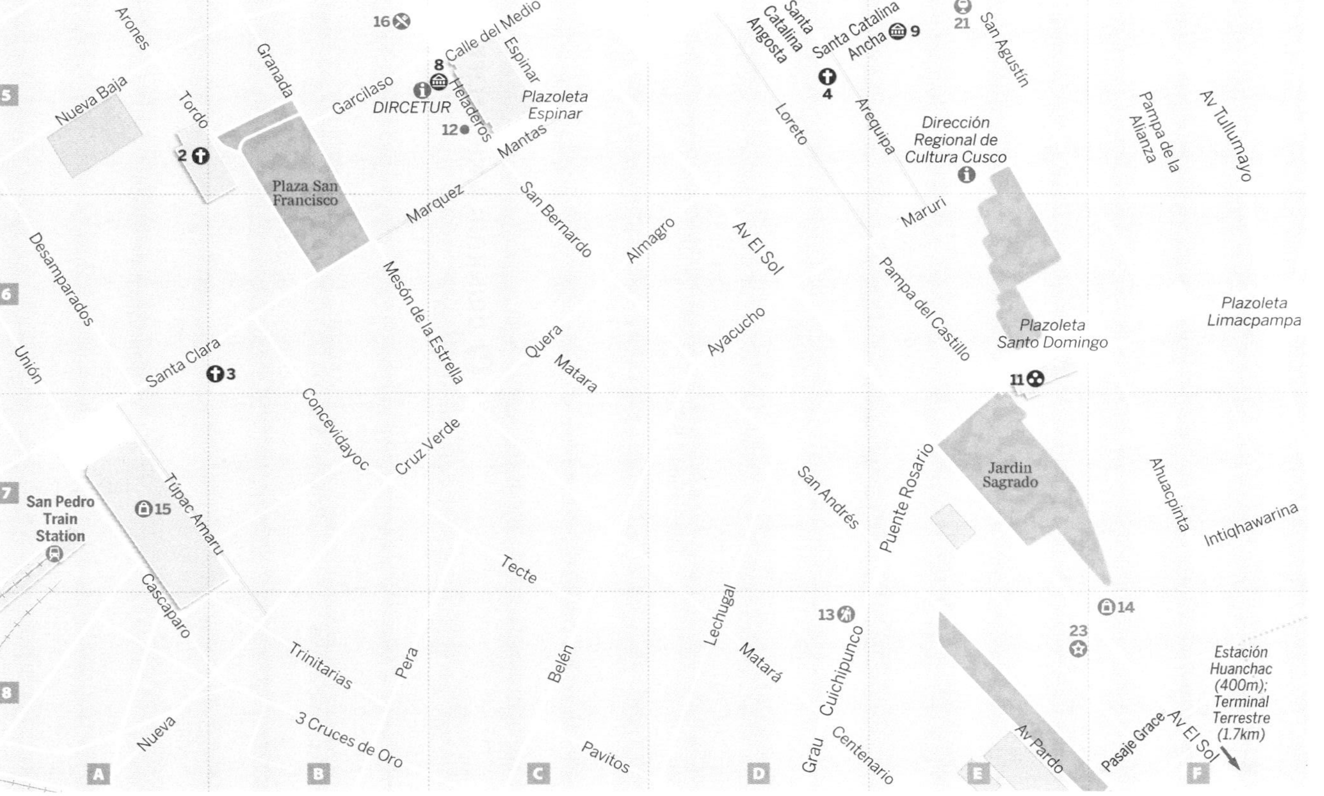
Arones
Nueva Baja
Tordo
2
Granada
Plaza San Francisco
Garcilaso
DIRCETUR
16
8
Calle del Medio
Espinar
Heladeros
12
Plazoleta Espinar
Mantas
Marquez
San Bernardo
Almagro
Av El Sol
Santa Catalina Angosta
Santa Catalina Ancha
9
4
Loreto
Arequipa
21
San Agustín
Dirección Regional de Cultura Cusco
Maruri
Pampa de la Alianza
Av Tullumayo
Desamparados
Unión
Santa Clara
3
Mesón de la Estrella
Quera
Matara
Ayacucho
Pampa del Castillo
Plazoleta Santo Domingo
11
Plazoleta Limacpampa
San Pedro Train Station
15
Túpac Amaru
Concevidayoc
Cruz Verde
San Andrés
Puente Rosario
Jardin Sagrado
Ahuacpinta
Intiqhawarina
Cascaparo
Tecte
Lechugal
13
Cuichipunco
14
23
Trinitarias
Pera
Belén
Matará
Estación Huanchac (400m); Terminal Terrestre (1.7km)
Nueva
3 Cruces de Oro
Pavitos
Grau
Centenario
Av Pardo
Pasaje Grace
Av El Sol
A
B
C
D
E
F
5
6
7
8

Cuzco

Sights
1 Iglesia del Triunfo........ D4
2 Iglesia San Francisco........ A5
3 Iglesia y Convento de Santa Clara........ B6
4 Iglesia y Monasterio de Santa Catalina........ D5
5 La Catedral........ D4
6 Museo de Arte Precolombino........ D3
7 Museo de Arte Religioso........ E4
8 Museo Histórico Regional........ C5
9 Museo Machu Picchu........ E5
10 Plaza de Armas........ C4
11 Qorikancha........ E6

Activities, Courses & Tours
12 Alpaca Expeditions........ C5
13 Apus Peru........ D8
Marcelo Batata Cooking Class........ (see 18)

Shopping
14 Center for Traditional Textiles of Cuzco........ F8
15 Mercado San Pedro........ A7

Eating
16 Chicha........ B5
17 Cicciolina........ E4
18 Marcelo Batata........ E4
19 Monkey Cafe........ E2

Drinking & Nightlife
20 Limbus........ F3
21 Museo del Pisco........ E5
22 Republica de Pisco........ C4

Entertainment
23 Centro Qosqo de Arte Nativo........ E8
24 Ukuku's........ C4

drinks feature double shots made with Peruvian-origin roasts. There are also very tasty sweets and hearty breakfasts ranging from healthy to heart-stopping.

Cicciolina International $$
(Map p276; 084-23-9510; www.cicciolinacuzco.com; Triunfo 393, 2nd fl; mains S38-59; 8am-11pm) On the 2nd floor of a lofty colonial courtyard mansion, Cicciolina may be Cuzco's best restaurant. The eclectic, sophisticated food is divine, starting with house-marinated olives, and continuing with crisp polenta squares with cured rabbit, huge green salads, charred octopus and satisfying mains like red trout in coconut milk, beetroot ravioli and tender lamb. With impeccable service and warmly lit seating.

Marcelo Batata Peruvian $$
(Map p276; 084-22-2424; www.cuscodining.com/marcelo-batata; Palacio 121; mains S43-56; 12:30-11pm) A sure bet for delectable Andean cuisine with a twist. Marcelo Batata innovates with traditional foods to show them at their best – like the humble *tarwi* pea, which makes a mean hummus. The chicken soup with *hierba Luisa* (a local herb) is exquisite, alongside satisfying beet *quinotto* (like risotto), tender alpaca and twice-baked Andean potatoes that offer crispy-creamy goodness.

Chicha Peruvian $$$
(Map p276; 084-24-0520; Regocijo 261, 2nd fl; mains S30-65) A Gastón Acurio venture serving up haute versions of Cuzco classics in an open kitchen. Its riff on *anticuchos* (beef skewers) is a delectable barbecued octopus with crisp herbed potato wedges. Other contenders include *papas rellenas* (stuffed potatoes), curried alpaca with quinoa, and *chairo* (lamb and barley soup) served in a clay pot.

DRINKING & NIGHTLIFE

Limbus Rooftop Bar
(Map p276; 084-43-1282; www.limbusrestobar.com; Pasñapakana 133; 8am-1am Mon-Sat, noon-midnight Sun) Billed as the best view in Cuzco, it's all that (even after climbing to the top of San Blas). Don't worry, if you come during peak hours you'll have plenty of time to catch your breath while you queue to get in. With gorgeous cocktails and glass-walled panoramas, this was the hottest city spot when we visited.

Republica de Pisco Bar
(Map p276; 084-24-4111; www.facebook.com/republicadelpiscocusco; Plateros 354; 5pm-2am) A wonderful, elegant bar with attentive bartenders and drinks that merit seconds. It's popular with locals and travelers alike.

ENTERTAINMENT

Ukuku's Live Music

(Map p276; ☎084-24-2951; Plateros 316; ⏰6pm-2am) The most consistently popular nightspot in town, Ukuku's plays a winning combination of crowd-pleasers – Latin and Western rock, reggae, *reggaetón*, salsa and hip-hop – and often hosts live bands. Usually full to bursting after midnight with as many Peruvians as foreign tourists, it's good, sweaty, dance-a-thon fun. Happy hour is 8pm to 10:30pm.

Centro Qosqo de Arte Nativo Performing Arts

(Map p276; ☎084-22-7901; www.centroqosqodeartenativo.com; Av El Sol 604) Has live nightly performances of Andean music and folk dancing at 6:45pm.

INFORMATION

iPerú (www.peru.travel; ☎084-59-6159; Portal de Harinas 177; ⏰9am-7pm Mon-Fri, to 1pm Sat) has excellent source for tourist information for both the region and entire country.

GETTING THERE & AWAY

AIR

Cuzco's **Aeropuerto Internacional Alejandro Velasco Astete** (CUZ; ☎084-22-2611) has regular flights to Lima, Bogota and La Paz.

BUS

All international and most long-distance buses depart from the **Terminal Terrestre** (☎084-22-4471; Vía de Evitamiento 429), about 2km out of town toward the airport. Take a taxi (S30) or walk via Av El Sol.

TRAIN

Cuzco has two train stations. **Estación Huanchac** (Wanchaq; ☎084-58-1414; Av Pachacutec s/n; ⏰7am-5pm Mon-Fri, to midnight Sat & Sun), near the end of Av El Sol, serves Juliaca and Puno on Lake Titicaca. **Estación Poroy** (Calle Roldan s/n, Carr Cuzco-Urubamba), east of town, serves Ollantaytambo and Machu Picchu.

Museo del Pisco

When you've had your fill of colonial religious art, investigate this **pisco museum** (Map p276; ☎084-26-2709; www.museodelpisco.org; Santa Catalina Ancha 398; ⏰noon-1am), where the wonders of the national drink are extolled, exalted and – of course – sampled. Opened by an enthusiastic expat, this museum-bar is Pisco 101, combined with a tapas lounge. Grab a spot early for show-stopping live music (9pm to 11pm nightly).

Pisco sour cocktails

VIENNETTA / SHUTTERSTOCK ©

GETTING AROUND

TAXI

There are no meters in taxis, but there are set rates. At the time of research, trips within the city center cost S8 and destinations further afield, such as El Molino, cost S12.

Pisac

It's not hard to succumb to the charms of sunny Pisac, a bustling and fast-growing colonial village with a fabulous market at the base of a spectacular Inca fortress perched on a mountain spur. Located just 33km northeast of Cuzco by a paved road, it's the most convenient starting point to the Sacred Valley.

From left: Local woman in Ollantaytambo; Mercado San Pedro (p275); A Quechua woman demonstrates traditional weaving

DONYANEDOMAM / GETTY IMAGES ©

AGUSTINA CAMILION / SHUTTERSTOCK ©

SIGHTS

Mercado de Artesanía Market

(Plaza Constitución; 8am-4pm) Pisac is known far and wide for its market, by far the biggest and most touristy in the region. While there are still some local arts and crafts of note, watch out for mass-produced goods invading from as far as Colombia. Its success has it filling the Plaza Constitución and surrounding streets every day.

ACTIVITIES & TOURS

Parque de la Papa Ecotour

(084-24-5021; www.ipcca.info/about-parque-de-la-papa; Pisac) Day treks and cooking workshops are some of the offerings of this wonderful nonprofit, which promotes potato diversity and communal farming.

EATING

Doña Clorinda Peruvian $$

(084-20-3051; Urb San Luis, La Rinconada; mains S18-35; 9am-5pm) In a lovely colonial home, this longtime Pisac mainstay serves up hearty Andean fare. Order some homemade *chicha morada* (blue-corn juice) to go with heaping plates of *arroz chaufa* (Peruvian fried rice), trout, beef and *rocoto relleno* (stuffed peppers) with *kapchi*. A classic.

GETTING THERE & AWAY

Minibuses to Pisac (S5, one hour) leave from terminals at Tullumayo 207 and Puputi 208 in Cuzco.

Ollantaytambo

Dominated by two massive Inca ruins, the quaint village of Ollantaytambo, also called Ollanta, is the best surviving example of Inca city planning, with narrow cobblestone streets that have been continuously inhabited since the 13th century. After the hordes passing through on their way to Machu Picchu die down around late morning, Ollanta is a lovely place to be. It's perfect for wandering the mazy, narrow byways, past stone buildings and babbling irrigation channels, pretending you've stepped back in time. It also offers access to excellent hiking and biking.

TOURS

Coffee & distillery tours Food

(☎084-20-4014; www.elalbergue.com; Estación de Tren, El Albergue; tours S50) Led by El Albergue B&B, these tours offer a fascinating behind-the-scenes look at a small-scale coffee roaster and distiller of *cañazo, a* sugarcane alcohol that's the oldest spirit in the Americas. Brought by the Spanish colony, the rustic Andean digestif is now taking on new dimensions as a high-end spirit. Participants get a free coffee or cocktail.

SHOPPING

Awamaki Arts & Crafts

(☎84-43-6744; www.awamaki.org; Ventiderio s/n; ⏲9am-6pm Mon-Fri, 10am-5pm Sat & Sun) A nonprofit boutique selling gorgeous locally woven sweaters, hats and gloves made with organic dyes, as well as handmade leather handbags and wallets. Products are high quality and design conscious; they're wonderful gifts for those back home. The foundation also runs worthwhile tours to nearby weaving villages.

EATING

El Albergue Restaurante International $$

(☎084-20-4014; Estación de Tren; mains S29-45; ⏲5:30-10am, noon-3pm & 6-9pm;) This whistle-stop cafe serves elegant and well-priced Peruvian fare. It's inviting, with an open kitchen bordered by heaping fruit bowls and candles adorning linen-topped tables. Start with the *causas* (potato dish) or organic greens from the garden. Lamb medallions with *chimichurri* (herb sauce) are a standout, as is as the molle-pepper steak spiced from the tree outside. Access via the train platform.

GETTING THERE & AWAY

Minibuses to Ollantaytambo (S12, two hours) leave from near the Puente Grau in Cuzco.

There are also several trains daily between Cuzco and Ollantaytambo.

MACHU PICCHU,
PERU

In this Chapter

Machu Picchu, Peru

For many visitors to Peru and even South America, a visit to the Inca city of Machu Picchu is the long-anticipated highpoint of their trip. In a spectacular location, it's the best-known archaeological site on the continent.

This awe-inspiring ancient city was never revealed to the conquering Spaniards and was virtually forgotten until the early part of the 20th century. Now, in the high season from late May until early September, 2500 people arrive daily. Despite this great tourist influx, the site manages to retain an air of grandeur and mystery, and is a must for all visitors to Peru.

Two Days in Machu Picchu

Machu Picchu is huge, so it's best to spend at least two days, using Aguas Calientes as a base camp to allow ample time to explore the ruins. Staying in town also allows you to get up early and beat the midday crowds at Machu Picchu. If you are also climbing **Wayna Picchu** (p292) or **Cerro Machu Picchu** (p292), you may need even more time.

Four Days in Machu Picchu

Put aside at least four days to hike the **Inca Trail** (p296), with time to return and recover from the strenuous trek. The ancient trail was laid by the Incas, from the Sacred Valley to Machu Picchu. You will push yourself up and down across mountains, and past rivers and lakes, and feel proud to reach Machu Picchu on day four.

Previous page: Aerial view of Machu Picchu

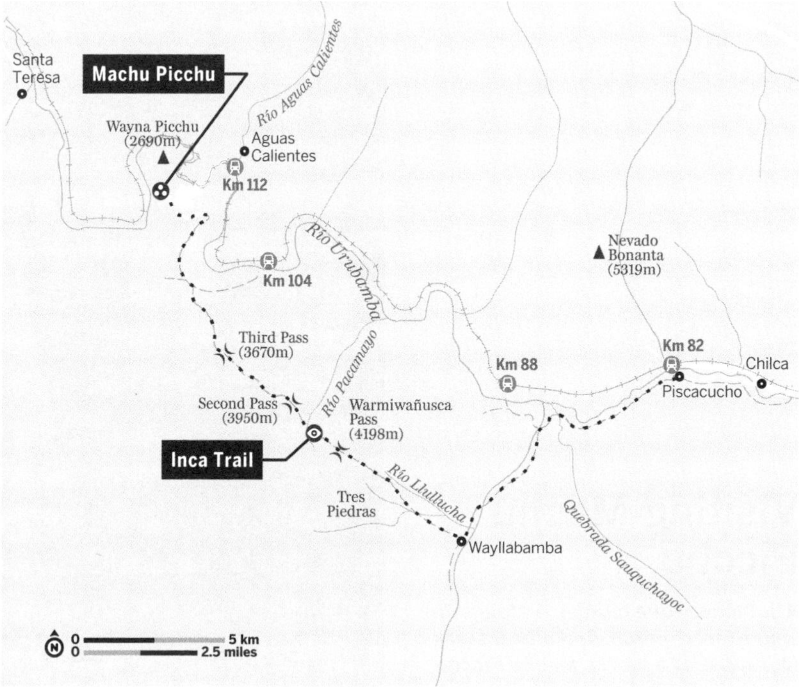

Arriving in Machu Picchu

Unless you are taking a trek on the Inca Trail, Aguas Calientes is the entry point to Machu Picchu. Cuzco is the launching point to Aguas Calientes.

Bus From Aguas Calientes, the only option up to Machu Picchu is a 20-minute bus ride.

Air The nearest airport is in Cuzco, which only serves Bolivia or domestic flights. Entry to Peru is always via Lima.

Where to Stay

Lodgings in Aguas Calientes are consistently overpriced – probably costing two-thirds more than counterparts in less-exclusive locations.

Travelers exploring Machu Picchu

Visiting Machu Picchu

A sublime stone citadel. A staggering cloud-forest perch. And a backstory that's out of a movie. Machu Picchu is an extraordinary Inca settlement and Unesco World Heritage Site.

Great For...

Need to Know

Machu Picchu Historical Sanctuary
(www.machupicchu.gob.pe; adult/student S152/77; 6am-6pm)

★ Top Tip

Try to visit outside peak times (between 10am and 2pm); June through August are the busiest months.

Unless you arrive via the Inca Trail, you'll officially enter the ruins through a ticket gate on the south side of Machu Picchu. About 100m of footpath brings you to the mazelike main entrance of Machu Picchu proper, where the ruins lie stretched out before you, roughly divided into two areas separated by a series of plazas.

Entrance tickets often sell out: buy them in advance in Cuzco. The site is limited to 5940 visitors daily, with 400 paid spots for hiking Wayna Picchu and Cerro Machu Picchu. Visitation is limited to a morning or afternoon ticket: morning tickets are valid between 6am and noon while afternoon tickets are valid between noon and 5:30pm.

Local guides (S150 per person, S30 for groups of six to 10) are readily available for hire at the entrance. Their expertise varies, but look for one wearing an official guide ID from Dircetur.

Buying Machu Picchu Tickets

You would think accessing the continent's number-one destination might be easier. Get ready. Currently, Machu Picchu tickets can be purchased online (www.machu picchu.gob.pe), though not all foreign credit cards go through. If you reserve online, can't get your card to work and happen to be in Cuzco, you can deposit the amount due at a Banco de la Nación outlet within a three-hour window; later check in via the website to print your ticket.

In Cuzco, you can also purchase tickets from the **Dirección Regional de Cultura Cusco** (DIRCETUR; Map p276; ☎084-58-2030; www.dirceturcusco.gob.pe; Maruri 340; ⏲7:15am-6:30pm Mon-Sat) or the **Dircetur**

Hut of the Caretaker of the Funerary Rock

outlet (Map p276; ☎084-58-2030, ext 2000; www.dirceturcusco.gob.pe; Garcilaso s/n, Museo Histórico Regional; ⏰7am-7:30pm Mon-Sat) in the Museo Histórico. Both outlets accept Peruvian soles, Visa or Mastercard. If you want to risk waiting, you can also purchase them from the Centro Cultural (p303) in Aguas Calientes, but only in Peruvian soles. Note that Aguas Calientes ATMs frequently run out of cash. Student tickets must be purchased in person with valid photo ID from the institution.

For a reasonable fee, travel agencies can also obtain tickets, which some readers recommend.

☑ Don't Miss

Museo de Sitio Manuel Chávez Ballón (p302) by Puente Ruinas at the base of the climb to Machu Picchu.

BRENT WINEBRENNER / GETTY IMAGES ©

Entry to Machu Picchu requires a valid photo ID.

Lastly, ticketing procedures can change, but iPerú (p303) can offer the latest updates. Good luck.

Inside the Complex

Hut of the Caretaker of the Funerary Rock — Ruins

An excellent viewpoint to take in the whole site. It's one of a few buildings that has been restored with a thatched roof, making it a good shelter in the case of rain. The Inca Trail enters the city just below this hut. The carved rock behind the hut may have been used to mummify the nobility, hence the hut's name.

Ceremonial Baths — Ruins

If you head straight into the ruins from the main entry gate, you pass through extensive terracing to a beautiful series of 16 connected ceremonial baths that cascade across the ruins, accompanied by a flight of stairs.

Temple of the Sun — Ruins

Just above and to the left of the ceremonial baths is Machu Picchu's only round building, a curved and tapering tower of exceptional stonework. This structure is off-limits and best viewed from above.

Royal Tomb — Ruins

Below the Temple of the Sun, this almost hidden, natural rock cave was carefully carved by Inca stonemasons. Its use is highly debated; though known as the Royal Tomb, no mummies were actually ever found here.

Sacred Plaza — Plaza

Climbing the stairs above the ceremonial baths, there is a flat area of jumbled rocks, once used as a quarry. Turn right at the top of the stairs and walk across the quarry

✕ Take a Break

Bring drinking water. Bringing food is not officially allowed.

on a short path leading to the four-sided Sacred Plaza. The far side contains a small viewing platform with a curved wall, which offers a view of the snowy Cordillera Vilcabamba in the far distance and the Río Urubamba below.

Temple of the Three Windows Ruins

Important buildings flank the remaining three sides of the Sacred Plaza. The Temple of the Three Windows features huge trapezoidal windows that give the building its name.

Principal Temple Ruins

The 'temple' derives its name from the massive solidity and perfection of its construction. The damage to the rear right corner is the result of the ground settling below this corner rather than any inherent weakness in the masonry itself.

House of the High Priest Ruins

Little is known about these mysterious ruins, located opposite the Principal Temple.

Sacristy Ruins

Behind and connected to the Principal Temple lies this famous small building. It has many well-carved niches, perhaps used for the storage of ceremonial objects, as well as a carved stone bench. The Sacristy is especially known for the two rocks flanking its entrance; each is said to contain 32 angles, but it's easy to come up with a different number whenever you count them.

Intihuatana Ruins

This Quechua word loosely translates as the 'Hitching Post of the Sun' and refers to the carved rock pillar, often mistakenly called a sundial, at the top of the Intihuatana hill. The Inca astronomers were able to predict the solstices using the angles of this pillar. Thus, they were able to claim control over the return of the lengthening summer days. Its exact use remains unclear, but its elegant simplicity and high craftwork make it a highlight.

Central Plaza Plaza

The plaza separates the ceremonial sector from the residential and industrial areas.

Prison Group Ruins

At the lower end of this area is the Prison Group, a labyrinthine complex of cells, niches and passageways, positioned both under and above the ground.

Temple of the Condor Ruins

This 'temple' is named for a carving of the head of a condor with rock outcrops as outstretched wings. It is considered the centerpiece of the Prison Group.

Ruins Outskirts

Intipunku Gate

(checkpoint closes around 3pm) The Inca Trail ends after its final descent from the

Inca Drawbridge

notch in the horizon called Intipunku (Sun Gate). Looking at the hill behind you as you enter the ruins, you can see both the trail and Intipunku. This hill, called Machu Picchu (Old Peak), gives the site its name.

Access from the Machu Picchu ruins may be restricted. It takes about an hour to reach Intipunku. If you can spare at least a half-day for the round-trip, it may be possible to continue as far as **Wiñay Wayna** (Huiñay Huayna). Expect to pay S15 or more as an unofficial reduced-charge admission fee to the Inca Trail, and be sure to return before 3pm, which is when the checkpoint typically closes.

Inca Drawbridge

A scenic but level walk from the Hut of the Caretaker of the Funerary Rock takes you right past the top of the terraces and out along a narrow, cliff-clinging trail to the Inca drawbridge. In under a half-hour's walk, the trail gives you a good look at cloud-forest vegetation and an entirely different view of Machu Picchu. This walk is recommended, though you'll have to be content with photographing the bridge from a distance; someone crossed the bridge some years ago and tragically fell to their death.

☑ Don't Miss

Hike an hour to Intipunku (Sun Gate) for a different angle overlooking Machu Picchu.

★ Top Tip

There are no signposts here – it's not a museum – so read up or hire a guide.

TIMOTHY MULHOLLAND / ALAMY STOCK PHOTO ©

Wayna Picchu

Wayna Picchu is the small, steep mountain at the back of the ruins. Wayna Picchu is normally translated as 'Young Peak,' but the word *picchu,* with the correct glottal pronunciation, refers to the wad in the cheek of a coca-leaf chewer. Access to Wayna Picchu is limited to 400 people per day – the first 200 in line are let in at 7am, and another 200 at 10am. A **ticket** (S48), which includes a visit to the Moon Temple, may only be obtained when you purchase your Machu Picchu entrance ticket. These spots sell out a week in advance in low season and a month in advance in high season, so plan accordingly.

At first glance, it would appear that Wayna Picchu is a challenging climb but, although the ascent is steep, it's not technically difficult. However, it is not recommended if you suffer from vertigo. Hikers must sign in and out at a registration booth located beyond the central plaza between two thatched buildings. The 45- to 90-minute scramble up a steep footpath takes you through a short section of Inca tunnel.

Take care in wet weather as the steps get dangerously slippery. The trail is easy to follow, but involves steep sections, a ladder and an overhanging cave, where you have to bend over to get by. Partway up Wayna Picchu, a marked path plunges down to your left, continuing down the rear of Wayna Picchu to the small **Temple of the Moon**. From the temple, another cleared path leads up behind the ruin and steeply onward up the back side of Wayna Picchu.

The descent takes about an hour, and the ascent back to the main Wayna Picchu trail longer. The spectacular trail drops and climbs steeply as it hugs the sides of Wayna Picchu before plunging into the cloud forest. Suddenly, you reach a cleared area where the small, very well-made ruins are found.

Cerro Machu Picchu (S48) is a very good alternative if you miss out on Wayna Picchu tickets.

The Mystery of Machu Picchu

Machu Picchu is not mentioned in any of the chronicles of the Spanish conquistadores. Nobody apart from local Quechua people knew of Machu Picchu's existence until American historian Hiram Bingham was guided to it by locals in 1911.

Despite scores of more recent studies, knowledge of Machu Picchu remains sketchy. Even today archaeologists are forced to rely heavily on speculation and educated guesswork as to its function. Some believe the citadel was founded in the waning years of the last Incas as

Descending steps at Wayna Picchu

an attempt to preserve Inca culture or rekindle their predominance, while others think that it may have already become an uninhabited, forgotten city at the time of the conquest.

A more recent theory suggests that the site was a royal retreat or the country palace of Pachacutec, abandoned at the time of the Spanish invasion. The site's director believes that it was a city, a political, religious and administrative center. Its location, and the fact that at least eight access routes have been discovered, suggests that it was a trade nexus between Amazonia and the highlands.

It seems clear from the exceptionally high quality of the stonework and the abundance of ornamental work that Machu Picchu was once vitally important as a ceremonial center. Indeed, to some extent, it still is: Alejandro Toledo, the country's first indigenous Andean president, impressively staged his inauguration here in 2001.

☑ Need to Know

Drones, tripods and backpacks over 20L are not allowed into the ruins. Walking sticks are allowed.

★ Top Tip

For really in-depth explorations, take along a copy of *Exploring Cuzco* by Peter Frost.

Machu Picchu

CITADEL HIGHLIGHTS

This great 15th-century Inca citadel sits at 2430m on a narrow ridgetop above the Río Urubamba. Traditionally considered a political, religious and administrative center, but new theories suggest that it was a royal estate designed by Pachacutec, the Inca ruler whose military conquests transformed the empire. Trails linked it to the Inca capital of Cuzco and important sites in the jungle. As invading Spaniards never discovered it, experts still dispute when the site was abandoned and why.

At its peak, Machu Picchu was thought to have some 500 inhabitants. An engineering marvel, its famous Inca walls have polished stone fitted to stone, with no mortar in between. The citadel took thousands of laborers 50 years to build – today its cost of construction would exceed a billion US dollars.

Making it habitable required leveling the site, channeling water from high mountain streams through stone canals and building vertical retaining walls that became agricultural terraces for corn, potatoes and coca. The drainage system also helped combat heavy rains (diverting them for irrigation), while east-facing rooftops and farming terraces took advantage of maximum sun exposure.

The site is a magnet to mystics, adventurers and students of history alike. While its function remains hotly debated, the essential grandeur of Machu Picchu is indisputable.

TOP TIPS

- Visit before midmorning crowds.
- Allow at least three hours to visit.
- Wear walking shoes and a hat.
- Bring drinking water.
- Gain perspective walking the lead-in trails.

Intihuatana

The 'Hitching Post of the Sun', an exquisitely carved rock, was likely used by Inca astronomers to predict solstices. It's a rare survivor since invading Spaniards destroyed *intihuatanas* throughout the kingdom to eradicate what they considered to be pagan blasphemy.

Temple of the Three Windows

Enjoy the commanding views of the plaza below through the huge trapezoidal windows framed by 3-ton lintels. Rare in Inca architecture, the presence of three windows may indicate special significance.

ayna Picchu

is 2720m peak with ladders, caves and mall temple can be climbed in a 45- to -minute scramble. Take care, the steep steps slippery when wet. Purchase a coveted rmit ahead with admission.

POWEROFFOREVER/GETTY IMAGES ©

Central Plaza

This sprawling green area with grazing llamas separates the ceremonial sector of Machu Picchu from the more mundane residential and industrial sectors.

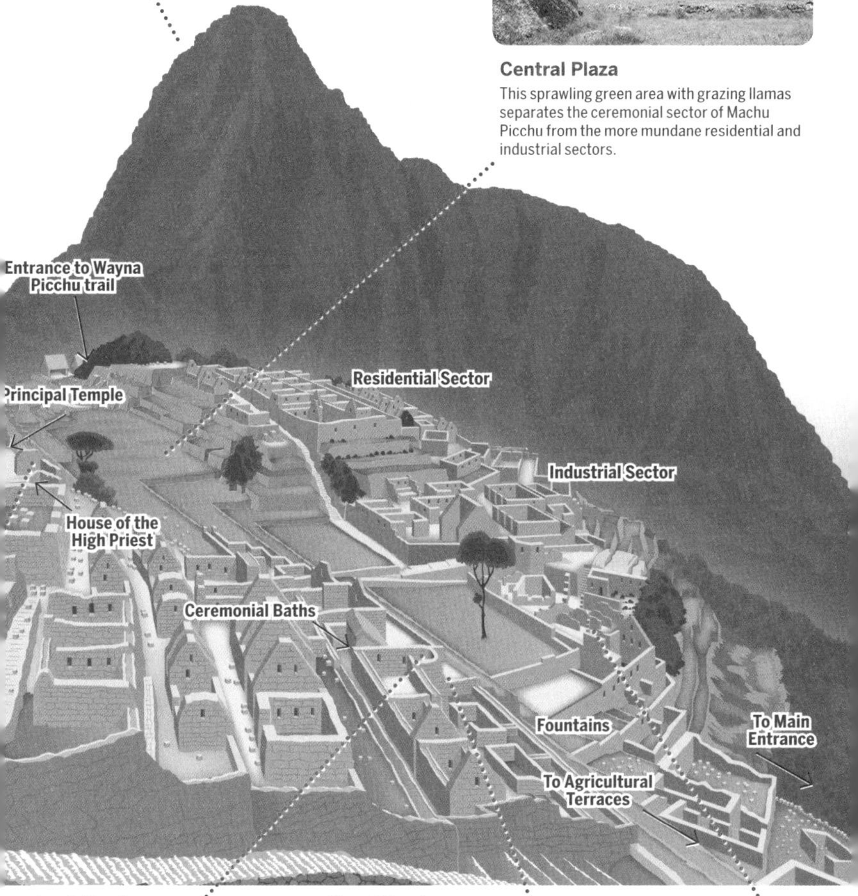

Entrance to Wayna Picchu trail

Residential Sector

Principal Temple

Industrial Sector

House of the High Priest

Ceremonial Baths

Fountains

To Main Entrance

To Agricultural Terraces

mple of the Sun

is off-limits rounded tower is best viewed m above. Featuring the site's finest stone-rk, an altar and trapezoidal windows, it may ve been used for astronomical purposes.

Royal Tomb

Speculated to have special ceremonial significance, this natural rock cave sits below the Temple of the Sun. Though it is off-limits, visitors can view its steplike altar and sacred niches from the entrance.

OSCAR ESPINOSA/SHUTTERSTOCK ©

Temple of the Condor

Check out the condor-head carving with rock outcrops that resemble outstretched wings. Behind, an off-limits cavity reaches a tiny underground cell that may only be entered by bending double.

Llamas

The Inca Trail

The views of snowy mountain peaks, distant rivers and cloud forests are stupendous – and walking from one cliff-hugging pre-Columbian ruin to the next is a mystical and unforgettable experience.

Great For...

☑ Don't Miss

Hot springs in the towns along the way will help weary hiking legs to recover.

The most famous hike in South America, the four-day Inca Trail is walked by thousands every year. Although the total distance is only about 24 miles, the ancient trail laid by the Incas from the Sacred Valley to Machu Picchu winds its way up and down and around the mountains, snaking over three high Andean passes en route, which have collectively led to the route being dubbed 'the Inca Trial.'

Booking Your Trip

It is important to book your trip at least six months in advance for dates between May and August. Outside these months, you may get a permit with a few weeks' notice, but it's very hard to predict. Only licensed operators can get permits, but you can check general availability at www.camino-inca.com.

Inside Machu Picchu

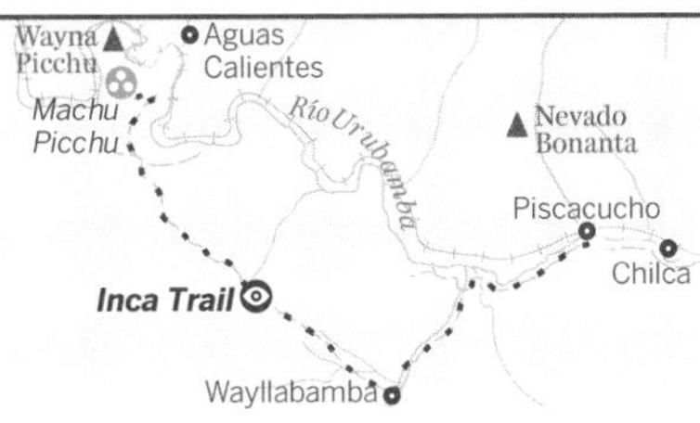

Need to Know

Most trekking agencies run buses to the start of the trail, also known as Piscacucho or Km 82.

Take a Break

Most tours include meals and snacks. Bring a refillable water bottle.

★ Top Tip

The Inca Trail is best visited in the dry season, April to October, and is closed in February.

Consider booking a five-day trip to lessen the pace and enjoy more wildlife and ruins. Other positives include less-crowded campsites and being able to stay at the most scenic one – Phuyupatamarka (3600m) – on the third evening.

Make sure you have international travel insurance that covers adventure activities.

Regulations & Fees

The Inca Trail is the only trek in the Cuzco area that cannot be walked independently – you must go with a licensed operator. Treks start at US$595 and can cost up to US$6000 or more.

Only 500 people each day (including guides and porters) are allowed to start the trail. You must go through an approved Inca Trail operator. Permits are issued to them on a first-come, first-served basis. You will need to provide your passport number to get a permit and carry the passport with you to show at checkpoints along the trail. Be aware that if you get a new passport but had applied with your old, it may present a problem.

Permits are nontransferrable: name changes are not allowed.

Choosing an Operator

While it may be tempting to quickly book your trek and move onto the next item on your to-do list, it's a good idea to examine the options carefully before sending that deposit. If price is your bottom line, keep in mind that the cheapest agencies may cut corners by paying their guides and porters lower wages. Other issues are substandard gear (ie leaky tents) and dull or lackadaisical guiding.

Yet paying more may not mean getting more, especially because international operators take their cut and hire local Peruvian agencies. Talk with a few agencies to get a sense of their quality of service. You might ask if the guide speaks English (fluently or just a little), request a list of what is included and inquire about group size and the kind of transportation used. Ensure that your tour includes a tent, food, a cook, one-day admission to the ruins and the return train fare.

Porters who carry group gear – tents, food etc – are also included. You'll be expected to carry your own personal gear, including sleeping bag. If you are not an experienced backpacker, it may be a good idea to hire a porter to carry your personal gear; this usually costs around US$50 per day for about 10kg.

If you prefer more exclusive services, it's possible to organize private trips with an independent licensed guide (US$1250 to US$2000 per person).

For a list of agencies and guides based in Cuzco, see p275.

The Two-Day Inca Trail

This 10km version of the Inca Trail gives a fairly good indication of what the longer trail is like. It's a real workout, and passes through some of the best scenery and most impressive ruins and terracing of the longer trail.

It's a steep three- or four-hour climb from Km 104 to Wiñay Wayna, then another two hours or so on fairly flat terrain to Machu Picchu. You may be on the trail a couple of hours longer, just to enjoy the views and explore. We advise taking the earliest train possible from Cuzco or Ollantaytambo.

The two-day trail means overnighting in Aguas Calientes, and visiting Machu Picchu

Warmiwañusca (Dead Woman's Pass; p300)

the next day, so it's really only one day of walking. Prices range from US$400 to US$535.

What to Expect

Even if you are not carrying a full backpack, this trek requires a good level of fitness. In addition to regularly exercising, you can get ready with hikes and long walks in the weeks before your trip (also a good time to test out your gear). Boots should be already worn in by the time you go. On the trail, you may have to deal with issues such as heat and altitude. Just don't rush it; keep a reasonable pace and you should do fine.

★ Top Tip

On the trail, get your next day's water hot in a well-sealed bottle; you can use it as a sleeping bag warmer and it will be cool to drink by the time you're hiking.

MIKAEL KVIST / GETTY IMAGES ©

Day One

After crossing the Río Urubamba (2600m) and taking care of registration formalities, you'll climb gently alongside the river to the trail's first archaeological site, **Llactapata** (Town on Top of the Terraces), before heading south down a side valley of the Río Cusichaca. (If you start from Km 88, turn west after crossing the river to see the little-visited site of **Q'ente**, about 1km away, then return east to Llactapata on the main trail.)

The trail leads 7km south to the hamlet of **Wayllabamba** (Grassy Plain; 3000m), near which many tour groups will camp for the first night. You can buy bottled drinks and high-calorie snacks here, and take a breather to look over your shoulder for views of the snow-capped **Nevado Verónica** (5750m).

Day Two

Wayllabamba is situated near the fork of Ríos Llullucha and Cusichaca. The trail crosses the Río Llullucha, then climbs steeply up along the river. This area is known as **Tres Piedras** (Three Stones; 3300m), though these boulders are no longer visible. From here it is a long, very steep 3km climb through humid woodlands.

The trail eventually emerges on the high, bare mountainside of **Llulluchupampa** (3750m), where water is available and the flats are dotted with campsites, which get very cold at night. This is as far as you can reasonably expect to get on your first day, though many groups will actually spend their second night here.

From Llulluchupampa, a good path up the left-hand side of the valley climbs for

ℹ Need to Know

Take cash (in Peruvian soles) for tipping; an adequate amount is S100 for a porter and S200 for a cook.

a two- to three-hour ascent to the pass of **Warmiwañusca**, also colorfully known as 'Dead Woman's Pass.' At 4200m above sea level, this is the highest point of the trek, and leaves many a seasoned hiker gasping. From Warmiwañusca, you can see the Río Pacamayo (Río Escondido) far below, as well as the ruin of Runkurakay halfway up the next hill, above the river.

The trail continues down a long and knee-jarringly steep descent to the river, where there are large campsites at **Paq'amayo**. At an altitude of about 3600m, the trail crosses the river over a small footbridge and climbs toward **Runkurakay**; at 3750m this round ruin has superb views. It's about an hour's walk away.

Day Three

Above Runkurakay, the trail climbs to a false summit before continuing past two small lakes to the top of the second pass at 3950m, which has views of the snow-laden Cordillera Vilcabamba. You'll notice a change in ecology as you descend from this pass – you're now on the eastern, Amazon slope of the Andes and things immediately get greener. The trail descends to the ruin of **Sayaqmarka**, a tightly constructed complex perched on a small mountain spur, which offers incredible views. The trail continues downward and crosses an upper tributary of the Río Aobamba (Wavy Plain).

The trail then leads on across an Inca causeway and up a gentle climb through some beautiful cloud forest and an **Inca tunnel** carved from the rock. This is a relatively flat section and you'll soon arrive at the third pass at almost 3600m, which has grand views of the Río Urubamba Valley, and campsites where some groups spend their final night, with the advantage of watching the sun set over a truly spectacular view, but with the disadvantage of having to leave at 3am in the race to reach the Sun Gate in time for sunrise. If you are camping here, be careful in the early morning as the steep incline makes the following steps slippery.

Just below the pass is the beautiful and well-restored ruin of **Phuyupatamarka** (City Above the Clouds), about 3570m above sea level. The site contains six beautiful ceremonial baths with water running through them. From Phuyupatamarka, the trail makes a dizzying dive into the cloud forest below, following an incredibly well-engineered flight of many hundreds of Inca steps (it's nerve-racking in the early hours, use a headlamp). After two or three hours, the trail eventually zigzags its way down to a collapsed red-roofed white building that marks the final night's campsite.

A 500m trail behind the old disused pub leads to the exquisite little Inca site of **Wiñay Wayna**, which is variously translated as 'Forever Young,' 'To Plant the Earth Young' and 'Growing Young' (as opposed to 'growing old'). Peter Frost writes that

Wiñay Wayna

the Quechua name refers to an orchid *(Epidendrum secundum)* that blooms here year-round. The semitropical campsite at Wiñay Wayna boasts one of the most stunning views on the whole trail, especially at sunrise. For better or worse, the famous pub located here is now deteriorated and no longer functioning. A rough trail leads from this site to another spectacular terraced ruin, called **Intipata**, best visited on the day you arrive to Wiñay Wayna (consider coordinating it with your guide if you are interested).

Day Four

From the Wiñay Wayna guard post, the trail winds without much change in elevation through the cliff-hanging cloud forest for about two hours to reach **Intipunku** (Sun Gate) – the penultimate site on the trail, where it's tradition to enjoy your first glimpse of majestic Machu Picchu while waiting for the sun to rise over the surrounding mountains.

The final triumphant descent takes almost an hour. Trekkers generally arrive long before the morning trainloads of tourists, and can enjoy the exhausted exhilaration of reaching their goal without having to push past enormous groups of visitors.

★ Top Tip

As a courtesy, don't occupy the dining tent until late if it's where the porters sleep.

Recommended Reading

Mark Adams' *Turn Right at Machu Picchu* (2011) is a humorous and fascinating travelogue about visiting the famous Lost City.

NIARKRAD / SHUTTERSTOCK ©

Aguas Calientes

Also known as Machu Picchu Pueblo, this town lies in a deep gorge below the ruins. A virtual island, it's cut off from all roads and enclosed by stone cliffs, towering cloud forest and two rushing rivers. Despite its gorgeous location, Aguas Calientes has the feel of a gold-rush town, with a large itinerant population, slack services that count on one-time customers and an architectural tradition of rebar and unfinished cement. With merchants pushing the hard sell, it's hard not to feel overwhelmed. Your best bet is to go without expectations.

SIGHTS

Museo de Sitio Manuel Chávez Ballón Museum

(admission S22; 9am-5pm) This museum has superb information in Spanish and English on the archaeological excavations of Machu Picchu and Inca building methods. Stop here before or after the ruins to get a sense of context (and to enjoy the air-conditioning and soothing music if you're walking back from the ruins after hours in the sun).

There's a small botanical garden with orchids outside, down a cool if nerve-testing set of Inca stairs. It's by Puente Ruinas, at the base of the footpath to Machu Picchu.

Las Termas Hot Springs

(admission S20; 5am-8:30pm) Weary trekkers soak away their aches and pains in the town's hot springs, 10 minutes' walk up Pachacutec from the train tracks. These tiny, natural thermal springs, from which Aguas Calientes derives its name, are nice enough but far from the best in the area, and get scummy by late morning.

Towels can be rented cheaply outside the entrance.

ACTIVITIES

Putucusi Hiking

This jagged minimountain sits directly opposite Machu Picchu. Parts of the walk are up ladders, which get slippery in the wet season. The view across to Machu Picchu is worth the trek. Allow three hours. Follow the railway tracks about 250m west of town and you'll see a set of stairs, the start of a well-marked trail.

EATING

Restaurants range from basic eateries to fine dining. Touts standing in the street will try to herd you into their restaurant, but take your time making a selection. Standards are not very high in most restaurants – if you go to one that hasn't been recommended, snoop around to check the hygiene first. Since refrigeration can be a problem, it's best to order vegetarian if you're eating in low-end establishments.

Indio Feliz French $$

(084-21-1090; Lloque Yupanqui 4; mains S34-48; 11am-10pm) Hospitality is the strong suit of French cook Patrik at this multi-award-winning restaurant, but the food does not disappoint. Start with *sopa a la criolla* (mildly spiced, creamy noodle soup with beef and peppers). There are also nods to traditional French cooking – like Provençal tomatoes, crispy-perfect garlic potatoes and a delicious apple tart.

Tree House Fusion $$

(084-21-1101; www.thetreehouse-peru.com; Huanacaure s/n; mains S38-60; 4:30am-10pm) The rustic ambience of Tree House provides a cozy setting for its inviting fusion menu served alongside South American wines, craft beers and cocktails. Dishes like stuffed wontons with tamarind sauce, alpaca tenderloin and crisp quinoa-crusted trout are lovingly prepared. For dessert, lip-smacking chocolate mousse. There are raw and vegan options. Reserve ahead. It's part of the **Rupa Wasi hotel**.

Mapacho Cafe $$

(984-759-634; Av Imperio de los Incas 614; mains S20-48; 10am-10pm) This friendly streetside cafe is popular with the backpacking set. Perhaps it's all the craft beer and burgers on offer. It's worth checking out the *arroz chaufa* (fried rice) and *lomo saltado* (strips of beef stir-fried with onions, tomatoes, potatoes and chili).

Chullpi Peruvian $$$

(914-169-687; Av Imperio de los Incas 140; mains S49-69; 11:30am-11pm) Touting *'cocina de autor,'* this stylish shoebox of a restaurant serves beautifully plated food, but in its mass production it might not quite live up to gourmet standards. The fare is classic Andean – including grilled trout, shredded pork and *wallpa chupe* (a chicken-tomato stew). There are also soups and *causas* (creamy potato dishes). Tour groups have a tendency to take over – reserve ahead.

Café Inkaterra Peruvian $$$

(084-21-1122; Machu Picchu Pueblo Hotel; menú lunch/dinner S93/122; 11:30am-4pm & 6-10pm;) Upstream from the train station, this tucked-away riverside restaurant is housed in elongated thatched rooms with views of water tumbling over the boulders. There's a set menu (starter, main dish and dessert), with gluten-free and vegetarian options, and a decent kids menu to entice the young ones. The *lomo saltado* bursts with flavor.

INFORMATION

BCP (Av Imperio de los Incas s/n) ATM.

Centro Cultural (Machu Picchu Tickets; 084-21-1196; Av Pachacutec s/n; 5:30am-8:30pm) This is the only spot in town selling Machu Picchu entrance tickets. It's cash only and never a sure thing last minute.

iPerú (084-21-1104; Av Pachacutec, cuadra 1; 9am-6pm Mon-Sun) A helpful information center for everything Machu Picchu.

GETTING THERE & AWAY

TRAIN

All train companies have ticket offices in the train station.

To Cuzco (three hours), **Peru Rail** (Map p276; 084-58-1414; www.perurail.com; Estación Poroy; 7am-5pm Mon-Fri, to noon Sat) has service to Poroy and taxis connect to the city, another 20 minutes away.

To Ollantaytambo (two hours), both Peru Rail and **Inca Rail** (Map p276; 084-25-2974; www.incarail.com; Portal de Panes 105, Plaza de Armas; 1 way S231-330; 8am-9pm Mon-Fri, 9am-7pm Sat, to 2pm Sun) provide service. Inca Rail offers a ticket with connecting bus service to Cuzco.

To **Santa Teresa** (via Hidroelectrica Station, 45 minutes), Peru Rail travels at 6:45am, 1:30pm and 3:40pm daily.

BUS

There is no road access to Aguas Calientes. The only buses go from the **bus stop** (where you can purchase tickets) up the hill to Machu Picchu (round-trip S80, 25 minutes) from 5:30am to 4pm; buses return until 6pm.

Porter Welfare on the Inca Trail

In the past, Inca Trail porters have faced excessively low pay, enormous carrying loads and poor working conditions. Relatively recent laws now stipulate a minimum payment of S170 to porters, adequate sleeping gear and food, and treatment for on-the-job injuries. At checkpoints on the trail, porter loads are weighed (each is allowed 20kg of group gear and 5kg of their own gear).

Yet there is still room for improvement and the best way to help is to choose your outfitter wisely. A quality trip will set you back at least US$500. The cheaper trips cut costs and often affect porter welfare.

Porters on the Inca Trail

THE CORDILLERAS, PERU

In this Chapter

The Cordilleras, Peru

Ground zero for outdoor-adventure worship in Peru, the Cordilleras are one of the preeminent hiking, trekking and backpacking spots in South America. Here are some of Peru's most majestic vistas, with glaciated white peaks razoring their way through expansive lime-green valleys, which hold scores of pristine jade lakes, ice caves and torrid springs.

Huaraz is a hotbed of hiking inspiration. New adventurers mix it up with experienced climbers to share their recent thrills and show off their snaps. Land here first to fill up on good food and plan your next adventure in the Cordilleras.

Two Days in the Cordilleras

Spend your first day in Huaraz (elevation 3091m) acclimatizing. Visit the Wari ruins of **Monumento Nacional Wilkahuaín** (p314) north of town, check out the Museo Regional de Ancash and eat well at **Manka** (p316). Get an early start the next day for a memorable visit to the stunning **Laguna Parón** (p310), either going solo or by organized tour from Huaraz.

Four Days in the Cordilleras

On your third day, head off on a two-wheeled outing with **Mountain Bike Adventures** (p316). Recover that night over craft beers and snacks at **Los 13 Buhos** (p317). The next morning set out for **Chavín de Huántar** (p312) and spend the day exploring the fascinating archaeological site and its top-notch **museum** (p313).

Previous page: Basecamp at Laguna Jahuacocha, Cordillera Huayhuash
JOERG STEBER / SHUTTERSTOCK ©

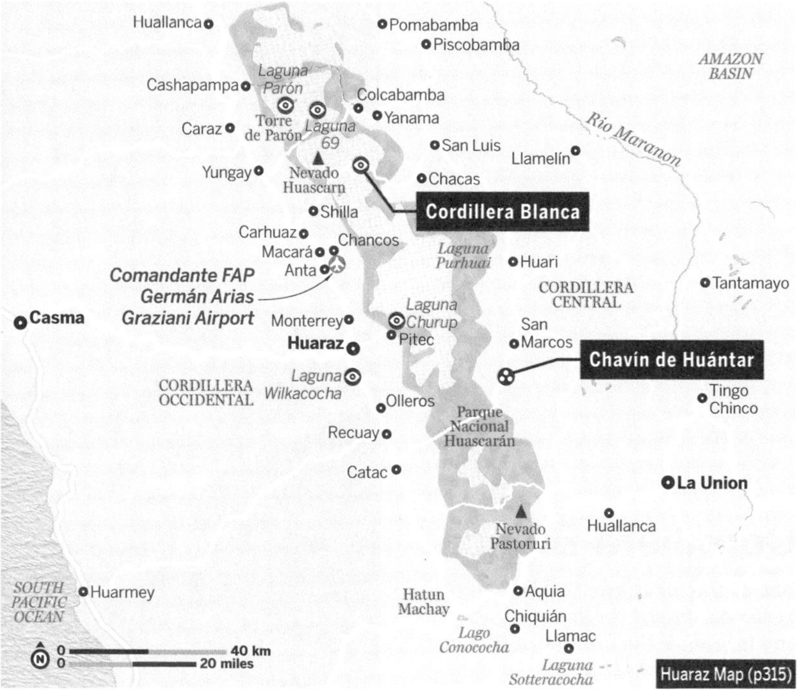

Huaraz Map (p315)

Arriving in the Cordilleras

Comandante FAP Germán Arias Graziani Airport The Huaraz airport is actually at Anta, 23km north of town. A taxi will cost about S40.

Bus Buses from Lima and most other destinations arrive in central Huaraz.

Where to Stay

Hotel prices can double during holiday periods and rooms become very scarce. Better hotels, at the southeast fringe of central Huaraz, are often perched higher, making for better views of Huascarán.

Laguna Parón and Pirámide de Garcilaso (p310)

Cordillera Blanca

One of the most breathtaking parts of the continent (both figuratively and literally), the Cordillera Blanca is the world's highest tropical mountain range and encompasses some of South America's highest mountains.

Great For...

Need to Know

Even experienced mountaineers would do well to add a local guide to their trekking group.

★ Top Tip

The dry season, May to September, offers the best trekking conditions.

Parque Nacional Huascarán

This 3400-sq-km park encompasses practically the entire area of the Cordillera Blanca above 4000m, including more than 600 glaciers and nearly 300 lakes, and protects such extraordinary and endangered species as the giant *Puya raimondii* plant, the spectacled bear and the Andean condor.

Visitors to the park can register (bring your passport) and pay the park fee at the park office (p317) in Huaraz, although most of the main entrances to the park also sell tickets. Fees are S30 per person for a day visit, S60 for a three-day visit and S150 for a month.

Laguna Parón

Silent awe enters people's expressions when they talk of **Laguna Parón** (Map p307; S5). Nestled at 4185m above sea level, along a bumpy road 25km east of Caraz, and surrounded by spectacular snow-covered peaks, many claim this to be the most beautiful lake in the Cordillera Blanca. It is certainly the largest, despite its water levels being lowered from 75m to 15m in the mid-1980s to prevent a collapse of Huandoy's moraine.

Ringed by formidable peaks, Parón offers close-up views of **Pirámide de Garcilaso** (5885m), **Huandoy** (6395m), **Chacraraju** (6112m) and several 1000m granite rock walls. The challenging rock-climbing wall of Torre de Parón, known as the Sphinx, is also found here.

Hiking in Parque Nacional Huascarán

Most people see the lake as part of an organized tour out of Huaraz or Caraz (from S50). Going solo, you can organize a taxi in Caraz for around S150 round-trip with wait. The journey from Caraz takes 1½ hours on an unpaved road.

Hiking

Laguna Churup — Hiking

If overnight trekking isn't your bag, but you'd like to experience the sight of some of the area's extravagant high-altitude lakes, this one-day hike is for you. It begins at the hamlet of Pitec (3850m), just above Huaraz, and takes you to the emerald green **Laguna Churup** (Map p307; 4450m), at the base of Nevado Churup. Note the altitudes and the ascent (it's a steep 600m straight up). The walk takes roughly six hours and is a good acclimatization hike.

Take a Break

Ask in Huaraz what amount of food and water is required for your trek, or bring a cook.

BYELIKOVA OKSANA / SHUTTERSTOCK ©

Laguna 69 — Hiking

This vivid blue **lake** (Map p307) surrounded by snow-covered peaks is the jewel of the Cordilleras. Set at 4600m, it's a challenging acclimatization hike (we recommend working up to it with an easier hike at altitude). 'Sixty-nine' is most commonly visited as a day trip from Huaraz and has become increasingly popular in recent years. Don't expect to have the place to yourself. Swimming in the lake is prohibited.

Acclimatize!

It is important that trekkers freshly arrived in the Cordilleras spend several days in Huaraz acclimatizing before sallying forth into the mountains. Huaraz is located at an altitude of 3091m – a sharp jump in elevation if you're arriving from sea level – but most Cordillera hikes go much higher, climbing to altitudes between 3500m and 5000m.

Rush into the high country and it's possible you'll end up suffering from dizziness, nausea or worse, putting a premature end to your trekking trip or, at best, turning the whole thing into one long miserable pain-fest.

On your first day, take it easy by pursuing some gentle, flat walks around town. On day two, depending on how you feel (everyone is different), you might want to try the **Laguna Wilkacocha hike** (Map p307), one of the few trails around Huaraz that doesn't climb above 4000m. On day three, well-trained hikers may feel strong enough to break the 4000m barrier by shinning it up to Laguna Churup.

☑ Don't Miss

Lakes, ruins and hot springs en route – it's not just about seeing the (spectacular) mountains.

Underground passageway

Chavín de Huántar

Chavín de Huántar is the most intriguing of the many relatively independent, competitive ceremonial centers constructed throughout the central Andes.

Great For...

☑ Don't Miss

The carved tenon heads at the Museo Nacional de Chavín.

The quintessential site of Peru's Mid–Late Formative Period (c 1200–500 BC), Chavín de Huántar is a phenomenal achievement of ancient construction, with large temple-like structures above ground and labyrinthine (now electronically lit) underground passageways. Although not as initially impressive as sites like Machu Picchu and Kuélap, Chavín tells an engrossing story together with its excellent affiliated museum.

Edificio A

The largest and most important building, Edificio A, has withstood some mighty earthquakes over the years. Built on three different levels of stone-and-mortar masonry, the walls here were at one time embellished with tenon heads (blocks carved to resemble human heads with animal or

Ancient stone tenon head

KLUBLU / SHUTTERSTOCK ©

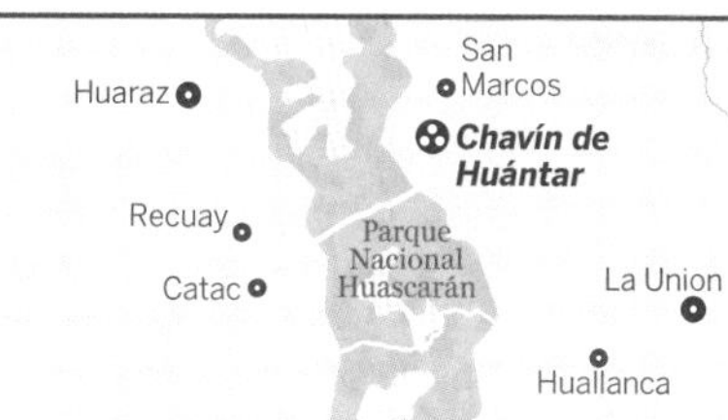

Need to Know

admission S15; 9am-4pm Tue-Sun

Take a Break

Buongiorno (Calle 17 de Enero Sur s/n; mains S20-35; 7am-7pm Tue-Sun) A sophisticated Peruvian-Italian restaurant in a pleasant garden setting right next to the ruins.

★ Top Tip

Stay overnight in under-appreciated Chavín town and have the ruins to yourself in the morning.

perhaps hallucinogen-induced characteristics backed by stone spikes for insertion into a wall). Only one of these remains in its original place, although around 30 others may be seen in the local museum.

Lanzón de Chavín

A series of tunnels underneath the Castillo are an exceptional feat of engineering, comprising a maze of complex corridors, ducts and chambers. In the heart of this complex is an exquisitely carved, 4.5m monolith of white granite known as the Lanzón de Chavín. In typical terrifying Chavín fashion, the low-relief carvings on the Lanzón represent a person with snakes radiating from his head and a ferocious set of fangs, most likely feline. The Lanzón, almost certainly an object of worship given its prominent, central placement in this ceremonial center, is sometimes referred to as the Smiling God – although its appearance seems anything but friendly.

Museo Nacional de Chavín

This outstanding **museum** (043-45-4011; 17 de Enero s/n; 9am-5pm Tue-Sun) FREE, funded jointly by the Peruvian and Japanese governments, houses most of the intricate tenon heads carved with horror-stricken expressions from Chavín de Huántar, as well as the magnificent Tello Obelisk, another stone object of worship with low relief carvings of a caiman and other fierce animals.

The museum is located around 2km from the ruins on the north side of town – an easy 25-minute walk.

Huaraz

Huaraz is the restless capital of this Andean adventure kingdom and its rooftops command exhaustive panoramas of the city's dominion: one of the most impressive mountain ranges in the world. Nearly wiped out by the earthquake of 1970, Huaraz isn't going to win any Andean-village beauty contests anytime soon, but it does have personality – and personality goes a long way.

This is first and foremost a trekking metropolis. During high season (May to September) the streets buzz with hundreds of backpackers and adventurers freshly returned from arduous hikes or planning their next expedition as they huddle in one of the town's many fine watering holes. Dozens of outfits help plan trips, rent equipment and organize a list of adventure sports as long as your arm.

SIGHTS

Monumento Nacional Wilkahuaín Ruins

(adult/student S5/2; 9am-5pm Tue-Sun) This small Wari ruin about 8km north of Huaraz is remarkably well preserved, dating from about AD 600 to 900. It's an imitation of the temple at Chavín done in the Tiwanaku style (square temples on raised platforms). Wilkahuaín means 'grandson's house' in Quechua. The three-story temple has seven rooms on each floor, each originally filled with bundles of mummies. The bodies were kept dry using a sophisticated system of ventilation ducts. A one-room museum gives some basic background information in English and Spanish.

To get here by foot take a taxi to 'El Pinar' (S7) from where there are two paths leading to the ruins – a direct route via the main road (6km) or a longer but more scenic route via Marian. Alternatively, a taxi direct to the ruins will set you back around S25.

There are actually two sets of ruins. Buy your ticket at the lower complex. It's a 10-minute walk along a dirt road to the smaller second complex (Wilkahuaín Pequeño).

Avoid taking the path from the ruins down to the baths at Monterrey as robberies have been reported on this stretch.

Museo Regional de Ancash Museum

(Plaza de Armas; adult/child S5/1; 8:30am-5:15pm Tue-Sat, 9am-2pm Sun) The Museo Regional de Ancash houses one of the most significant collections of ancient stone sculptures in South America lined up in a garden out back. Most of them are from the Recuay culture (400 BC–AD 600) and the Wari culture (AD 600–1100). Otherwise the collection is limited to a few mummies and some trepanned skulls.

Jirón José Olaya Architecture

On the east side of town, Jirón José Olaya is the only street that remained intact through the earthquakes and provides a glimpse of what old Huaraz looked like; go on Sunday when a street market sells regional foods.

ACTIVITIES & TOURS

Quechuandes Trekking

(943-386-147; www.quechuandes.com; Santa Gadea 995; 9am-8pm Mon-Sat, from 11am Sun) A very well organized agency that gets rave reviews for its quality guides and ethical approach to treks. Management will assess your level before sending you out into the mountains or renting gear, to ensure you are up to the task. In addition to offering treks, summit expeditions and mountaineering courses, its staff are experts in rock climbing and bouldering.

Owners Marie and David researched and wrote the Cordillera's definitive climbing guidebook. Prices vary depending on activity, number of people and type of trip. Contact them via their website for a quote.

Eco Ice Peru Trekking

(www.ecoice-peru.com; Figueroa 1185; 3- to 4-day treks from US$240; 8am-6pm) Run by a gregarious and passionate young guide, this agency gets top reviews from travelers for its customer service, guides, *arrieros* (mule drivers) and food. Treks often end with a dinner at the owner's pad in Huaraz.

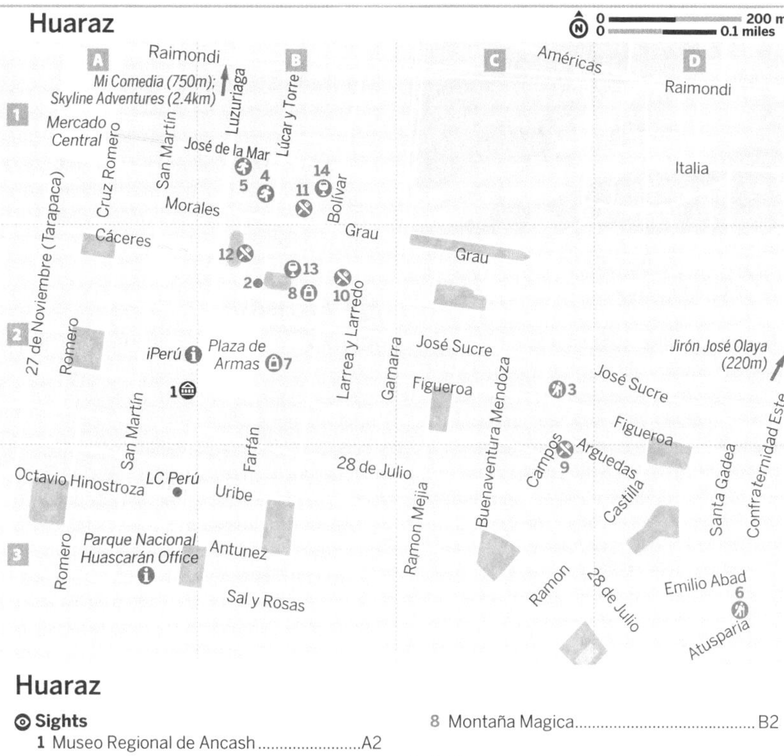

Huaraz

Sights

1 Museo Regional de Ancash A2

Activities, Courses & Tours

2 Andean Kingdom B2
3 Eco Ice Peru C2
4 Mountain Bike Adventures B1
5 Pablo Tours B1
6 Quechuandes D3

Shopping

7 Feria Artesanal La Plaza B2
8 Montaña Magica B2

Eating

9 La Casona Huaracina C3
10 Manka B2
11 Rinconcito Mineiro B1
12 Trivio B2

Drinking & Nightlife

13 Los 13 Buhos B2
14 Tio Enrique B1

Andean Kingdom Adventure
(944-913-011; www.andeankingdomhuaraz.com; Parque Ginebra; climbing trips from S120; 9am-9pm Mon-Sat) A laid-back but enthusiastic agency offering day courses for aspiring climbers, logistical support for experts and the usual day excursions, with an obvious bias toward climbing trips (Los Olivos and Hatun Machay feature highly).

Skyline Adventures Mountaineering
(043-42-7097; www.skyline-adventures.com; Pasaje Industrial 137) Based just outside Huaraz, this high-end operator comes highly recommended and provides guides for treks and mountain climbs. Leads six- and 12-day mountaineering courses (from US$1000).

Mountain Biking

Mountain Bike Adventures (☎972-616-008; www.chakinaniperu.com; Lúcar y Torre 530, 2nd fl; 2-day tours from US$380; ⏰9am-1pm & 3-8pm) has been in business for well over a decade and receives repeated visits from mountain bikers for its decent selection of bikes, knowledgeable and friendly service, and good safety record. It offers guided tours, ranging from an easy five-hour cruise to 12-day circuits around the Cordillera Blanca.

Involved owner, Julio, is a lifelong resident of Huaraz who speaks English and will tailor-make a trip for your specific requirements. No one knows the region's single-track possibilities better than he does.

Mountain biking in the Cordillera Blanca

PAWEL CEBO / SHUTTERSTOCK ©

Pablo Tours Sightseeing Tours
(☎043-42-1145; www.pablotours.com; Luzuriaga 501; ⏰9am-8pm) An agency selling the standard Huaraz day tours to places like Chavín de Huántar (S40), Lagunas Llanganuco (S40) and Laguna 69 (S45).

SHOPPING

Feria Artesanal La Plaza Arts & Crafts
(Plaza de Armas; ⏰10am-10pm) Huaraz' main craft market is made up of an association of local artisans and has sprawling digs next to the unfinished cathedral in the Plaza de Armas. Here you can buy everything from alpaca wool jumpers to brightly colored canvas bags. It's a great place for browsing aimlessly.

Montaña Magica Sports & Outdoors
(☎949-680-107; Parque Ginebra 25; ⏰10am-2pm & 4-8pm Mon-Sat) Forget your kit? Head to Mountain Magic where you can stock up on a full gamut of decent trekking and mountaineering gear from rain jackets to camping stoves.

EATING

Manka Peruvian, Italian $
(☎043-23-4306; Bautista 840; menú S10; ⏰8:30am-11pm) If you were curious about what happens when Peruvian *cocina* (cuisine) collides with Italian *cucina* then, let us tell you, it's a taste worth savoring. For proof, head straight to this simply decorated restaurant whose mix-and-match menu can deliver bruschetta for starters, *lomo saltado* (strips of beef stir-fried with onions, tomatoes, potatoes and chili) for a main and a delectable chocolate mousse for desert.

Trivio International $$
(☎043-22-0416; Parque del Periodista; mains S21-37; ⏰8am-midnight) Cementing a three-way marriage of craft beer, micro-roasted coffee and food made with local ingredients, Trivio joins a few Huaraz restaurants that wouldn't be alien in Lima. The decor is North America hip, the clientele predominantly gringo, and the food clever enough to excite the taste buds but filling enough to cover the hole left by your recent four-day trek.

Mi Comedia Italian $$
(☎043-58-7954; Centenario 351; mains S22-38; ⏰5-11pm Mon-Sat) Many restaurants claim great pizzas with some even uttering the word 'Naples' blasphemously in the description. But at Mi Comedia the Italian boasts are no exaggeration. This is about as Neapolitan as a pizza can get in Peru.

Rinconcito Mineiro Peruvian $$
(Morales 757; menú S8-16, mains S12-35; ⏰7am-11pm; 📶) This popular place is *the* spot to tuck into homey and cheap Peruvian daily

menús (set meals). The daily blackboard of 10 or so options includes an excellent *lomo saltado*, plus grilled trout, *tacu-tacu* (a Peruvian fusion dish of rice, beans and a protein) and the like.

La Casona Huaracina Peruvian **$$$**
(43-39-6420; Campos 735; mains S22-42; 11am-10pm) The colonial architectural style is noticeably absent in Huaraz until you step into the sparkling new Huaracina, the clever designers of which have drawn inspiration from the graceful buildings of Arequipa. The business is split into three interconnecting spaces: a smart lounge bar, a *pastelería* (pastry shop) and the restaurant, all decked out with astute attention to detail (glass lampshades, elaborate balustrades, bookshelves).

DRINKING & NIGHTLIFE

Los 13 Buhos Bar
(Parque Ginebra; 11am-2am) Halfway up some monstrous Andean pass with a 15kg pack on your back, it's not uncommon to start dreaming of 13 Buhos with its Luchos craft beer, pool table and delectable afternoon 'snacks' (waffles anyone?).

Tio Enrique Bar
(Bolivar 572; 4-11pm) In an energy-sapping mountain town like Huaraz, this cozy Swiss-themed drinking hole with a long bar and communal pine tables is just what the doctor ordered. Popular with hardcore climbers, it serves around three dozen varieties of imported beers from the UK, Belgium and Germany as well as sausages grilled at the door by the charismatic apron-toting owner.

INFORMATION

English newspaper the *Huaraz Telegraph* (www.thehuaraztelegraph.com) is a good source of information about the region.

iPerú (043-42-8812; iperuhuaraz@promperu.gob.pe; Pasaje Atusparia, Oficina 1, Plaza de Armas; 9am-6pm Mon-Sat, to 1pm Sun) Has general tourist information but little in the way of trekking info.

Parque Nacional Huascarán Office (043-42-2086; www.sernanp.gob.pe; Sal y Rosas 555; 8:30am-1pm & 2:30-6pm Mon-Fri) Staff have some limited information about visiting the park. You can also pay your park fees here.

GETTING THERE & AWAY

AIR

LC Perú (043-42-4734; www.lcperu.pe; Luzuriaga 904; 9am-7pm Mon-Fri, to 6pm Sat) is currently the only company offering service, with flights to/from Lima (US$120, one hour) on Tuesdays, Thursdays and Saturdays.

BUS

Buses leave from different company offices: most are located in and around Raimondi and Bolívar streets a few blocks north of the Plaza de Armas.

A plethora of companies have departures for Lima. The top four for comfort and reliability are Cruz del Sur, Oltursa, Linea and Movil Tours. Most depart midmorning or late evening.

QUITO & THE CENTRAL HIGHLANDS, ECUADOR

In this Chapter

Quito & the Central Highlands, Ecuador

Quito is dramatically situated, squeezed between high Andean peaks whose greenery is concealed by the afternoon mist. The city's crown jewel is its 'Old Town,' a Unesco World Heritage Site packed with colonial monuments and architectural treasures. There is no sterile museum mile: here everyday life pulses along the handsomely restored blocks with 17th-century facades, picturesque plazas and magnificent art-filled churches.

Quito is also the launchpad for attractions in the Andean highlands, including adventure activities in Baños and stunning alpine scenery in the Parque Nacional Cotopaxi.

Two Days in Quito

Spend a full day in Quito's Old Town. Visit the decadent **Iglesia de la Compañía de Jesús** (p325), take in pre-Columbian treasures at the **Casa del Alabado** (p325) and admire the view from the **Plaza San Francisco** (p326).

On day two head to **Parque Nacional Cotopaxi** (p330). Check into a hacienda, take short walks, admire the views and adjust to the serious elevation!

Four Days in Quito

On day three, rise early for a sunrise in the park. then go horseback riding or trekking amid the breathtaking scenery.

On the fourth day continue to Baños for a bit of adventure. Make the (mostly downhill) mountain-biking trip towards Puyo, stopping at waterfalls along the way. At day's end soak your weary gams in the **Termas de la Virgen** (p338).

Previous page: Plaza Grande (p324), Quito's Old Town (p322)
JESS KRAFT / SHUTTERSTOCK ©

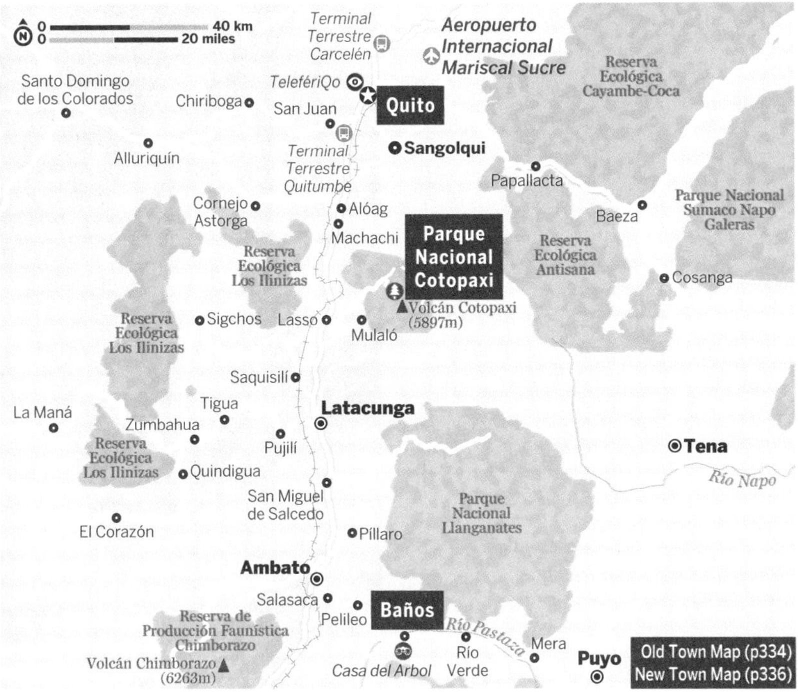

0 40 km
0 20 miles
Terminal Terrestre Carcelén
Aeropuerto Internacional Mariscal Sucre
Reserva Ecológica Cayambe-Coca
Santo Domingo de los Colorados
Chiriboga
TelefériQo
San Juan
Quito
Alluriquín
Terminal Terrestre Quitumbe
Sangolqui
Papallacta
Cornejo Astorga
Alóag
Machachi
Parque Nacional Cotopaxi
Baeza
Parque Nacional Sumaco Napo Galeras
Reserva Ecológica Los Ilinizas
Reserva Ecológica Antisana
Cosanga
Volcán Cotopaxi (5897m)
Reserva Ecológica Los Ilinizas
Sigchos
Lasso
Mulaló
Saquisilí
Tigua
La Maná
Zumbahua
Latacunga
Reserva Ecológica Los Ilinizas
Pujilí
Tena
Quindigua
Río Napo
San Miguel de Salcedo
Parque Nacional Llanganates
El Corazón
Píllaro
Ambato
Salasaca
Pelileo
Baños
Reserva de Producción Faunística Chimborazo
Río Pastaza
Mera
Río Verde
Puyo
Volcán Chimborazo (6263m)
Casa del Arbol
Old Town Map (p334)
New Town Map (p336)

Arriving in Quito

Quito's modern **Aeropuerto Internacional Mariscal Sucre** (p402) is 37km northeast of the city in a broad valley near Tababela. There is a **tourist information booth** (p338) in the arrivals hall.

Taxi prices into the city center are fixed at $26 to Mariscal Sucre or the Old Town (allow 45 to 75 minutes travel time).

Where to Stay

In Quito, most travelers tend to stay near the Mariscal, a guesthouse- and hostel-packed district. The quieter neighborhood of La Floresta is a pleasant alternative and begins only a few blocks away. There's a good range of accommodations in the Old Town, including most of Quito's best top-end hotels. You'll also find atmospheric haciendas near Cotopaxi and ample guesthouses in Baños.

Quito's Old Town

With its narrow streets, restored colonial architecture and lively plazas, Quito's Centro Histórico is a marvel to wander. Built centuries ago by indigenous artisans and laborers, Quito's churches, convents, chapels and monasteries are cast in legend and steeped in history. It's bustling but magical: the more you look, the more you find.

Great For...

☑ Don't Miss

The Last Supper painting with subtle Ecuadorian elements (including roasted guinea pig) at the Catedral Metropolitana (p324).

★ **Top Tip**

Avoid visiting on Monday when some sights are closed.

Plaza Grande

The heart of the Old Town is the **Plaza Grande** (Map p334), a picturesque, palm-fringed square surrounded by historic buildings and bustling with everyday life. The benches are great for soaking up the Andean morning sun and watching the day unfold. On Monday, the changing of the guards takes place on the plaza at 11am.

Catedral Metropolitana

On Plaza Grande's southwest side stands Quito's **cathedral** (Map p334; cathedral adult/child $3/2, cathedral & dome [adults only] $6; 9am-5pm Mon-Sat). Although not the most ornate of the Old Town's churches, it has some fascinating works by artists from the Quito School and houses the tomb of independence hero Antonio José de Sucre. Behind the main altar is a plaque marking where President Gabriel García Moreno died on August 6, 1875; after being slashed with a machete outside the Palacio del Gobierno, he was carried, dying, to the cathedral.

Don't miss the painting of the Last Supper, with Christ and disciples feasting on *cuy* (guinea pig), and a nativity painting that features a llama and a horse peering over the newborn Jesus. Admission includes a free guided tour in Spanish and entry to the small cathedral museum. For an extra $3 you can climb up a narrow spiral staircase and onto the cathedral's domed roof; the views are impressive but there is some clambering along narrow ledges involved.

Palacio Arzobispal

On the northeast side of Plaza Grande, this former **archbishop's palace** (Map p334) is

Palacio Arzobispal

now a colonnaded row of small shops and restaurants, located between Avenidas García Moreno and Venezuela. Concerts are often held on the covered patio on weekends.

Iglesia de la Compañía de Jesús

Capped by green-and-gold domes, **La Compañía de Jesús** (Map p334; www.fundacioniglesiadelacompania.org.ec; García Moreno & Sucre, adult/student $5/2.50; 9:30am-6:30pm Mon-Thu, to 5:30pm Fri, to 4pm Sat, 12:30-4pm Sun) is Quito's most ornate church and a standout among the baroque splendors of Old Town. Free guided tours in English or Spanish highlight the church's unique features, including its Moorish elements, perfect symmetry (right down to the trompe l'oeil staircase at the rear), symbolic elements (bright-red walls are a reminder of Christ's blood) and its syncretism (Ecuadorian plants and indigenous faces are hidden along the pillars).

★ Andean High

Quito's elevation of about 2850m can leave you breathless. To minimize symptoms of altitude sickness, take things easy upon arrival, eat light and lay off the alcohol.

PETER ADAMS / GETTY IMAGES ©

Museo de la Ciudad

This first-rate **museum** (Map p334; 02-228-3883; www.museociudadquito.gob.ec; García Moreno S1-47 near Rocafuerte; adult/child $3/1.50; 9am-5pm Tue-Sun) depicts daily life in Quito through the centuries, with displays including dioramas, model indigenous homes and colonial kitchens. The 1563 building itself (a former hospital) is a work of art. There are also a number of temporary exhibitions. Entry is free on the last Sunday of the month.

The museum sits just past the 18th-century arch, Arco de la Reina, built to give shelter to churchgoers.

Casa del Alabado

Housed in an elegant colonial-era home, this privately owned **museum** (Map p334; 02-228-0940; www.alabado.org; Cuenca N1-41 near Bolívar; adult/child $6/1; 9:30am-5:30pm), with contemporary displays, showcases an impressive collection of pre-Columbian artifacts. Thematically organized around subjects such as shamans, pigmentation and the afterlife, explanations in English and Spanish (audioguides are available) explore the indigenous beliefs represented by the finely crafted ceramic pieces and jewelry.

Need to Know

The Old Town **tourist office** (Corporación Metropolitana de Turismo; Map p334; 02-257-2445; www.quito-turismo.gob.ec; Venezuela near Espejo; 9am-6pm Mon-Sat, 9:30-4:30pm Sun;) is well located on Plaza Grande.

La Ronda

La Ronda (Map p334; 24hr) is a completely restored narrow cobblestone lane lined with postcard-perfect 17th-century buildings housing festive restaurants, bars and colorful shops. Sleepy by day, it comes alive on Friday and Saturday nights when *canelazo* (*aguardiente* with hot cider and cinnamon) vendors keep the crowds nice and warm and live music spills outdoors. Placards along the walls describe (in Spanish) some of the street's history and the artists, writers and political figures who once resided here.

Plaza San Francisco

Walking from the Old Town's narrow colonial streets into this open **plaza** (Map p334) reveals one of the finest sights in all of Ecuador: a sweeping cobblestone plaza backed by the mountainous backdrop of Volcán Pichincha, and the long, white-washed walls and twin bell towers of Ecuador's oldest church.

Museo Camilo Egas

Inside this restored colonial home is a small but iconic **collection** (Map p334; Venezuela 1302 near Esmeraldas; 8:30am-5pm Tue-Fri, 10am-4pm Sat) FREE of work by painter Camilo Egas (1899–1962), Ecuador's first *indigenista* (indigenous-led movement) painter. One of the galleries showcases temporary exhibitions by contemporary painters.

Museo Franciscano

To the right of the Iglesia de San Francisco's main entrance, and within the Convent of St Francis, this **museum** (Museo Fray Pedro

Interior of Iglesia de San Francisco

Gocial; Map p334; www.museofraypedrogocial.com; Cuenca 477 near Sucre, Plaza San Francisco; adult/child $3/1; ⌚9am-5:30pm Mon-Sat, to 1pm Sun) contains the church's finest artwork, including paintings, sculpture and 16th-century furniture, some of which is fantastically wrought and inlaid with thousands of pieces of mother-of-pearl. The admission fee includes a guided tour in English or Spanish.

Good guides will point out Mudejar (Moorish) representations of the eight planets revolving around the sun in the ceiling and will explain how the light shines through the rear window during the solstices, lighting up the main altar. They'll also demonstrate an odd confessional technique, where two people standing in separate corners can hear each other while whispering into the walls.

Cumandá Parque Urbano

Old Town's old bus terminal has been converted into a sparkling covered **cultural center** (☎02-257-3645; www.facebook.com/quitocumanda; Av 24 de Mayo; ⌚7am-8pm Tue-Fri, 8am-6pm Sat & Sun) FREE and sports complex with a volleyball court, soccer pitch, climbing wall, yoga studios and several small swimming pools – all free of charge. Temporary art exhibitions, theater performances, live music and other cultural events are also held here. It's accessed from La Ronda.

★ Easter Processions

Colorful religious processions are held during Easter Week, the most spectacular being the procession of *cucuruchos* (penitents wearing purple robes and conical masks) on Good Friday.

Ruta de las Cascadas, Baños

Adventures in Baños

Baños offers unrivaled adventures: you can visit thundering waterfalls, hike down impossibly steep forest-lined gorges and bike all the way to the Amazon Basin. Afterwards, you can rejuvenate in the town's steaming thermal springs.

Great For...

☑ Don't Miss

The views over the countryside from Bellavista, high above Baños.

Mountain Biking

The most popular ride is the dramatic descent past a series of waterfalls on the road to Puyo, a jungle town 61km to the east. Various other mountain-biking options are available and the outfitters will be happy to tell you about them.

Many companies around town rent mountain bikes (it's worth paying extra for disk brakes and suspension). From Puyo (or any point on the way), you can simply take a bus back to Baños, putting your bike on the roof (or in the luggage compartment).

Hiking

The tourist office provides a useful map showing some of the trails around town. Reports of assaults on nearby hikes have dropped in recent years. Nevertheless, it's advisable to bring just the cash you need and leave the expensive camera at your hotel.

Rainforest zip-lining

Need to Know

Near the Parque Central, the **tourist office** (03-274-0483; www.facebook.com/gadbanosdeaguasanta; Halflants near Rocafuerte; 8am-noon & 2-5pm) has lots of info and free maps.

Take a Break

You'll find filling South American dishes at the lively Cafe Hood (p339).

★ Top Tip

Be sure to bring your swimsuit, so you can take a dip in the thermal springs.

Going south on Maldonado takes you to a path that climbs to **Bellavista**, where a white cross stands high over Baños. The path then continues to the settlement of **Runtún**, some two hours away, where the views are outstanding. From here, you can continue up to the **Casa del Arbol** ($1; 7am-6:30pm), or loop around and back down to Baños, ending up at the southern end of Mera. This takes you past the statue of **La Virgen del Agua Santa**, about half an hour from town. The whole walk takes four to five hours.

Climbing

The climbing conditions on Tungurahua (5016m), an active volcano, are naturally in flux. At the time of research, climbing to the peak was allowed, but only with a licensed guide (six hours for those in optimum condition; others may be well advised to take the two-day approach and sleep at the refuge). You can also climb just to the refuge at 3830m, a steep three- to four-hour climb from the village of Pondoa.

Andean Summit Adventure (968-959-533; www.andeansummitadventure.com; Ambato & Reyes) is an experienced and certified Aseguim/IFMGA team of European and South American mountaineers with an excellent success rate for scaling Tungurahua and other Ecuadorian peaks.

Rafting

The town's tour operators offer guided trips (half-day $30) on the Río Patate and Pastaza. The trips bring you to Class III and IV water (Class IV is enough to really get your heart pumping). Kayak classes are also available ($80).

Horseback Riding

José & Two Dogs (098-420-6966; paulo_climb@hotmail.com; cnr Maldonado & Martínez) offers horseback riding excursions to nearby springs as well as canyoning, zip-lining and salsa classes.

Andean condor

Parque Nacional Cotopaxi

Covered in a draping glaciated skirt that gives way to sloping gold-and-green páramo, the flanks of Cotopaxi are home to wild horses, llamas and fox, with Andean condors soaring overhead. Whether you come for trekking, horseback riding or simply to admire the view, the setting is spectacular.

Great For...

☑ Don't Miss

The sunrise views against the backdrop of majestic Volcán Cotopaxi.

Climbing Cotopaxi

Although the climb is not technical – save for a few basic crevasse crossings and heart-pounding shimmies up fallen seracs – it is physically demanding, freezing and, for some people, vertigo-inducing.

The ascent starts around midnight from Refugio José Rivas. Even experienced, fit and acclimatized climbers can only reach the summit at dawn about once out of every two tries (no guarantees, baby!). The reward for those who make it to the top (on a clear day) are awesome views of other mountains and a peek at the crater's smoking fumaroles.

Many outfitters lead climbs, including the reputable Quito-based Condor Trekk (p333).

Hikers near Volcán Cotopaxi

ECUADORPOSTALES / SHUTTERSTOCK ©

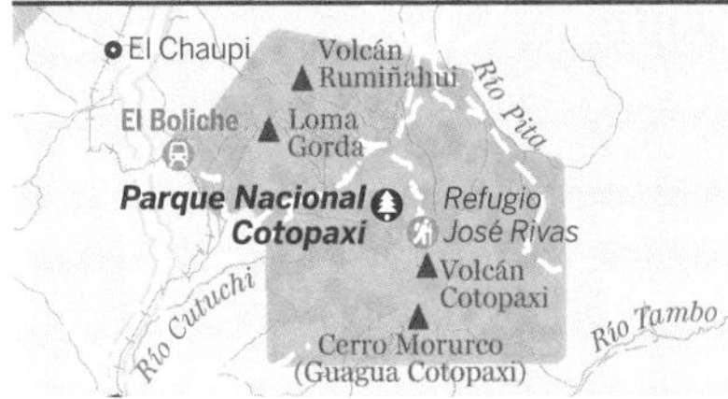

Need to Know

All of the haciendas provide transportation from Quito, often at an additional cost.

Take a Break

Within the park itself, **Tambopaxi** (02-600-0365; www.tambopaxi.com; camping per person $16, dm $24, s/d/tr incl breakfast $92/115/140;) serves food all day in its cozy dining room with spectacular views of Cotopaxi.

★ Top Tip

The skies are clearest around sunrise. Get up early for the best views.

Mountain Biking

Cruising around the park's circuit of relatively flat dirt roads is popular, as is a descent down from the *refugio* (mountain refuge) parking lot to the Control Caspi. Tour operators in Latacunga and Quito, such as Biking Dutchman (p333), can arrange trips.

Bird-Watching

Keep your eyes peeled for the giant, soaring Andean condor and the Ecuadorian hill star, one of the world's highest-altitude hummingbirds. Andean lapwing, Baird's sandpiper, Andean coot, caracara, Andean teal, Andean gull and solitary sandpiper are common visitors to **Laguna Limpiopungo**.

Haciendas

The luxurious lodges located in and around Cotopaxi National Park are some of the best in the country, and well worth the extra bucks you pay for the views. You can arrange all manner of activities, and all lodges have restaurants on site.

The modern adobe dwelling of **Hacienda Los Mortiños** (02-334-2520; www.losmortinos.com; dm/s/d/ste incl breakfast $30/80/103/151;) has jaw-dropping views of the neighboring volcanoes and comfortable rooms.

Located within the national park boundaries, Tambopaxi is perfectly positioned for hikes, though you could spend all day gazing at the volcano, llamas and wild horses through the windows of the stove-heated main lodge.

A lovely rustic property on the way to the northern entrance of Parque Nacional, **Secret Garden Cotopaxi** (099-357-2714; www.secretgardenquito.com/the_secret_garden_cotopaxi; near Santa Ana del Pedregal; incl full board dm $40, d $100-120) has superb views and loads of activities.

Quito

In Quito, warm and relaxed, traditional Ecuadorian Sierra culture – overflowing market stands, shamanistic healers, fourth-generation hatmakers – mixes with a vibrant and sophisticated culinary and nightlife scene.

SIGHTS

TelefériQo Cable Car

(Map p321; https://teleferico.com.ec; Av Occidental near Av La Gasca, New Town; adult/child $8.50/6.50; 9am-8pm Tue-Thu, 8am-8pm Fri-Mon) For spectacular views over Quito's mountainous landscape, hop aboard this sky tram. This is one of the world's highest aerial lifts and it takes passengers on a 2.5km ride (10 minutes) up the flanks of Volcán Pichincha to the top of Cruz Loma. Once you're at the top (a mere 4100m), you can hike to the summit of Rucu Pichincha (4680m), a 4km (five-hour) round-trip – ask about the safety situation before attempting the climb and bring warm clothes.

...warm and relaxed, traditional Ecuadorian Sierra culture...

Capilla del Hombre Gallery

(Chapel of Man; www.guayasamin.org; Calvache E18-94 & Chávez, Bellavista; adult/child incl Casa Museo Guayasamín $8/4; 10am-5pm) One of the most important works of art in South America, Ecuadorian artist Oswaldo Guayasamín's Capilla del Hombre stands next to the **Casa Museo Guayasamín** (www.guayasamin.org; Calvache E18-94 & Chávez, Bellavista; adult/child incl Capilla del Hombre $8/4; 10am-5pm). The fruit of Guayasamín's greatest vision, this giant monument-cum-museum is a tribute to humankind, to the suffering of Latin America's indigenous poor and to the undying hope for something better. It's a moving place and tours (in English, French and Spanish, included in the price) are highly recommended. Admission includes entrance to the Casa Museo.

Museo Nacional Museum

(Map p336; http://muna.culturaypatrimonio.gob.ec; cnr Avs Patria & 12 de Octubre, Eugenio

TeleféríQo's cable cars and a view over Quito's landscape

Espejo, New Town; 9am-6pm Tue-Sun) FREE Located in the circular, glass-plated, landmark building of the Casa de la Cultura is one of the country's largest collections of Ecuadorian art, with magnificent works of pre-Hispanic and colonial religious art. The museum collection includes more than 1000 ceramic pieces dating from 12,000 BC to AD 1534. Highlights are 'whistle bottles' from the Chorrera culture, figures showing skull deformation practiced by the Machalilla culture, wild serpent bowls from the Jama-Coaque and ceramic representations of *tzantzas* (shrunken heads).

TOURS

Quito is one of the easiest places in Ecuador to arrange a guided tour, be it a Galápagos cruise, mountain-climbing, Amazon lodge, biking tour or whitewater rafting.

Happy Gringo Tours
(02-512-3486; www.happygringo.com; Aldaz N34-155 near Portugal, Edificio Catalina Plaza, 2nd fl, La Carolina, New Town; 9am-6pm Mon-Fri) A British- and Dutch-owned company catering to a midrange market, Happy Gringo can organize week- to month-long customized itineraries throughout the country, from the Galápagos to the Amazon. Professionally run with English-speaking guides and private drivers available, it's one of the best all-around tour companies in the city.

CarpeDM Adventures Tours
(Map p334; 02-295-4713; www.carpedm.ca; Antepara E4-70 near Los Rios, San Blas, Old Town; day tours per person $50) CarpeDM earns high marks for its affordable prices and wide range of tours, though it's the excellent service that makes this agency stand out from many others. Day trips to Cotapaxi, Otavalo and Mindo for those short on time.

Condor Trekk Adventure
(Map p336; 02-222-6004; https://condortrekkexpeditions.com/; Reina Victoria N24-281 near Rodriguez, Mariscal Sucre, New Town; 9:30am-6pm Mon-Fri, to noon Sat & Sun) Reputable climbing operator offering single- and multiday guided climbs and tough hikes up and around most of Ecuador's peaks. It is best to pop into its office to discuss what you are looking for.

Biking Dutchman Cycling
(Map p336; 02-256-8323; www.bikingdutchman.com; La Pinta E-731 near Reina Victoria, New Town; 1-day tours from $59; office 9:30am-5:30pm Mon-Fri) Ecuador's pioneer mountain-biking operator has good bikes and guides, and an outstanding reputation. It offers one- to eight-day tours. The office is just north of Mariscal Sucre.

Biking in Quito

Every Sunday, the entire length of Avenida Amazonas and most of the Old Town closes to cars from 9am to 2pm as thousands of cyclists take to the street for the weekly **ciclopaseo**. The entire ride (some 30km), which you can cycle part or all of, stretches past the old airport, through the Old Town and into the southern reaches of Quito. It's a marvelous way to experience the city. Bikes can be hired along the way for $3 an hour.

Another good place for cyclists to check out is the bicycle-loving cafe **La Cleta Bici Café** (Map p336; 02-223-3505; www.facebook.com/lacleta.bicicleta; Lugo N24-250 near Guipuzcoa, La Floresta, New Town; pizzas $6-14; 11am-11pm Mon-Thu, to 11:45pm Fri, 5:30-11pm Sat;).

Cyclists enjoying the weekly ciclopaseo
MARGIE POLITZER / GETTY IMAGES ©

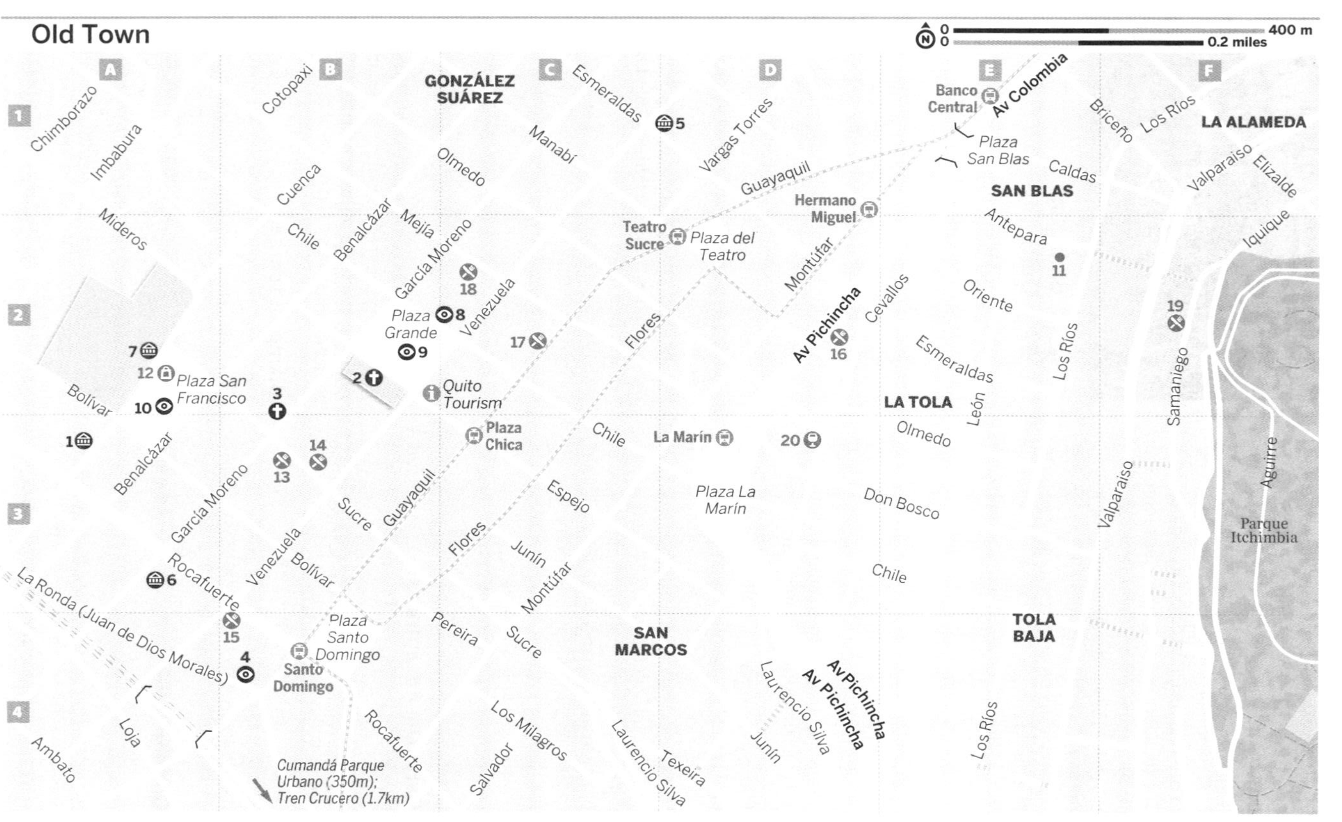
Old Town
0
0
400 m
0.2 miles
GONZÁLEZ SUÁREZ
SAN BLAS
LA ALAMEDA
LA TOLA
TOLA BAJA
SAN MARCOS
Parque Itchimbia
Banco Central
Plaza San Blas
Hermano Miguel
Teatro Sucre
Plaza del Teatro
Plaza Grande
Quito Tourism
Plaza Chica
La Marín
Plaza La Marín
Plaza San Francisco
Plaza Santo Domingo
Santo Domingo
Cumandá Parque Urbano (350m); Tren Crucero (1.7km)
Av Colombia
Av Pichincha
La Ronda (Juan de Dios Morales)
Chimborazo
Imbabura
Mideros
Cotopaxi
Cuenca
Chile
Benalcázar
Mejía
García Moreno
Olmedo
Manabí
Esmeraldas
Vargas Torres
Guayaquil
Montúfar
Flores
Venezuela
Bolívar
Sucre
Espejo
Junín
Pereira
Rocafuerte
Los Milagros
Salvador
Laurencio Silva
Texeira
Loja
Ambato
Don Bosco
Cevallos
Oriente
Antepara
Caldas
Briceño
Los Ríos
Valparaiso
Elizalde
Iquique
Samaniego
Aguirre
León

Old Town

Sights
1 Casa del Alabado A3
2 Catedral Metropolitana B2
3 Iglesia de la Compañía de Jesús B2
4 La Ronda B4
5 Museo Camilo Egas D1
6 Museo de la Ciudad A3
7 Museo Franciscano A2
8 Palacio Arzobispal C2
9 Plaza Grande B2
10 Plaza San Francisco A2

Activities, Courses & Tours
11 CarpeDM Adventures E2

Shopping
12 Tianguez A2

Eating
13 Cafetería Modelo B3
14 Cafetería Modelo II B3
15 Masaya Bistro B4
16 Mercado Central D2
17 San Agustín C2
Tianguez .... (see 12)
18 Vista Hermosa C2
19 Vista Hermosa Itchimbia F2

Drinking & Nightlife
20 Bandido Brewing D3

SHOPPING

Tianguez — Arts & Crafts

(Map p334; www.tianguez.org; Plaza San Francisco, Old Town; 9am-6pm) Next to **Tianguez cafe**, this fair-trade shop sells a wide selection of quality handmade crafts from across Ecuador. Items are arranged by region, with information on the techniques used to produce them.

Galería Latina — Arts & Crafts

(Map p336; www.galerialatina-quito.com; Mera N23-69 near General Banquedano, Mariscal Sucre, New Town; 10am-7pm Mon-Sat, 11am-6pm Sun) One of the finest handicraft and clothing shops in the city, Galería Latina has a huge selection of beautifully made pieces: tagua carvings, colorful Andean weavings, textiles, jewelry, sweaters and handmade items from across Latin America. Prices are high, but so is the craftsmanship.

EATING

Masaya Bistro — Bistro $

(Map p334; www.masaya-experience.com/en/hostel-quito; cnr Venezuela & Rocafuerte, Old Town; mains $3-8; 7am-midnight;) This large, inviting space with bare brick pillars and long wooden tables spills onto the peaceful enclosed garden of the affiliated **Masaya Hostel**. Ecuadorian-international food is served up in this casual, relaxed setting, where beef in chimichurri sauce, quinoa croquettes, Ecuadorian-style ceviche, burgers, wraps and pastas are all possibilities.

Cafetería Modelo — Ecuadorian $

(Map p334; www.facebook.com/cafeteriamodelocentrohistorico; Sucre 391 near García Moreno, Old Town; mains $4-6.25; 8am-7:30pm Mon-Sat, 9am-6pm Sun) Opened in 1950, Modelo is one of the city's oldest cafes and a great spot to try traditional snacks such as *empanadas de verde* (empanadas made with plantain dough), *quimbolitos* (sweet, cake-like corn dumplings) and tamales. It's also a popular spot for ice cream. The fun, slightly kitsch Ecuador-of-yore trappings make the wait for the food interesting.

Nearby **Cafetería Modelo II** (Map p334; Sucre OE4-48; mains $4-6.25; 9am-6:30pm Mon-Thu, to 7:30pm Fri & Sat, to 5:30pm Sun) offers similar environs plus live music on Friday afternoons.

San Agustín — Ecuadorian $$

(Map p334; 02-228-5082; http://heladeriasanagustin.net; Guayaquil N5-59 near Mejia, Old Town; mains $5.50-12.50; restaurant 10am-3pm, ice-cream shop 10am-5pm;) Kitschy religious icons and old-fashioned radios decorate this old-school classic serving Ecuadorian fare to workday crowds. Opt for first-rate *seco de chivo* (goat stew), *corvina* (sea bass) or *arroz marinero* (seafood rice) – there are so many options, the menu takes an age to peruse. Follow these up with old-fashioned *helados de paila:* ice cream handmade in big copper bowls.

New Town

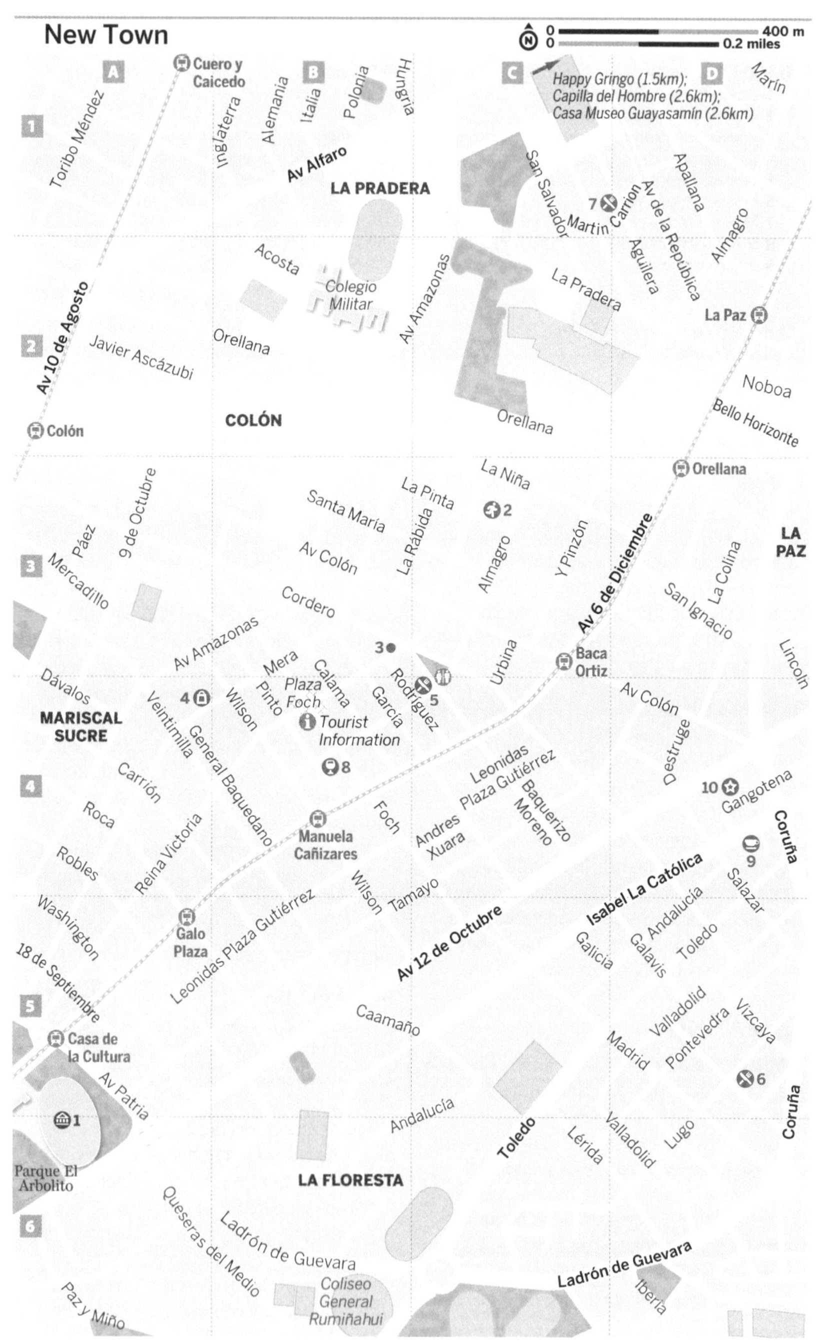
0 400 m
0 0.2 miles
Happy Gringo (1.5km);
Capilla del Hombre (2.6km);
Casa Museo Guayasamín (2.6km)
Cuero y Caicedo
LA PRADERA
COLÓN
Colegio Militar
La Paz
Colón
Orellana
LA PAZ
MARISCAL SUCRE
Plaza Foch
Tourist Information
Baca Ortiz
Manuela Cañizares
Galo Plaza
Casa de la Cultura
Parque El Arbolito
LA FLORESTA
Coliseo General Rumiñahui
Av 10 de Agosto
Av Amazonas
Av 6 de Diciembre
Av 12 de Octubre
Av Colón
Av Alfaro
Av Patria
Isabel La Católica
Ladrón de Guevara
Leonidas Plaza Gutiérrez
Toledo
Coruña

New Town

Cosa Nostra Italian $$

(Map p336; 02-252-7145; https://pizzeriacosanostra.ec; cnr Baquerizo Moreno & Almagro, Mariscal Sucre, New Town; mains $11-18; 12:30-3:30pm & 6-11pm Mon-Wed, 12:30-4pm & 6-11pm Thu & Sat, 12:30-4pm & 6-11:30pm Fri, 12:30-3:30pm & 6-10pm Sun;) Italian-owned Cosa Nostra has a pleasant front patio, cozy dining room and nearly three-dozen varieties of pizza piled with generous toppings and fired up in a brick oven – we consider it the best in town. It has good gnocchi and other pastas, and tiramisu for dessert.

Zazu Fusion $$$

(Map p336; 02-254-3559; www.zazuquito.com; Aguilera 331, La Pradera, New Town; mains $13-25, tasting menu $70; 12:30-3:30pm & 6:30-11pm Mon-Fri, 6:30-11pm Sat) One of Quito's best restaurants, Zazu serves beautifully prepared seafood dishes, grilled meats and ceviches in a stylish setting of light brick, ambient electronica and an inviting, backlit bar. The menu showcases the best of Ecuadorian cuisine with dishes such as Andean grains and veg, confit guinea pig empanada and seafood tamale.

DRINKING & NIGHTLIFE

Isveglio Cafe

(Map p336; www.isveglio.com; Isabel La Católica N24-682 near La Coruña, La Floresta, New Town; coffee & snacks $2-6; 9am-8:30pm Mon-Fri, 11am-8:30pm Sat, 2-8pm Sun) The standard of artisan coffee has been on an upward trajectory in Quito and Isveglio is at the forefront of the movement. This cafe, coffee education center and barista training school serves up organic brews from Ecuador's various coffee-growing regions, plus some beans from further afield.

Bandido Brewing Microbrewery

(Map p334; http://bandidobrewing.com; Olmedo E1-136 near Cevallos, San Blas, Old Town; 4-11pm Mon-Fri, 2-11pm Sat) These guys from Oregon produce their own creative brews such as La Gran Calabaza Imperial Pumpkin Ale (made with cinnamon, cloves and pumpkin spice) and La Gua.Pa (an American Pale Ale flavored with *guayusa*, a tea leaf native to the Ecuadorian Amazon). The bar has a vaguely Gothic feel, with stone walls, wooden benches and even a small chapel.

Finn McCool's Irish Pub

(Map p336; www.facebook.com/FinnMcCoolsQuito; Almagro E24-64 near Pinto, Mariscal Sucre, New Town; 1pm-1am Mon-Wed, to 3am Thu, 11am-3am Fri & Sat, 11am-7pm Sun) Proudly flying the green, white and gold, this Irish-owned bar attracts a mix of locals and foreigners who come for games of pool, table football, pub grub and theme nights (pub quiz on Tuesdays, regular live bands that often play Celtic music, open-mic nights, game nights whenever there's soccer on).

ENTERTAINMENT

La Juliana Live Music

(Map p336; www.lajuliana.com.ec; Av 12 de Octubre N24-722 near Coruña, La Floresta, New Town; admission incl drink $25; 9pm-2:30am Fri & Sat) In an old converted house, La Juliana is a colorfully decorated space with a good mix

Vista Hermosa

A much-loved spot in El Centro, **Vista Hermosa** (Map p334; 02-295-1401; http://vistahermosa.ec; Mejía 453, 5th fl, Old Town; mains $13-28; 1pm-midnight Mon-Sat, noon-8pm Sun) lives up to its name ('beautiful view') with a magnificent 360-degree panorama over the Old Town from its open rooftop terrace. Ecuadorian specials include *seco de chivo* (goat stew). Live music on Friday and Saturday from 10pm adds to the magic. Arrive early to beat the crowds.

There is another **Vista Hermosa** (Map p334; https://vistahermosa.ec/; Samaniego s/n, Parque Itchimbia, Old Town; mains $13-28; 3pm-midnight Mon-Sat) up by Parque Itchimbia serving up similar food and impressive views (truth be told, the views are still loftier here).

Quito's Old Town

F11PHOTO / HUTTERSTOCK ©

of bands (rock, salsa, merengue) lighting up the dance floor most weekend nights.

INFORMATION

Quito Tourism (Corporación Metropolitana de Turismo; 02-257-2445; www.quito-turismo.gob.ec; Venezuela near Espejo, Plaza Grande, Old Town; 9am-6pm Mon-Sat, 9:30-4:30pm Sun;).

Tourist Information (02-281-8363; aeropuerto@quito-turismo.gob.ec; Aeropuerto Internacional Mariscal Sucre) At the airport.

Tourist Information (02-382-4815; quitumbre@quito-turismo.gob.ec; Terminal Terrestre Quitumbre) At Terminal Terrestre Quitumbre.

Tourist Information (Map p336; cnr Reina Victoria & Foch; 9am-6pm Mon-Sat) Small booth on Plaza Foch in Mariscal Sucre.

GETTING THERE & AWAY

AIR

Quito's Aeropuerto Internacional Mariscal Sucre (p402) is 37km northeast of the city in a broad valley near Tababela.

BUS

Quito has two main bus terminals that are a long way from the center; allow at least an hour by public transport, 30 minutes or more by taxi.

Terminal Terrestre Quitumbe (cnr Cóndor Ñan & Sucre), 10km southwest of the Old Town, has buses to Baños and other destinations in the Central and Southern Andes, the coast, and the Oriente.

Terminal Terrestre Carcelén (Av Eloy Alfaro s/n), located in the north, services northern destinations including Otavalo, Ibarra, Mindo and Tulcán.

Baños

Baños is the central highlands' premiere destination for outdoor activities. Not surprisingly, it's often packed with out-of-towners, with abundant guesthouses and diverse restaurants to serve the international crowd.

SIGHTS & ACTIVITIES

Termas de La Virgen Thermal Baths (Montalvo; adult/child $2/1, after 6pm $3/1.50; 5am-4pm & 6-9:30pm) These are the only hot pools in the town proper. This community project built in 1928 was named for the Virgin Mary, who is said to have come here to dip her own feet. Some baths are cold, others warm and one reaches an intense 42°C (118°F). The rooftop pools have lovely views of a nearby waterfall. There are two locations; the 'old' pools at the top of the street, and the newer building below, which is open Wednesday to Sunday ($6/3).

Termas El Salado Thermal Baths

(Salado; adult/child $3/1.50; ⏰5am-8pm) These wonderful hot springs are located in a verdant canyon, 2.5km from town. There are hot, medium and cool pools surrounded by tree-covered hills, with the soothing sounds of a fast-flowing river close by. You'll need a swimming cap. Buses to here ($0.25, 10 minutes) depart from the stop on **Rocafuerte**.

SHOPPING

Maki Awashka Arts & Crafts

(Montalvo, near Santa Clara; ⏰8am-7pm) The family from Salasaca who own this shop weave many of the gorgeous wool rugs and tapestries in their workshop upstairs. There's a good selection of artisan crafts for sale here, including tablecloths, scarves and blankets.

EATING

Cafe Hood International $

(☎03-274-1609; www.cafehoodecuador.com; Montalvo & Rafael Viera; mains $4-8; ⏰noon-10pm; 📶🌱) Named for owner Ray Hood, a long-standing gringo-in-residence, this excellent cafe has cheap *almuerzos* (set lunches) and a menu of Asian and South American dishes. The cafe is a welcoming place to meet with friends or just chill *solito* (alone). If you don't feel like leaving there's a comfy *hostal* in the back with nice views.

La Tasca de Baños Spanish $$

(12 de Noviembre, near Montalvo; tapas $3.50-6; ⏰6:30-10:30pm Wed-Fri, 12:30-4:30pm & 6:30-10:30pm Sat & Sun) It may be difficult to get a table at this tiny tapas restaurant. The selection of small dishes is excellent, ranging from perennial favorites like *tortilla española* (Spanish omelet) to Andalusian meatballs and shellfish. Order up five to share.

DRINKING & NIGHTLIFE

Mocambo Bar

(☎03-274-1329; Alfaro near Ambato; ⏰8pm-midnight) Tired of the bus *bachata*? Guitar-hungry gringos need look no further than this joint, where the owner's laptop always has a classic playlist cued up, from Guns N' Roses to Metallica, while revisiting some classics from further back. And he takes requests. You'll likely *hear* Mocambo before you see it. Best bar sign in Ecuador: 'No wi-fi. Talk amongst yourselves.'

Stray Dog Brewpub

(www.facebook.com/straydoginbanos; cnr Rocafuerte & Maldonado; ⏰4pm-midnight Mon-Thu, to 2am Fri & Sat) This brewpub features artisanal offerings like light Llamas' Breath Belgian and bold Stray Dog Stout. There's a small bar menu to balance out the bevvies.

GETTING THERE & AWAY

From Quito's Terminal Terrestre Quitumbe, Transportes Baños offers frequent buses direct to Quito ($4.45, 3½ hours).

Andes by Rail

After massive investment, the country's **train network** (☎1-800-873-367; http://trenecuador.com; cnr Guayllabamba & Sincholagua, Estación de Ferrocarril Chimbacalle, Chimbacalle) is once again ferrying passengers on slow-motion journeys through breathtaking high-altitude scenery. Routes include the **Tren de los Volcanes** (☎1-800-873-637; www.trenecuador.com; adult/child $53/37; ⏰8am-5:30pm Fri-Sun), which makes the round-trip to El Boliche in Cotopaxi National Park, and the luxurious **Tren Crucero** (Train of Wonders; ☎1-800-873-637; www.trenecuador.com; adult/child $1650/1485; ⏰Tue-Fri), a four-day, four-night luxury train tour from Quito to Guayaquil.

Trains depart from Quito's beautifully renovated **Estación de Ferrocarril Chimbacalle** (Chimbacalle Train Station; cnr Guayllabamba & Sincholagua) 2km south of the Old Town. Book tickets online or at the booking desk at Quito Tourism.

GALÁPAGOS
ISLANDS,
ECUADOR

In this Chapter

Galápagos Islands, Ecuador

The Galápagos Islands may just inspire you to think differently about the world. The creatures that call the islands home, many found nowhere else in the world, act as if humans are nothing more than slightly annoying paparazzi.

This isolated group of volcanic islands and its fragile ecosystem has taken on almost mythological status as a showcase of biodiversity. Yet you don't have to be an evolutionary biologist or an ornithologist to appreciate one of the few places left on the planet where the human footprint is kept to a minimum.

Two Days in the Galápagos

Starting in Isla San Cristóbal, spy marine iguanas and sea lions at **La Lobería** (p346). Visit the intriguing **Interpretation Center** (p347), then stroll up to Cerro de las Tijeretas.

Take a boat to Isla Santa Cruz, and eye giant tortoises at **El Chato Tortoise Reserve** (p344), followed by a peak through **Lava Tunnels** (p345). End the day at lovely **Tortuga Bay** (p350).

Four Days in the Galápagos

On day three take a boat to Isla Isabela and go snorkeling at **Los Túneles** (p348), then bike out to **Muro de las Lágrimas** (p347).

Rise early for a visit to **Volcán Sierra Negra** (p347). Look for abundant birdlife and admire the views from the fumarole-dotted Volcán Chico.

Previous page: Galápagos giant tortoise

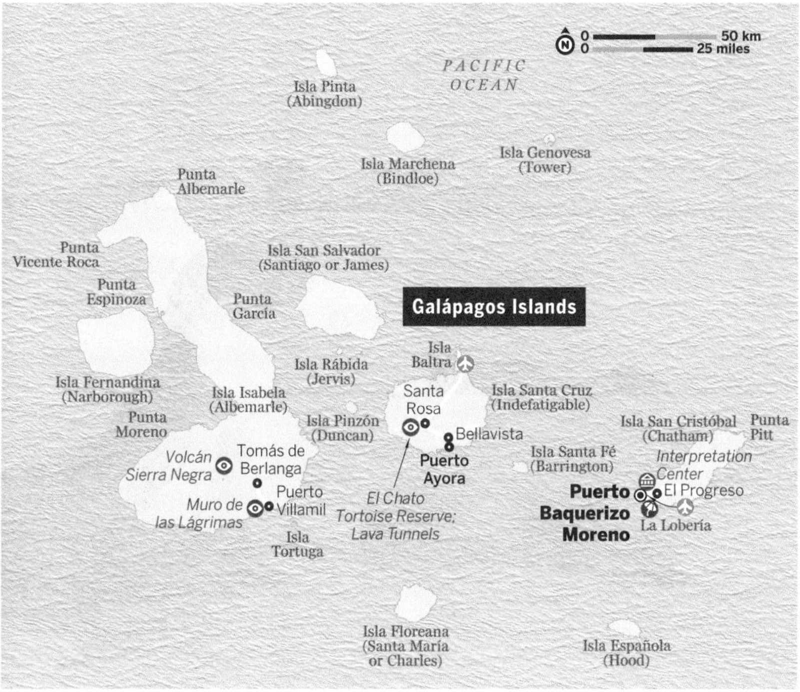

0 50 km
0 25 miles
PACIFIC OCEAN
Isla Pinta (Abingdon)
Isla Marchena (Bindloe)
Isla Genovesa (Tower)
Punta Albemarle
Punta Vicente Roca
Isla San Salvador (Santiago or James)
Punta Espinoza
Punta García
Galápagos Islands
Isla Baltra
Isla Rábida (Jervis)
Isla Fernandina (Narborough)
Isla Isabela (Albemarle)
Santa Rosa
Isla Santa Cruz (Indefatigable)
Punta Moreno
Isla Pinzón (Duncan)
Bellavista
Isla San Cristóbal (Chatham)
Punta Pitt
Volcán Sierra Negra
Tomás de Berlanga
Puerto Ayora
Isla Santa Fé (Barrington)
Interpretation Center
Puerto Villamil
El Chato Tortoise Reserve; Lava Tunnels
Puerto Baquerizo Moreno
El Progreso
Muro de las Lágrimas
La Lobería
Isla Tortuga
Isla Floreana (Santa María or Charles)
Isla Española (Hood)

Arriving in the Galápagos

Flights from the mainland arrive at two airports: Isla Baltra just north of Santa Cruz, and Isla San Cristóbal. There are almost an equal number of flights to Baltra and San Cristóbal.

Most flights come via Guayaquil, though there are a few direct options from Quito.

Where to Stay

Whether you're tacking a night on to either end of a cruise or looking for a land-based way to enjoy the Galápagos, you'll find perfect places to sleep on the inhabited islands of Santa Cruz, San Cristóbal, Isabela and Floreana. Options range from bustling, budget-friendly hostels and guesthouses to five-star luxury lodges.

Sea lions, Isla Española

Visiting the Galápagos

There are three kinds of tours in the Galápagos: the most common and recommended are boat-based trips with nights spent aboard (for their relatively low environmental impact and the exposure to a variety of wildlife and geography). There are also day trips returning to the same island each night and hotel-based trips staying on different islands.

Great For...

☑ Don't Miss

The sight of massive tortoises lumbering through the misty highlands at El Chato Tortoise Reserve.

Isla Santa Cruz

The island of Santa Cruz has the largest and most developed town in the Galápagos. Though many people are just passing through (from airport to cruise ship), the island is a destination in itself, full of visitor sites. It has easily accessible beaches and remote highlands in the interior, making it a base for adventurous activities far from the tourism trail.

El Chato Tortoise Reserve

South of Santa Rosa is **El Chato Tortoise Reserve** (Map p343), where you can observe giant tortoises in the wild. When these virtually catatonic, prehistoric-looking beasts extend their accordionlike necks to feed, it's an impressive sight. The reserve is also a good place to look for short-eared owls, Darwin's finches, yellow warblers, Galápagos rails and paint-billed crakes (these last

two are difficult to see in the long grass). The reserve is part of the national park and a guide is required.

Rancho Primicias

Next to El Chato is this private ranch, where there are dozens of giant tortoises, and you can wander around at will. The entrance is beyond Santa Rosa, off the main road – ask locals for directions. Remember to close any gates that you go through. There is a cafe selling cold drinks and hot tea, which is welcome if the highland mist has soaked you.

Lava Tunnels

These impressive underground **tunnels** (Map p343) southwest of the village of Santa Rosa are more than 1km in length and were formed when the outside skin of a molten-lava flow solidified. When the lava flow ceased, the molten lava inside the flow kept going, emptying out of the solidified skin and thus leaving tunnels. Because they are on private property, the tunnels can be visited without an official guide. The tunnels have electrical lighting (you can also hire flashlights/torches).

Tours to the lava tunnels are offered in Puerto Ayora.

Cerro Crocker

A path north from Bellavista leads toward Cerro Crocker (864m) and other hills and extinct volcanoes. This is a good chance to see the vegetation of the scalesia, miconia and fern-sedge zones and to look for birds such as the vermilion flycatcher, the elusive Galápagos rail and the paint-billed crake. It's around 5km from Bellavista to the crescent-shaped hill of Media Luna, and 3km further to the base of Cerro Crocker. This is a national park, so a guide is required.

El Garrapatero Beach

A 30-minute taxi ride from Puerto Ayora through the highlands, plus a 15-minute walk, brings you to this beautiful beach. It has tidal pools that are good for exploring and snorkeling on calm days, and a lagoon with flamingos, white-cheeked ducks and black-necked stilts.

Need to Know

The 13 major islands of the Galápagos Archipelago straddle the equator about 1000km west of Ecuador's mainland.

Take a Break

Hit the seafood kiosks along Charles Binford in Puerto Ayora for a satisfying al fresco meal.

★ Top Tip

Bring an underwater camera for photographing/filming sea lions, sea turtles and other aquatic life.

Isla San Cristóbal

San Cristóbal is the only island with fresh water and an airport in town, and it has several easily accessible visitor sites. It's also the fifth-largest island and home to the second-largest population in the archipelago. The Chatham mockingbird, common throughout the island, is found nowhere else.

Cerro Brujo

Possibly one of the nicest beaches in the Galápagos, Cerro Brujo is a huge white expanse found on the west side of the island. The sand here feels like powdered sugar. A colony of sea lions and blue-footed boobies call Cerro Brujo home, and behind the beach is a lagoon where you'll find great egrets and great blue herons. There's also good snorkeling in the turquoise waters.

El Junco Lagoon

Around 10km east of El Progreso along the main road, you'll find El Junco Lagoon – a freshwater lake some 700m above sea level. It's one of the few permanent fresh water bodies in the Galápagos. Here you can see frigate birds shower in the freshwater to remove salt from their feathers; white-cheeked pintails and common gallinules; and the typical highland miconia vegetation and endemic tree ferns. The weather is often misty or rainy.

La Lobería

Southwest of the town of Puerto Baquerizo Moreno, a road leads 2.5km (about a 30-minute walk) to La Lobería, a rocky beach with a lazy sea-lion colony. It's good for year-round surfing, and there are lots of iguanas along the trail leading past the

Isla Isabela

beach. Bring water and sun protection. Taxis charge about $3 to take you out here and you can walk back. Once there, a cliffside path takes you past marine iguanas, lava lizards and soaring frigate birds. To get here on foot, take Av Alsacio Northia toward the airport, turn left after the stadium (look for the murals) and then take the first right.

Interpretation Center

This modern and easily digestible **center** (☎05-252-0021; https://galapagos.unc.edu/gsc; Av Alsacio Northia; ⌚8:30am-5:30pm Mon-Sat) FREE explains the history and significance of the Galápagos better than anywhere else in the country. Exhibits deal with the biology, geology and human history of the islands – it deserves a visit even if you've been inundated with facts from boat guides. From the center there are also many well-marked trails that wind around the cacti and scrub of Cerro de las Tijeretas (Frigate-Bird Hill).

Punta Pitt

The northeasternmost point of the island is Punta Pitt, whose volcanic tuff formations are of interest to geologists (and attractive in their own right), but the unique feature of the site is that it's the only one where you can see all of the Galápagos booby species nesting. The walk is a little strenuous, but rewarding.

Isla Isabela

At 4588 sq km, Isabela is the largest island in the archipelago. Despite its size and imposing skyline of active volcanoes, it's the delicate sights, like frigates flying as high as the clouds or penguins making their way tentatively along the cliffs, that reward visitors.

It's a relatively young island that consists of a chain of five intermittently active volcanoes, including Volcán Sierra Negra, which erupted in late 2005 and sent up a 20km-high smoke column.

Volcán Sierra Negra

Northwest of the tiny settlement of Tomás de Berlanga lies the massive **Volcán Sierra Negra** (Map p343; 1490m), which last erupted in late 2005. An 8km trail leads around the east side of the volcano. It's possible to walk all the way around the caldera, but the trail peters out.

ℹ Wall of Tears

On Isla Isabela, you can visit the *Muro de las Lágrimas* (Map p343; Wall of Tears), a 100m-long wall of lava rocks built by convicts when the island was a penal colony.

UWE-BERGWITZ / GETTY IMAGES ©

☑ Surfing

There's excellent surfing in the Galápagos, especially in Isla San Cristóbal near Puerto Baquerizo Moreno (with board hire in town).

Galápagos hawks, short-eared owls, finches and flycatchers are among the birds commonly seen on this trip. The summit is often foggy and it is easy to get lost. There are spectacular views from nearby Volcán Chico, a subcrater where you can see fumaroles. Several agencies in Puerto Villamil offer all-day tours.

Darwin Lake

A dry landing deposits you at the beginning of a 2km-long trail that brings you past this postcard-perfect saltwater lagoon. It has twice the salinity of the ocean, and is a tuff cone, like a chimney from the main volcano. The trail leads to the lower lava slopes of **Volcán Darwin** (1280m), where various volcanic formations and stunning views of surrounding slopes can be observed. There are some steep sections on this trail. A panga ride along the cliffs to Tagus Cove will enable you to see the historical graffiti and various seabirds, usually including Galápagos penguins and flightless cormorants. There are snorkeling opportunities in the cove.

Los Túneles

Around a 30- to 40-minute boat ride from Puerto Villamil is this outstanding spot for snorkeling, formed by convoluted lava formations standing between mangroves and the open sea. Look out for white-tipped sharks, manta rays, eagle rays, sea lions, turtles and even sea horses in the shallows. Tour operators in Puerto Villamil run daily five-hour trips here for around $90.

Isla Floreana

Floreana is known for the mysterious history of its first residents – a small contingent of European settlers who became entangled in power struggles, peculiar disappearances and alleged murders. It's also home to intensely pink flamingos and top-flight snorkeling sites.

Devil's Crown

This ragged semicircle of rocks, poking up out of the ocean a few hundred meters from Punta Cormorant, is one of the most outstanding marine sites in all of the Galápagos. A strong current sweeps snorkelers briskly past thousands of bright tropical fish, a small coral formation, sea lions, marine turtles and the occasional shark. A *panga* ride around the semi-submerged volcanic cone will give views of red-billed tropic birds, pelicans, herons and lava gulls nesting on the rocks.

Post Office Bay

Most groups spend several perfunctory minutes on the north coast at Post Office Bay, where scraps of wood covered in graffiti surround a a few gone-to-seed barrels. It was a functioning mailbox for American

Diver viewing a Galápagos green turtle

and British whalers from the late 18th century, but these days it's tourists who leave postcards, hoping they will find their way, like a message in a bottle. Actually, it's more prosaic than that: visitors are asked to grab a few to post when they return to their home countries.

Isla Fernandina

The one visitor site at Punta Espinoza, just across from Tagus Cove on Isabela, is a memorable one. Marine iguanas, too many to count, can be seen sunning themselves on the black-lava formations, a dramatic sight that looks like a museum diorama on dinosaurs come to life. Flightless cormorants nest nearby, hawks soar overhead and Galápagos penguins, turtles and sea lions sometimes frolic in an admirable display of multispecies tolerance in the lagoon near the landing.

Isla Santiago

Once a hideout for British buccaneers and one of the stops on Darwin's itinerary, Isla Santiago is the fourth largest of the islands. Its terrain of rough lava fields is an example of the island's challenging beauty.

Evolution in Action

A fascinating account of the sometimes rapid changes unfolding on the islands is *The Beak of the Finch: A Story of Evolution in Our Time* by Jonathan Weiner.

☑ Biking the Galápagos

In the main towns on Isla Santa Cruz and Isla San Cristóbal you can hire bikes for a ride (uphill) to the misty interior.

Puerto Ayora

This town, the largest in terms of population and size in the Galápagos, is a surprise to most visitors, who don't expect to find anything but plants and animals on the islands. Puerto Ayora looks and feels like a fairly prosperous mainland Ecuadorian coastal town, despite the sea lions and pelicans hanging around the waterfront.

SIGHTS

MAPRAE Museum

(Museo de Arte Precolombino de Realidad Aumentada; ☎05-252-5197; www.maprae.com; Av Darwin & Av Binford; $5-10, includes tablet with headphones; ⏰10am-10pm) The first of its kind in the world, this museum uses augmented reality to showcase a permanent exhibition of 55 pre-Columbian artifacts. The ancient cultures of Ecuador's Amazon and coastal regions are brought to life as visitors point smart phones or tablets at one of the relics, with historical information and three-dimensional images appearing directly on the devices.

Charles Darwin Research Station Wildlife Reserve

(☎05-252-6146; www.darwinfoundation.org; Av Darwin; ⏰7:30am-12:30pm & 2-5:30pm) FREE Just northeast of Puerto Ayora is this iconic national-park site, where over 200 scientists and volunteers are involved with research and conservation efforts, the most well known of which involves a captive breeding program for giant tortoises. Paths leading through arid-zone vegetation take you past tortoise enclosures, where you can look at these Galápagos giants. There's also a baby-tortoise house with incubators (when the tortoises weigh about 1.5kg or are about four years old, they're repatriated to their home islands).

Several of the 11 remaining subspecies of tortoise can be seen here. Other attractions include a small enclosure containing several land iguanas, with explanations in Spanish and English concerning efforts to restore their populations on islands where they've been pushed to the brink of extinction. Follow paths through arid-zone vegetation such as saltbush, mangroves and prickly pear, and see a variety of land birds, including Darwin's finches. The research station is supported by contributions to the Galápagos Conservancy (www.galapagos.org).

Tortuga Bay Beach

In terms of sheer white-sand beauty, this beach is the rival of any in South America. You'll find it at the end of a 2.5km paved trail southwest of Puerto Ayora. In addition to swimming (a spit of land provides protection from the strong and dangerous currents on the exposed side), surfing or just sunbathing, you can see sharks, marine iguanas, pelicans and the occasional flamingo. There's no drinking water or other facilities.

It's about a half-hour walk from the start of the path – often used by local runners – where you must sign in between 6am and 6pm.

Playa Mansa Lagoon

If you walk the length of Tortuga Bay, you'll reach this picturesque lagoon lined with mangroves. Here you can spot marine iguanas, brown pelicans and blue herons, among other species. On the nearby dunes, sea turtles lay their eggs. The placid, shallow water is a great swimming spot for kids. **Kayaks** (per person per hr $10; ⏰9am-6pm) are available for hire.

Laguna de las Ninfas Lagoon

FREE This peaceful lagoon has a short boardwalk path, where you can stop to take in the mangroves while looking for stingrays, baby sharks, sea turtles and other creatures sometimes spotted here.

EATING

More than a half-dozen popular food kiosks sell inexpensive and hearty meals – mainly seafood – along Charles Binford, just east of Avenida Baltra. It's liveliest at night, particularly on weekends, when there's a festive atmosphere among the outdoor tables set out on the street.

Galápagos Deli Deli, Pizzeria **$$**
(Berlanga; mains $4.50-10; ⏰7am-9:45pm Tue-Sun; 📶) Tired of standard *almuerzos* (set lunches)? Head to this sleek and modern place for brick-oven pizza (small $6.50 to $9.75) and high-quality deli sandwiches ($4.70 to $8.75), as well as fish and chips, espresso and delicious gelato. Because it's on a block with few pedestrians, it feels like a secret.

Almar Japanese **$$$**
(Av Darwin, Red Mangrove Aventura Lodge; mains from $16-24; ⏰8am-10pm; 📶) Located inside **Red Mangrove Aventura Lodge**, Almar prepares its seafood dishes with ingredients sourced from local suppliers. The big draw is sitting on the back waterside deck where sea lions have free rein.

Garrapata Ecuadorian **$$$**
(Av Darwin; mains $15-30; ⏰11am-10:30pm Mon-Sat) Good tunes, cool breezes and tasty Ecuadorian and international dishes (seared tuna, grilled seafood platters and fish in coconut sauce) draw a lively crowd most nights. It's pricey but casual, with open sides and a pebble floor.

DRINKING

Bongo Bar Bar
(Av Darwin; ⏰7pm-2am; 📶) What nightlife there is in Puerto Ayora centers mainly on this bar, a trendy 2nd-floor spot replete with flat-screen TVs, music and a lubricated mix of hip locals, guides and tourists. Surprisingly, you'll also find some of the best sushi on the islands here (rolls $10 to $14).

INFORMATION

i-Tur (Av Darwin, entrance to water-taxi pier) A small kiosk with flyers, maps and basic hotel and travel-agency info.

GETTING THERE & AWAY

Three airlines fly to the Isla Baltra, a small island practically touching the far northern edge of Isla Santa Cruz: **Avianca** (☎1-800-003-434; www.avianca.com; Av Francisco de Orellana), **LAN** (☎05-269-2850; Av Darwin; ⏰8am-6pm Mon-Sat, 10am-1pm Sun) and **TAME** (☎05-252-6527; cnr Av Darwin & Av 12 de Febrero; ⏰8am-noon & 2-5pm Mon-Fri, 8am-1pm Sat).

Las Grietas

For nice swimming and snorkeling, head to Las Grietas, a water-filled crevice in the rocks. Talented and fearless locals climb the nearly vertical walls to plunge gracefully (and sometimes clumsily) into the water below. Take a water taxi (per person around US$1, from 6am to 7pm) to the dock for the Angermeyer Point restaurant, then walk past the Finch Bay Hotel, then past an interesting salt mine, and finally up and around a lava-rock-strewn path to the water. Good shoes are recommended for the 700m walk from the dock. Keep an eye on any valuables that you leave on the rocks.

Las Grietas, Puerto Ayora

GETTING AROUND

Lanchas (speedboats) head daily to the islands of Isabela (two to 2¼ hours) and San Cristóbal (two hours). Boats depart to Isabela/San Cristóbal at 7am and 2pm. There's also boat service to Floreana (1¾ hours) at 8am, but this service is irregular, often running on demand only.

CARTAGENA,
COLOMBIA

In this Chapter

Cartagena, Colombia

Cartagena de Indias is a historic city of superbly preserved beauty and the undisputed queen of the Caribbean coast. Cartagena's Old Town – a maze of cobbled alleys, balconies covered in bougainvillea and massive churches that cast their shadows across leafy plazas – is a Unesco World Heritage Site.

This is a place to drop all sightseeing routines. Instead of trying to tick off all the sights, just stroll through the Old Town day and night. Soak up the sensual atmosphere, pausing to ward off the brutal heat and humidity in one of the city's many excellent bars and restaurants.

Two Days in Cartagena

Delve into Cartagena's Old Town, visiting the photogenic **Plaza de Bolívar** (p356), the chilling **Palacio de la Inquisición** (p357) and the glittering **Museo del Oro Zenú** (p357). Dine at **El Boliche** (p365).

On day two, explore the atmospheric **Castillo de San Felipe de Barajas** (p363) and enjoy a memorable view from the **Convento de la Popa** (p362). Afterwards, have dinner and drinks in **Getsemaní** (p362).

Four Days in Cartagena

On day three, take a trip out to the Islas del Rosario for a Caribbean escape. Overnight on **Isla Grande** (p360) and enjoy the beach without the daytrippers.

After a morning on the sands, make your way back to Cartagena for a final night on the town. Enjoy dinner at **La Cevichería** (p366) followed by dancing and drinks at **Bazurto Social Club** (p367).

Previous page: Cartagena balconies and Catedral (p356)
JESS KRAFT / 500PX ©

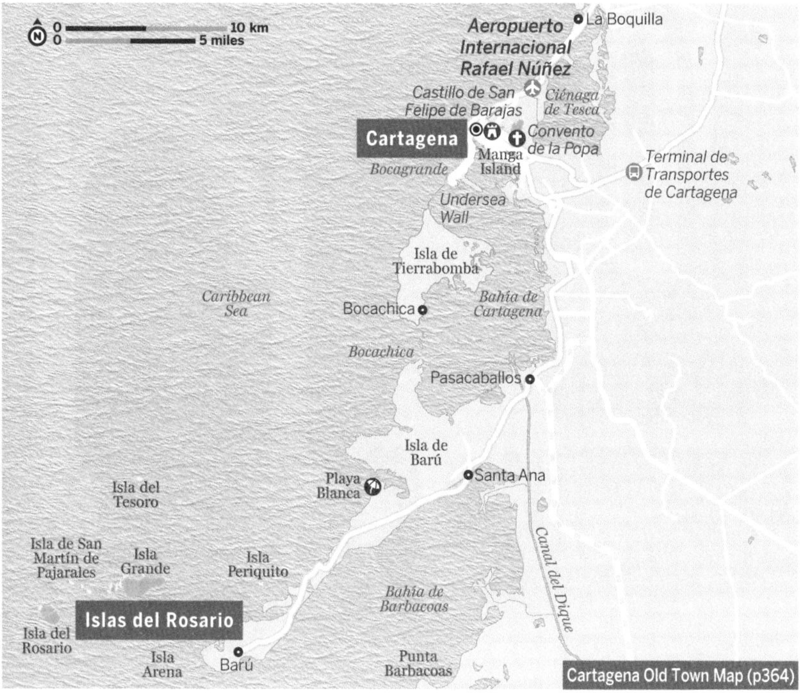

Cartagena Old Town Map (p364)

Arriving in Cartagena

Cartagena's Aeropuerto Internacional Rafael Núñez is just 3km from the city. *Colectivos* (COP$2000), as well as nicer air-conditioned shuttles called **Metrocar** (p367), go to the Old Town.

By taxi, expect to pay between COP$10,000 and COP$15,000 to Getsemaní, San Diego and El Centro.

Where to Stay

Cartagena has a huge choice of places to sleep, though you'll pay a pretty penny for anything above a hostel or a very simple midrange hotel. Catering to wealthy Colombian and US weekenders, the town's top-end accommodations have truly stratospheric rates, and there's an enormous number of beautifully restored boutique colonial options to choose from.

Entrance to the Catedral

Cartagena's Old Town

The Old Town is packed with perfectly preserved colonial churches, monasteries, plazas, palaces and mansions, with balconies and shady patios that overflow with bright flowers.

Great For...

☑ Don't Miss

Pre-Columbian pottery and Spanish colonial torture instruments at the Palacio de la Inquisición (p357).

Plaza de Bolívar

Formerly the Plaza de Inquisición, this leafy and shaded **plaza** (Map p364) is surrounded by some of the city's most elegant balconied colonial buildings. It's one of Cartagena's most alluring plazas and offers wonderful respite from the Caribbean heat. A statue of the eponymous Simón Bolívar stands in the middle of the square.

Catedral

Work on Cartagena's **cathedral** (Map p364; Calle de los Santos de Piedra) began in 1575, but in 1586, while still under construction, it was partly destroyed by the cannons of Francis Drake. The structure known officially as the Basilica Santa Catalina de Alejandría wasn't completed until 1612, although the distinctive terracotta dome visible all over town was added later.

Need to Know

Cartagena's old city consists of the historical districts of El Centro in the west and San Diego in the northeast.

Take a Break

Munch on creative, mouth-watering ceviche at La Cevichería (p366).

★ Top Tip

A beautiful walkway alongside the **Muelle Turístico de los Pegasos** (Map p364) links the neighborhood of Getsemaní with the Old Town.

Further alterations were carried out in the early 20th century.

Museo del Oro Zenú

This **museum** (Map p364; Plaza de Bolívar; 9am-5pm Tue-Sat, 10am-3pm Sun) FREE is like a miniature version of Bogotá's world-class gold museum, the Museo del Oro. Though small, it offers a fascinating collection of the gold and pottery of the Zenú people, who inhabited the region of the present-day departments of Bolívar, Córdoba, Sucre and northern Antioquia before the Spanish Conquest. Some pieces are exquisitely detailed.

Convento & Iglesia de San Pedro Claver

Founded by Jesuits in the first half of the 17th century as Convento San Ignacio de Loyola, this **convent** (Map p364; 5-664-4991; Plaza de San Pedro Claver; adult/child COP$13,000/8000; 8am-5:30pm) later changed its name to honor Spanish-born monk Pedro Claver (1580–1654), who lived and died here. Called the 'Apostle of the Blacks' or the 'Slave of the Slaves,' the monk spent his life ministering to enslaved people brought from Africa. A series of lucid paintings inside the building relates his life story.

Palacio de la Inquisición

The **Palace of the Inquisition** (Map p364; Plaza de Bolívar; adult/child COP$20,000/17,000; 9am-6pm Mon-Sat, 10am-4pm Sun) may today be one of the finest buildings in the city, but in the past it housed the notoriously grisly Inquisition, whose bloody task it was to stamp out heresy in colonial Cartagena. The palace is now a museum, displaying the inquisitors' instruments of torture, some of which are quite horrific. The museum also houses pre-Columbian pottery and plots a historical trajectory of the city using armaments, paintings, furniture and even church bells.

Islas del Rosario

An archipelago about 35km southwest of Cartagena, these 27 islands are surrounded by coral reefs, where the color of the sea is an incredible combination of cerulean and turquoise.

Great For...

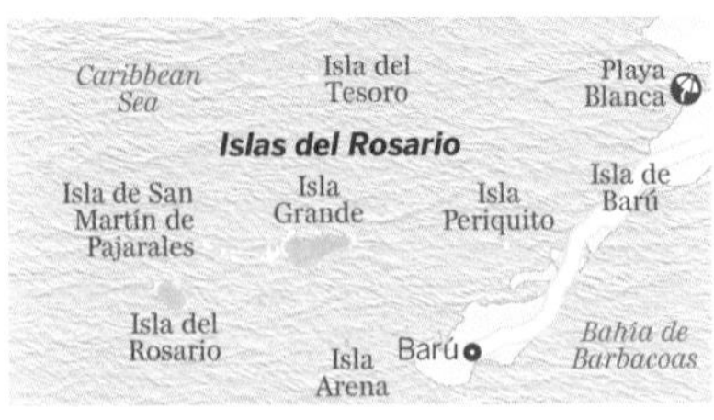

☑ Don't Miss

Basking on the pretty sands of Playa Blanca on Isla de Barú.

★ **Top Tip**

Get an early start to make a full day out on the islands, or better yet spend the night.

Isla Grande

The most developed of the islands, Isla Grande is indeed also the biggest. There's a large lagoon perfect for swimming in the unbelievably blue waters, and several sleeping options.

Isla del Rosario

The smaller neighbor to Isla Grande has several stretches of gorgeous beach, a huge lagoon perfect for swimming, and a handful of hotels and guesthouses.

Tours

The usual way to visit the park is on a one-day boat tour of the islands. Tours depart year-round from the **Muelle Turístico de la Bodeguita** (Map p364) in Cartagena; contact the cruise office at the *muelle* (pier; tours from COP$60,000 per person). Boats leave between 8am and 9am daily and return roughly between 4pm and 6pm.

A number of smaller operators at the pier offer cheaper tours. Popular budget hotels in Cartagena sell tours, too, and may offer lower prices – COP$50,000 per person is common.

Tours all take a similar route to the islands, though the trip may differ a little between small and large boats. All vessels go through the Bahía de Cartagena and into the open sea through the Bocachica strait, passing between Batería de San José and, directly opposite, the Fuerte de San Fernando. Boats then cruise among the islands (there's generally Spanish commentary along the way) and stop at the tiny **Isla de**

Playa Blanca, Isla de Barú

San Martín de Pajarales. Here there's an aquarium and a shady wooded area to chill out in or a beach to swim at while you wait for the trip to continue. Boats then go to Playa Blanca, on the Isla de Barú, for lunch and two hours or so of free time.

Tours usually include lunch but not port taxes, the national-park entrance fee and aquarium entry; check with your operator to confirm. Some higher-end hotels offer their own boat transfers from Cartagena.

Overnighting on the Islands

It's worth spending more than a day on the Islas del Rosario if you're looking for true escape, peace and quiet, and are happy with slow or nonexistent wi-fi. Most hotels are on Isla Grande and tend to be very rustic no matter how much you pay – and at the top end that won't be an insignificant amount. A few standout options include **Coralina Island** (313-245-9244; www.coralinaisland.com; Isla del Rosario; r from COP$680,000;) and **Eco Hotel Las Palmeras** (314-584-7358; Isla Grande; hammock/r per person incl full board COP$80,000/120,000).

Need to Know

Most people visit the islands on organized tours from Cartagena, but you can also arrange private transfers with the hotels on the island.

Take a Break

Beach shacks serve simple but filling dishes, including fresh seafood.

STREETFLASH / SHUTTERSTOCK ©

SIGHTS

Getsemaní Area

(Map p364) Getsemaní, the outer walled town, is less obviously impressive than Cartagena's old city but has some charming parts and is well worth exploring. In recent years it has been the focus of Cartagena's exploding gentrification and growing hotel industry, and boasts excellent bars, restaurants and cafes, as well as some superb street art on its derelict buildings.

The plaza in front of the Iglesia de la Santísima Trinidad is a massive draw for locals and travelers alike come sundown, when street-food vendors set up their stalls and a crowd of revelers sticks around until well after midnight.

Convento de la Popa Church

(Map p355; adult/child COP$11,000/8000; 8am-6pm) On a 150m-high hill, the highest point in Cartagena, stands this convent. The views from here are outstanding and stretch all over the city. The convent's name literally means the 'Convent of the Stern,' after the hill's similarity to a ship's back end. Founded by Augustine fathers in 1607, it was initially just a small wooden chapel, but when the hill was fortified two centuries later it was replaced by a stouter construction.

Las Murallas Fortress

(Map p364) The Old Town is surrounded by Las Murallas, the thick walls built to protect it. Construction was begun toward the end of the 16th century after the attack by Francis Drake; until that time, Cartagena was almost completely unprotected. The project took two centuries to complete, due to repeated storm damage and pirate attacks. It's possible to walk along large stretches of these magnificent structures, with wonderful sea views and a cooling breeze from the the northern and western sides.

ACTIVITIES & TOURS

Cartagena has grown into an important scuba-diving center, taking advantage of the extensive coral reefs along its coast. La Boquilla, just outside town, is also popular for kitesurfing.

Vibrant Getsemaní

Sico Cycling

(Map p364; ☎300-339-1728; www.sicobikerental.com; Calle Puntales 37-09; ⏰9am-10pm) This friendly outfit in the middle of the Old Town offers two-hour guided bicycle tours of the city and its surroundings. It also rents out good-quality hybrids and mountain bikes (COP$24,000 per half-day). Multilingual two-hour city tours depart at 8am and 4:30pm daily.

Diving Planet Diving

(Map p364; ☎310-657-4926, 320-230-1515; www.divingplanet.org; Calle Estanco del Aguardiente No 5-09; ⏰8am-6pm Mon-Sat) This five-star PADI diving school offers two-tank dives in the Islas del Rosario, including transportation, equipment, lunch and instructors, for COP$408,000. Discounts of 10% are available if you pay in cash.

Backpackers Tours

(Map p364; ☎5-664-8594, 300-504-9929; www.backpackersctg.com; cnr Calle de los 7 Infantes & Calle del Pilar; day tours from COP$70,000; ⏰8am-6pm) Highly recommended English-speaking agency offering a raft of day trips and tours aimed at budget travelers. These include daily departures to Playa Blanca, Volcán de Lodo El Totumo and Islas del Rosario, for which prices are some of the lowest in town. There are also less-standard tours available, such as trips to the Aviario Nacional de Colombia.

SHOPPING

Cartagena has a wide range of shops selling crafts and souvenirs, and the quality of the goods is usually high. The biggest tourist shopping center in the walled city is **Las Bóvedas** (Map p364; Playa del Tejadillo), which offers handicrafts, clothes and kitschy souvenirs. You'll find more interesting things for sale by wandering in Getsemaní, San Diego and El Centro, however.

Ábaco Books

(Map p364; ☎5-664-8338; cnr Calle de la Iglesia & Calle de la Mantilla; ⏰8am-10pm Mon-Sat, 10am-8pm Sun; 📶) An erudite-looking bookshop-cafe that's short on space but big on atmosphere, with the obligatory ladder to reach the higher shelves. Search carefully and you'll encounter Cervantes tomes, English-language titles and pretty much everything Gabriel García Márquez ever wrote. There's also Italian beer, Spanish wine and strong espresso.

Castillo de San Felipe de Barajas

The greatest fortress ever built by the Spaniards in any of their colonies, the **Castillo de San Felipe de Barajas** (Map p355; Av Arévalo; adult/child COP$25,000/10,500; ⏰8am-6pm) still dominates an entire section of Cartagena's cityscape. It should definitely be the first fortress you visit. The original edifice was quite small. It was commissioned in 1630, and construction began in 1657 on top of the 40m-high San Lázaro hill. In 1762 an extensive enlargement was undertaken, which resulted in the entire hill's being covered with this powerful bastion.

It was truly impregnable and was never taken despite numerous attempts to storm it. A complex system of tunnels connected strategic points to allow provisions to be distributed and to facilitate evacuation. Some of the tunnels are lit and are open to visitors – an eerie walk not to be missed. Take an audio tour or hire a guide for the full story.

The fortress is a short walk over the bridge from Getsemaní.

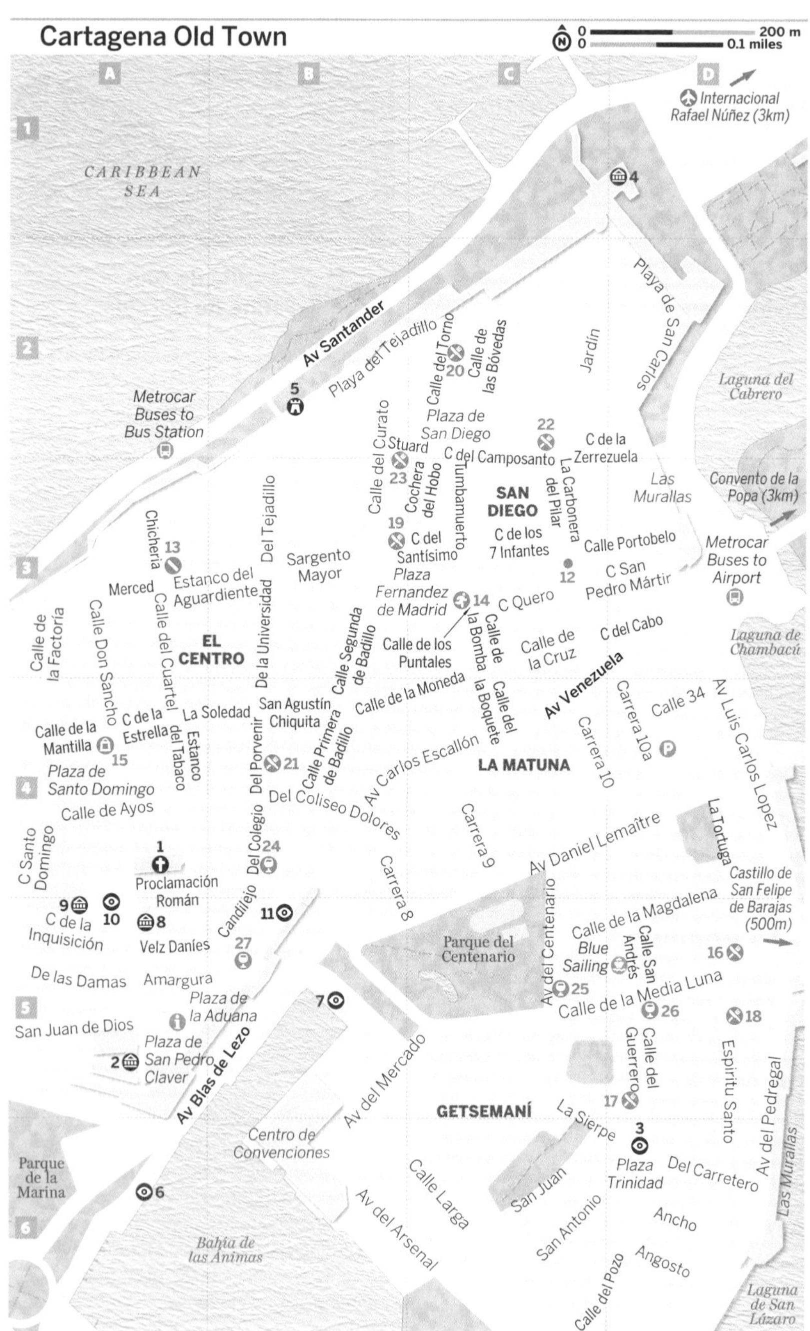
Cartagena Old Town
0 200 m
0 0.1 miles
A
B
C
D
Internacional Rafael Núñez (3km)
CARIBBEAN SEA
Av Santander
Playa del Tejadillo
Calle del Torno
Calle de las Bóvedas
Jardín
Playa de San Carlos
Laguna del Cabrero
Metrocar Buses to Bus Station
Calle del Curato
Plaza de San Diego
Stuard
C del Camposanto
C de la Zerrezuela
Cochera del Hobo
Tumbamuerto
La Carbonera
del Pilar
SAN DIEGO
Las Murallas
Convento de la Popa (3km)
Del Tejadillo
Chichería
C del Santísimo
C de los 7 Infantes
Calle Portobelo
Metrocar Buses to Airport
Sargento Mayor
Merced
Estanco del Aguardiente
Plaza Fernandez de Madrid
C Quero
C San Pedro Mártir
Calle de la Factoría
Calle Don Sancho
Calle del Cuartel
De la Universidad
EL CENTRO
Calle Segunda de Badillo
Calle de los Puntales
Calle de la Bomba
Calle de la Cruz
C del Cabo
Laguna de Chambacú
Calle de la Moneda
Calle del la Boquete
Av Venezuela
Carrera 10a
Calle 34
Av Luis Carlos Lopez
Calle de la Mantilla
C de la Estrella
La Soledad
San Agustín Chiquita
Del Porvenir
Estanco del Tabaco
Calle Primera de Badillo
Av Carlos Escallón
LA MATUNA
Carrera 10
Plaza de Santo Domingo
Calle de Ayos
Del Coliseo
Dolores
Carrera 9
La Tortuga
C Santo Domingo
Del Colegio
Av Daniel Lemaître
Carrera 8
Proclamación
Román
Castillo de San Felipe de Barajas (500m)
C de la Inquisición
Velz Daníes
Candilejo
Av del Centenario
Calle de la Magdalena
Blue Sailing
Calle San Andrés
Parque del Centenario
De las Damas
Amargura
Plaza de la Aduana
Calle de la Media Luna
San Juan de Dios
Plaza de San Pedro Claver
Av Blas de Lezo
Av del Mercado
Calle del Guerrero
Espiritu Santo
Av del Pedregal
GETSEMANÍ
La Sierpe
Las Murallas
Centro de Convenciones
Parque de la Marina
Plaza Trinidad
Del Carretero
Calle Larga
San Juan
San Antonio
Ancho
Av del Arsenal
Angosto
Bahía de las Ánimas
Calle del Pozo
Laguna de San Lázaro
1
2
3
4
5
6
7
8
9
10
11
12
13
14
15
16
17
18
19
20
21
22
23
24
25
26
27

Cartagena Old Town

Sights
1 Catedral....A4
2 Convento & Iglesia de San Pedro Claver....A5
3 Getsemaní....D6
4 Las Bóvedas....D1
5 Las Murallas....B2
6 Muelle Turístico de la Bodeguita....A6
7 Muelle Turístico de los Pegasos....B5
8 Museo del Oro Zenú....A5
9 Palacio de la Inquisición....A5
10 Plaza de Bolívar....A5
11 Plaza de los Coches....B5

Activities, Courses & Tours
12 Backpackers....C3
13 Diving Planet....A3
14 Sico....C3

Shopping
15 Ábaco....A4

Eating
16 Beer & Laundry....D5
17 Beiyu....D5
18 Caffé Lunático....D5
19 El Boliche....B3
20 El Santísimo....C2
21 Espíritu Santo....B4
22 Interno....C2
23 La Cevichería....B3

Drinking & Nightlife
24 Alquímico....B4
25 Bazurto Social Club....C5
26 Café Havana....D5
27 Donde Fidel....B5

EATING

Espíritu Santo — Colombian $

(Map p364; Calle del Porvenir No 35-60; mains COP$16,000; 11:30am-3:30pm) In a city full of tourists, Espíritu Santo is where you come to meet the locals – hundreds of 'em in one sitting. (The restaurant is small from the outside but deceptively large within.) Choose your protein plus three sides and, in the true spirit of *comida corriente* (set menu of the day), it'll arrive in the blink of an eye.

Beer & Laundry — Pizza $

(Map p364; www.beerandlaundry.com; Calle de la Media Luna No 10-113; pizzas from COP$12,000; 8am-7pm Mon-Sat;) It's the bane of every backpacker: where to get your laundry done with minimal fuss. Here's the answer: deposit it with the friendly English-speaking staff at this Getsemaní laundry-bar and enjoy beer and a pizza while you wait (two hours max). It's possibly the best pizza in Cartagena – and definitely the best laundry!

Beiyu — Cafe $$

(Map p364; Calle del Guerrero No 29-75; breakfast COP$10,000-13,000; 7am-9pm Mon-Sat, 9am-6pm Sun;) A simple little cafe plying excellent Colombian coffee, fresh juices, full breakfasts and an innovative selection of lunch and dinner dishes, Beiyu is a slice of organic, sustainable heaven in the heart of Getsemaní. It's top pick as the place to slowly eat off the effects of a late night. Portions are supergenerous. Don't miss the açai bowl.

Caffé Lunático — Tapas $$

(Map p364; 320-383-0419; Calle Espíritu Santo No 29-184; tapas COP$12,000-20,000, mains COP$26,000-53,000; 11am-3pm & 7-11pm;) There's nothing remotely looney about this artsy little spot in the hosteling hub of Gestemaní that pays homage to Amy Winehouse in a head-and-shoulders mural that takes up a whole wall. The perfect solution to minor lunchtime hunger pangs, midafternoon cake yearnings or early-evening cocktail urges, the Lunático does a full range of small plates and desserts exceedingly well.

El Boliche — Ceviche $$$

(Map p364; 5-660-0074, 310-368-7908; Cochera del Hobo No 38-17; mains COP$48,000-60,000; 12:30-3pm & 7-11pm Mon-Sat;) Small, delightful and not so well known that it's inundated, El Boliche basks in its relative obscurity. If you're reticent about raw fish, Boliche offers hot and cold ceviche daubed with bold and adventurous ingredients such as tamarind, coconut milk and mango. The handsome six-table

Street Food

Cartagena is strong on street food: plenty of snack bars all across the Old Town serve local snacks such as *arepas de huevo* (fried maize dough with an egg inside), *dedos de queso* (deep-fried cheese sticks), empanadas and *buñuelos* (deep-fried maize-and-cheese balls). Try the region's sweets at confectionery stands lining El Portal de los Dulces on the **Plaza de los Coches** (Map p364).

interior features a glass waterfall and a bar that dispatches spot-on mojitos.

Interno Colombian $$$

(Map p364; ☎310-260-0134, 310-327-3682; www.restauranteinterno.com; Cárcel San Diego, Calle Camposanto; 3-course set meal COP$90,000; ⏰7-11pm Tue-Sun) Interno is a restaurant inside Cartagena's women's prison that raises money for the rehabilitation of its inmates, who cook for and wait on you. Trained by a top Bogotá chef, the cooks prepare set meals that are delectable takes on modern Colombian cuisine. Meals are served on a gorgeously repurposed open-air patio.

You'll need to make reservations 24 hours ahead with your passport number, and you'll need to bring your passport with you when you come.

La Cevichería Seafood $$$

(Map p364; ☎5-664-5255; Calle Stuart No 7-14; mains COP$39,000-120,000; ⏰noon-11pm Wed-Mon; 📶) A once little-known spot prized by locals, La Cevichería was given ample publicity in an episode of Anthony Bourdain's *No Reservations* in 2008. Cue the crowds but, thankfully, no real slide in the excellent quality of the food. Each dish is prepared with panache; the octopus in peanut sauce is incredible, as is the black-squid-ink rice and Peruvian ceviche.

El Santísimo Colombian, Fusion $$$

(Map p364; ☎5-660-1531, 314-541-2117; www.elsantisimo.com; Calle del Torno No 39-62; mains COP$45,000-60,000; ⏰noon-11pm) A family-friendly restaurant that won't scare off romantic couples, Santísimo indulges in a bit of creative recycling. The chandeliers are made from empty wine bottles, while wood from rescued packing cases lines the walls and ceiling. There's nothing secondhand about the food, though; it's a trip through Colombian cuisine, combining ingredients and reinventing classics as it goes.

DRINKING & NIGHTLIFE

There's a long-standing bar scene centered on the Plaza de los Coches in El Centro for salsa and vallenato, while most of the hotter and hipper action can be found in thumping Getsemaní, where the venues are bigger and the crowd younger.

Alquímico Cocktail Bar

(Map p364; ☎318-845-0433; www.alquimico.com; Calle del Colegio No 34-24; ⏰5pm-2am Sun-Thu, to 3:30am Fri & Sat) Anyone remotely hip ultimately gravitates to this Old Town bar with a pharmaceutical theme. Occupying a gorgeous colonial building, the bar is spread over three floors: the ground floor is a sleek, low-lit lounge perfect for an aperitif, while upstairs there's a kitchen and pool table. One more floor up is the always-packed roof-terrace bar, serving imaginative aguardiente cocktails.

Café Havana Club

(Map p364; cnr Calle del Guerrero & Calle de la Media Luna; cover COP$30,000; ⏰8:30pm-4am Thu-Sat, 5pm-2am Sun) Havana has it all: live salsa from horn-blowing Cubans, strong drinks, a gorgeous horseshoe-shaped bar surrounded by brilliant eccentrics, wood-paneled walls and a ceiling full of whirring fans. While it's no secret these days, it's still worth a pilgrimage. Expect sweaty crowds and the odd elbow in the ribs when you're trying out your salsa moves at 1am. No shorts.

Bazurto Social Club Club
(Map p364; www.bazurtosocialclub.com; Av del Centenario No 30-42; cover COP$5000; 8pm-4am Wed-Sat) Join the crowds at this lively spot where locals dance in unison under an enormous glowing red fish to live *champeta* music, sip knockout cocktails and catch up on the Getsemaní gossip. The music's great, and after a few drinks you'll find yourself being dragged in, though your ears will likely ring for days.

Donde Fidel Bar
(Map p364; 5-664-3127; El Portal de los Dulces No 32-09; 11am-2am) Old salts meet salsa-seeking tourists at this usually packed and always loud Old Town bar characterized by glaring florescent lighting and busy walls covered with photos of owner Fidel posing with a Wikipedia's worth of Latin celebrities from A-list to D-list. Order a bottle of rum along with an ice bucket and some mixers, and hunker down.

ENTERTAINMENT

Estadio Olímpico Jaime Morón León Stadium
(Villa Olímpico) Cartagena's local football team, Real Cartagena, plays games at this stadium located 5km south of the city.

INFORMATION

The city's main **tourist office** (Turismo Cartagena de Indias; Map p364; 5-660-1583; Plaza de la Aduana; 9am-noon & 1-6pm Mon-Sat, 9am-5pm Sun) can be found on Plaza de la Aduana. There are also small booths in Plaza de San Pedro Claver and Plaza de los Coches.

GETTING THERE & AWAY

AIR

All major Colombian carriers operate flights to and from Cartagena's **Aeropuerto Internacional Rafael Núñez** (5-693-1351; www.sacsa.com.co; Calle 71 No 8-9), 3km from the city, in Crespo.

BUS

For most destinations, you'll need to head to Cartagena's **Terminal de Transportes de Cartagena** (304-577-5743; www.terminaldecartagena.com; Calle 1A No 3-89). It's on the eastern outskirts of the city, around 45 minutes from the center.

GETTING AROUND

Large green-and-red-signed **Metrocar buses** (Map p364; Av Santander; COP$2000) shuttle between the city and the bus terminal every 15 to 30 minutes (COP$3000, 40 minutes). In the center you can catch them on Av Santander. A taxi between the bus station and El Centro costs COP$15,000, plus COP$5000 after 8pm.

Peruvian dancers in Cuzco (p262)

In Focus

Rio de Janeiro (p40), Brazil

South America Today

The past decade has witnessed a rising middle class and strong economic growth in large swaths of South America. Poverty rates have fallen, and addressing the large gap between rich and poor seems to be the hot topic nearly everywhere. Big challenges, however, remain. Deforestation is once again on the rise and the political leadership has tacked sharply to the right, threatening to put an end to recent social progress.

Breaking Down Barriers

Machismo has taken a blow, with the first female presidents in South America helping to break down barriers. Cristina Fernández de Kirchner of Argentina, Dilma Rousseff of Brazil and Michelle Bachelet of Chile have all recently served as presidents of some of South America's largest economies. Speaking of historic elections, Evo Morales (now in his third term) also deserves special mention, becoming the first president of Bolivia to hail from an indigenous background. He follows on the heels of Alejandro Toledo, who became Peru's first indigenous president back in 2001. On other fronts, there have been equally dramatic changes in recent years. Gay marriage has been legalized in Argentina, Brazil and Uruguay, and three other countries (Chile, Colombia and Ecuador) have a form of same-sex civil union. Gay marriage is also legal in French Guiana, which is considered part of France.

Social & Environmental Threats

Despite economic growth in many countries, not all have benefited. Rural poverty remains a gripping problem in every country in South America, with many families still struggling with basic needs: adequate nutrition, health care and clean water. And one in seven still live in extreme poverty, subsisting on less than US$2.50 per day.

When it comes to the environment, there's a mix of good and bad news. On the plus side, there's increased interest in a green future. Sustainable sources meet more than 70% of Brazil's energy needs. Chile has greatly expanded its protected areas, creating five new national parks and expanding three existing parks in the process; in total it has added more than 40,500 sq km – an area larger than Switzerland.

Sadly, deforestation has risen once again in the Amazon. After falling year-on-year from 2005 to 2015, it surged again in the last few years, rising by 38% over the course of 2018. At the same time, oil production will soon begin in Ecuador's Parque Nacional Yasuní, a pristine area of the Amazon that holds one of the country's largest reserves. Petroamazonas began drilling in this Unesco World Heritage Site in early 2016. The building of access roads and pipelines – not to mention the possibility of oil spills – could be devastating for Yasuní.

In Peru, coca and cocaine production not only have serious social repercussions, but also affect Peru's environment through deforestation in remote growing areas and chemical contamination. The Amazon is also now bisected by the Interoceanic Highway, an overland trade route that links Peru to Brazil. Economics aside, there's great concern about the irrevocable impact this could have on the world's most biologically rich rainforest.

Corruption Scandals

Political corruption remains pervasive in South America. In Brazil, one of the largest scandals in the nation's history (a staggering US$3 billion bribery and money-laundering scheme) brought down many politicians and heads of industry, and led to the impeachment of President Dilma Rousseff in 2016. In Argentina, former president Cristina Kirchner had to deal with damaging allegations that she and her late husband (who was president before her) enriched themselves at taxpayers' expense. Likewise, former Chilean president Michelle Bachelet also found herself briefly embroiled in a corruption scandal involving abuse of power by her son. Her name was ultimately cleared, and after her term ended she was appointed by the UN to the prestigious role of Human Rights High Commissioner.

Machu Picchu, Peru (p282)

ALEX ROBINSON / GETTY IMAGES ©

History

South America has a long and tumultuous history. It was the birthplace of one of the world's great empires, sadly brought to ruin upon European arrival, and the destination for millions of men, women and children who were enslaved and brought over from Africa. Independence movements freed the continent from foreign rule, but did little to address the yawning divide between rich and poor, which still remains today.

14,000–23,000 BC

Humans traveling from Asia, probably across the Bering land bridge, reach the Americas during great human migration.

1493

Inca Huayna Cápac begins his reign, pushing his vast empire north; his untimely death in 1525 leaves the kingdom divided.

1494

Spain and Portugal sign the Treaty of Tordesillas, dividing colonized lands in the Americas between them.

Andean women in Quito, Ecuador (p318)

GABRIEL PEREZ / GETTY IMAGES ©

First Peoples

There are various competing theories about how the indigenous peoples arrived in the Americas. Until recently, it was generally believed that early inhabitants traveled from present-day Siberia to Alaska over a land bridge across the Bering Strait. Some scholars estimate this epic migration occurred around 14,000 years ago. In the last several decades, new evidence of older sites in the southern reaches of South America has challenged the land-bridge theory. Early humans may have arrived by a combination of foot and boat travel following the coastline south as early as 23,000 years ago. In Monte Verde, Chile, scientists have discovered some of the oldest undisputed evidence of human occupation in the Americas. Apparently, early peoples were seafarers (or at least seafood lovers): among the artifacts found there were 10 different species of seaweed.

The earliest peoples were nomadic hunter-gatherers who lived in small groups. Agriculture likely developed around 5000 BC with the planting of wild tubers such as manioc and sweet potato under systems of shifting cultivation. About the same time, highland people

1548
Wine comes to Chile via missionaries and conquistadores. Jesuit priests cultivated early vineyards of rustic pais grapes.

1550
Facing a labor shortage, Portugal turns to the African slave trade; open-air slave markets flourish in the growing colony.

1807
Napoleon invades Portugal; the Portuguese prince regent (future Dom João VI) and his entire court of 15,000 flee to Brazil.

began to farm seed crops, such as beans, and to domesticate animals, such as the llama. One of South America's greatest foodstuffs is the humble but versatile potato, a root crop domesticated in the Andean highlands. Today, more than 6000 varieties of potato are cultivated there.

Complex societies first developed in the valleys of coastal Peru. Their growth was unsustainable, however – it's thought that the population of some of these valleys grew until all the cultivable land was occupied. The need to expand into neighboring valleys led the inhabitants to organize, innovate and conquer. Not dissimilar from what would happen after the Europeans arrived, conquerors became the rulers and the conquered became their subjects; this helped develop the social and economic hierarchies of these early states and beyond.

These embryonic societies ultimately developed into major civilizations, such as the Wari empire of the Peruvian central highlands, the Tiahuanaco culture of highland Bolivia, the Chimú culture of northern coastal Peru and the Inca empire of Cuzco.

Inca Empire

According to legend, the Inca civilization was born when Manco Cápac and his sister Mama Ocllo, children of the sun, emerged from Lake Titicaca to establish a civilization in the Cuzco Valley. Whether Manco Cápac was a historical figure is up for debate, but what is certain is that the Inca civilization was established in the area of Cuzco at some point in the 12th century. The reign of the first several incas (kings) was largely unremarkable, and for a couple of centuries the Incas remained a small, regional state.

Expansion took off in the early 15th century, when the ninth king, Inca Yupanqui, defended Cuzco – against incredible odds – from the invading Chanka people to the north. After the victory, he took on the new name of Pachacutec (Transformer of the Earth) and spent the next 25 years bagging much of the Andes. Under his reign, the Incas grew from a regional fiefdom in the Cuzco Valley into a broad empire of about 10 million people known as Tawantinsuyo (Land of Four Quarters). The kingdom covered most of modern Peru, in addition to pieces of Ecuador, Bolivia and Chile. The empire traversed the Andes with more than 8000km of highways and managed to control peoples from 100 separate cultures and 20 different language groups for about a century. This was made more remarkable by the fact that the Incas, as an ethnicity, never numbered more than about 100,000.

Pachacutec allegedly gave Cuzco its layout in the form of a puma and built fabulous stone monuments in honor of Inca victories, including Sacsaywamán, the temple-fortress at Ollantaytambo and possibly Machu Picchu. He also improved the network of roads that connected the empire, further developed terrace agricultural systems and made Quechua the lingua franca.

1819
Simón Bolívar defeats the Spanish army at Boyacá near Bogotá; the Republic of Gran Colombia is founded.

1830
Gran Colombia splits into Colombia, Ecuador and Venezuela. Bolívar sends himself into exile; he dies in Santa Marta.

1834–35
HMS Beagle explores South America with Charles Darwin on board; the expedition gives Darwin fodder for his theory of evolution.

Portuguese Arrival

The Portuguese were the first Europeans to set foot on the South American continent. In 1500 a fleet of 12 Portuguese ships carrying nearly 1200 men dropped anchor near what is today Porto Seguro. There they erected a cross and held Mass in the land they baptized Terra da Vera Cruz (Land of the True Cross) before taking to the waves once again. Over the next century, the Portuguese set up coastal colonies in present-day Salvador, Rio de Janeiro and other coastal areas. There they harvested the profitable *pau brasil* (brazilwood), which gave the country its name.

Over the following centuries a four-front war was waged on the indigenous way of life. It was a cultural war, as well as a physical, territorial and biological one. Many indigenous peoples fell victim to the *bandeirantes* – groups of roaming raiders who spent the 17th and 18th centuries exploring Brazil's interior, pillaging indigenous settlements as they went. Those who escaped such a fate were struck down by the illnesses which traveled from Europe, against which they had no natural resistance. Others were worked to death on sugar plantations.

Defeat of the Incas

The vast Inca empire was in trouble even before the Spanish arrived in present-day Peru. Smallpox and other epidemics transmitted by European soldiers were sweeping through the entire American continent. Thousands of indigenous people were killed by the disease – including, in all likelihood, Inca emperor Huayna Cápac, who died in 1525.

Without a clear plan of succession, the emperor's untimely death left a power vacuum. The contest turned into a face-off between two of his many children: the Quito-born Atahualpa, who commanded his father's army in the north, and Huáscar, who was based in Cuzco. The ensuing struggle plunged the empire into a bloody civil war, reducing entire cities to rubble. Atahualpa emerged as the victor in April 1532. But the vicious nature of the conflict left the Incas with a lot of enemies throughout the Andes – which is why some tribes were so willing to cooperate with the Spanish when they arrived just five months later.

While the Portuguese were battling for control over the eastern half of the continent, the Spaniards set their sights on South America's Pacific coast. Following rumors of golden splendor in the interior, Francisco Pizarro led an exploratory journey to the north coast of Peru in 1528. There, near Tumbes, a crew of welcoming indigenous people offered them meat, fruit, fish and corn beer. To their delight, a cursory examination of the city revealed an abundance of silver and gold. The group quickly returned to Spain to court royal support for a bigger expedition.

They returned in September 1532, with a shipload of arms, horses and slaves, as well as a battalion of 168 troops. Tumbes, the rich town Pizarro had visited just four years earlier, had been devastated by epidemics, and the recent Inca civil war. Atahualpa, in the meantime,

1865–70

Brazil, allied with Uruguay and Argentina, wages the 'War of the Triple Alliance' on Paraguay, which leaves untold thousands dead.

1879–83

Chile wages war against Peru and Bolivia over nitrate-rich lands in the Atacama Desert; Bolivia loses its coastline.

1888

Slavery is abolished in Brazil, the last country in South America to do so.

★ Best Historical Reads

1491: New Revelations of the Americas before Columbus (Charles C Mann)

Last Days of the Incas (Kim MacQuarrie)

Open Veins of Latin America (Eduardo Galeano)

Prisoner without a Name, Cell without a Number (Jacobo Timerman)

Traveler on an Inca trail, Lake Titicaca, Peru (p250)

was in the process of making his way down from Quito to Cuzco to claim his hard-won throne. When the Spanish arrived, he was in the highland settlement of Cajamarca, enjoying the area's mineral baths.

Pizarro quickly deduced that the empire was in a fractious state. He and his men charted a course to Cajamarca and approached Atahualpa with royal greetings and promises of brotherhood. But the well-mannered overtures quickly devolved into a surprise attack that left thousands of Incas dead and Atahualpa a prisoner of war. (Between their horses, their armor and the steel of their blades, the Spanish were practically invincible against fighters armed only with clubs, slings and wicker helmets.)

In an attempt to regain his freedom, Atahualpa offered the Spanish a bounty of gold and silver. Thus began one of the most famous ransoms in history – with the Incas attempting to fill an entire room with the precious stuff in order to placate the unrelenting appetites of the Spanish. But it was never enough. The Spanish held Atahualpa for eight months before executing him with a garrote at the age of 31.

The Inca empire never recovered from this fateful encounter. The arrival of the Spanish brought on a cataclysmic collapse of the indigenous society. It is estimated that the local population – around 10 million when Pizarro arrived – was reduced to 600,000 within a century.

The Dark Era of Slavery

The slave trade practiced by early European traders from the 1500s to 1866 enslaved as many as 12.5 million people – with just around 10.7 million surviving the grueling journey from Africa to the Americas. Only a fraction (around half a million) ended up in North America. The rest were destined for Latin America and the Caribbean with the majority (as many as six million) ending up in Brazil, most of them working on the backbreaking sugarcane plantations. They were torn from a variety of tribes in Angola, Mozambique and Guinea, as well as the Sudan and Congo. Whatever their origins and cultures, their destinations were identical: slave markets such as Salvador's Pelourinho or Belém's Mercado

1890s
Brazil opens its borders. Millions arrive from Italy, Portugal, Spain, Germany and later Japan and other countries.

1967
Argentine revolutionary Ernesto 'Che' Guevara is executed by a US-backed military squad in Bolivia.

1970
A 7.7-magnitude earthquake in northern Peru kills almost 80,000 people, leaves 140,000 injured and another 500,000 homeless.

Ver-o-Peso. Elsewhere, smaller numbers of Africans were taken to Peru, Colombia, the Guianas and all along the Caribbean coast.

For those who survived the ordeal of removal and transfer, arrival in the Americas meant only continued suffering. A slave's existence was one of brutality and humiliation. Kind masters were the exception, not the rule, and labor on the plantations was relentless. Slaves were required to work as many as 17 hours each day, before retiring to the squalid *senzala* (slave quarters), and with as many as 200 slaves packed into each dwelling, hygiene was a concept as remote as the distant coasts of Africa. Dysentery, typhus, yellow fever, malaria, tuberculosis and scurvy were rife, and malnutrition was a fact of life.

Syphilis also plagued a slave population sexually exploited by its masters. Sex slavery was so common that a large mixed-race population soon emerged. Off the plantations there were greater numbers of white men than white women, and many black or indigenous women were used by white men as live-in sex slaves.

Many slaves escaped from their masters to form *quilombos*, communities of runaway slaves that quickly spread across the countryside. The most famous, the Republic of Palmares, which survived through much of the 17th century, was home to some 20,000 people before it was destroyed by Brazilian federal troops.

Most countries in South America banned slavery between 1816 and 1831, but in Brazil, it wasn't until 1888 that slavery was finally outlawed. Unsurprisingly, this didn't make a huge immediate difference to the welfare of the 800,000 freed slaves, who were largely illiterate and unskilled. Thousands were cast into the streets without any kind of infrastructure to support them. Many died, while others flooded to Brazil's urban centers, desperately in search of jobs.

Critics point out that the end of slavery didn't really bring justice to newly freed people. Gross inequalities continue to plague South America up to the present day. One 2015 study in Brazil showed that people of color earn 59% of what whites earn, and that 132% more Afro-Brazilians than whites are killed by violence each year.

Settlements in the Amazon

New discoveries are reshaping the dominant thinking about pre-Columbian societies. The Amazon, once thought to be a wilderness incapable of supporting large populations, is now viewed as home to mound-building societies with some settlements containing as many as 100,000 inhabitants. At least 12% (and probably more) of the nonflooded Amazon forest is of anthropogenic origin (directly or indirectly altered by humans). Evidence of agriculture in the rainforest exists as far back as 4000 years ago, with as many as 140 different crops grown. Anthropologists have even found proof that early peoples used complex farming techniques to enrich the earth with microorganism-rich *terra preta* (black soil).

1970

Salvador Allende, Chile's first democratically elected Marxist president, introduces radical social reform and massive income redistribution.

1973–89

Following a military coup, General Augusto Pinochet takes charge of Chile. He dissolves Congress and rules by decree.

1976–83

A military junta takes control of Argentina, launching the 'Dirty War.' In eight years an estimated 30,000 people 'disappear.'

Independence

By the early 19th century, *criollos* (creoles, born in South America to Spanish parents) in many Spanish colonies had grown increasingly dissatisfied with their lack of administrative power and the crown's heavy taxes – leading to revolutions all over the continent. Argentine revolutionary José de San Martín led independence campaigns in Argentina and Chile (1818), before sailing up the coast to take Lima in 1821. From the opposite direction came Simón Bolívar, the Venezuelan revolutionary who had been leading independence fights in Venezuela, Colombia and Ecuador.

The two liberators met in Guayaquil, Ecuador, in 1822. At this famous meeting, the apolitical San Martín found himself in conflict with Bolívar, who had strong political ambitions. San Martín considered the installation of a powerful leader, even a monarch, as essential to avoid the disintegration of Peru, while Bolívar insisted on a constitutional republic. In a complicated exchange, which aroused ill feeling in both camps, Bolívar won the day and San Martín returned to the south. In the long run, both were disappointed. The proliferation of *caudillos* (local warlords) set a deplorable pattern for most of the 19th century.

Ever in its own world, Brazil followed quite a different path to independence. Unlike its neighboring countries, Brazil had a European monarch living within its borders in the early 1800s. Brazil became a temporary sanctuary to the Portuguese royal family, who fled from the advance of Napoleon in Iberia in 1807. The prince regent – and future king, Dom João VI – fell in love with Rio, naming it the capital of the United Kingdom of Portugal, Brazil and the Algarves. His affection for Brazil was so strong that he didn't want to return to Portugal even after Napoleon's defeat at Waterloo in 1815. He finally returned to Europe six years later, leaving his son Pedro as prince regent. When the Portuguese parliament attempted to restore Brazil to its previous status as subservient colony, Dom Pedro rebelled and declared Brazil independent, announcing himself the country's head as Emperor Dom Pedro I. Portugal was too weak to fight its favorite son, so without spilling blood, Brazil attained its independence in 1822.

Military Dictatorships

The 20th century was a tumultuous period for South America, with political turmoil and economic crises paving the way for the rise of military dictatorships. The social unrest that followed the Great Depression of 1929 provided justification for the army to intervene in countries across the continent. In Argentina, the pro-fascist general José Félix Uriburu seized control during a military coup in 1930, ushering in the so-called Infamous Decade. Likewise the 1930s saw military coups and repressive regimes rise in Peru and Chile. In Brazil, it was the era of the autocratic Getulio Vargas, when rival political parties were banned, the press was muzzled and opponents were imprisoned.

1992
Thousands of indigenous protesters march in Quito. In ensuing negotiations they are granted title to 2.5 million acres in Amazonia.

2001
A vast financial crisis hits Argentina. Interim president Duhalde devalues the peso and defaults on US$140 billion in debt.

2014
Brazil hosts the 2014 FIFA World Cup, spending around US$12 billion in preparation for the event.

Unfortunately, this was just the beginning, with far more horrifying dictatorships on the horizon. The 1960s and 1970s were an even darker period in South America when military dictatorships ruled in Argentina, Bolivia, Brazil, Chile, Paraguay, Peru, Suriname and Uruguay. Student- and worker-led movements crying out for social justice were met with increasing brutality.

In the late 1960s and '70s in Argentina, antigovernment feeling was rife and street protests often exploded into all-out riots. Armed guerrilla organizations emerged as radical opponents of the military, the oligarchies and US influence in Latin America. In 1976 the army general Jorge Rafael Videla seized power, ushering in a bloody seven-year period known as the Dirty War. Security forces went about the country arresting, torturing and killing anyone on their hit list of suspected leftists. As many as 30,000 people were 'disappeared' – that is, murdered.

In Chile, there was hope for a brighter future when socialist candidate Salvador Allende was elected in 1970. This was soon crushed, however, when Augusto Pinochet led a coup in 1973. Ruling until 1989, he became Latin America's most notorious dictator, with thousands of suspected leftists jailed, tortured and executed, and hundreds of thousands fleeing the country.

Meanwhile in Brazil, military dictators ran the show from 1964 to 1984. Though not as brutal as the Chilean or Argentine regimes, it was still a period when dissent was crushed, political parties were banned and the media was muzzled. Things remained grim throughout South America until the early 1990s, when democracy at last returned to most of the continent..

The 21st Century

Towards the end of the 1990s and into the 21st century, things took a remarkable turn for the better in South America. A rising middle class, falling poverty rates and strong economies were hallmarks of the early 2000s. As the continent veered to the left, wage disparities fell slightly and social justice seemed to be the hot topic of the day.

Progressives like former Brazilian president Lula helped pave the way, demonstrating that you could both grow an economy and help lift people out of poverty. Machismo took a blow, with the first female presidents in South America helping to break down barriers. Cristina Kirchner of Argentina, Dilma Rousseff of Brazil and Michelle Bachelet of Chile all recently served as presidents of some of South America's largest economies. Leaders from indigenous backgrounds also emerged on the political stage, including Evo Morales of Bolivia and Alejandro Toledo of Peru.

In the last few years, the political landscape has again shifted dramatically. As of 2019, no women were serving as heads of state in any South American country. Right-wing governments seemed everywhere on the rise, and some leaders – like Brazil's firebrand Jair Bolsonaro – even spoke fondly of the military dictatorship of the past.

2015
Pope Francis visits Bolivia and begs forgiveness for the grave sins committed against indigenous peoples in the name of God.

2016
Rio becomes the first city in South America to host the Summer Olympics. The city spends US$13 billion in preparations.

2018
Peruvian President Pedro Pablo Kuczynski resigns from office and is succeeded by Vice President Martín Vizcarra.

Peruvian woman in the Sacred Valley (p262), Peru

People & Culture

There are many layers to South American culture. Religion is a key component of life on the continent, where Christianity, indigenous beliefs and African religions have all shaped identity. South America is also the birthplace of samba, tango, Andean sounds and countless other regional genres. While religion and music can be a great unifier, there is still a huge gulf between haves and have-nots in this stratified society.

Multiculturalism

South America boasts astonishing diversity. The continent has been shaped by the original indigenous inhabitants, European colonists and Africans brought over as slaves to toil in the plantations and mines. The level of intermixing varies greatly from country to country, which has led to the relative diversity or homogeneity of the population.

Immigration has also added to the complex ethnic tapestry of the continent. For decades, the US was a major destination for migrants from South America. These days, there's much more migration happening internally (ie between South American countries), with Brazil, Argentina and Chile attracting the largest numbers of migrants, largely from neighboring countries. There are also complicated dynamics at work in each of the continent's 13 countries. Ecuador for instance, with a population of just 16 million, has an

Baby llama

MEDIAPRODUCTION / GETTY IMAGES ©

estimated two million emigrants, living in the US, Italy and Spain; in the latter, they make up the largest contingent of Latin Americans. On the flipside, Ecuador has seen an influx of refugees (in the 1980s and 1990s) fleeing from conflicts in neighboring Colombia, and opportunity-seeking migrants from Peru.The situation, however, remains quite fluid. Since 2008, with improved job opportunities in Ecuador, a growing number of Ecuadorians are choosing to return home.

In the 19th century Brazil and Argentina saw mass immigration from Europe: Spaniards, Italians, Germans and Eastern Europeans were the most frequent immigrants moving to the Americas. Brazil also welcomed immigrants from Japan, Portugal and the Middle East. They worked in a wide variety of fields, from coffee plantations and farming to heavy industry in the continent's growing cities. The influx of new arrivals continued well into the 20th century, with tumult in Europe causing the flight of Jews from Nazi persecution. They were soon followed by Nazis looking to avoid being put on trial for war crimes, in addition to Italians and others escaping their ravaged cities in the postwar period.

Lifestyles

No matter where you go in South America, you'll likely encounter a yawning divide between rich and poor. Modern-day South Americans inherited a highly stratified society from the slave-owning European colonists, and this dispiriting chasm persists centuries later between the haves and have-nots of both urban and rural society. At the bottom of the heap are those struggling in low-wage jobs in the city, or scraping out a meager existence in the countryside – many are barely able to put food on the table. Those who live in rural areas are practically invisible to the urban middle and upper classes.

★ Best Classic Albums

Volver (Carlos Gardel; 1934)

Contigo Peru (Arturo 'Zambo' Cavero; 2008)

Elis & Tom (Elis Regina & Tom Jobim 1977)

Gracias a La Vida (Violeta Parra; 1966)

Ojos que matan (Julio Jaramillo; 1970)

Flower seller, Quito (p318), Ecuador

The middle and upper class live in comfortable apartments or houses, with all the trappings of the developed world, including good health care in private clinics, cars, vacations away and easy access to the latest gadgets and trends (though iPhones and laptops are pricier here). Owing to low wages, maids are common, even among the middle class. Crime is of high concern, and those that can afford it live in high-security buildings or gated residential complexes.

The divide is greatest in struggling countries like Bolivia, where nearly half the population lives below the poverty line. There many live without running water, electricity and heat, and the threat of illness looms high over children – with the majority of childhood deaths associated with malnutrition and poverty.

Religion

Christianity

The dominant religion in South America is Roman Catholicism, a legacy from the early Spanish and Portuguese colonizers. The number of followers varies by region, with no small degree of complexity from country to country (in Argentina, for instance, 92% of the population call themselves Catholic, though less than 20% practice regularly). On average though, 70% or more of each country's population professes to be Roman Catholic. The ranks are declining from year to year, and many people (particularly in urban areas) merely turn up to church for the basics: baptism, marriage and burial. Nevertheless, the church still has a strong visible presence here. Nearly every city, town or village has a central church or cathedral, and the calendar is loaded with Catholic holidays and celebrations.

Evangelical Christianity, meanwhile, is booming. All across the continent, especially in poor communities where people are most desperate, simple, recently built churches are full of worshippers. The religion has done particularly well here, with converts from Catholicism often citing a more personal relationship with God, as well as receiving more direct guidance in the realm of health, jobs and living a moral life. The firebrand Pentecostal branch attracts many new followers, with its emphasis on divine healing, speaking in tongues and receiving direct messages from God. With the current growth of the Evangelical church, some predict that the majority of South America will be Protestant by 2050.

Indigenous Beliefs

Among indigenous peoples, allegiance to Catholicism was often a clever veneer adopted to disguise traditional beliefs ostensibly forbidden by the church. In parts of the interior, the Amazon and the Andes, shamanism and animism still flourish. There is also a strong belief in powerful spirits that inhabit the natural world – the sky, mountains, lightning and the wind. Some groups, like the Andean Aymará, practice a syncretic religion that pays equal homage to both deities and Catholic saints. They may attend mass, baptisms and saint's day celebrations, while also paying respect to Pachamama (Mother Earth) come harvest time. The old Inca celebration of Inti Raymi (Festival of the Sun) is celebrated with fervor in some parts of the Andes. It happens on the winter solstice (late June) and commemorates the mythical birth of the Inca.

A Visionary Leader

One of the most famous figures from the Amazon is Raoni Metuktire, chief of the Kayapó people. Born in 1930, Chief Raoni was an early advocate for indigenous rights and the preservation of the Amazon, and his hard-fought campaigns have brought worldwide attention to the plight of the rainforest and its inhabitants. Though made more than 40 years ago, the French-Belgian documentary *Raoni* (1978) sheds more light on his tireless efforts to protect the Amazon that continue up to the present. There's also a surprising cameo by Marlon Brando, a strong supporter of the Kayapó.

African Religions

Enslaved peoples brought over ancient African religions to the Americas, which were adapted over the centuries. The best known and most orthodox is Candomblé, which arrived in Brazil via the Nago, Yoruba and Jeje peoples. It later found root in Bahia, where it is still practiced today. Candomblé denotes a dance in honor of the gods and indeed trancelike dancing is an essential part of the religion. Afro-Brazilian rituals are directed by Candomblé priests, the *pai de santo* or *mãe de santo* (literally 'saint's father' or 'saint's mother'), and practiced in a *casa de santo* or *terreiro* (house of worship).

The religion centers upon the *orixás*. Like the gods in Greek mythology, each *orixá* has a unique personality and history. Although *orixás* are divided into male and female types, there are some that can switch from one sex to the other, such as Logunedé, the son of two male gods, or Oxumaré, who is male for six months of the year and female for the other six months. (Candomblé, not surprisingly, is much more accepting of homosexuality and bisexuality than other religions.)

Candomblé followers believe that every person has a particular deity watching over them, and followers give food or other offerings to their respective *orixá*.

Music

South America has given the world a rich musical heritage. This is the birthplace of tango, samba, bossa nova and haunting Andean folk music, but this is just the beginning of the dizzying soundtrack, of wide-ranging rhythms with roots in Europe, Africa and indigenous pre-Columbian villages.

Tango

Music plays a key part in festivities across the continent, and it also takes center stage when it comes to nightlife in many cities. The tango is deeply linked to Buenos Aires (though the music also has ties to lesser-known Montevideo in Uruguay). It emerged from the country's bordellos in the late 19th century, though it didn't become mainstream until Carlos Gardel helped popularize the songs in the 1920s and 1930s. Although Gardel was born in France, he was brought by his destitute single mother to Buenos Aires when he was three years old. In his youth he entertained neighbors with his rapturous singing, then went on to establish a successful performing career. He single-handedly helped bring tango out of the tenement and onto the world stage. He died tragically in a plane crash at the height of his career and was mourned around the world.

Another seminal figure in the tango world was Astor Piazzolla, who moved the genre from the dance halls into the concert halls. Tango nuevo, as it was called when it emerged in the 1950s, was given a newfound respect, with its blend of jazz and classical elements and new forms of melodic structures. Piazzolla also paved the way for the tango fusion, which emerged in the 1970s and continues to this day with *tango electrónico* groups such as Gotan Project, Bajofondo Tango Club and Tanghetto.

Samba & Bossa Nova

The birth of modern Brazilian music essentially began with the birth of samba, first heard in the early 20th century in a Rio neighborhood near present-day Praça Onze. Here, Bahian immigrants formed a tightly knit community in which traditional African customs thrived – music, dance and the Candomblé religion. Such an atmosphere nurtured the likes of Pixinguinha, one of samba's founding fathers, as well as Donga, one of the composers of 'Pelo Telefone,' the first recorded samba song (1917) and an enormous success at the then-fledgling Carnaval.

Samba continued to evolve in the homes and *botequims* (neighborhood bars) around Rio. The 1930s are known as the golden age of samba. Sophisticated lyricists such as Dorival Caymmi and Noel Rosa wrote popular songs featuring sentimental lyrics and an emphasis on melody (rather than rhythm), foreshadowing the later advent of cool bossa nova. The 1930s were also the golden age of samba songwriting for Carnaval.

In the 1950s came bossa nova (literally, 'new wave'), sparking a new era of Brazilian music. Bossa nova's founders – songwriter and composer Antônio Carlos (Tom) Jobim and guitarist João Gilberto, in association with the lyricist-poet Vinícius de Moraes – slowed down and altered the basic samba rhythm to create a more intimate, harmonic style. Bossa nova was also associated with the new class of university-educated Brazilians. Its lyrics reflected the optimistic mood of the middle class in the 1950s, and by the following decade it had become a huge international success.

Andean Sounds

The breathy, mournful songs played by groups across the western half of the continent (from Chile up to Venezuela) are all part of the legacy of Andean folk music. Its roots date back to pre-Inca times when music was largely played during religious ceremonies. It was viewed as a sacred art with connections to the divine world, and it paid homage to the spirits that were believed to inhabit the natural world.

Musical styles vary from region to region (with four-, five-, six- or seven-note scales), but the instruments are often quite similar. Panpipes are a staple: usually made of bamboo, these instruments consist of a single or double row of hollow tubes, and come in a bewildering variety of sizes. These are often accompanied by a smaller flutelike *quena,* a bass drum and a stringed instrument (an influence adopted from Europe), such as the 10-string *charango,* which is similar to a mandolin. Prior to the Spaniards, wind and percussion were the dominant sounds – fitting for a region of fiery volcanoes and bone-chilling gales that blow across the highlands.

Traveler exploring Machu Picchu (p282), Peru

GLEB AITOV / SHUTTERSTOCK ©

Outdoor Activities

South America has countless activities for adventure seekers. There's fabulous trekking throughout the continent (particularly in the Andes), whitewater rafting on rushing mountain rivers, and legendary surfing on both the Pacific and the Atlantic coasts. Wildlife-watching here is among the best on earth, whether you're traveling through the Amazon, the Pantanal, the Galapagos or the cloud forests of Peru.

Hiking & Trekking

The opportunities for hiking are practically limitless. Stunning scenery is a guarantee wherever you go, with snow-covered peaks, cloud forests and verdant lowland jungle setting the stage for hiking and wildlife-watching. If you head to the mountains, be prepared to spend a few days acclimating to the dizzying altitudes – or face a heavy-duty bout of altitude sickness.

The Andean countries are famous for their old Inca roads, which are ready-made for scenic excursions. The four-day tramp along the Inca Trail to Machu Picchu is, of course, the classic, but there are alternative routes around Cuzco, including a six-day trek around the venerated Ausangate (6372m). This takes you over 5000m passes, through huge herds of alpacas and past tiny hamlets unchanged in centuries. In the Peruvian Andes, trekking is most rewarding during the dry season (May to September). Avoid the wet season (December to March), when rain makes some areas impassable.

In Peru, Cuzco and Huaraz have outfitters that can provide equipment, guides and even *arrieros* (mule drivers). If you prefer to trek ultralight, you might want to purchase your own gear, especially a sleeping bag, as old-generation rental items tend to be heavy. Whether you'll need a guide depends on where you trek. Certain areas of Peru, such as along the Inca Trail, require guides; in other places, like the Cordillera Blanca, you'll find many trekking routes that are wonderfully DIY. Equip yourself with topographic maps for major routes in the nearest major gateway towns.

Chile's sublime Torres del Paine is one of the continent's most beloved hiking destinations, graced by glaciers, gemstone lakes and the world-famous granite spires. The park has good public access, *refugios* (huts) and campsites that allow for multiday treks. To combat overcrowding, new regulations require reservations for all camping and lodgings on the 'W' and Paine Circuit hikes. For awe-inspiring isolation, Tierra del Fuego's Dientes de Navarino hiking circuit is also stunning but harder to access.

Chile's Lakes District abounds with trails and tantalizing terrain. Across the border Argentina's storm-pounded but spectacular Fitz Roy Range (located in the northern section of Parque Nacional Los Glaciares) is a superb setting for trekking. It's blessed with excellent trail infrastructure and accessibility.

Hiking in Brazil is best done during the cooler months of April to October. During the summer, the tropical sun heats the rock to oven temperatures and turns the jungles into steamy saunas. If you plan to hike in the Amazon, aim to come when the water levels are low (roughly August to December); at other times the forest is flooded and virtually all your activities will be by canoe.

Hiking Safety

Many trails in South America are poorly marked or not marked at all. Trekkers should always inquire ahead, as navigation may be a major component of hiking and many travelers come unprepared. When it comes to packing, quality mountain gear is a must. Even in summer the Andes can have extreme temperatures – summer sleeping bags and nonwaterproof gear will not work!

What to Bring

Trekking poles are recommended, as some hikes (particularly the Inca Trail) feature a cartilage-crunching number of downhill steps. Other items that will come in handy: first-aid kit, sunscreen, sandals for camp, a down jacket for cold nights, a waterproof jacket, a warm hat and gloves, sun hat, travel towel, broken-in hiking boots, warm trekking socks, thermal underwear top and bottom, a fleece, water bottle or hydration pack, insect repellent, long pants and sunglasses. Make sure that the weight of your pack is comfortable and that you have enough juice (portable battery packs) for cameras and other electronics.

Mountaineering

On the continent with one of the world's greatest mountain ranges, climbing opportunities are almost unlimited. Ecuador's volcanoes and the high peaks of Peru's Cordillera Blanca all offer outstanding mountaineering opportunities. Despite its relatively low elevation, Argentina's Fitz Roy Range – home to Cerro Torre, one of the world's most challenging peaks – chalks in as a major climbing destination.

In Chile, a charm bracelet of lower volcanic cones rises through the Lakes District and Torres del Paine. Popular climbs here include Volcán Osorno, which has summit ice caves.

Rock Climbing

Argentina's Parque Nacional Los Glaciares, home to Cerro Torre and Cerro Fitz Roy, is one of the world's most important rock-climbing destinations. Cerro Torre is considered one of the five toughest climbs on the planet. The nearby town of El Chaltén is a climber's haven, and several shops offer lessons and rent equipment. If you don't have the time or talent for climbs of Cerro Torre's magnitude, there are plenty of other options.

Mountain Biking & Cycling

From a leisurely ride around enchanting lowland scenery to bombing down smouldering volcanoes, South America has some exciting destinations for mountain bikers. The Andes are blessed with some of the most dramatic mountain-biking terrain in the world, and offer relatively easy access to mountain ranges, magnificent lakes, precolonial ruins and trails, and myriad eco-zones connected by an extensive network of footpaths and jeep roads. Mountain bikes are widely available for hire, though quality varies considerably. Make a thorough inspection of key components (brakes, tires, gears) before committing. For longer multiday trips, it's better to bring your own bike.

There is no shortage of incredible terrain in Peru. Single-track trails ranging from easy to expert await mountain bikers outside Huaraz. If you're experienced, there are incredible mountain-biking possibilities around the Sacred Valley and downhill trips to the Amazon jungle, all accessible from Cuzco.

One of Bolivia's most famous mountain-biking experiences is the thrilling 3600m trip down the World's Most Dangerous Road from La Cumbre to Coroico. Outfitters in La Paz arrange excursions.

A favorite mountain-biking destination in Chile's north is San Pedro de Atacama. Fabulous trips in the Lakes District access pristine areas with limited public transportation. The bike lane around Lago Llanquihue is very popular, while Río Puelo Valley and Río Cochamó Valley (also in the Lakes District) are fabulous destinations. In the south, the Carretera Austral remains one of the most popular biking destinations in South America. From December to March the road is packed with cyclists.

At outdoor hot spots in Argentina you can rent a mountain bike for a day of independent pedaling or for guided mountain-bike rides. Patagonia is a popular and mythical destination, with its desolate, beautiful landscapes and wide-open skies. However, be ready for fierce, multidirectional winds and rough gravel roads. Take four-season gear, even in summer, when long days and relatively warm weather make for the best touring. The classic road down here is RN 40, but cycling is tough because of the winds and lack of water; most cyclists alternate sections with Chile's Carretera Austral.

In recent years, Buenos Aires has become a more bike-friendly destination, with an expanding system of dedicated bike lanes, along with a free bike-share program.

It's hard to beat the adrenaline-charged downhills on the flanks of Cotopaxi in Ecuador. From Baños, you can travel 'La Ruta de las Cascadas' (Highway of the Waterfalls), a 61km (mostly) downhill ride to Puyo, with some refreshing dips in waterfalls along the way.

Horseback Riding

Saddling up and following in the path of Chile's *huasos* (cowboys) is a fun and easy way to experience the wilderness. Chilean horses are compact and sturdy, with amazing skill for fording rivers and climbing Andean steps. Now more than ever, multiday horseback-riding trips explore cool circuits, sometimes crossing the Andes to Argentina, on terrain that

★ Best Hiking Destinations

The Inca Trail (p296), Peru

Torres del Paine (p202), Chile

Cordillera Blanca (p308), Peru

Fitz Roy Range (p158), Argentina

Hiker in Parque Nacional Torres del Paine (p206)

would be inaccessible otherwise. Except in the far north, opportunities can be found just about everywhere.

With strong initiatives for community-based rural tourism in the south, guided horseback riding and trekking with packhorses is a great way to discover remote areas. Rural guides charge affordable rates, provide family lodging in their own homes and offer invaluable cultural insight.

Adventure outfitters offer multilingual guides and a more elaborate range of services. Most places offer first-time riders preliminary lessons before taking to the trails. Favorites for single- or multiday horse treks are San Pedro de Atacama and around Torres del Paine.

Ecuador also has some fine horseback-riding opportunities, particularly on the slopes of Cotopaxi, a few hours south of Quito.

Wildlife-Watching

The number of creatures great and small reaches epic proportions in the land of cloud forests, Andean mountains and Amazon rainforest. Whether you're an avid birdwatcher or just want to see monkeys in the wild, South America is hard to top. Its biodiversity is staggering.

Brazil has superb places for seeing wildlife. You can look for toucans, sloths, river dolphins and various monkey species at a jungle lodge in the Amazon. Odds are higher that you'll see even more species in the Pantanal, an extensive wetlands area that can also be accessed from Bolivia or Paraguay.

Ecuador is a major birdwatching hotspot. The Galápagos Islands have their own feathery appeal, owing to their 28 endemic species, which have evolved in extraordinary ways. Isla Santa Cruz boasts the highest bird count overall, and it's a good place to begin to find the 13 species of Darwin's finches. Various large species are easily seen around Puerto Ayora harbor, including blue-footed boobies, magnificent frigate birds and lava herons.

River Rafting

You'll find churning white water all over the continent. The settings are spectacular: splashing through deep canyons or pounding down the forest-lined banks of a Class IV rapid.

The wealth of scenic rivers, lakes, fjords and inlets in southern Chile makes it a dream destination. Chile's rivers, raging through narrow canyons from the Andes, are world class. Northern Patagonia's Futaleufú River offers memorable Class IV and V runs. Less technical runs include the beautiful Petrohué, near Puerto Varas. Near Santiago, the Cajón del Maipo offers a gentle but enjoyable run.

In Peru, Cuzco is the launch point for the greatest variety of river-running options. Choices range from a few hours of mild rafting on the Urubamba to adrenaline-pumping rides on the Santa Teresa to several days on the Apurímac, technically the source of the Amazon. A river-running trip on the Tambopata, available from June through October, tumbles down the eastern slopes of the Andes, culminating in a couple of days of floating in unspoiled rainforest.

Skiing & Snowboarding

Powder junkies rejoice: world-class resorts in the Chilean and Argentine Andes, South America's most important downhill ski areas, offer myriad possibilities for skiing, snowboarding and even heliskiing (the season is roughly June to September). Don't expect too many bargains; resorts are priced to match their quality. 'First descents' of Chilean Patagonia's numerous mountains is a growing (but limited) trend.

Most resorts in Chile are within an hour's drive of Santiago, including a wide variety of runs at family-oriented La Parva, all-levels El Colorado, and Valle Nevado, with a lot of terrain and renowned heliskiing. Legendary Portillo, the site of several downhill speed records and the summer training base for many of the Northern Hemisphere's top skiers, is northeast of Santiago near the Argentine border crossing to Mendoza.

Responsible Trekking

- Exercise caution with campfires on the windy Andean slopes and the Patagonian steppe.
- Cook on a camp stove (not an open fire) and dispose of butane cartridges responsibly.
- Carry out all rubbish.
- If there's no toilet, the best practice is to carry out waste. If you decide to bury it, dig a small hole 15cm deep and at least 100m from any watercourses. Cover with soil and a rock. Pack out toilet paper (take it with you in a ziplock bag).
- Wash with biodegradable soap at least 50m away from any watercourses.
- Do not feed wildlife.
- Stick to existing trails. Avoid cutting corners; it contributes to erosion.
- Trails can pass through private property. Ask permission before entering, and leave all livestock gates as you found them.

Surfing

Brazil is South America's best-known surfing destination, with great breaks near Rio and in the southeast, and sprinkled all along the coast.

With breaks lining the long Pacific coast, Chile nurtures some serious surf culture, most active in middle and northern Chile. Keep in mind, you'll need a wetsuit. The coastal Ruta 1 is lined with waves.

Ecuador's best breaks are off Isla San Cristóbal in the Galápagos.

Hang-Gliding & Paragliding

Rio de Janeiro is probably one of the world's most scenic places to go hang-gliding, offering memorable tandem flights over tropical rainforest with views of the beach and island-filled ocean in the distance. Paragliding *(parapente)* can also be arranged in Rio.

Travelers on the Inca Trail (p296), Peru

Survival Guide

DIRECTORY A–Z 391

TRANSPORT 401

Directory A–Z

Accessible Travel

In general, South America is not well set up for travelers with disabilities, but the more modernized Southern Cone countries are more accommodating – notably Chile, Argentina and the bigger cities of Brazil. For city travel, Santiago is the most accessible city in South America. Things are slowly improving in some places, particularly in Ecuador, which now has a president who uses a wheelchair.

Unfortunately, cheap local lodgings probably won't be well equipped to deal with physically challenged travelers; air travel will be more feasible than most local buses (although this isn't impossible); and well-developed tourist attractions will be more accessible than off-the-beaten-track destinations. Start your research here:

Lonely Planet (http://lptravel.to/AccessibleTravel) Free Accessible Travel guides.

Emerging Horizons (www.emerginghorizons.com) Features well-written articles and regular columns full of handy advice.

Go Wheel the World (http://gowheeltheworld.com) Chile-based outfit that leads excellent adventure tours. Check the website for inspiring documentaries about traveling off the beaten path.

Mobility International (www.miusa.org) This US-based outfit advises travelers with disabilities and runs educational-exchange programs overseas.

Royal Association for Disability and Rehabilitation (www.disabilityrightsuk.org) Good resource for travelers.

Society for Accessible Travel & Hospitality (www.sath.org) Good, general travel information; based in the USA.

Accommodations

South America has plenty of variety, with options for all budgets. Be sure to book well in advance when visiting during big festivals (particularly Carnaval time in Brazil) and in popular resort areas during high season.

Costs

Costs vary from country to country, with Andean countries (especially Bolivia) being the cheapest (from around US$10 per night) and Chile, Brazil and Argentina the costliest (upwards of US$30).

Camping

Camping is an obvious choice in parks and reserves and is a useful budget option in pricier countries such as Chile. Bring all your own gear. While camping gear is available in large cities and in trekking and activities hubs, it's expensive and choices are usually minimal. Camping gear can be rented in areas with substantial camping and trekking action (eg the Lakes District and Huaraz), but quality is sometimes dubious.

An alternative to tent camping is staying in *refugios* (simple structures within parks and reserves), where a basic bunk and kitchen access are usually provided. For climbers, most summit attempts involve staying in a *refugio*.

Hostels

Albergues (hostels) have become increasingly popular throughout South America and, as throughout the world, are great places to socialize with other travelers. Across South America, there are numerous private hostels as well as scores of official *albergue juvenil* (youth hostel), where you can get a small discount if you're a card-carrying member of Hostelling International–American Youth Hostel (HI-USA).

Book Your Stay

For more accommodation reviews by Lonely Planet authors, check out http://hotels.lonelyplanet.com/southamerica. You'll find independent reviews, as well as recommendations on the best places to stay. Best of all, you can book online.

Hotels & Guesthouses

When it comes to hotels, both terminology and criteria vary. The costliest in the genre are *hoteles* (hotels) proper. A step down in price are *hostales* (small hotels or guesthouses). The cheapest places are *hospedajes, casas de huéspedes, residenciales, alojamientos* and *pensiones.* A room in these places includes a bed with (hopefully) clean sheets and a blanket, maybe a table and chair and sometimes a fan. Showers and toilets may be shared; there may not be hot water. Cleanliness varies widely, but many places are remarkably tidy. In some areas, especially southern Chile, the cheapest places may be *casas familiares,* family houses whose hospitality makes them excellent value.

In Brazil, Argentina and some other places, prices often include breakfast, the quality of which is usually directly related to the room price.

Hot-water supplies are often erratic, or may be available only at certain hours of the day. It's something to ask about (and consider paying extra for), especially in the highlands and far south, where it gets cold.

When showering, beware the electric showerhead, an innocent-looking unit that heats cold water with an electric element. Don't touch the shower head or anything metal when the water is on or you may get shocked – never strong enough to throw you across the room, but hardly pleasant.

Customs Regulations

Customs vary slightly from country to country, but you can generally bring in personal belongings, camera gear, laptops, handheld devices and other travel-related gear. All countries prohibit the export (just as home countries prohibit the import) of archaeological items and goods made from rare or endangered animals. Avoid carrying plants, seeds, fruits and fresh meat products across borders.

Electricity

Electricity is not standard across South America. Voltage ranges from 100V to 240V, with the most common plug types being flat-pronged American style and rounded European style.

Discount Cards

The HI-USA membership card can be useful in some places (particularly in Brazil, where there are dozens of HI-affiliated lodging options.

An International Student Identity Card (ISIC) can provide discounted admission to archaeological sites and museums. It may also entitle you to reductions on bus, train and air tickets. In less developed countries, student discounts are rare, although high-ticket items such as the entrance to Machu Picchu (discounted nearly 50% for ISIC holders under 26) may be reduced. In some countries, such as Argentina, almost any form of university identification will suffice where discounts are offered.

Emergency & Important Numbers

There is no continent-wide emergency number.

Argentina	☎107 ambulance, ☎100 fire, ☎101 police
Bolivia	☎123 ambulance, fire & police
Brazil	☎192 ambulance, ☎193 fire, ☎190 police
Chile	☎131 ambulance, ☎132 fire, ☎133 police
Colombia	☎123 ambulance, fire & police
Ecuador	☎131 ambulance, ☎102 fire, ☎101 police
Peru	☎106 ambulance, ☎116 fire, ☎105 police

Food

Reservations aren't necessary for casual eateries, but are recommended for midrange and top-end restaurants. Reserve several weeks in advance for the best places.

Cafes Snacking and sipping with less formality amid a bar or coffeeshop vibe.

Cevicherías In Peru and Ecuador you'll find casual lunch spots serving up fresh fish marinated in lime juice, with many variations on the theme.

Grill houses Known as *parrillas* in Argentina and *churrascarias* in Brazil, these places specialize in barbecue meat.

Pay-by-Weight You'll find extensive lunch buffets in some places (particularly in Brazil), where you select what you want and then pay per 100 grams.

Restaurants Ranging from fine dining to basic, these sometimes serve a discounted set menu known as *menú del día* at lunch.

Health

Prevention is the key to staying healthy while in South America. Travelers who receive the recommended vaccines and follow common-sense precautions usually go away with nothing more than a little diarrhea.

Before You Go

Recommended Vaccinations

Since most vaccines don't produce immunity until at least two weeks after they're given, visit a physician four to eight weeks before departure. Ask your doctor for an International Certificate of Vaccination (otherwise known as the yellow booklet), which will list all the vaccinations you've received.

The only required vaccine is yellow fever, and that's only if you're arriving from a yellow-fever-infected country in Africa or the Americas. However, a number of vaccines are recommended.

Health Insurance

If your health insurance doesn't cover you for medical expenses abroad, consider getting extra insurance. Find out in advance if your insurance plan will make payments directly to providers or reimburse you later for overseas health expenditures. (In many countries doctors expect payment in cash.)

Websites

There is a wealth of travel health advice on the internet. The World Health Organization (www.who.int/ith) maintains up-to-date info on disease outbreaks. Another resource of general interest is MD Travel Health (www.mdtravelhealth.com), which provides complete travel health recommendations for every country in the world.

It's usually a good idea to consult your government's travel health website before departure, if one is available:

Australia (www.smartraveller.gov.au)

Canada (www.travelhealth.gc.ca)

UK (www.fco.gov.uk)

USA (wwwnc.cdc.gov/travel)

In South America

Good medical care may be more difficult to find in smaller cities and impossible to locate in rural areas. Many doctors and hospitals expect payment in cash, regardless of whether you have travel health insurance. If you develop a life-threatening medical problem, you'll probably want to be evacuated to a country with state-of-the-art medical care. Since this may cost tens of thousands of dollars, be sure you have insurance to cover this before you depart. You can find a list of medical-evacuation and travel-insurance companies on the US State Department website (http://travel.state.gov).

Infectious Diseases

Dengue

Dengue fever is a viral infection found throughout South America. Dengue is transmitted by Aedes mosquitoes, which bite preferentially during the daytime and are usually found close to human habitations, often indoors. Dengue is especially common in densely populated, urban environments.

Dengue usually causes flu-like symptoms, including fever, muscle aches, joint pains, headaches, nausea and vomiting, often followed by a rash. The body aches may be quite uncomfortable, but most cases resolve uneventfully in a few days.

There is no treatment for dengue fever except to take analgesics such as acetaminophen/paracetamol (Tylenol) and drink plenty of fluids. Severe cases may require hospitalization for intravenous fluids and supportive care. There is no vaccine. The cornerstone of prevention is protection against insects.

Keep an eye out for outbreaks in areas where you plan to visit. A good website on the latest information is the CDC (wwwnc.cdc.gov/travel).

Hepatitis A

Hepatitis A is the second most common travel-related infection (after traveler's diarrhea). It's a viral infection of the liver that's usually acquired by ingestion of contaminated water, food or ice, though it may also be acquired by direct contact with infected persons. Symptoms may include fever, malaise, jaundice, nausea, vomiting and abdominal pain. Most cases resolve themselves without complications, though hepatitis A occasionally causes severe liver damage.

The vaccine for hepatitis A is extremely safe and highly effective. If you get a booster six to 12 months later, it lasts for at least 10 years. You really should get it before you go to any developing nation.

Malaria

Malaria occurs in every South American country except Chile and Uruguay. It's transmitted by mosquito bites, usually between dusk and dawn. The main symptom is high spiking fevers, which may be accompanied by chills, sweats, headache, body aches, weakness, vomiting or diarrhea. Severe cases may involve the central nervous system and lead to seizures, confusion, coma and death.

There is a choice of three malaria pills, all of which work about equally well. Protecting yourself against mosquito bites is just as important as taking malaria pills, since none of the pills are 100% effective.

If you develop a fever after returning home, see a physician, as malaria symptoms may not occur for months.

Typhoid

Typhoid fever is caused by ingestion of food or water contaminated by a species of salmonella known as *Salmonella typhi*. Fever occurs in virtually all cases. Other symptoms may include headache, malaise, muscle aches, dizziness, loss of appetite, nausea and abdominal pain. Either diarrhea or constipation may occur. Possible complications include intestinal perforation, intestinal bleeding, confusion, delirium or (rarely) coma.

Unless you expect to take all your meals in major hotels and restaurants, the typhoid vaccine is a good idea.

Yellow Fever

Yellow fever is a life-threatening viral infection transmitted by mosquitoes in forested areas. The illness begins with flu-like symptoms, which may include fever, chills, headache, muscle aches, backache, loss of appetite, nausea and vomiting. These symptoms usually subside in a few days, but one person in six enters a second, toxic phase characterized by recurrent fever, vomiting, listlessness, jaundice, kidney failure and hemorrhage, leading to death in up to half of the cases. There is no treatment except for supportive care.

Yellow-fever vaccine can be given only in approved yellow-fever vaccination centers, which provide validated International Certificates of Vaccination (yellow booklets). The vaccine should be given at least 10 days before any potential exposure to yellow fever and remains effective for approximately 10 years.

Zika

Zika virus is primarily transmitted by infected mosquitoes, typically active from dawn to dusk. It can be transmitted from a pregnant woman to her fetus. Human transmission can also occur through unprotected sex, and on occasion through saliva and urine. Symptoms include mild fever, headache, muscle and joint pain, nausea, vomiting and general malaise. Symptoms may present three to 12 days after being bitten.

The best prevention is to wear long sleeves, repellent with 20% to 30% DEET and avoid being outdoors at dawn and dusk when mosquitoes are most common. High-altitude destinations are not considered a risk.

Altitude Sickness

Altitude sickness may develop in those who ascend rapidly to altitudes greater than 2500m. Being physically fit offers no protection. Those who have experienced altitude sickness in the past are prone to future episodes. The risk increases with faster ascents, higher altitudes and greater exertion. Symptoms may include headaches, nausea, vomiting, dizziness, malaise, insomnia and loss of appetite. Severe cases may be complicated by fluid in the lungs (high-altitude pulmonary edema) or swelling of the brain (high-altitude cerebral edema).

When traveling to high altitudes, it's also important to avoid overexertion, eat light meals and abstain from alcohol.

If your symptoms are more than mild or don't resolve promptly, see a doctor. Altitude sickness should be taken seriously; it can be life-threatening when severe.

Cold Exposure & Hypothermia

Cold exposure may be a significant problem in the Andes, particularly at night. Be sure to dress warmly, stay dry, keep active, consume plenty of food and water, get enough rest, and avoid alcohol, caffeine and tobacco.

Hypothermia occurs when the body loses heat faster than it can produce it and the core temperature of the body falls. If you're trekking at high altitudes or simply taking a long bus trip over mountains, particularly at night, be prepared. In the Andes, you should always be prepared for cold, wet or windy conditions even if it's just for a few hours. It is best to dress in layers. A hat is also important.

Traveler's Diarrhea

To prevent diarrhea, avoid tap water unless it has been boiled, filtered or chemically disinfected (with iodine tablets); only eat fresh fruits or vegetables if cooked or peeled; be wary of dairy products that might contain unpasteurized milk; and be highly selective when eating food from markets and street vendors.

If you develop diarrhea, be sure to drink plenty of fluids, preferably an oral rehydration solution containing salt and sugar. Gastrolyte works well for this. A few loose stools don't require treatment but you may want to take antibiotics if you start having more than three watery bowel movements within 24 hours, and it's accompanied by at least one other symptom – fever, cramps, nausea, vomiting or generally feeling unwell. Effective antibiotics include Norfloxacin, Ciprofloxacin or Azithromycin – all will kill the bacteria quickly. Note that an antidiarrheal agent (such as loperamide) is just a 'stopper' and doesn't get to the cause of the problem. Don't take loperamide if you have a fever or blood in your stools. Seek medical attention quickly if you don't respond to an appropriate antibiotic.

Tap Water

Tap water is generally not safe to drink. Vigorous boiling for one minute is the most effective means of water purification. At altitudes greater than 2000m, boil for three minutes.

Other methods of treating water include using a handheld ultraviolet light purifier (such as a SteriPEN), iodine and water filters.

Argentina Generally safe to drink, but best to check in rural areas.

Bolivia Not safe to drink.

Brazil Generally safe to drink in major cities; not safe in rural areas.

Chile Tap water is generally safe to drink from Santiago down to Patagonia, but generally unwise in the Atacama Desert.

Recommended Vaccinations

Vaccine	Recommended for	Dosage	Side effects
Chickenpox	Travelers who've never had chickenpox	2 doses one month apart	Fever; mild case of chickenpox
Hepatitis A	All travelers	One dose before trip; booster 6-12 months later	Soreness at injection site; headaches; body aches
Hepatitis B	Long-term travelers in close contact with the local population	3 doses over 6-month period	Soreness at injection site; low-grade fever
Measles	Travelers born after 1956 who've had only one measles vaccination	1 dose	Fever; rash; joint pains; allergic reactions
Rabies	Travelers who may have contact with animals and may not have access to medical care	3 doses over 3- to 4-week period	Soreness at injection site; headaches; body aches
Tetanus-diphtheria	Travelers who haven't had booster within 10 years	1 dose lasts 10 years	Soreness at injection site
Typhoid	All travelers	4 oral capsules, 1 taken every other day	Abdominal pain; nausea; rash
Yellow fever	Travelers to jungle areas at altitudes below 2300m	1 dose lasts 10 years	Headaches; body aches; severe reactions are rare

Colombia Not safe to drink, except in Bogotá and Cartagena.

Ecuador Not safe to drink.

Peru Not safe to drink.

Insurance

A travel-insurance policy covering theft, loss, accidents and illness is highly recommended. Many policies include a card with toll-free numbers for 24-hour assistance, and it's good practice to carry it with you. Note that some policies compensate travelers for misrouted or lost luggage. Baggage insurance is worth its price in peace of mind. Also check that the coverage includes worst-case scenarios: ambulances, evacuations or an emergency flight home. Some policies specifically exclude 'dangerous activities,' such as scuba diving, motorcycling or even trekking. If such activities are on your agenda, avoid this sort of policy.

There are a wide variety of policies available and your travel agent will be able to make recommendations. The policies handled by student-travel organizations usually offer good value. If a policy offers lower and higher medical-expense options, the low-expenses policy should be OK for South America – medical costs are not nearly as high here as elsewhere in the world.

If you have baggage insurance and need to make a claim, the insurance company may demand a receipt as proof that you bought the stuff in the first place. Make a list of stolen items and their value. At the police station, you complete a *denuncia* (statement), a copy of which is given to you for your insurance claim.

Worldwide travel insurance is available at www.lonelyplanet.com/bookings. You can buy, claim and extend online anytime – even if you're already on the road.

Internet Access

Wi-fi access is widely available, with many hostels, cafes and guesthouses offering free wi-fi. In contrast, internet cafes are a rarity.

Legal Matters

In city police stations, an English-speaking interpreter is rare. In most cases you'll either have to speak the local language or provide an interpreter. Some cities have a tourist police service, which can be more helpful.

If you are robbed, photocopies (even better, certified copies) of original passports, visas and air tickets and careful records of credit-card numbers and traveler's checks will prove invaluable during replacement procedures. Replacement passport applications are usually referred to your home country, so it helps to leave a copy of your passport details with someone back home.

LGBT Travelers

Buenos Aires, Rio de Janeiro, São Paulo and Santiago are the most gay-friendly cities, though gay couples are openly out only in certain neighborhoods. Elsewhere on the continent, where public displays of affection by same-sex couples may get negative reactions, do as the locals do – be discreet to avoid problems.

Despite a growing number of publications and websites devoted to gay travel, few have specific advice on South America. One exception is Purple Roofs (www.purpleroofs.com), an excellent guide to gay-friendly accommodations throughout South America.

Maps

International Travel Maps & Books (www.itmb.com) produces a range of excellent maps of Central and South America. For the whole continent, it has a reliable reference map at a 1:4,000,000 scale and a commemorative edition of its classic 1:5,000,000 map. The maps are huge for road use, but they're helpful for pretrip planning. More detailed ITMB maps are available for the Amazon Basin and every country in South America. All are available on the ITMB website.

Maps of the South American continent as a whole are widely available; check any well-stocked map or travel bookstore.

Money

It's convenient to have a small wad of US dollars tucked away (in US$20 denominations and less; US$100 bills are difficult to exchange). US currency is by far the easiest to exchange throughout South America. Of course, unlike traveler's checks, nobody will give you a refund for lost or stolen cash. When you're about to cross from one country to another, it's handy to change some cash. Trying to exchange worn notes can be a hassle, so procure crisp bills before setting out.

In some countries, especially in rural areas, *cambio* (change) can be particularly hard to come by. Businesses even occasionally refuse to sell you something if they can't or don't want to change your note. So break down those larger bills whenever you have the opportunity, such as at busy restaurants, banks and larger businesses.

ATMs

ATMs are available in most cities and large towns, and are almost always the most convenient, reliable and economical way of getting cash. The rate of exchange is usually as good as any bank or legal money changer. Many ATMs are connected to the Cirrus or Plus network, but many countries prefer one over the other. If your ATM card gets swallowed by a machine, generally the only thing you can do is call your bank and cancel the card. Although such events are rare, it's well worth having an extra ATM card (to a different account), should something go wrong.

If possible, sign up with a bank that doesn't charge a fee for out-of-network ATM withdrawals. Also, find a bank that offers a low exchange-rate fee (1% to 2%). Before hitting the road, call your bank, informing them of your travel plans – that way the bank won't put a hold on foreign withdrawals while you're on the road.

Many ATMs will accept a personal identification number (PIN) of only four digits; find out whether this applies to the specific countries you're traveling to before heading off.

Bargaining

Bargaining is accepted and expected when contracting long-term accommodations and when shopping for craft goods in markets. Haggling is a near sport in the Andean countries, with patience, humor and respect serving as the ground rules of the game. Bargaining is much less common in the Cono Sur (Southern Cone; a collective term for Argentina, Chile, Uruguay and parts of Brazil and Paraguay).

Credit Cards

Visa and MasterCard are accepted at most large stores, travel agencies and better hotels and restaurants. Credit-card purchases sometimes attract an extra *recargo* (surcharge) on the price (from 2% to 10%), but they are usually billed to your account at favorable exchange rates. Some banks issue cash advances on major credit cards. The most widely accepted card is Visa, followed by MasterCard (those with UK Access should insist on its affiliation with MasterCard). American Express is accepted at fewer places.

Exchanging Money

Traveler's checks and foreign cash can be changed at *casas de cambio* (currency-exchange offices) or banks. Rates are usually similar, but *casas de cambio* are quicker, less bureaucratic and open longer hours.

It is preferable to bring money in US dollars, although banks and *casas de cambio* in capital cities will change euros, pounds sterling, Japanese yen and other major currencies. Changing these currencies in smaller towns and on the street is next to impossible.

Traveler's Checks

Traveler's checks are not nearly as convenient as ATM cards, and you may have difficulty cashing them – even at banks. High commissions (from 3% to upwards of 10%) also make them an unattractive option. If you do take traveler's checks, American Express is the most widely accepted brand, while Visa, Thomas Cook and Citibank are the next best options. To facilitate replacement in case of theft, keep a record of check numbers and the original bill of sale in a safe place. Even with proper records, replacement can be a tedious, time-intensive process.

Tipping

Restaurants In some countries (such as Brazil and Chile), a 10% service charge is typically included.

Tours When booking tours (such as to the Galápagos or the Amazon), it's customary to tip your guide – from a few dollars per day to 15%, depending on service.

Taxis Not expected, though you can round up the bill.

Bars Not expected.

Fraud

Unfortunately, ATM-card cloning is a big worry in Brazil and your account can be drained of thousands of dollars before you even realize it.

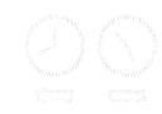

Opening Hours

On Sunday, nearly everything is closed. In the Andean countries, businesses tend to close earlier.

Banks Monday to Friday (for money changing).

Businesses 8am or 9am–noon and 2pm–8pm or 9pm Monday to Friday. Shorter hours on Saturday.

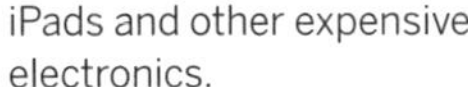

Photography

Consumer electronics are readily available throughout South America, but taxes can kick prices through the roof. You'll probably find better deals at home. *Lonely Planet's Guide to Travel Photography* is full of helpful tips for photography while on the road.

Post

International postal rates can be quite expensive. Generally, important mail and parcels should be sent by registered or certified service; otherwise, they may go missing. Sending parcels can be awkward: often an *aduana* (customs) officer must inspect the contents before a postal clerk can accept them, so wait to seal your package until after it has been checked. Most post offices have a parcels window, usually signed *encomiendas* (parcels). The place for posting overseas parcels is sometimes different from the main post office.

UPS, FedEx, DHL and other private postal services are available in some countries, but are prohibitively expensive.

Safe Travel

To avoid becoming a victim, use common sense and take general precautions throughout South America:

- Carry only the minimum cash needed when out for the day.
- Dress down, leave the jewelry at home and don't walk around flashing iPhones, iPads and other expensive electronics.
- Be alert and walk purposefully. Criminals home in on dopey, hesitant, disoriented-looking individuals.
- Use ATMs inside buildings. Before doing so, be very aware of your surroundings.
- Check windows and doors of your room for security, and don't leave anything valuable lying around.

Theft

Theft can be a problem, but remember that fellow travelers can also be accomplished crooks, so where there's a backpacker scene, there may also be thievery. Here are some common-sense suggestions to limit your liability:

- Even if you're just running down the hall, never leave your hotel door unlocked.
- Always conceal your money belt and its contents, preferably beneath your clothing.
- Keep your spending money separate from the big stuff (credit cards, tickets etc).
- Be aware of the risk of bag slashing and the theft of your contents on buses. Keep close watch on your belongings – the bag isn't safe under your seat, above your head or between your legs (it's better on your lap). Be mindful in crowded markets or terminals where thefts are more likely to occur.

Etiquette

Greetings These are important. In Spanish-speaking countries, greet people you encounter with *buenos días* (good morning), *buenas tardes* (good afternoon) or *buenas noches* (good evening). Use *bom dia, boa tarde* and *boa noite* in Brazil.

Shops Always greet people when entering and exiting a shop.

Cheek kissing When meeting people socially, give *besos* (kisses) on the cheek (both cheeks for Brazilians). Men shake hands.

Shorts Dress for the occasion; for example, usually only tourists and athletes wear shorts in Buenos Aires.

Photographs Ask before photographing people, particularly in indigenous communities – payment may be requested.

- When exploring cities, consider ditching the daypack and carrying what you need in a plastic bag to deter potential thieves.

Tours

There are loads of great adrenaline activities on offer, from rafting to mountain biking, but do your research on an agency before joining a tour. Travelers have lost their lives owing to poorly maintained equipment and reckless, ill-prepared guides. It's never wise to choose an operator based on cost alone.

Druggings

Lonely Planet has received correspondence from travelers who were unwittingly drugged and robbed after accepting food from a stranger.

Be very careful in bars as there are occasional reports of folks being unwittingly drugged then raped or robbed. Always keep a close eye on your drink and be cautious when meeting new friends.

Telephone

Mobile Phones

Cell (mobile) phone numbers in South America often have different area codes that are different to fixed-line numbers, even if the cell-phone owner resides in the same city. Calling a cell-phone number is always more expensive (sometimes exorbitantly so) than calling a fixed line.

If you plan to travel with a smartphone, you may want to purchase an international plan or local SIM to minimize (what could be) enormous costs. Remember it's possible to call internationally for free or very cheaply using Skype or other Voice over Internet Protocol (VoIP) systems.

Phone Cards

Aside from Skype, the cheapest way to make an international call is by using a phone card, the type you purchase at a kiosk or corner store. These allow you to call North America or Europe for as little as US5¢ per minute with a good card. The caveat is that you need a private phone line or a permissive telephone kiosk operator to use them.

Toilets

There are two toilet rules for South America: always carry your own toilet paper and don't ever throw anything into the toilet bowl. Except in the most developed places, South American sewer systems can't handle toilet paper, so all paper products must be discarded in the wastebasket. Another general rule is to use public bathrooms whenever you can, as you never know when your next opportunity will be. Folks posted outside bathrooms proffering swaths of paper require payment.

Tourist Information

Every country in South America has government-run tourist offices, but their quality and breadth of coverage vary.

Visas

Some travelers – including those from the USA – may require visas to enter several countries, including Bolivia and Brazil. Arrange these well in advance of your departure. Some countries don't generally require visas but may require a reciprocity fee (such as the $117 fee Chile charges to Australian travelers), paid upon arrival. If no visa is required, a tourist card is issued upon arrival. See individual countries for more details. Suriname charges U$35 for a tourist card, available upon arrival if flying in; if coming overland, get this from a Surinamese embassy before heading to the border.

Carry a handful of passport-sized photos for visa applications. Hold onto any entry-exit cards you are given. There can be serious fines and complications if you lose them!

If you need a visa for a country and arrive at a land border without one, be prepared to backtrack to the nearest town with a consulate to get one. Airlines won't normally let you board a plane for a country to which you don't have the necessary visa. Also, a visa in itself does not guarantee entry: you may still be turned back at the border if you don't have 'sufficient funds' or an onward or return ticket.

Women Travelers

At one time or another, solo women travelers will find themselves the object of curiosity – sometimes well intentioned, sometimes not. Avoidance is an easy, effective self-defense strategy. In the Andean region, particularly in smaller towns and rural areas, modest dress and conduct are the norm, while in Brazil and the more liberal Cono Sur, standards are more relaxed, especially in beach areas.

Machista (macho) attitudes, stressing masculine pride and virility, are fairly widespread among South American men (although less so in indigenous communities). They are often expressed by boasting and in exaggerated attention toward women. Snappy put-down lines or other caustic comebacks to unwanted advances may make the man feel threatened, and he may respond aggressively. Most women find it easier to invent a husband.

There have been isolated cases of South American men raping women travelers. Women trekking or taking tours in remote or isolated areas should be especially cautious. Some cases have involved guides assaulting tour group members, so it's worth double-checking the identity and reputation of any guide or tour operator. Also be aware that women (and men) have been drugged, in bars and elsewhere, using drinks, cigarettes or pills. Police may not be very helpful in rape cases – if a local woman is raped, her family usually seeks revenge instead of calling the police. Tourist police may be more sympathetic, but it's possibly better to see a doctor and contact your embassy before reporting a rape to police.

Tampons are generally difficult to find in smaller towns, so stock up in cities or bring a supply from home.

Transport

Getting There & Away

Flights, cars and tours can be booked online at lonelyplanet.com/bookings.

Air

North American, European and Australian airlines offer regular South American connections.

Argentina The main airports are **Aeropuerto Internacional Ministro Pistarini** (Ezeiza; ☎011-5480-6111; www.aa2000.com.ar) and **Aeroparque Jorge Newbery** (☎011-5480-6111; www.aa2000.com.ar; Av Rafael Obligado; 🚌33, 45), both in Buenos Aires. There are several other international airports around Argentina; find info online at Aeropuertos Argentina 2000 (www.aa2000.com.ar). Aerolíneas Argentinas (www.aerolineas.com.ar) is the national carrier.

Bolivia The principal international airport is La Paz' **El Alto International Airport** (LPB; Héroes Km 7, El Alto). The national airline is the state-owned Boliviana de Aviación (www.boa.bo), which has international flights to Madrid, Barcelona and Miami.

Brazil The most popular international gateways are **Galeão International Airport** (Aeroporto Internacional Antônio Carlos Jobim; ☎21 3004-6050; www.riogaleao.com; Domestic Arrival Hall, Av Vinte de Janeiro) in Rio de Janeiro and São Paulo's **GRU Airport** (Aeroporto Guarulhos; ☎11 2445-2945; www.gru.com.br; Rod Hélio Smidt s/n). **Salvador** (SSA; ☎71 3204-1010; Praça Gago Coutinho s/n, São Cristóvão) receives a few direct scheduled flights from Europe. Though headquartered in Chile, LATAM (www.latam.com) is Brazil's largest international carrier.

Chile Santiago's **Aeropuerto Internacional Arturo Merino Benítez** (Santiago International Airport, SCL; ☎2-2690-1796; www.nuevopudahuel.cl) is the country's main gateway. LATAM (www.latam.com) is the chief international airline serving Chile.

Colombia Aeropuerto Internacional El Dorado (☎1-266-2000; www.eldorado.aero; Av El Dorado) in Bogotá is the main gateway. Avianca (www.avianca.com) is the national carrier.

Ecuador Quito (☎02-395-4200; www.aeropuertoquito.aero) and **Guayaquil** (GYE; ☎04-216-9000; www.tagsa.aero; Av de las Américas) airports are both international hubs. TAME (www.tame.com.ec) is the national carrier but Avianca (www.avianca.com), based in Quito, is close behind.

Peru Lima's **Aeropuerto Internacional Jorge Chávez** (☎01-517-3500, schedules 01-511-6055; www.lima-airport.com; Callao) is the country's major hub. LATAM (www.latam.com) has the most flights domestically and internationally.

Land

From North America, you can journey overland only as far south as Panama. There is no road connection onward to Colombia: the Carretera Panamericana (Pan-American Hwy) ends in the vast wilderness of the Darién Province, in southeast Panama. This roadless area between Central and South America is called the Darién Gap. In the past it has been difficult, but possible, to trek across the gap with the help of local guides, but since around 1998 it has been prohibitively dangerous, especially on the Colombian side. The region is overrun with smugglers and is positively unsafe.

Sea

One of the most popular modes of travel between South and Central America is by booking passage on one of the foreign sailboats that travel between Cartagena (Colombia) and the San Blás islands, with some boats continuing to Colón (Panama). The typical passage takes about five days and costs between US$450 and US$650. A good source of information regarding schedules and available berths is at **Blue Sailing** (☎310-704-0425, 300-829-2030; www.bluesailing.net; Calle San Andrés No 30-47; 5-day trips US$450-650; ⌚9am-5pm Mon-Sat) in Cartagena. Do some serious research before joining any tour; there are many unsavory operators out there and a few boats have even sunk.

A less expensive way to reach Panama from Colombia is via small boat from Capurgana to Puerto Obaldia (COP$30,000 for the 30-minute trip), from where you can take a domestic flight to Panama City (US$115, flying Tuesdays, Thursdays and Sundays) or continue up through the San Blás islands.

Officially, both Panama and Colombia require an onward or return ticket as a condition of entry. This may not be enforced in Colombia, but it's wise to get one anyway, or have lots of money and a plausible itinerary. Panama requires a visa or tourist card, an onward ticket and sufficient funds, and has been known to turn back arrivals who don't meet these requirements.

There are occasional reports of pirate attacks off

Climate Change & Travel

Every form of transport that relies on carbon-based fuel generates CO_2, the main cause of human-induced climate change. Modern travel is dependent on aeroplanes, which might use less fuel per kilometre per person than most cars but travel much greater distances. The altitude at which aircraft emit gases (including CO_2) and particles also contributes to their climate change impact. Many websites offer 'carbon calculators' that allow people to estimate the carbon emissions generated by their journey and, for those who wish to do so, to offset the impact of the greenhouse gases emitted with contributions to portfolios of climate-friendly initiatives throughout the world. Lonely Planet offsets the carbon footprint of all staff and author travel.

the coast of South America, most of which occur in the Caribbean region.

Getting Around

Air

There is an extensive network of domestic flights, with refreshingly low price tags, especially in the Andean countries (Bolivia, Ecuador and Peru). After 18-hour bus rides across mountainous terrain on atrocious roads, you may decide to take the occasional flight.

There are drawbacks to flying, however. Airports are often far from city centers, and public buses don't run all the time, so you may end up spending a bit on taxis (it's usually easier to find a cheap taxi *to* an airport than *from* one). Airport taxes also add to the cost of tickets; they are always higher for international departures. If safety concerns you, check out the 'Fatal Events by Airline' feature at www.airsafe.com.

Avoid scheduling a domestic flight with a close connection for an international flight or vice versa. Reconfirm all flights 48 hours before departure and allow ample extra time at the airport.

Air Passes

A few South America air passes exist and can save you a bit of money, provided you can deal with a fixed itinerary. These mileage-based passes allow travelers to fly between cities in a limited set of countries. The restrictions vary, but flights must be completed within a period ranging from 30 days to 12 months. You'll pay higher rates (or be ineligible) if you arrive in South America on a carrier other than the one sponsoring the air pass.

Gol South America Airpass (www.voegol.com.br) Includes Brazil, Argentina, Bolivia, Chile, Paraguay and Uruguay.

One World Alliance Visit South America Airpass (www.oneworld.com) Includes Argentina, Bolivia, Brazil, Chile, Colombia, Ecuador, Paraguay, Peru, Uruguay and Venezuela.

LATAM South American Airpass One of the most extensive networks around the continent; covers some 124 different destinations in Argentina, Bolivia, Brazil, Chile, Colombia, Ecuador, Paraguay, Peru, Uruguay and Venezuela.

Bicycle

Cycling South America is a challenging yet highly rewarding alternative to public transport. While better roads in Argentina and Chile make the Cono Sur (Southern Cone; a collective term for Argentina, Chile, Uruguay and parts of Brazil and Paraguay) countries especially attractive, the entire continent is manageable by bike, or – more precisely – by mountain bike. Touring bikes are suitable for paved roads, but only a *todo terreno* (mountain bike) allows you to tackle the spectacular back roads (and often main roads!) of the Andes.

There are no multicountry bike lanes or designated routes. Mountain bikers have cycled the length of the Andes. As for road rules, forget it – except for the logical rule of riding with traffic on the right-hand side of the road, there are none. Hunt down good maps that show side roads, as you'll have the enviable ability to get off the beaten track at will.

Bring your own bicycle since locally manufactured ones are less dependable and imported bikes are outrageously expensive. Bicycle mechanics are common even in small towns, but will almost invariably lack the parts you'll need. Before setting out, learn bicycle mechanics and purchase spares for the pieces most likely to fail. A basic road kit will include extra spokes and a spoke wrench, a tire patch kit, a chain punch, inner tubes, spare cables and a cycling-specific multitool. Some folks box up spare tires, leave them with a family member back home and have them shipped to South America when they need them.

Drawbacks to cycling include the weather (fierce rains, blasting winds), high altitude in the Andes, poor roads and reckless drivers – the biggest hazard for riders. Safety equipment such as reflectors, mirrors and a helmet are highly recommended. Security is another issue:

always take your panniers with you and lock your bike (or pay someone to watch it) while you sightsee and bring your bike into your hotel room overnight.

Boat

From cruises through the mystical fjords of Chilean Patagonia and riverboat chugs up the Amazon to outboard canoe travel in the coastal mangroves of Ecuador, South America offers ample opportunity to travel by boat. Safety is generally not an issue, especially for the established ferry and cruise operators in Chile and Argentina. There have been a couple of problems with tourist boats in the Galápagos (including a few that have sunk over the years), so do some research before committing to a cruise.

Bus

In general, bus transport is well developed throughout the continent. Note that road conditions, bus quality and driver professionalism vary widely. Much depends on the season: vast deserts of red dust in the dry season become oceans of mud in the rainy season. In Argentina, Ecuador, and coastal and southern Brazil, roads are generally better. Chile and much of Argentina have some of the best-maintained roads and most comfortable and reliable bus services in South America.

Most major cities and towns have a *terminal de autobuses* or *terminal de ómnibus* (bus terminal); in Brazil, it's called a *rodoviária,* and in Ecuador it's a *terminal terrestre.* Terminals are often on the outskirts of town and you'll need a local bus or taxi to reach it. The biggest and best terminals have restaurants, shops, showers and other services, and the surrounding area is often a good (but frequently ugly) place to look for cheap sleeps and eats. Village 'terminals' in rural areas often amount to dirt lots flanked by dilapidated metal hulks called 'buses' and men hawking various destinations to passersby; listen for your town of choice.

Some cities have several terminals, each serving a different route. Sometimes each bus company has its own terminal, which is particularly inconvenient. This is most common in Colombia, Ecuador and Peru, especially in smaller towns.

Car & Motorcycle

Driving around South America can be mentally taxing and at times risky, but a car allows you to explore out-of-the-way places – especially parks – that are totally inaccessible via public transport. In places like Patagonia and other parts of Chile and Argentina, a short-term rental car can be well worth the expense.

There are some hurdles to driving. First off, it's a good idea to have an International Driving Permit to supplement your license from home. Vehicle security can be a problem anywhere in South America. Avoid leaving valuables in your car, and always lock it. Drive carefully. Throughout South America, if you are in an accident that injures or kills another person, you can be jailed until the case is settled, regardless of culpability.

Driver's License

If you're planning to drive anywhere, obtain an International Driving Permit or Inter-American Driving Permit (Uruguay theoretically recognizes only the latter). For about US$10 to US$15, any motoring organization will issue one, provided you have a current driver's license.

Insurance

Home auto-insurance policies generally do not cover you while driving abroad. Fender benders are generally dealt with on the spot, without involving the police or insurance agents. When you rent, be certain your contract includes *seguro* (insurance).

Rental

Major international rental agencies such as Hertz, Avis and Budget have offices in South American capitals, major cities and at major airports. Local agencies, however, often have better rates. To rent a car, you must be at least 25 years old and have a valid driver's license from home and a credit card. Some agencies rent to those under 25 years, but charge an added fee. If your itinerary calls for crossing borders, know that some rental agencies restrict or forbid this; ask before renting.

Rates can fluctuate wildly (ranging from US$40 to US$80 per day).

Road Conditions & Road Rules

South Americans drive on the right-hand side of the road. Road rules are frequently ignored and seldom enforced; conditions can be hazardous; and many drivers, especially in Argentina and Brazil, are reckless and even willfully dangerous. Driving at night is riskier than during the day due to lower visibility and the preponderance of tired and/or intoxicated nighttime drivers sharing the road.

Road signs can be confusing, misleading or nonexistent – a good sense of humor and patience are key attributes. Honking your horn on blind curves is a simple, effective safety measure; the vehicle coming uphill on a narrow road usually has the right of way. If you're cruising along and see a tree branch or rock in the middle of the road, slow down: this means there's a breakdown, rock slide or some other trouble up ahead. Speed bumps can pop up anywhere, most often smack in the center of town, but sometimes inexplicably in the middle of a highway.

Local Transportation

Local and city bus systems tend to be thorough and reliable throughout South America. Although in many countries you can flag a bus anywhere on its route, you're best off finding the official bus stop. Still, if you can't find the stop, don't hesitate to throw your arm up to stop a bus you know is going in your direction. Never hesitate to ask a bus driver which is the right bus to take; most of them are very generous in directing you to the right bus.

As in major cities throughout the world, pickpockets are a problem on crowded buses and subways. Avoid crowded public transport when you're loaded down with luggage.

Taxis in most big cities (but definitely not all) have meters. When a taxi has a meter, make sure the driver uses it. When it doesn't, always agree on a fare *before* you get in the cab.

Train

Trains have slowly faded from the South American landscape, but several spectacular routes still operate. Ecuador has invested heavily in rehabilitating its old lines.

For great scenery with a touch of old-fashioned railway nostalgia, try the **Puno–Juliaca–Cuzco** route in Peru. This train runs for group bookings in high season. Departures are unpredictable, but when it does run, it's open to nongroup passengers.

Language

Portuguese pronunciation is not difficult because most sounds are also found in English. The exceptions are the nasal vowels (represented in our pronunciation guides by 'ng' after the vowel), which are pronounced as if you're trying to make the sound through your nose; and the strongly rolled 'r' (represented by 'rr' in our pronunciation guides). Also note that the symbol 'zh' sounds like the 's' in 'pleasure'. The stress generally falls on the second-last syllable of a word. In our pronunciation guides stressed syllables are indicated with italics. Portuguese has masculine and feminine forms of nouns and adjectives. Both formsare given where necessary, indicated with 'm' and 'f' respectively.

Spanish pronunciation is not difficult as most of its sounds are also found in English. You can read our pronunciation guides below as if they were English and you'll be understood just fine. If you pronounce 'th' in our guides with a lisp and 'kh' as a throaty sound, you'll even sound like a real Spanish person.

To enhance your trip with a phrasebook, visit **lonelyplanet.com**.

Portuguese

Basics

Hello.
Olá. o·*laa*

Goodbye.
Adeus. a·de·*oosh*

How are you?
Como está? *ko*·moo shtaa

Fine, and you?
Bem, e você? beng e vo·*se*

Yes.
Sim. seeng

No.
Não. nowng

Please.
Por favor. poor fa·*vor*

Thank you.
Obrigado. o·bree·*gaa*·doo (m)
Obrigada. o·bree·*gaa*·da (f)

You're welcome.
De nada. de *naa*·da

Excuse me.
Faz favor. faash fa·*vor*

Sorry.
Desculpe. desh·*kool*·pe

Do you speak English?
Fala inglês? *faa*·la eeng·*glesh*

I don't understand.
Não entendo. nowng eng·*teng*·doo

Accommodations

Do you have a single/double room?
Tem um quarto de solteiro/casal? teng oong *kwaar*·too de sol·*tay*·roo/ka·*zal*

How much is it per night/person?
Quanto custa por noite/pessoa? *kwang*·too *koosh*·ta poor *noy*·te/pe·*so*·a

Spanish

Basics

Hello.
Hola. *o*·la

How are you?
¿Qué tal? ke tal

I'm fine, thanks.
Bien, gracias. byen *gra*·thyas

Excuse me. (to get attention)
Disculpe. dees·*kool*·pe

Yes./No.
Sí./No. see/no

Thank you.
Gracias. *gra*·thyas

You're welcome./That's fine.
De nada. de *na*·da

Goodbye. /See you later.
Adiós./Hasta luego. a·*dyos*/*as*·ta *lwe*·go

Do you speak English?
¿Habla inglés? *a*·bla een·*gles*

I don't understand.
No entiendo. no en·*tyen*·do

Accommodations

I'd like to make a booking.
Quisiera reservar una habitación. kee·*sye*·ra re·ser·*var* *oo*·na a·bee·ta·*thyon*

How much is it per night?
¿Cuánto cuesta por noche? *kwan*·to *kwes*·ta por *no*·che

Behind the Scenes

Acknowledgements

Climate map data adapted from Peel MC, Finlayson BL & McMahon TA (2007) 'Updated World Map of the Köppen-Geiger Climate Classification', *Hydrology and Earth System Sciences*, 11, 163–344.

Cover image: Iguazú Falls, Brazil; Giordano Cipriani/4Corners ©

Illustrations pp294–95 by Michael Weldon.

This Book

This 1st edition of Lonely Planet's *Best of South America* guidebook was curated by Regis St Louis and researched and written by Regis, Isabel Albiston, Robert Balkovich, Alex Egerton, Anthony Ham, Mark Johanson, Brian Kluepfel, Tom Masters, Carolyn McCarthy, MaSovaida Morgan, Kevin Raub, Brendan Sainsbury, Andy Symington, Phillip Tang, and Luke Waterson. This guidebook was produced by the following:

Destination Editor Bailey Freeman

Senior Product Editors Martine Power, Saralinda Turner

Regional Senior Cartographer Corey Hutchison

Product Editor Jenna Myers

Book Designer Meri Blazevski

Assisting Editors Sarah Bailey, Michelle Bennett, Nigel Chin, Jacqueline Danam, Andrea Dobbin, Emma Gibbs, Carly Hall, Victoria Harrison, Gabrielle Innes, Alison Morris, Lauren O'Connell, Charlotte Orr, Monique Perrin, Christopher Pitts, Maja Vatrić

Cover Researcher Naomi Parker

Thanks to Shona Gray, Angela Tinson

Send Us Your Feedback

We love to hear from travellers – your comments keep us on our toes and help make our books better. Our well-travelled team reads every word on what you loved or loathed about this book. Although we cannot reply individually to postal submissions, we always guarantee that your feedback goes straight to the appropriate authors, in time for the next edition. Each person who sends us information is thanked in the next edition, the most useful submissions are rewarded with a selection of digital PDF chapters.

Visit lonelyplanet.com/contact to submit your updates and suggestions or to ask for help. Our award-winning website also features inspirational travel stories, news and discussions.

Note: We may edit, reproduce and incorporate your comments in Lonely Planet products such as guidebooks, websites and digital products, so let us know if you don't want your comments reproduced or your name acknowledged. For a copy of our privacy policy visit lonelyplanet.com/privacy.

Index

D

E

F

G

000 Map pages

H

I

N

P

Symbols & Map Key

Look for these symbols to quickly identify listings:

- Sights
- Activities
- Courses
- Tours
- Festivals & Events
- Eating
- Drinking
- Entertainment
- Shopping
- Information & Transport

These symbols and abbreviations give vital information for each listing:

- Sustainable or green recommendation
- FREE No payment required

- Telephone number
- Opening hours
- Parking
- Nonsmoking
- Air-conditioning
- Internet access
- Wi-fi access
- Swimming pool
- Bus
- Ferry
- Tram
- Train
- English-language menu
- Vegetarian selection
- Family-friendly

Find your best experiences with these Great For... icons.

 Art & Culture

Beaches

 Budget

 Cafe/Coffee

Cycling

 Detour

Drinking

 Entertainment

 Events

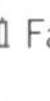 Family Travel

 Food & Drink

 History

Local Life

 Nature & Wildlife

 Photo Op

Scenery

 Shopping

 Short Trip

 Sport

 Walking

 Winter Travel

Sights

- Beach
- Bird Sanctuary
- Buddhist
- Castle/Palace
- Christian
- Confucian
- Hindu
- Islamic
- Jain
- Jewish
- Monument
- Museum/Gallery/Historic Building
- Ruin
- Shinto
- Sikh
- Taoist
- Winery/Vineyard
- Zoo/Wildlife Sanctuary
- Other Sight

Points of Interest

- Bodysurfing
- Camping
- Cafe
- Canoeing/Kayaking
- Course/Tour
- Diving
- Drinking & Nightlife
- Eating
- Entertainment
- Sento Hot Baths/Onsen
- Shopping
- Skiing
- Sleeping
- Snorkelling
- Surfing
- Swimming/Pool
- Walking
- Windsurfing
- Other Activity

Information

- Bank
- Embassy/Consulate
- Hospital/Medical
- Internet
- Police
- Post Office
- Telephone
- Toilet
- Tourist Information
- Other Information

Geographic

- Beach
- Gate
- Hut/Shelter
- Lighthouse
- Lookout
- Mountain/Volcano
- Oasis
- Park
- Pass
- Picnic Area
- Waterfall

Transport

- Airport
- BART station
- Border crossing
- Boston T station
- Bus
- Cable car/Funicular
- Cycling
- Ferry
- Metro/MRT station
- Monorail
- Parking
- Petrol station
- Subway/S-Bahn/Skytrain station
- Taxi
- Train station/Railway
- Tram
- Underground/U-Bahn station
- Other Transport

Andy Symington

Andy has written or worked on over a hundred books and other updates for Lonely Planet (especially in Europe and Latin America) and other publishing companies, and has published articles on numerous subjects for a variety of newspapers, magazines and websites. He part-owns and operates a rock bar, has written a novel and is currently working on several fiction and non-fiction writing projects. Andy, from Australia, moved to Northern Spain many years ago. When he's not off with a backpack in some far-flung corner of the world, he can probably be found watching the tragically poor local football side or tasting local wines after a long walk in the nearby mountains.

Phillip Tang

Phillip grew up on a typically Australian diet of *pho* and fish'n'chips before moving to Mexico City. A degree in Chinese- and Latin-American cultures launched him into travel and then writing about it for Lonely Planet's *Canada*, *China*, *Japan*, *Korea*, *Mexico*, *Peru* and *Vietnam* guides.

Luke Waterson

Raised in the remote Somerset countryside in Southwest England, Luke quickly became addicted to exploring out-of-the-way places. Completing a Creative Writing degree at the University of East Anglia, he shouldered his backpack and vowed to see as much of the world as possible. Luke specialises in writing on South America (he writes for the *Peru* and *Ecuador* Lonely Planet guides). His other areas of expertise are the Caribbean (LP's *Cuba* and *Puerto Rico* guides), Scandinavia and Eastern Europe. That's alongside contributing to travel reference books such as *Food Lover's Guide to the World*, *Best in Travel* and *National Parks of Europe*.

Alex Egerton

A news journalist by trade, Alex has worked for magazines, newspapers and media outlets on five continents. Having had his fill of musty newsrooms and the insatiable corporate appetite for superficial news, Alex decided to leap into travel writing in order to escape the mundane. He spends most of his time on the road checking under mattresses, sampling suspicious street food and chatting with locals as part of the research process for travel articles and guidebooks. A keen adventurer, Alex has hiked through remote jungles in Colombia, explored isolated tributaries of the mighty Mekong and taken part in the first kayak descent of a number of remote waterways in Nicaragua. When not on the road, you'll find him at home amongst the colonial splendor of Popayán in southern Colombia.

Anthony Ham

Anthony is a freelance writer and photographer who specialises in Spain, East and Southern Africa, the Arctic and the Middle East. When he's not writing for Lonely Planet, Anthony writes about and photographs Spain, Africa and the Middle East for newspapers and magazines in Australia, the UK and US.

Mark Johanson

Mark Johanson grew up in Virginia and has called five different countries home over the last decade while circling the globe reporting for British newspapers (the *Guardian*), American magazines (*Men's Journal*) and global media outlets (CNN, BBC). When not on the road, you'll find him gazing at the Andes from his current home in Santiago, Chile.

Brian Kluepfel

Brian lived in three states and seven different residences by the time he was nine years old. From then, he just kept moving, making stops in Berkeley, Bolivia, the Bronx and the 'burbs further down the line. His journalistic work across the Americas has ranged from the Copa America soccer tournament in Paraguay to an accordion festival in Quebec. Brian has covered far-flung destinations for Lonely Planet such as Venezuela, Costa Rica, Belize, Guatemala, Bolivia and Ecuador.

Tom Masters

Dreaming since he could walk of going to the most obscure places on earth, Tom has always had a taste for the unknown. This has led to a writing career that has taken him all over the world, including North Korea, the Arctic, Congo and Siberia. Despite a childhood spent in the English countryside, as an adult Tom has always called London, Paris and Berlin home.

Carolyn McCarthy

Carolyn McCarthy specializes in travel, culture and adventure in the Americas. She has written for *National Geographic*, *Outside*, *BBC Magazine*, *Sierra Magazine*, *Boston Globe* and other publications. A former Fulbright fellow and Banff Mountain Grant recipient, she has documented life in the most remote corners of Latin America. Carolyn has contributed to 40 guidebooks and anthologies for Lonely Planet, including Colorado, USA, Argentina, Chile, Trekking in the Patagonian Andes, Panama, Peru and USA National Parks guides.

MaSovaida Morgan

MaSovaida is a travel writer and multimedia storyteller whose wanderlust has taken her to more than 40 countries and all seven continents. Previously, she was Lonely Planet's Destination Editor for South America and Antarctica for four years and worked as an editor for newspapers and NGOs in the Middle East and United Kingdom.

Kevin Raub

Atlanta native Kevin Raub started his career as a music journalist in New York, working for *Men's Journal* and *Rolling Stone* magazines. He ditched the rock 'n' roll lifestyle for travel writing and has written over 70 Lonely Planet guides, focused mainly on Brazil, Chile, Colombia, USA, India, the Caribbean and Portugal. Raub also contributes to a variety of travel magazines in both the USA and UK. Along the way, the self-confessed hophead is in constant search of wildly high IBUs in local beers.

Brendan Sainsbury

Born and raised in the UK in a town that never merits a mention in any guidebook (Andover, Hampshire), Brendan spent the holidays of his youth caravanning in the English Lake District and didn't leave Blighty until he was nineteen. Making up for lost time, he's since squeezed 70 countries into a sometimes precarious existence as a writer and professional vagabond. His rocking chair memories will probably include staging a performance of 'A Comedy of Errors' at a school in war-torn Angola, running 150 miles across the Sahara Desert in the Marathon des Sables, and hitchhiking from Cape Town to Kilimanjaro with an early, dog-eared copy of LP's *Africa on a Shoestring*.

Our Story

A beat-up old car, a few dollars in the pocket and a sense of adventure. In 1972 that's all Tony and Maureen Wheeler needed for the trip of a lifetime – across Europe and Asia overland to Australia. It took several months, and at the end – broke but inspired – they sat at their kitchen table writing and stapling together their first travel guide, *Across Asia on the Cheap*. Within a week they'd sold 1500 copies. Lonely Planet was born. Today, Lonely Planet has offices in Franklin, London, Melbourne, Oakland, Dublin, Beijing and Delhi, with more than 600 staff and writers. We share Tony's belief that 'a great guidebook should do three things: inform, educate and amuse'.

Our Writers

Regis St Louis

Regis grew up in a small town in the American Midwest – the kind of place that fuels big dreams of travel – and he developed an early fascination with foreign dialects and world cultures. He spent his formative years learning Russian and a handful of Romance languages, which served him well on journeys across much of the globe. Regis has contributed to more than 50 Lonely Planet titles, covering destinations across six continents. His travels have taken him from the mountains of Kamchatka to remote island villages in Melanesia, and to many grand urban landscapes. When not on the road, he lives in New Orleans.

Isabel Albiston

After six years working for the *Daily Telegraph* in London, Isabel left to spend more time on the road. A job as writer for a magazine in Sydney, Australia was followed by a four-month overland trip across Asia and five years living and working in Buenos Aires, Argentina. Isabel started writing for Lonely Planet in 2014 and has contributed to 12 guidebooks. She's currently based in Ireland.

Robert Balkovich

Robert was born and raised in Oregon, but has called New York City home for almost a decade. When he was a child and other families were going to theme parks and grandma's house he went to Mexico City and toured Eastern Europe by train. He's now a writer and travel enthusiast seeking experiences that are ever so slightly out of the ordinary to report back on.

More Writers

STAY IN TOUCH LONELYPLANET.COM/CONTACT

AUSTRALIA The Malt Store, Level 3, 551 Swanston St, Carlton, Victoria 3053 ☎ 03 8379 8000, fax 03 8379 8111

IRELAND Digital Depot, Roe Lane (off Thomas St), Digital Hub, Dublin 8, D08 TCV4, Ireland

USA 124 Linden Street, Oakland, CA 94607 ☎ 510 250 6400, toll free 800 275 8555, fax 510 893 8572

UK 240 Blackfriars Road, London SE1 8NW ☎ 020 3771 5100, fax 020 3771 5101

 twitter.com/lonelyplanet

 facebook.com/lonelyplanet

 instagram.com/lonelyplanet

 youtube.com/lonelyplanet

 lonelyplanet.com/newsletter